W9-CGO-177

Greenhill Books

HITLER TRIUMPHANT

Other Greenhill Alternate History books include:

DIXIE VICTORIOUS
An Alternate History of the Civil War
Peter G. Tsouras (ed.)
ISBN-13 978-1-85367-689-5
ISBN-10 1-85367-689-6

HITLER'S ARDENNES OFFENSIVE
The German View of the Battle of the Bulge
Danny S. Parker (ed.)
ISBN-13 978-1-85367-683-3
ISBN-10 1-75367-683-7

BATTLE OF THE BULGE
Hitler's Alternate Scenarios
Peter G. Tsouras (ed.)
ISBN-13 978-1-85367-607-9
ISBN-10 1-85367-607-1

DISASTER AT D-DAY
The Germans Defeat the Allies, June 1944
Peter G. Tsouras
ISBN-13 978-1-85367-603-1
ISBN-10 1-85367-603-9

THIRD REICH VICTORIOUS
The Alternate History of How the Germans Won the War
Peter G. Tsouras (ed.)
ISBN-13 978-1-85367-492-1
ISBN-10 1-85367-492-3

Greenhill offers selected discounts and special offers on books ordered directly from us. For more information on our books please visit www.greenhillbooks.com. You can also write to us at Park House, 1 Russell Gardens, London, NW11 9NN, England.

HITLER TRIUMPHANT

ALTERNATE DECISIONS OF WORLD WAR II

Edited by Peter G. Tsouras

GREENHILL BOOKS, LONDON
MBI PUBLISHING, ST PAUL

In Memory of
KENNETH J. MACKSEY
1923–2005

Soldier and Historian – no more noble epitaph

Greenhill Books

Hitler Triumphant
Alternate Decisions of World War II

First published in 2006 by Greenhill Books/Lionel Leventhal Ltd, Park House,
1 Russell Gardens, London NW11 9NN
and
MBI Publishing Co., Galtier Plaza, Suite 200, 380 Jackson Street, St Paul, MN 55101-3885, USA

Text and maps © Lionel Leventhal Ltd 2006

British Library Cataloguing in Publication Data
Hitler triumphant : alternate decisions of World War II
1.World War, 1939-1945 2.Imaginary histories
I.Tsouras, Peter
940.5'3

ISBN-13 978-1-85367-699-4
ISBN-10 1-85367-699-3

Library of Congress Cataloging-in Publication Data available
For more information on our books, please visit www.greenhillbooks.com, email
sales@greenhillbooks.com, or telephone us within the UK on 020 8458 6314. You can also write
to us at the above London address.

Maps drawn by John Richards
Typeset by Palindrome

Printed and bound in the United States of America

Contents

Contents

Illustrations

Illustrations

Maps

Map key

⊠	infantry unit	**XXXXX**	army group or front
		XXXX	army
		XXX	corps
⊠	airborne	**XX**	division
	infantry unit	**X**	brigade
		I I I	regiment
⬭	tank unit	**I I**	battalion

* Axis units are shaded

8

Contributors

Dr Stephen Badsey MA (Cantab.) FRHistS is a Senior Lecturer in the Department of War Studies at the Royal Military Academy Sandhurst, and a Senior Research Associate of the Centre for Defence Studies, King's College, London. He has previously held research or teaching positions for the Imperial War Museum, the BBC, De Montfort University, The Open University, and the University of Southern Mississippi. He is a specialist on military theory, and on media presentations of warfare, and he has also made particular studies of airborne and amphibious operations. He has written or contributed to over sixty books and articles about warfare, including *Utah Beach; Omaha Beach; The Battle for Caen; The Falklands Conflict Twenty Years On; Britain, NATO and the Lessons of the Balkan Conflicts; The Media and International Security; World War II Battle Plans; The Gulf War Assessed; Arnhem 1944;* and *Normandy 1944.* He appears frequently on television as a military and media historian. He contributed the chapter 'Disaster at Dunkirk' to Peter G. Tsouras, *Third Reich Victorious.*

John D. Burtt is currently the editor of *Paper Wars* magazine, an independent review journal devoted to wargames. In his day-job personna, he is a contract nuclear engineer consulting for the US Navy. However, his real love is military history. A former marine sergeant and a veteran of Vietnam, he holds a Master's degree in Military History and is pursuing a PhD in the same field. He has written a wide range of articles for *Command* magazine, *Strategy & Tactics, The Wargamer,* and was the original editor of *CounterAttack* magazine. He contributed to *Rising Sun Victorious: How the Japanese Won the PacificWar, Third Reich Victorious: How the Germans Won the War, Cold War Hot: Alternate Decisions of the Cold War,* and *Dixie Victorious: An Alternate History of the Civil War.*

Kim H. Campbell was a regular officer in the United States Army serving thirteen years in combat arms and intelligence. For the last fifteen years he has been a senior analyst with the Air Force Intelligence Analysis Agency. He holds a Master's degree in strategic intelligence and a BA in European history. He contributed a chapter to the Greenhill alternate history *Battle of the Bulge*. He has appeared in 'Battlefield Detectives' on The History Channel discussing intelligence failures and successes during the Gettysburg Campaign. He has written numerous book reviews for the *Friday Review* and authored numerous articles on military operations for official United States Army and Air Force publications. He has been a student of military history for over forty years.

Wade G. Dudley holds a Master's degree in maritime history and nautical archaeology from East Carolina University (1997) and a doctorate in history from the University of Alabama (1999). Dr Dudley is the author of *Drake: For God, Queen, and Plunder* and the award winning *Splintering the Wooden Wall: The British Blockade of the United States, 1812–1815*. His short stories appear in Greenhill's *Rising Sun Victorious, Third Reich Victorious, Cold War Hot*, and *Dixie Victorious*. He is an assistant professor at East Carolina University in Greenville, NC, where he teaches Sea Power, North Carolina History, and Historical Research and Methods among other courses.

Paddy Griffith is a freelance military historian and publisher based in Manchester, England. He has written a series of books about battlefield tactics, from *Forward into battle* (1981 and 1990) to *Battle tactics of the Western Front 1916–18* (1994); but he has not yet written about paratroop attacks. He did, however, run a relevant series of wargames while he was a civilian lecturer at the Royal Military Academy, Sandhurst, during the 1970s and 1980s. The first was an investigation into what might have been if the Germans, including their paratroops, had invaded Britain in 1940. The remainder were based on the airborne capture of Crete in 1941, which might well have turned out in a variety of ways other than the glorious but pyrrhic victory that is recorded by history.

David Isby has written and edited over twenty books, including (by Greenhill), *G. I. Victory* (with the late Jeff Ethell), *Fighting the Bombers; The Luftwaffe Fighter Force: The View From the Cockpit; Fighting the Invasion, Fighting in Normandy;* and *Fighting the Breakout*. He has contributed to several previous volumes of alternative history published by Greenhill including *Battle of the Bulge; Cold War Hot; Rising Sun Victorious;* and *Third Reich Victorious*. He has designed 19 conflict simulations and holds two Charles Roberts awards for excellence in the field. A Washington-based national security consultant and attorney, he holds a BA in history from Columbia University and a JD from New York University. He was awarded the title 'bourgeois falsifier of history' by the Soviet government (pre-glasnost).

Nigel Jones is a historian, journalist, biographer and broadcaster. His books include *The War Walk: A Journey along the Western Front* (1984, updated 2004); *Hitler's Heralds: The Story of the Freikorps* (1987, updated as *A Brief History of the*

Birth of the Nazis 2004); *Rupert Brooke: Life Death & Myth* (1999); and biographies of the British fascist leader Sir Oswald Mosley (2004) and the writer Patrick Hamilton (1991). A former deputy editor of *History Today* and BBC *History* magazines, he now edits and writes for the *Daily Mail's Weekend* magazine. He is married with three children and lives in Sussex, England.

Dr David M. Keithly combines professional writing with a wide range of business interests. He has published several books, most recently *The USA and the World 2005*, and over seventy-five articles in journals and magazines. He is the American editor of *Civil Wars*. He teaches at American Military University and the Joint Military Intelligence College. He has twice been a Fulbright Fellow in Europe, was a Fellow of the Institute for Global Conflict and Cooperation at the University of California, a scholar-in-residence at the Friedrich Naumann Foundation in Bonn, Germany, and a legislative fellow in the parliament of the German state of Thüringen. He serves on the executive board of the Fulbright Association. He has a PhD from Claremont Graduate School and an MA from the German University of Freiburg. He did additional graduate work at the French University of Rennes. Thrice selected to 'Outstanding Young Men of America', he was designated a Navy 'National Reserve Officer of the Year' in 1993. He was named the IMA (Individual Mobilization Augmentee) Officer of the Year at the Defense Intelligence Agency in 2000, and received the annual faculty research award at the Joint Military Intelligence College in 2001. After sixteen years as an officer in the Navy Reserve, he transferred to the Air Force Reserve, where he presently holds the rank of lieutenant colonel.

John Prados is an author and historian of national security based in Washington, DC. He holds a PhD from Columbia University and focuses on presidential power, international relations, intelligence, military affairs, and policy issues. He is author of many articles and eighteen books on different military, intelligence, and policy issues. Prados' books include *Combined Fleet Decoded: The Secret History of U.S. Intelligence and the Japanese Navy in World War II; The Secret Wars of CIA Director William Colby; White House Tapes: Eavesdropping on the President; The Hidden History of the Vietnam War; Operation Vulture; The Blood Road: The Ho Chi Minh Trail and the Vietnam War; Presidents' Secret Wars; CIA and Pentagon Covert Operations from World War II through the Persian Gulf.* His most recent World War II publications include articles on the Japanese at Leyte Gulf for *World War II* magazine and *Battle of the Bulge: Hitler's Alternate Scenarios.* He has contributed chapters to 14 other books and entries in four reference works. Prados is a contributing editor to *MHQ: The Quarterly Journal of Military History*, and a contributing writer to *The VVA Veteran.* He is a senior fellow of the National Security Archive.

Peter G. Tsouras, Lieutenant Colonel, USAR (ret) is a military historian and recently retired from the Defense Intelligence Agency as a Senior Intelligence

Officer. He also served at the National Ground Intelligence Agency (NGIC). In the US Army he served with the 1st Battalion, 64th Armor, in Germany. He is the author/editor of twenty-three books on current military operations, military history, and alternate history. In the latter genre, he has written the widely acclaimed *Disaster at D-Day* and *Gettysburg: An Alternate History* which was banned at the Gettysburg National Military Park for being too realistic while at the same time nominated for the Lincoln Prize. He is also the editor of the popular Greenhill Books alternate history series of which *Hitler Triumphant* is the latest effort. Other titles include: *Rising Sun Victorious, Third Reich Victorious, Cold War Hot, Dixie Victorious*, and *Battle of the Bulge*. He has also edited a series on the WWII memoirs of General Erhard Raus, most notably *Panzers on the Eastern Front*. His military histories include *The Great Patriotic War, Changing Orders, Alexander: Invincible King of Macedonia, Montezuma: Warlord of the Aztecs, Warlords of Ancient America*. He is also noted for his military quotations books, the finest collections in English, which include: The *Greenhill Dictionary of Military Quotations* and the *Daily Telegraph Dictionary of Military Quotations*. He is married with three children and resides in Alexandria, Virginia.

Charles Vasey LLB FCA FTII is an itinerant finance director and game designer/publisher based in London. After reading law in London he qualified with Binder Hamlyn and worked with KPMG in both Taxation and Corporate Finance before starting his own business. A man of frighteningly few achievements he has written for *Military Modelling* and *Strategy & Tactics*, and publishes intermittently his own magazine *Perfidious Albion*. He has published a number of board games on such disparate topics as Mars-La-Tour 1870, biblical warfare, Tsushima, and the English Civil War.

Introduction

This book is dedicated to the late Kenneth Macksey (1923–2005), one of the last of the heroes of WWII, an eminent military historian in his own right. The experience of battle does indeed inform the historian, as Edward Gibbon wrote of his military experience long ago, '[T]he captain of the Hampshire grenadiers (the reader may smile) has not been useless to the historian of the Roman Empire.'[1] How much more did Ken Macksey's experience at D-Day and in the fighting across north-west Europe inform his masterful histories of World War II. In particular, Ken's biography of Guderian and the editing of the great panzer general's memoirs are the historical standards. Ken also excelled at that other variant of military history, the field of alternate history.

Alternate history has a surprisingly long pedigree, but until the last two decades it has been of intermittent interest to the public. Ken was fortunate to jump-start a field that had languished. The field may have had its origin in Geoffrey Château's 1836 *Napoleon et la conquête de la monde 1812–1823* written for Louis Napoleon. That was followed by *The Battle of Dorking*, a British speculation on a German invasion, the first of what was to become almost a British obsession before World War I. That war saw it take on serious life. The Germans reciprocated British fears of an invasion with the wishful-thinking *Hindenburg's March into London* in 1916. The consequences of a German victory appeared after the war in 1919 in Stephen Leacock's *The Hohenzollerns in America*. Echoing that in 1921 Gaston Omsey published *Si les Allemands Avaient Gagne la Guerre*. Already the fascination with the Germans actually winning was finding a niche. However, there was still room for showing how the Allies could have done better as in Bernard Newman's *The Cavalry Went Through*. By that same year the genre of alternate history in general had been well enough known for Walter Carruthers Sellar and Robert Julian Yeatman to satirise it in *1066 And All That*. The first alternate history best seller was the collection edited by J.C. Squire in 1932, *If It Had Happened Otherwise: Lapses into Imaginary History*.[2]

After World War II writing naturally focused on the Russian Revolution and the current consequences, but by the early 1960s it was wandering into

13

other channels. McKinley Cantor's *If the South had Won the Civil War* and Philip K. Dick's *The Man in the High Castle*, a novel set in a future that followed a German victory, came out in 1962. The next noteworthy attempt was Robert Sobel's *For Want of a Nail* in 1973 and explored the consequences of American defeat at Saratoga in 1779. Another novel set in the future created by a German victory was Len Deighton's *SS-GB* in 1979.

Ken Macksey set down a new marker for the genre in 1980 with his well-received *Invasion: The German Invasion of England 1940* (1980) – the execution of Operation SEA LION. It was a serious attempt to depict the actual military operations of such an event written not as novel but as an actual history book. As a soldier at the time, I remember reading it and being intrigued by the opportunities to understand history's twists and turns by playing out the 'what ifs' and 'might have beens'. Ken's book was the model I used for my alternate histories published by Greenhill, *Disaster at D-Day: The Germans Defeat the Allies, June 1944* (1994) and *Gettysburg: An Alternate History* (1996). Ken's book, I believe, had an influence in the now popular style of writing alternate history as actual military operational history. It also was a sign that the public retains a vicarious fascination with reading about the very dark subject of German victory in World War II. A simple review of Uchronia's database establishes that fact beyond any doubt. Fifteen years after *Invasion: The German Invasion of England 1940* came out, I sent Ken a replica of a pin designed by Himmler himself, embossed with a Viking longship, to commemorate the 'invasion of England' so that he might have one last laugh.

But Ken was not finished with this approach and edited the very well-received *The Hitler Options: Alternate Decisions of World War II* (1995) which explored, in ten chapters by different authors, the possible outcomes of the many operational-strategic initiatives the Germans had planned but never executed. This book, in turn, fathered the follow-on efforts in Greenhill's successful alternate history anthology series.[3]

'You will never know war until you fight Germans.'

Even in this new 'Age of Terror', the attraction of the history of World War II exerts an enormous force. Movies, such as *Saving Private Ryan* and *U-571* as well as countless documentaries on the History Channel and others prove that this vanished era has entered almost the realm of myth. Certainly the straightforward combat of great armies is easier to grasp than the shadow war against terrorists. There is as noble a struggle of heroes as there was in the fighting beneath the walls of Troy. There are heroes on both sides, as at Troy, though one side in World War II was ruled by a hideous villainy. In comparison, the terrorist opponent is utterly without nobility of any sort. Perhaps our anger is fuelled in part by the very impossibility to find any redeeming nobility in him.

Not so in the war against Germany. Such was the fighting ability of this nation after World War I, that George Orwell commented on the impression of the Germans gained on the level of man-to-man, 'During the war of 1914–18 the English working class were in contact with foreigners to an extent that is rarely possible. The sole result was that they brought back a hatred of all Europeans, except the Germans whose courage they admired.'[4] Captain Basil Liddell Hart drew the institutional comparison, 'The German generals of this war were the best-finished product of their profession – anywhere. They could have been better if their outlook had been wider and their understanding deeper. But if they had become philosophers they would have ceased to be soldiers.'[5] On a personal level, General Claude Auchinleck saluted his foe much as Hector saluted Telemonian Ajax.

Rommel gave me and those who served under my command in the Desert many anxious moments. There could never be any question of relaxing our efforts to destroy him, for if ever there was a general whose sole preoccupation was the destruction of the enemy, it was he. He showed no mercy and expected none. Yet I could never translate my deep detestation of the regime for which he fought into personal hatred of him as an opponent. If I say, now that he is gone, that I salute him as a soldier and a man and deplore the shameful manner of his death, I may be accused of belonging to what Mr. Bevin calls the 'trade union of generals'. So far as I know, should such a fellowship exist, membership in it implies now more than recognition in an enemy of the qualities one would wish to possess oneself, respect for a brave, able, and scrupulous opponent and a desire to see him treated, when beaten, in the way one would have wished had he been the winner and oneself the loser. This used to be called chivalry: many will now call it nonsense and say that the days when such sentiments could survive a war are past. If they are, then I, for one, am sorry.[6]

Again and again this martial race in two world wars came close to victory in its contests with opponents that aggregated vaster resources in manpower and industry. And when defeat stared them in the face, their soldiery hung on tenaciously until their nation itself cracked under the force of an aroused world. 'Like the warriors of the Teutonic tribes of old, they were resolved if necessary to die where they stood, should that be necessary to protect the uprooted population from the eastern invader.'[7]

Yet, how close they came to victory, especially in the first three years of the war, sends a chill through the student of this struggle. Churchill in the House on 11 December 1941 was only too prescient when he said, 'Who fight the Germans, fight a stubborn and resourceful foe – a foe in every way worthy of the doom prepared for him.' For the victory would have consigned the world to a hell little different from that planned by Osama bin Ladin and his Islamofascist swarm. But, while there is little to choose between Hitler and bin Ladin, surely no one in the future will write as glowing a tribute to the nineteen hijackers of 9/11 or his blood-soaked protégé, Zarqawi, the butcher of Baghdad, as Auchinleck wrote of Rommel. Churchill was also not afraid to praise a chivalrous and great enemy, praises that nearly earned him the censure of the House – 'we have a very daring and skilful opponent against us, and, may I say across the havoc of war a great general' (27 January 1942). Perhaps Churchill, again before the House, paid the ultimate salute to the enemy, 'You will never know war until you fight Germans.'[8]

This book follows that trail of German victories that might have been to breathe life into them and explore the 'hows' and 'whys' of such alternate realities. For the reader of military history as well as the historian will find value in such an exploration. History is definitely not, as the ever foolish Marxists claim, only the product of great, impersonal, and inexorable forces. It is the product of living, breathing men and women – their will, courage, and vision, even in death. It is individuals who stand repeatedly at a crossroads of time and direct mankind down the road to the future in one direction and not another. History is, in effect, a struggle for the crossroads that mark this way to the future. Life is indeed choice. And it is the choices made by heroes and villains that make the future.

Clarifications

The eleven chapters in this book do not form a continuous thread or single plot line. Rather they are the stories woven by eleven authors each charged with examining a different episode in war against Hitler's Germany and Mussolini's Italy in the light of the very real potential for different outcomes. Each is self-contained within its own alternate reality.

Our accounts of this alternate reality naturally need their own explanatory references, which appear in the endnotes that follow each chapter. The use of these 'alternate reality' endnotes, of course, poses a risk to the unwary reader who may make strenuous efforts to acquire a new and fascinating source. To avoid an epidemic of frustrating and futile searches, the 'alternate notes' are indicated by an asterisk (*) before the number of the endnote within the notes themselves. All works appearing within the bibliographies are, however, 'real'.

The Chapters

In chapter 1, 'May Day: The Premiership of Lord Halifax', Nigel Jones explores what may well have happened had Churchill not been at that most critical of mankind's signposts after the fall of France when Britain stood siege alone against the might of aroused tyranny. The British political establishment's alternatives to Churchill were meagre, and none of them could give voice to the lion's roar. The world truly lay on the shoulders of one man. Lesser men would have buckled under the strain with consequences of misery beyond reckoning for future generations.

One advantage of great price the Allies maintained was ULTRA, the ability to read some of the Germans' most encrypted message system, ENIGMA. In chapter 2, 'Peace in Our Time: Memories of Life at the Führer Headquarters', Charles Vasey writes in the guise of a German memoir of the war in which that advantage was lost.

The next three chapters concentrate on events in the Mediterranean and its Gibraltar gateway, areas where alternate histories, save for the campaign in the Western Desert, have trodden lightly if at all. John Prados in chapter 3, 'The Spanish Gambit: Operation FELIX', speculates on the course of the actual German plan to seize the great British fortress of Gibraltar. In this story, Italy's contribution could have been critical and offers an interesting sidelight into Italy as an advantage to its German ally, rather than a deadweight.

Wade Dudley, in chapter 4, '*Navigare Necesse Est, Vivere Non Est Necesse*': Mussolini and the Legacy of Pompey the Great', continues to explore the possibilities inherent in Italy's strengths, if well handled. It draws a decisive role for Italy's Royal Navy had it embarked on the building of aircraft carries as was seriously proposed in the early 1930s.

David Isby picks up the rich Italian thread of possibilities in chapter 5, 'The Health of the State: Italy and Global War'. For the sake of contrast, Isby shows Italy staking her own course in a world at war, emerging in a surprising state that does not necessarily follow the theme of the rest of the book.

Another area in the alternate histories of World War II that has received little if any attention is the role of the German airborne. The slaughter of the 7th Airborne Division in the capture of Crete so traumatised Hitler that he confined it to a ground role thereafter. A less blood-soaked victory on the island of Minos might well have given new wings to the German Fallschirm-jäger. In chapter 6, 'Black Cross, Green Crescent, Black Gold: The Drive to the Indus', David Keithly redirects German concentration after a quick and easy victory in Crete, to Aphrodite's island – Cyprus. But Cyprus is only a stepping stone for the follow-on panzers, in a Teutonic version of 'shock and awe' to oil-soaked sands of Iraq and Arabia, with a horrific detour to Jerusalem.[9] Keithly also makes the point that Hitler's hatred of Christianity and the Jews resonated within an important element of Muslim opinion and could have eased his path had he chosen to go into the Middle East.

In chapter 7, 'Wings Over the Caucasus: Operation LEONARDO', Paddy Griffith also uses a clean victory in Crete for greater feats for the German airborne arm, also in the search for oil. But in this telling, the airborne rather than the panzers have the main role in seizing the oil wealth of the Soviets in the Caucasus.

Griffith's chapter ushers the reader into the Eastern Front, the setting of the next two chapters. Kim Campbell, in chapter 8, 'To the Last Drop of Blood: The Fall of Moscow', avoids the diversion of German armour to the Ukraine in the critical months of late summer and early autumn. Thus, Russia's two most ferocious generals, January and February, are kept waiting in the wings as Guderian and Hoth direct their panzers in fine weather towards Moscow.

Chapter 9, 'The Stalingrad Breakout: "Raus Pulls You Through"', I focus my story on the potential to save the mighty German 6th Army from its doom at Stalingrad. It is a story of moral courage in two men, one to break into the Stalingrad pocket, and the other to break out. This story explores the theme of what would have been possible had a different man from the inadequate Paulus been standing at the crossroads of history.

The final two chapters explore from different directions the consequences of a 1943 invasion of France for ultimate victory over Germany. John Burtt in chapter 10, 'For Want of an Island: The Fall of Malta and German Victory', takes the loss of that bone-in-the-throat Mediterranean island and follows the ripples of that disaster to a fateful rendezvous along the coast of France.

Finally, Steven Badsey plants the pivot of his story (chapter 11, 'Ike's COCKADE: The Allied Invasion of France 1943') in the increasingly poisoned relationship of the Combined Chiefs of Staff that would lead to the disaster of Operation COCKADE.

Peter G. Tsouras
Alexandria, VA
2005

Notes

1   Edward Gibbon, *Autobiography*, 1962, quoted in Peter G. Tsouras, *The Greenhill Dictionary of Military Quotations*, London: Greenhill Books, 2000, p. 307.

2   Stephen Badsey, 'If It Had Happened Otherwise' – First World War Exceptionalism in Counterfactual History,' 2006.

3   *Rising Sun Victorious: The Alternate History of How the Japanese Won the Pacific War* (2000); *Third Reich Victorious: Alternate Decisions of World War II* (2002); *Cold War Hot: Alternate Outcomes of the Cold War* (2003); *Dixie Victorious: An Alternate History of the Civil War* (2004); *Battle of the Bulge: Hitler's Alternate Scenarios* (2004).

4   George Orwell, *England Your England*, 1941.

5   Erich von Manstein, *Lost Victories*, 1958, p. 17. Von Manstein quotes Liddell Hart in his introduction.

6   Field Marshal Sir Claude Auchinleck, quoted in the foreword to Desmond Young, *The Desert Fox* (1953), cited in Peter G. Tsouras, *The Greenhill Dictionary of Military Quotations*, London: Greenhill Books, 2000, p. 83.

7   John Keegan, *Six Armies in Normandy*, New York: Viking Press, 1982.

8   Eric Margolis, 'Soviet pride, shame,' *Toronto Sun*, 8 May 2005.

9   'Nazis planned to kill Palestine Jews,' *Washington Times*, 13 April 2006, p. A16; story from Agence France Presse.

1 May Day

The Premiership of Lord Halifax

Nigel Jones

7 May 1940

The House of Commons was packed. Members of Parliament crowded the green leather benches like tinned sardines, and an unmistakable buzz of excitement tinged with anxiety created the low murmur of an angry hive. The newest and youngest member of the ancient assembly, 23-year-old John Profumo, was especially anxious. Elected only a few weeks before as the Tory member for the Midlands constituency of Kettering, Profumo, like many younger MPs, was dressed in his army uniform. For Britain was at war – had been so for nine months – and one month previously, the long winter of inaction that had led wits to dub the conflict 'the phoney war' or 'the bore war', burst apart. Hostilities had suddenly got hot.

On 9 April *Fall Weserubung* (Operation WESER EXERCISE) Germany's invasion of Denmark and Norway, had begun at dawn. Totally surprised, the Danes offered virtually no resistance, and by breakfast the country was occupied. In Norway, it was less of a walkover – particularly for the German navy. Three cruisers, the *Karlsruhe*, *Königsberg* and *Blücher* and several destroyers were sunk and another cruiser badly damaged as they landed *Wehrmacht* troops from the capital Oslo in the south to the northern port of Narvik.

Inland, airborne troops secured key strongpoints as the Luftwaffe swept the skies above the surprised Scandinavian country. Five days later, on 15 April, British and French troops landed at Narvik, and, after hard fighting, re-took the port. Allied troops also landed at Åndalsnes and Namsos on either side of Trondheim. The Allied toeholds in Norway remained precarious as the crack German 3rd Mountain Division under General Eduard Dietl fought to regain control of Narvik.

The attack on Norway had come as a shock to the Anglo-French allies as well as to the Norwegians. Only a day before the Germans struck, the British Prime Minister, Neville Chamberlain, had boasted vaingloriously that 'Hitler has missed the bus'. He spoke just a little too soon. The invasion of Norway, and the Allies' failure to expel the Germans, provoked a serious political crisis in London that led to the calling of a two-day debate on the conduct of the campaign which Profumo, on leave from his unit's base in nearby Essex, was attending.

Despite a normally unassailable majority of 240, Chamberlain's Tory-dominated National Government was worried about the outcome of the Norway debate. Discontent with Chamberlain's supine pre-war policy of appeasement of Hitler's Germany had grown into worries over the lacklustre and passive conduct of the whole war. The recall of the belligerent and maverick Tory Winston Churchill to the Admiralty, a position he had also held at the beginning of World War I, on the outbreak of war had silenced the critics for a while, but the manifest inadequacy of the elderly, wing-collared, reedy-voiced Chamberlain as a war leader (demonstrated for all to see in the ham-fisted conduct of the Norway campaign) had stoked discontent – not least among those MPs who were also serving in the armed forces – up to boiling point. The paradoxical fact that Churchill's aggressive policy of mining Norwegian waters may have provoked the invasion, and that as First Lord of the Admiralty he was directly responsible for the disastrous campaign they were criticising, was an irony in many MPs' minds as the debate got under way, since it was Churchill who, as one of the two obvious candidates for the post, stood to gain the ultimate prize of the Premiership if the Chamberlain government fell.

The speeches rumbled on all day until, at 8 p.m., the diminutive Tory MP Leo Amery rose.[1] A friend and old colleague of both Chamberlain and Churchill, Amery had come into politics under the spell of Chamberlain's Imperialist father, Joseph, and held his parliamentary seat in the Chamberlain family fiefdom of Birmingham; and he had been a friend and contemporary of Churchill's at the exclusive Harrow school. Amery was notorious for his long and often dull speeches, but this time his fears and growing anxiety lent wings to his words. Of Jewish extraction himself, and a frequent visitor to German ski slopes, Amery had heard Hitler speak at first hand and knew the menace that Nazism represented to all that he held dear. Ambitious and, like his friend Churchill, long excluded from government for his anti-appeasement views, Amery's aim was simple: to bring down that government and bring in another – possibly with Churchill at its head – in its place.

Amery looked around as his typically long-winded peroration neared its climax. Over the gangway, the eyes of the old Lloyd George – Britain's Premier in World War I and a bitter foe to Chamberlain – twinkled encouragement.[2] The little man took a deep breath and ended, 'This is what Cromwell said to the Long Parliament when he thought it was no longer fit to conduct the affairs of the nation. "You have sat here too long for any good you have been doing. Depart, I say, and let us have done with you. In the name of God, go!"'

A shock as of electricity raced around the chamber as Amery sat down. There was a collective intake of breath, and not a few 'Oohs' and 'Aahs' – followed by a new excited buzz of talk. All – supporters and opponents of the Government alike – felt that Amery's words had breached a dam of restraint – that the wall of critical water that had been building up was now gushing into the open – and that it might not be possible for Chamberlain to save his embattled premiership from being swept away by the flood.

8 May

The next day, the opposition Labour party forced the issue to a vote. Forty-one rebel Tories – including a score of those in uniform, and with young John Profumo courageously among their number – trooped into the 'No' lobby to cast their votes against their Government. Up to sixty more sat on their hands in abstention. It was enough. The Government's majority was slashed by more than half – falling to eighty-one. White-faced, Chamberlain stumbled from the Chamber, to cries of 'Go!' and ironic jeers of 'Missed the bus!' John Profumo, in a state resembling shell-shock, also staggered rather than strode from the Commons and made his way to a nightclub.

9 May

In London, as his opponents met to plot his downfall, Chamberlain desperately cast around for ways to save his Government – and his job. His officials and minions had been scurrying and telephoning, trying to bribe rebels with job offers, promises to get rid of incompetent dead wood – anything, in fact, to buy them off and purchase precious time.

But Chamberlain, fearing the worst, had already begun to prepare a fallback position. Depressed by gloomy reports of the Government's sliding support from David Margesson, his trusty Chief Whip (party manager) in the Commons, he made dispositions to ensure that if he could not cling on in 10 Downing Street, the Prime Minister's official London residence, he would at least see that his successor would be his closest political friend and staunchest ally in the appeasement of Germany, 'a safe pair of hands' (or in this case, 'hand' since the gentleman in question had been born with just the one): Edward Wood, Earl of Halifax.[3]

There were two, and only two candidates for the Premiership should Chamberlain fall. The tottering Prime Minister's personal and political preference was for his Foreign Secretary. Halifax, a tall, gaunt aristocrat from rural Yorkshire was an austere nobleman whose two consuming passions – fox-hunting and the Church of England – were summed up in his nickname, a triple pun on his title, his hobbies and his political cunning: 'The Holy Fox'. Despite the disability of lacking a left hand, Halifax was a crack shot who relaxed from the hurly burly of politics either on the grouse moors near his Yorkshire home at Garrowby, on the hunting field, or on his knees wrestling with his God in prayer.

Born into wealth and privilege at the high tide of Britain's nineteenth-century power, Halifax – a one-time Viceroy of India, the jewel in Britain's imperial crown – had watched with grim resignation the slow but steady ebbing of that tide. He had gone to Germany to meet and treat with Hitler personally, and, though his contempt for the little corporal and failed artist who had made himself master of Germany's destiny was concealed behind a mask of icy courtesy, Halifax was painfully aware where the new powerhouse in European affairs was located; and he knew it was not in London.

His rival could not have been a more different man. Different in appearance, different in character and different in belief, Winston Churchill was also born into Britain's ruling aristocracy at the height of the Victorian age. But whereas the crane-like Halifax was the ultimate Establishment insider, a calm and cautious Conservative,the short and squat Churchill was the ultimate political romantic: a rumbustious, explosive and volcanic man of action, happy to upset applecarts, leap before he looked and even willing to swap political parties if it benefited his career or whatever policies he favoured at that moment. Unlike the gently defeatist Halifax (who would have called it 'realism'), Churchill reacted with titanic, if hitherto impotent, rage to the slow seepage of British pomp and power. He had more than once declared that he would never become prime minister to preside over the demise of the British Empire, but few doubted that his ultimate goal had been to occupy the seat of Government in Downing Street, whatever the circumstances of his arrival there.

His progress towards that goal had resembled a game of snakes and ladders: spectacular leaps forward, matched by equally extraordinary descents. His changes of party – starting as a Conservative, switching to the Liberals when they looked likelier to achieve power, then tacking back to the Tories again as Liberal popularity waned – had made many of his fellow politicians distrust him, even though most regarded 'Winston' – as he was universally known – with a sort of exasperated affection. His record as a war leader had reinforced that distrust. The chief architect of the disastrous attempt to force Turkey's Dardanelles straits at Gallipoli in 1915 – he had stubbornly persisted with the campaign when it was clear that it was lost – Churchill's attempts to evade responsibility for the débâcle had won him a host of new enemies.

Churchill's career between the wars was equally controversial: a ferocious anti-Bolshevik, he had favoured armed intervention to stop Communism in Russia even before the guns had fallen silent on the Western front; he had been an inept Chancellor of the Exchequer (Finance Minister) and a strike-buster during Britain's brief General Strike of 1926; and he had even made sympathetic noises about Mussolini's fascism before the rise of Hitler's Nazis had increasingly occupied his fertile mind and boundless energy. Kept out of office through the thirties by what he saw as the jealousy of lesser, little men like Chamberlain, who were distrustful of his belligerence towards the rising new power in Europe, Churchill had fumed in frustration on the sidelines through his wilderness years. But now he was back; an old man in a hurry, and torn between his loyalty to the failing administration of which he was part, and his urgent need to get his own hands on the steering-wheel of power.

At the Felsennest

Meanwhile, in Germany, the Führer, Adolf Hitler, moved gratefully from his civilian role to his position as Commander-in-Chief of the *Wehrmacht* as he travelled on his special train *Amerika* from Berlin via Hanover to his Spartan western HQ, the *Felsennest* (Cliff Nest), a small group of bunkers in the wooded Eifel hills close to the Belgian frontier, to oversee personally the next and most daring of the stages by which he planned to overrun all Europe. The Rhineland – Austria – the Sudetenland – Czechoslovakia – Memel – Poland – Denmark – Norway – and now, this, the most giant leap of all: *Fall Gelb* (Operation YELLOW), the invasion of France and the Low Countries (Belgium, the Netherlands and Luxembourg) that, if as daringly successful as he hoped and planned, would make him the most powerful man in the world.

The crucial component of YELLOW, *Fall Sichelschnitt* (Operation SICKLE CUT), had been devised by one of his wiliest commanders, Erich von Manstein,[4] a taciturn, hook-nosed Prussian, whose scheme was essentially a reprise in reverse of the Schlieffen Plan[5] that had brought the Germans tantalisingly close to taking Paris and winning World War I in a lightning six weeks in the high summer of 1914. To bypass the much-trumpeted French Maginot Line, a vast defensive chain of fixed underground fortifications stretching south from Luxembourg to the Swiss border at Basle, Manstein proposed a sweeping slash through the hilly terrain of the Ardennes, a well-wooded region of sparsely populated highland covering southern Belgium and Luxembourg, generally considered impassable to armour.

Where the Schlieffen Plan had launched six armies in a gigantic, swinging right hook curling north-east to south-west through Belgium and down on Paris, Manstein planned to use the new power of the *Wehrmacht*'s panzer armour, backed in the air by the crook-winged Junkers Ju87 Stuka dive-bombers, equipped with terrifying screaming sirens, to spearhead a sharp left-hand jab, moving from south-east to north-west, leapfrogging the river Meuse, and then sweeping all the French and British troops to the north and east of the German line of advance: Liege – Dinant – Sedan – Amiens – Lille – Calais into a gigantic bag and destroying the Allied will to resist in a matter of a month. And so it came to pass.

10 May

As the roar of gunfire heralding *Fall Gelb* split the spring night air, Hitler turned to his staff, most of whom had been kept in the dark as to the timing of the attack on the west, and were still unsure why they had been brought to this remote spot. 'Meine Herren,' rasped the Führer portentously, 'The offensive against the western powers has just begun.' By dawn the Luftwaffe were battering pre-selected targets across Belgium and eastern France, while elite units, sometimes dressed in the uniforms of their opponents, seized key strongpoints in the path of the advance.

In Britain, diarist Harold Nicolson,[6] a diplomat, journalist, broadcaster and MP, noted that it was a beautiful spring day, with flowers in bloom as he drove to catch a train up to London from Sissinghurst, his country home in Kent. The capital was awash with rumours about the attack and the political crisis. Events were moving speedily to a climax.

The Day Before – 9 May

Soon after he arrived for work at the Foreign Office on the morning of Thursday, 9 May, Lord Halifax received a summons to see the Prime Minister at 10 Downing Street. The Foreign Secretary did not have far to go. The vast Italianate pile of the Foreign Office lay on the opposite side of Downing Street to Number 10 – a minute's walk at most. Exchanging a meaning glance with his deputy, and political soulmate, the flabby-faced young 'Rab' Butler,[7] Halifax donned his bowler hat and with his gangling stride, nonchalantly loped across the street. Held by an unseen hand, the black, highly polished door of Number 10 swung open.

'Ah. Edward. Thank you for coming so soon.'

The Prime Minister was tired, Halifax thought. His neck, beneath his stiff wing-collar, looked as scrawny as a chicken's and his hair seemed grey and lifeless. Neville was, he reflected, seventy years old – and this afternoon every year showed.

Swiftly, his voice husky with lack of sleep, Chamberlain explained the situation in precise and unemotional tones. Though he was ready and willing to carry on, the country needed unity for the fight that lay ahead. Unity meant a new and truly national government, one uniting all three major parties – Tories, Labour and Liberals. The Labour party, for whom he had never troubled to conceal his contempt, would never enter such a coalition under his leadership said Chamberlain; but under Halifax, they just might. Above all it was vital to keep Winston out. The mercurial Churchill was the only man who could (and probably would) – as Winston himself had said of Admiral Jellicoe in World War I – lose the war in an afternoon, or fight on, as he had at Gallipoli, in a hopeless battle already lost. No one was questioning his great gifts – his energy, his eloquence, his burning patriotism. It was his judgement that so many who knew him doubted.

The first grumblings of a nervous stomach ache gnawed at the Foreign Secretary's guts. He knew where this was heading. Chamberlain was offering him the Premiership on a plate. Though unable to stay in office himself, the old man still had the power – and the will – to decide his successor. If he advised King George VI to send for Halifax, send for Halifax he would.

'You have only to say the word, Edward,' Chamberlain urged. 'The king has already told me that you are the obvious choice.' Halifax did not doubt this. His own old-world courtesy, the perfect manners of a bygone age, made him the ideal courtier, and his relations with the Royal family were accordingly cordial – even intimate. He had been given the unique privilege of a key to the gardens of Buckingham Palace, the King's London residence, and while taking his daily constitutional in the grounds, he not infrequently came across the King and Queen.[8] Despite the king's stammer and his paralysing shyness, they thought alike. More than once recently the king, and still more often, his tough-minded wife, had questioned why Britain was at war. With Poland gone, the original *casus belli* had disappeared. Surely it would be possible to make some accommodation with Herr Hitler? After all, the Royals knew the Germans – they were blood of their kin; they often spoke to their German cousins who asked why this absurd fraternal quarrel was being allowed to continue.

'Well, Edward?' Chamberlain's imperious question jerked Halifax out of his reverie.

'I'm sorry, Prime Minister – a moment's inattention...'

'I said: will you take the job?'

There followed a silence, broken only by the ticking of a clock on the mantle-piece and the distant bawled order of an officer drilling soldiers on Horse Guard's Parade.

Halifax rehearsed his objections: he was not sure whether he was up to the strain of being a war leader; he was a peer, a member of the House of Lords, and unable to speak for the Government in the Commons; he had been closely associated with the outgoing regime. As a man of privilege in a democratic age, he knew little of military matters – the very thought of it brought on a stomach ache. Chamberlain brushed these hesitations aside.

'Your modesty does you credit, Edward. But we have worked together. We cannot see our work for peace put into the careless hands of Winston. All we have done, all we have built up, would be smashed in minutes. It's your clear and bounden duty to accept. And you can have Winston in the Cabinet as War Minister. I'd be there at your side too. Together we would stop him ruining everything.'

At teatime, shortly after 4 p.m., it was Churchill's turn to be summoned to Number 10. He too had not far to come from the Admiralty building at the top of Whitehall.

He was ushered into the Cabinet room where he found the formidable triumvirate of Chamberlain, Halifax and the Chief Whip, David Margesson, a bitter and inveterate enemy, assembled across the Cabinet table.

'Winston, I won't beat around the bush,' Chamberlain began. 'I'm going; I've been to the Palace to tender my resignation and I've recommended that the King sends for Edward as my successor. He has indicated that he will ask you to be Minister of Defence – a new role in which you would have the political supervision of all three armed services. I would go back to being Chancellor.'

Churchill smelt a rat. As Chancellor, Chamberlain would be living literally next door at 11 Downing Street. The pliable Halifax in Number 10 might be the front man – but Chamberlain would still be running the show behind the scenes. It was yet another plot to keep the old gang in power. He had become all too familiar with such manoeuvres during his long wilderness years. Without speaking, he turned and faced the tall windows, with the rays of the waning day burnishing them gold. Later that day he told a friend, 'As I remained silent a very long pause ensued. It certainly seemed longer than the two minutes one observes on Armistice Day.'

At last Halifax broke the silence, 'Well, Winston, what do you say?'

Churchill, shoulders hunched, hands locked behind his back, slowly turned to face them, his face dark with frustrated rage. 'Say? What can I say?'

Chamberlain broke in, 'Of course, Winston, we all know that you desire to be Prime Minister yourself. We all think you would bring great abilities to that role. But there are obstacles...'

'What obstacles?' Churchill growled, louder than he had intended.

Chamberlain coughed nervously, 'Well, David can tell you some of them.'

Churchill glowered at his old foe. Undaunted, Margesson frowned back.

'The party won't wear you, Winston. The vast majority of our people remain loyal to Neville, but they would accept Edward. You, however, are a different proposition. Untrustworthy. A chancer. Dangerous. Those are the words that I am hearing in the tearoom.'

Churchill bristled, 'I do not believe it. Everyone knows I would go to the wall for the country.'

Chamberlain intervened again, 'We don't doubt it, Winston. The problem is, not everyone wants to go to the wall with you.'

Churchill grunted like a rooting boar. Chamberlain continued, 'Anyhow, the thing is this. The King is minded to appoint Edward as Prime Minister to oversee events, while you effectively run the war under his general supervision. David will ensure that the government gets the full support of the party in the Commons.'

'And Labour?' Churchill asked.

'David tells me that Labour is willing to serve under Edward.'

'Some of them have not forgotten Tonypandy,' added Margesson cruelly – a not-so-subtle reference to the time when Churchill, as Home Secretary, had sent troops to intimidate striking miners in South Wales. Churchill grunted again.

'Well, Winston,' said Halifax silkily, 'What do you say: Yes or No?'

Another long silence ensued. At last Churchill spoke. 'You leave me no choice.'

Halifax left the meeting and took his ministerial car up Whitehall, round the corner through Trafalgar Square, under Admiralty Arch and up the Mall straight to the gates of Buckingham Palace. His mission was to 'kiss hands' formally as Prime Minister, and the King received him like the old friend he was. Churchill returned to the Admiralty to continue running the war.

There was much to run. After retiring late, Churchill was awoken in the small hours to hear the first tidings of the onslaught on the west. Reports began to flood in of German bombers striking Brussels, Rotterdam, Strasbourg, Orleans, Lyons. Like flood waters bursting through broken Dutch dykes, tanks and troops were pouring across the frontiers into the flatlands of the Low Countries.

11 May
Fort Eben Emael, an almost impregnable Belgian stronghold on the banks of the Albert Canal was taken in a daring airborne attack by elite troops in

gliders which landed directly on the fort's superstructure. In the wake of its seizure two panzer divisions moved across the Belgian border.

12 May

General Ewald von Kleist's panzers knifed through Belgium and headed south-west towards Sedan, the scene of Napoleon III's disastrous defeat in the Franco-Prussian war. The leading division of Kleist's armoured columns was commanded by a thrusting young General, Erwin Rommel.

13 May

Fearing German encirclement, French General Henri Giraud, who had moved forward into Belgium to support the Dutch army on his left flank, decided to withdraw, leaving the Dutch exposed and alone. French attempts to bomb bridges already seized by the Germans were beaten off as the Luftwaffe established air command over the battle zone.

14 May

The Dutch port of Rotterdam was heavily bombed. Fifty-seven Heinkel 111 bombers dropped ninety-seven tons of high explosives on the city centre. The old houses, mainly composed of wood, burned furiously, incinerating an unknown number of victims.

General Gerd von Rundstedt's Army Group A continued its advance through southern Belgium, with the crucial Ardennes sector assigned to the tanks of General Heinz Guderian, a noted pre-war apostle of armoured warfare.[9]

The advance units of Rommel's 7th Panzer Division paddled across the River Meuse in inflatable dinghies and, after a short, sharp action, established a vital bridgehead on the west bank. By the end of the day, Guderian's panzers were across, fanning out over the open country beyond.

15 May

The Dutch army surrendered. Queen Wilhelmina and her ministers fled into exile in London.

16 May

The Belgian port of Antwerp fell. The British and French armies in Belgium, now in full retreat west along roads already clogged by columns of civilian refugees, and harassed by raids from strafing Stukas, reached the Belgian border, finding defensive blockhouses unmanned and abandoned. A French officer, Captain Denis Barlone noted, 'The men want to know where I am leading them but I conceal the fact that we are returning to France. They feel that things are not going too well.'

17 May

The Belgian capital, Brussels, fell. After a bitter wrangle, Guderian successfully begged his Chief, von Kleist, for permission for his tanks to exploit the crossing of the Meuse and forge ahead. He advanced an extraordinary fifty-five miles to reach the River Oise.

18 May
The Germans reached the French town of St Quentin. Alarmed, the combative French Premier, Paul Reynaud, personally took over the Ministry of Defence. The Germans reached the River Somme.

19 May
Reynaud reshuffled his Government, appointing two aged and pessimistic World War I veterans to key positions. Marshal Philippe Pétain becomes Vice-Premier, while Marshal Maxine Weygand replaced Gamelin as French Commander-in-Chief.[10] The Commander of the British Expeditionary Force (BEF), Lord Gort, advised the War Cabinet that he might be forced to retreat to the Channel port of Dunkirk.

20 May
The French city of Amiens and the town of Abbeville fell. The Germans reached the Channel ports, severing the BEF and the French army in north-east France from Paris, and cutting the Allied armies in two.

21 May
An attempted counter-attack by British tanks at Arras failed.

22 May
The Germans began a bombardment of the Channel port of Boulogne.

'Grave – but by no means desperate'

The King had given special dispensation for Halifax, as a peer, to appear in the House of Commons to present his Government on 12 May. He told MPs that the situation in France forty-eight hours into the German invasion was 'Grave – but by no means desperate', and he was confident that, working closely with 'Our gallant French allies' the *Blitzkrieg* offensive could be stemmed. The House listened to him in sombre silence, but its mood briefly brightened when the new Prime Minister announced that he was sending the new Minister for Defence, Winston Churchill, to France as his first duty as soon as he had organised his newly created department, to oversee the closer coordination of the war effort between the two allies.

On the day he was due to depart, 16 May, Churchill was awakened early by a call from Reynaud. He should not bother coming to France that day as planned, the normally ebullient little Frenchman said, in a broken, husky voice. Still sleepy, Churchill did not take in at first the full import of Reynaud's meaning.

'We are beaten,' the embattled Premier said. 'The war is lost.'

'Lost? What are you talking about?' demanded Churchill. 'The offensive is only four days old. France has more than a hundred divisions. We British have ten divisions in the field. How can the battle be lost?'

'They have crossed the Meuse. We are beaten,' Reynaud repeated.

Churchill flung aside the silk sheets of his bed. 'Nonsense!' he roared, attempting to stiffen the fighting sinews of his ally, as if by bawling down the crackling cross-Channel wire he could instill the faltering French with his own iron will and sense of purpose. 'We went through much worse than this in the last war. Take no irrevocable decisions. I am on my way.'

He slammed down the phone with such force that a chip of bakelite flew off the receiver.

'Goddamn and blast the French!' he muttered to himself. 'They run around like headless chickens at the first setback.' He grimaced at a portrait of Admiral Lord Nelson that adorned his bedroom wall in the Old Admiralty building. '*He* would have known what to do with them.'

Three hours later at Heston airport, Churchill hoisted himself up the steps leading into the cabin of the Dakota aircraft and squeezed his bulk through the tiny doorway. Though he had no right to do so, he was wearing the uniform of a Marshal of the Royal Air Force, privately believing that such props might help impress the French with his determination to fight on at all costs, no matter what the odds.

Various members of his staff, clutching briefcases and files, followed him into the plane while Churchill, lighting up one of his beloved Havana cigars, fumed with impatience.

Minutes later they were airborne, the pilot circling over the west London suburbs, scanning the skies for his allocated escort of fighter planes. At last they were there, skimming towards him, a flight of three new-fangled Supermarine Spitfires, only just coming into service, and reportedly faster and more manoeuvrable than the old warhorse Hawker Hurricanes that were the RAF's standard fighter weapon. Well, they were certainly more stylish, thought Churchill, as he admired the fresh-painted planes streaking in perfect symmetry across the sky, waggling the flaps of their wings in salute. The Spits took up their allotted station on either wing of the Dakota, while the lead fighter nosed ahead on a course out over the Channel at Dungeness.

Günther Ahlberg could not believe his luck. As his Messerschmitt 109 fighter broke out of the grey bolster of cloud over Calais at some 8,000 feet the bright spring sunshine yielded a magical scene to his feasting eyes. The blue counterpane of the Channel lay smooth and unruffled, reflecting the clear, sunlit skies above it – empty except for the flight of aircraft winging south-west some thousand feet below him. Three of the new English Spitfires, plus a civilian Dakota lumbering along between them. The fighters were clearly an escort, and, equally clearly, his duty must be to attack the civilian plane – whoever was on board must be important to merit such a trio of shotgun riders. All these thoughts coiled through his mind in a couple of seconds while instinctively he was already preparing for the attack. Flicking the gun control into the *'Auf'* ('on') setting, he banked the yellow and black camouflaged plane, gazing out of the long cockpit at his prey. Astonishingly, despite the clear conditions, they had not seen him yet, and he had the elements of height and surprise on his side plus the rising sun behind him in the west to cancel out their advantage in numbers. He was – how had they called it in World War I? – 'the Hun in the sun'. He smiled grimly then tilted his stick forward to commence his attacking dive.

Ahlberg struck lucky. The first machine-gun bullet that entered the Dakota's cockpit killed its pilot. The rest of the burst, though they found targets too among the cockpit crew and the instruments, were redundant, as the Dakota, with its pilot hanging insensibly over his controls, his life's blood gushing out across his instruments, began its steep and irreversible dive towards the gulping sea, carrying with it Britain's Minister of Defence, his staff, its crew and the hopes of a desperate nation as it careered down, down, down.

Night was coming on

It took some forty-five minutes for the news of Churchill's dramatic demise to reach Lord Halifax. The commander of the Spitfire escort had reported to his base at Tangmere in Sussex that the 'Dakota had gone into the drink' with its distinguished passenger and that, far too late, his planes had chased and shot down the Me 109 that had carried out the fatal attack. Tangmere control, in consternation, had immediately reported the disaster to Fighter Command in north London, who had relayed it direct to Downing Street. Halifax called a Cabinet meeting at noon.

The six surviving Cabinet members, looking shrunken and lost, gathered around the long table, faces drawn and desperately worried. Although, with one or two exceptions, none of them had actually liked the dead statesman, all of them had respected his energy, his purpose, his patriotism and his popularity with the people. Without him, they felt like children lost in a wood, abandoned by their wise guide. And night was coming on.

Halifax cleared his throat. 'Well, gentlemen,' he began. 'This is a bad blow.' Heads nodded lugubriously around the table. 'Whatever else he was, Winston was a great man and we shall miss him grievously. Personally, and, I dare say, politically.' After a few more platitudes about the dead man, Halifax, devout High Churchman that he was, led a prayer for the repose of Winston's turbulent soul; and then deftly moved on to other business. News from the front continued bad, he reported; indeed worse by the hour. What was needed, Halifax said, harking back to World War I, was some new figurehead to rally and inspire the nation. In 1914, it had been the towering figure of Lord Kitchener, the nation's most famous soldier, who had been seconded to the Cabinet as Secretary for War, and whose fiercely moustachioed face and pointing finger had become the most famous and successful recruiting poster of all time, luring millions of young men into the armed forces.

He proposed to bring in a second Kitchener, said Halifax, in the shape of the current Chief of the Imperial General Staff, the ironically nicknamed Field Marshal Sir Edmund 'Tiny' Ironside. Standing nearly six-foot-six in his gleaming topboots, Ironside's very name suggested fortitude, strength and calmness – let alone his towering physical presence. A steady soldier, most famous for his command of the Allied intervention in Bolshevik Russia after the World War I, Ironside would be the perfect replacement for the dead Churchill. Halifax did not need to push the parallel with Kitchener too far – since 'K', like Churchill, had died at sea at a crucial moment of the war through enemy action while shoring up a faltering ally – in his case a mine that had sunk the cruiser *Hampshire* on which he had been sailing to Russia.

Finally, said the Prime Minister, as Ironside, like Kitchener, would be a non-party Cabinet member, he would have to name a new Cabinet minister from his own Conservative party to keep up Tory parity with Labour. He proposed 'Rab' Butler, the young Under Secretary at the Foreign Office, since he had worked in close and smooth proximity with the young man, and besides, the Cabinet needed young blood – even if, he allowed with a thin smile, young Butler's blood might be a trifle pallid compared to the black treacle that had flowed through old Winston's veins.

Charleville – 24 May

The news of Churchill's death, announced by the BBC, caused as much delight in Hitler's entourage as corresponding despair among the British public. Hitler even permitted himself a little dance of joy when he heard of it. On 24 May he flew from the *Felsennest* to Charleville, just south of the Ardennes, where General von Rundstedt, commander of Army Group A, spearheading the invasion of the west, had established his forward HQ.[11] On his arrival Hitler called a midday conference at which Rundstedt proposed that the panzers, currently converging on the port of Dunkirk, should halt – or pause, to regroup. There were several reasons for his request, he nervously told the silently brooding Führer: communications between the forward armour and the rear echelons had become taut and overstretched by their rapid advance; supplies of food and fuel were getting patchy; the men were exhausted and prone to make mistakes because of their tiredness; and the flat plain behind Dunkirk was – as the Führer himself well knew, having fought in Flanders during the last war – criss-crossed with canals which made it unsuitable for the rapid armoured advances that had carried the panzers across France.

Rundstedt paused. Never a courageous man, he almost flinched at the storm his words might unleash. He did not have long to wait.

'Never!' Hitler yelled, moving from slumped silence to screaming fury in a second. 'Never will I permit my *Wehrmacht* to be deprived of the victory they have fought and died for by the miserable...' he savoured the word, and repeated it, 'miserable and... and cowardly hesitations of my so-called Generals.' He sneered out the phrase *'So-gen-nante Gen-e-ral-e'*, his tongue lashing round every syllable, as though he was pronouncing the word *'kriminale'*.

Working himself into a frenzy, his spittle flecking his moustache, Hitler pounded the map table as he raved and ranted at the hesitations of his commanders. The ordinary soldiers, he claimed, were more heroic than the Generals, pointedly ignoring the Iron Crosses and *Pour le mérite* medals that adorned the chests and clustered at the throats of every officer around the table. If he had not overruled their advice before – before the *Anschluss*, before taking the Sudetenland, Czechoslovakia, Poland, Norway – he would not be where he was today – *they* would not be either – on the verge of scooping up all western Europe. His audience were silent. There was no stopping the Führer when he was in the full flood of his fury; and besides, no one could gainsay him: he had been right before, and who was to say that he was not right now? 'The English are within our grasp,' Hitler concluded, his forefinger jabbing down on the map of Dunkirk. 'One more push and we will have them. Goering will hammer them from the skies; Guderian's tanks will punch through the perimeter defences. Within forty-eight hours we will have won the greatest victory since Sedan. No, Rundstedt, you will not have your little *Mittags-pause*. We will kick through their puny defences and roll them into our bag. To work, gentlemen.' Exhausted by the force of his own verbosity, the Führer collapsed into a chair, the torrent of his anger spent. Aides rushed to telephones to transform his words into operational orders.

The Front – 24 May

German forces bombarded Boulogne, besieged Calais and pressed through the defensive perimeter around Dunkirk.

25 May
Boulogne fell.

26 May
The Germans broke through the Dunkirk defences – the major part of the British Expeditionary Force, some 300,000 men, and the remaining French army in the north-east were made prisoner, and their equipment was destroyed or seized.

27 May
Calais fell.

28 May
King Leopold of Belgium capitulated.

29 May
The French city of Lille fell.

30 May – London
It was another fine and cloudless spring day. The sky over St James's Park was azure blue, but the three men circling the ponds that had been laid out by King Charles II for his daily walks were not in a mood to observe or talk about the weather. One, a soft-faced young man in a bowler hat, was 'Rab' Butler, the newly appointed Foreign Secretary. The second, brash and bespectacled and clad in an expensively cut double-breasted suit, was Joseph P. Kennedy, Ambassador of the United States to the court of St James; and the third, wrapped in a fawn-coloured coat more suitable to harsher northerly climes than this balmy spring day in London was Birgir Dahlerus, a Swedish businessman who had been, since the war began, using his neutral status to act as a liaison channel between Britain and the more pro-British elements of the Nazi hierarchy, particularly Reichsmarschall Hermann Goering, the corpulent overlord of the Luftwaffe.[12]

'Well,' said Kennedy in his steely-hard Boston accent, 'It doesn't seem that events have left you much choice, Rab. Not exactly the ideal situation to start your new job.'

Butler, whose motto was that politics was the art of the possible, nodded in agreement. 'You put it, as ever, Joe, most succinctly.'

The American envoy ploughed on, his hand-made leather brogues treading heedlessly, almost sadistically, on the British politicians' delicate sensibilities.

'You've lost your army. You've lost half your air force. You're in the process of losing France, and you've lost the one man ready and able to put up more of a fight.'

Silence fell briefly, broken only by the crunch of the three men's footfalls and the splatter of a mallard's wings as it took off from the lake in a blue-green flash, as they considered the import of Kennedy's words. 'Oh, and you have also lost Poland – the ostensible reason for you going into this goddamn war.'

'So what would your advice be to me?' queried Butler mildly.

'It's staring you in the face, Rab. Your going to have to ask Uncle Adolf for peace terms – and you're going to have to move pretty fast – before Italy declares war on you and muscles in on your Mediterranean possessions.'

'Spain too,' murmured the Swede. 'I understand that Franco wants to get his hands on Gibraltar.'

'Once the jackals see a wounded beast they won't stop tearing at the flesh until the bones are picked clean,' added the Ambassador.

'But what reception do you think a peace feeler would receive in Berlin, Mr Dahlerus?' Butler asked.

'I can tell you that for sure,' replied the Swede, 'I was with Goering only four days ago. He has Hitler's ear and knows his mind. The Führer respects Britain. Believes the Empire is a force for stability and order in the world. His favourite film is *Night Riders of Bengal* you know. He admires the English – we are all of the same stock, after all.'

'What that means in concrete terms,' put in Kennedy with his usual blunt brutality, 'is that he's kicked your asses out of Europe, and he will expect you to go along with whatever settlement he chooses to impose on the Europeans. No opposition to the new order. No British interference either. You will have to turn your attention exclusively to running the Empire, while Adolf runs Europe. A straightforward cutting of the cake.'

'Which, under the military circumstances that you face,' added Dahlerus silkily, 'is more than generous.'

'And the alternative?' asked Butler.

'The alternative, my young British friend,' said Kennedy, 'is that you fight on. Alone, since the US will not intervene; starving, since Hitler will step up the U-Boat attacks on merchant shipping; bombed, since the RAF will be shot out of the sky; and threatened with ultimate invasion and occupation, since your army is in German captivity.' There was another long pause.

'Since you put it that way,' said Butler, 'I will attempt to convince my colleagues of the wisdom of your arguments. My word,' he added, 'it is certainly a beautiful day.'

The BBC radio announcer's tone was serious, but calm. 'We are now going direct to Downing Street,' he said, 'where the Prime Minister, Lord Halifax, will address the nation.'

There was a click and then listeners heard a dry preparatory clearing of the throat. For once, Halifax did not mince his words but made his meaning plain. He spoke of 'an unmitigated and catastrophic defeat', of 'the bravery of our forces borne down by the enemy's sheer superiority'. He looked ahead to 'the practical impossibility of continuing an unequal struggle with no identifiable outcome... a protracted war with no realistic hope of a positive end'. He mixed in the suffering of the ordinary people, and the uncertainty of the fate of the hundreds of thousands of men who had fallen into German hands. He spoke frankly of the difficulty of maintaining links with the Empire and the sources of food, 'on which we all – every man, woman and child in Britain – depended'. He recalled 'an honourable struggle, entered into for honourable motives', and then offered a backhanded compliment to the military skill of 'determined, ruthless, and worthy foes'.

Finally, he got to the nub of his address. Although he would not preside over a government that would 'compromise or erode 1,000 years of British freedom,' he was asking 'Herr Hitler for an immediate armistice to end hostilities,' and would himself, along with his Foreign Secretary, R. A. Butler, be travelling to Berlin as soon as a visit could be arranged, to negotiate a permanent and lasting peace in Europe with Germany's victorious leaders. Finally, he said, he hoped that he carried the prayers of the British people with him. 'Goodnight, and God bless you all.'

The Reality

While following the outline of events as they actually happened in the crucial month of May 1940, I have posited five vital differences. All five, I believe, to have been plausible – even likely – and I have tried to imagine, on the available evidence, what would have happened next had they occurred. The five 'what if' events which, in my account, differ from the reality are:

1 Halifax succeeding Chamberlain as Prime Minister rather than Churchill on 10 May.
2 Churchill being killed by enemy action flying to France soon after taking up his new post as Minister of Defence on 16 May.
3 Hitler rejecting Rundstedt's plea for a pause in the headlong advance of his panzers as they converged on Dunkirk on 24 May and ordering the armour to continue and capture the port.
4 As a consequence of 3, the BEF being overwhelmed and falling into German hands between 24–29 May, resulting in the abortion of the planned evacuation of Dunkirk by an armada of small ships.
5 Prime Minister Halifax being compelled by the accumulating disasters since 10 May to announce an armistice and personally sue for a Hitler-dictated peace.

As the whole world well knows, Halifax was the preferred choice as Prime Minister of Chamberlain, the King, and the majority of the Conservative party's MPs. The opposition Labour party, though less keen, would have served in a Halifax-led government. It was a combination of Halifax's own diffidence, and a feeling that Churchill, despite his well-known faults, had the qualities necessary in a war leader, that propelled him into office.

Churchill would most certainly have accepted the likely job offer that Halifax would have made: that of Minister of Defence to run the war effort under Halifax's overall supervision. As Prime Minister Churchill did take a panicky call from the French Premier Reynaud, and he did fly to France on 16 May. However, he survived the flight and three subsequent flying visits, as he attempted to stiffen the failing French will to resist.

Halifax, supported by his rabidly pro-appeasement Under Secretary, R. A. Butler, did push for sounding out neutral parties (Italy and Sweden) to ascertain whether Germany would entertain a compromise peace. Halifax, prompted by Butler, raised this issue in the War Cabinet during the crucial days of the Dunkirk evacuation at the end of May. Churchill, with the support of other Ministers – particularly junior Ministers – firmly crushed such peace moves.

At their Charleville conference on 24 May Hitler acceded to Rundstedt's plea for a pause in the advance of the panzers around Dunkirk. Forty-eight hours later, he changed his mind and rescinded the 'halt order' but by then the bulk of the BEF had escaped from the Dunkirk pocket, living – albeit without their equipment – to fight another day.

What Really Happened To Them?

JOHN PROFUMO: He had a 'good war' but lost his Parliamentary seat in the 1945 Labour election landslide which ousted Churchill's Conservative party from office. He returned five years later as MP for Stratford-upon- Avon, and eventually became Secretary for War. Embroiled in a sex scandal in 1963, he quitted politics and devoted the rest of his life to social work in the East End of London. He died in March 2006.

LEO AMERY: Appointed Secretary for India in Churchill's wartime Government. His disturbed pro-Nazi eldest son, John, was executed after the war for making treasonable broadcasts from Berlin. His second son, Julian, had a fine war as a Commando in the Balkans, and served in post-war Conservative cabinets. Leo Amery died in 1955.

WINSTON CHURCHILL: Britain's wartime Premier was unexpectedly defeated in the general election of July 1945. He returned to writing history, but came back to power for a second term in 1951. He resigned due to age and ill-health in 1955 and died ten years later in 1965.

NEVILLE CHAMBERLAIN: He became Lord President in Churchill's cabinet, and was treated by him with wary respect. He died of cancer in December 1940.

LORD HALIFAX: Replaced as Foreign Secretary by Anthony Eden, he was sent to Washington as British Ambassador later in the war. He died in 1959.

R. A. BUTLER: Sidelined as Education Minister by Churchill, he presided over egalitarian reforms in the education system. Post-war he became a leading Conservative politician but was repeatedly passed over for the post of Prime Minister and ended his career as Vice-Chancellor of Cambridge University and mentor to the Prince of Wales. He died in 1982.

JOSEPH P. KENNEDY: Recalled from London by President Roosevelt, partly on account of his freely expressed defeatist views of Britain's prospects for survival, and his barely concealed admiration for Nazi Germany, Kennedy devoted his post-war career to furthering the political ambitions of his sons. His eldest son, Joe Junior, was killed in the war; but his second son, John F. Kennedy, became president in 1960. He was assassinated at Dallas in 1963. Joe Senior, crippled by a stroke, died in 1969.

PAUL REYNAUD: The pugnacious if emotional Reynaud resigned as France fell, to be succeeded by the defeatist and aged Marshal Philippe Pétain. Reynaud was put on trial by Pétain's collaborationist Vichy regime, along with other leaders of the Third Republic. He survived the war, and returned to politics under the Fourth Republic, fathering a family in his seventies. He died in 1966.

Notes

*1   Leo Amery, *End of Empire*, Ottawa: 1953. Amery's memoirs, written while he was posted as High Commissioner to Canada, give a full – if characteristically dull – portrait of the decline of Britain's Empire in the first forty years of the twentieth century. There are unsubstantiated reports that the German Ambassador to Britain, Rudolf Hess, put pressure on Halifax to send the gadfly Amery into comfortable 'exile' as High Commissioner to Canada.

*2   David Lloyd George , *Partners for Peace*, London: 1944. The aged World War I Premier's last book – written a year before his death in 1945, is a typically eloquent plea for 'eternal friendship' between the 'racial cousins' Britain and Germany. It is remarkable for its fulsome praise of Hitler as 'Germany's, perhaps Europe's, greatest son'.

*3   Lord Halifax, *Saving the Day*, London: 1958. Halifax's somewhat self-serving memoirs portray him as a realist who managed the decline of Britain and the end of Empire which as little pain to its people as possible. It was written in his Yorkshire home after he was replaced as Premier by R. A. Butler in 1945.

*4   Erich von Manstein, *Vorwaerts mit dem Fuehrer*, Berlin: 1947. Manstein's memoirs set out the details of his strategy for SICHELSCHNITT – while being careful to praise Hitler for approving the conception of the plan and putting it into effect.

*5   *Der Schlieffen Plan: wie es wirklich war*, Berlin: 1964. The results of an international symposium of military historians in Berlin on the fiftieth anniversary of the outbreak of World War I. This revisionist verdict praised Schlieffen as the greatest strategist since Hannibal, and lauded Hitler – who had died the previous year – as the pupil who defeated France with his revised version of Schlieffen. 'Schlieffen with tanks' as Britain's Basil Liddell-Hart called the Führer's plan.

*6   *A Patriot's Diary*, Washington: 1956. The manuscript of his father's diary was smuggled out of Britain by Harold Nicolson's son Nigel in the early 1950s. The book gives a frank and unvarnished inside account of the anti-Halifax opposition in Britain in the 1940s; and their determined but futile attempt to build a 'British resistance'. Nicolson was arrested in 1943, held in the Tower of London, and executed in 1945 in reprisal for a resistance bomb at London's Halifax House (formerly 10 Downing Street).

*7   R. A. Butler, *Peace and its Possibilities*, London: 1970. Butler's political testament are marked by their silky venom against what he calls 'The Winstonians' – Churchill, Eden and other political rivals who failed to appreciate what he called 'The stubbornness of facts' – i.e., the need to bow before the might of Germany and the wisdom of making an accommodation with 'The man who saved Europe' as Butler flatteringly referred to Hitler.

*8   George Windsor, (formerly His Majesty King George VI) *The Last Emperor*, Sydney: 1950. The ghosted memoirs of the last King of Britain after he agreed to go into exile in Australia for the sake of his declining health in 1947. The book, despite his wooden style, gives a remarkable glimpse into behind the scenes life at the palace and concludes with the ex-king's satisfaction with his new role as a sailing instructor in Sydney harbour.

*9   J. F. C. Fuller and Basil Liddell-Hart (eds), *The Tank War*, London: 1942. An academic congress bringing together armoured commanders and military historians and theorists in postwar London gave rise to this valuable assessment of the role of tanks in the 1940 campaign. Its contributors included Guderian, Rommel and de Gaulle.

*10   Paul Reynaud, *Defaite*, Paris: 1944. Paul Reynaud's memoirs are uninformative about the unhealthy influence upon him of his pro-Nazi mistress, Comtesse Helene de

Portes. 'You have no idea,' he told a friend, 'what, at the end of a hard day, a man will do to secure a little peace.' The Countess was killed when she was struck on the back of the neck by a heavy suitcase when Reynaud braked their car sharply soon after the armistice of June 1940.

*11   Rundstedt's memoirs, *Kriegs Erinnerungen,* Berlin: 1953 unsurprisingly make no mention of Hitler's outburst. My account relies on the gossipy recollections of Rudolf Schandt '*Mein Fuehrer- zum Befehl!'*, Munich: 1960, one of Hitler's favourite adjutants, who was present at the Charleville conference.

*12   Hermann Goering, *Im Dienst meines Vaterlands,* Munich: 1962, his second volume of memoirs, is remarkably revealing about his attempts to reach an accommodation with the British 'peace party' around Butler.

Bibliography

The literature on the fall of France – military, political and personal accounts – is immense. For ease of reference I have confined myself to a personal selection of sources available in English.

For an account of the role of John Profumo – from private sources – see *Churchill* by Roy Jenkins, London: Macmillan, 2001. Profumo himself has never published his memoirs. Jenkins also points out how unreliable Churchill's account is in his *The Second World War,* London: Cassell, six volumes 1948–54 (see especially volume III, *Their Finest Hour*) regarding the circumstance of his rise to the Premiership. Although Martin Gilbert's multi-volume official *Life of Churchill,* London: Heinemann, 1991, is massive and magisterial, it is also pretty unreadable. The best single volume life is by Geoffrey Best *Churchill: A Study in Greatness,* London: Hambledon & London, 2001; see also the same author's *Churchill and War,* London: Hambledon & London, 2005; for the anti-Churchill case see John Charmley's *Churchill: The End of Glory,* London: Hodder & Stoughton, 1993, and Clive Ponting's *1940: Myth and Reality,* London: Hamilton 1989. For Leo Amery see the third volume of his memoirs *My Political Life,* London: Hutchinson, 1955. See also David Faber's *Speaking for England,* London: Free Press, 2005, a fascinating triple life of Leo Amery and his two sons John and Julian.

There are numerous biographies and studies of Neville Chamberlain. The most exhaustive, recent and, it must be said, pro-Chamberlain account is by David Dilks, *Neville Chamberlain,* Cambridge: CUP, 1984. A more balanced consideration is *Neville Chamberlain* by David Dutton, London: Arnold, 2001.

Halifax's own memoirs *Fullness of Days,* London: Collins, 1957; and his first biography *Halifax* by the Earl of Birkenhead, London: Hamish Hamilton, 1965, should be read alongside Andrew Roberts' more revealing and brilliant biography *The Holy Fox,* London: Weidenfeld & Nicolson, 1991.

Anthony Howard's biography of Butler *RAB: The Life of R. A. Butler,* London: Cape, 1987, is too indulgent to its subject.

Harold Nicolson's *Diaries and Letters 1939–45,* London: Collins, 1967, are a vivid and honest account by a well-connected insider with Churchillian sympathies – albeit one on the outer fringes of the ruling circle.

Indispensable accounts of the political jockeying during the desperate days of May and June 1940 include *Five Days in London: May 1940* by John Lukacs, New Haven: Yale University Press, 1999; John Colville's *Fringes of Power: Downing Street Diaries,*

1939–1955, London: Hodder & Stoughton 1985, are the journals of Chamberlain's secretary who performed the same role for Churchill. Colville's conversion from a committed Chamberlainite to a convinced Churchillian are as interesting as his intimate glimpses of the great man at work. Other relevant accounts include Philip Bell's *A Certain Eventuality: Britain and the Fall of France,* [Farnborough]: Saxon House, 1974; Eleanor M. Gates' *The End of the Affair: the collapse of the Anglo-French Alliance 1939–1940,* London: Allen & Unwin, 1981; and Andrew Roberts's *Eminent Churchillians,* London: Weidenfeld & Nicolson, 1994 is fascinating in exposing the precariousness of Churchill's position in 1940 and after, and the abiding hostility of large sections of the Establishment towards the wartime Prime Minister. For an interesting view from an American 'outsider-insider' see Henry Channon's *Chips: The Diaries of Sir Henry Channon,* London: Weidenfeld & Nicolson, 1967. Channon was an American Anglophile who married into the wealthy Guinness family, and became a naturalised Briton, a Tory MP, and a fanatical Chamberlainite. His journals are waspish but highly readable.

On the scene in France see *To Lose a Battle* by Alistair Horne, London: Macmillan, 1969; *Assignment to Catastrophe,* London: Heinemann, 1954, by Major General Sir Edward Spears – a confidante of Churchill who, remarkably, was the top British liaison man to the French army both in 1914 and in 1940; *The Fall of France* by Julian Jackson, Oxford: OUP, 2003; and Philip Warner's *The Battle of France, 1940,* London: Cassell, 1990.

2 Peace in Our Time
Memories of Life at Führer Headquarters

Charles Vasey

Berlin, 2 June 1970

It has been a long day, a glorious day, and a day that represented all that I have worked and struggled for, a day that has sealed my military and civil career. And yet a day of sadness for today I stood at the Führer's funeral and said goodbye to a man with whom I have worked for decades, a man who led us to victory in the war, and who has been instrumental in winning the peace. As a member of the personal staff, albeit now retired from the armed forces, I was seated in the forefront of the mourners. In front of the diplomats, in front of the damned Prussians and their army, within two rows of his Majesty, the King of Prussia; in the midst of our colleagues, those who had served in the headquarters for so long. Even with my old rank though my favoured position was based on the decoration that hangs still around my neck – the Grand Cross of the Iron Cross, an award previously only given to a few men by the old Kaiser, the present King's grandfather.[1]

Why I wear that award and how these things came to pass is the purpose of my story. A story I prepare for my grandchildren. I hope they will be plural, but my son has at last married and my daughter-in-law is pregnant. I wish them to know what was done. The death of the Führer and the birth of a grandchild seem symbolic. Is it the Druzes who believe in reincarnation of the dead at a coterminous birth? I am not sure for my knowledge of such matters is poor. But what I do know, I set out below.

I, Hermann Sulzbach, was born in 1917 in the Rhineland provinces of the old Brandenburg lands. I am not a 'von' and have never sought entry to the Junker class. I always remember my Führer saying he had a Christian Fleet, a Prussian Army and a National Socialist Luftwaffe. I was a loyal Party member, who was not in defeated Germany, and when I joined the armed services I picked the parachute arm. Yet this non-traditional choice should not make you think my family was not a loyal German family used to combat. My father had died in the Great War, I never knew him. His father had died in the Franco-German war, killed storming toward St Privat.[2]

My grandfather, also Hermann, hid a secret though – he was a converted

40

Jew. Considering what was to happen later, I find this amusing, but until the recent improvements of the sixties and the Civil Rights Movement, I would not have mentioned it. Indeed, I have not mentioned it outside the family at all. Though I suspect both the traitor Admiral Canaris and his rival Himmler either knew or suspected. Why was I a Nazi and yet a quarter Jewish? Was I a traitor to my country or to my ancestor? Frankly, I neither know nor cared. My grandfather died like a good German, killing Frenchmen. He was not a moneylender or a Jew by religion, though perhaps his father was both. By all accounts he was a decent man. However, having regard to the possibility that I have Jewish relatives I have always avoided attacking Jews – which is more than I can say for the Bolsheviks whom I loathe. But who is to say? Perhaps old Hermann did not die killing Frenchmen. Maybe he never saw a Frenchman and only heard the whine of their bullets. He died long before my birth and he died a secretive man, with good reason as it turned out.

It seemed clear to me when I joined the Fallschirmjäger that war was coming, but equally I had neither career nor wealth. I would have joined anyway. I was blessed with blond hair and blue eyes, I loved flying (but lacked the skill to be a pilot), I was healthy and I wished to avoid serving in the trenches, where my father had died. An elite service beckoned me. Of course, things did not turn out quite as I intended both as to trenches and fighting, but more of that in a moment. I looked the part of a good German soldier and had the dead-pan courage required of a Fallschirmjäger. I was even included in a propaganda film by Miss Riefenstahl; this impressed a number of young women, one of whom later became my wife.

The Fallschirmjäger service was an exciting one, but I can now confess our equipment was not of the best. After the war I met both Soviet and British paratroopers and compared their equipment. As it happened my career was not to involve many jumps. But my start on the road to where I now am did commence in blood and by glider.

I was a solid student and had self-confidence (or at least it appeared that I did) and I was proud to be commissioned and take my oath to my Führer. My unit was, of course, the best battalion in the service, which was the best in the German Armed forces. It was fitting then that we should be selected to attack Fort Eben-Emael in Belgium.[3] This fortress complex had to be knocked out to permit the advance by our armed forces into Belgium. Much as the Liège fortifications in the Kaiser's War required the huge Skoda guns to crack, so this fortification was to be cracked by our paratroops. Instead of advancing through the minefields and wire we were to drop on to the target and use surprise to knock out the weapons and kill the garrison. We had studied the fall of Douamont and Vaux at Verdun. We believed implicitly in our ability to do this.

The glider assault was most exciting and the combat most confusing. I never cease to be amazed when I read the accounts how difficult it is to remember things that way. Even the citation on my Iron Cross, even my promotion, cannot clear my memory. I do remember landing and clearing our targets. But our flank company had come under heavy fire and suffered losses. I crossed the fire zone, destroyed the machine-gun cupolas and took the surrender of a stunned Belgian colonel. I mean stunned too, the poor man had been hit in the aftershock underground and his ears were bleeding. I was, I think, deranged with combat but fortunately my Feldwebel was at hand to calm me down. The Belgian colonel was kind enough to offer me a chair as well as his side arm. I lacked the grace to refuse the latter but was suitably grateful for the former. I must confess that I never thought of myself as brave but merely foolhardy. Once I had started forward it was difficult to stop and in my excited state I thought it safer to keep moving. Perhaps I was right. Certainly I enjoyed being a hero and saw no reason to protest the accounts of my heroism, difficult though I found them to believe after the fact. Of course old soldiers love to recount their deeds, but I remain prouder of other actions and skate over this. I have left the documents in my papers with my lawyer if you wish to read them. My eldest son Baldur has my first medal. The Grand Cross I retain.

An act of heroism was a common thing in the Fallschirmjäger service and my good fortune over my fellow heroes arose from, I think, a number of causes. First, a field photographer had landed with us, for which he deserved a medal, and caught me blowing up two cupolas and receiving the surrender of the Colonel, generously missing out the chair. Second, one should never forget service rivalry – the Fallschirmjägers demanded a hero to match those of the Panzerwaffe. Third, I do look the part with blond hair and blue eyes I looked the true German hero. I was selected to meet my Führer and to receive my medal from him personally.

Although the German armed forces have evinced a courage and professionalism second to none, we of the Fallschirmjäger, as our colleagues in the panzers, carry an air of modernity that compares in reputation to the Hussars of the Baroque era. We were the darlings of all, especially when, like me, we were men of the people. My family was not a 'von' whose military bravery was hallowed and bred by centuries of military service, and by duelling scars and hunting. Any German lad could look at me and see himself as he might prefer to be. And, I am saddened to think many joined and died in Crete for no other reason. But we are all free agents, and I was in any case only obeying orders.

The fourth reason for my fame appears singularly odd now, but those were heady days. My first name was not a Christian name at all but that of the great German hero, Hermann of the Cherusci (or Arminius if you read Tacitus, as I now did). The Reichsmarschall pointed this out and my Führer joined in the laughter; there were some obscure jokes about defeating the Belgii which demonstrated a love of Latin but little else. My Führer decided there and then I was to receive more than just an award; I was to join his headquarters staff. I could scarcely believe my luck. A man may think meanly of himself for never having been a soldier but once his courage is established he finds a warm billet a more immediate desire. It is now fashionable to sneer at the views of ancient history which the Reich had in those days. Since then we have seen how well a Slav can fight, and how well Polish bandits keep fighting to this day. Archaeology has also demonstrated that the warrior Aryan very quickly became a trader. However, in those days with the insult of Versailles so close to us we embraced the vision of the German warrior free and unfettered. We particularly saw this Volk model as better than the Roman model (now appropriated by Il Duce) or the Athenian model (much favoured in the West). Speaking as a man without university education (though an honorary doctor at many fine universities) I can say that the deviant and devious Athenian was not a model that I felt I wanted to follow. But all nations need a myth (even if the myth is the absence of a myth) – and this was ours.

I shall not dwell on the arrangements of my Führer's headquarters. Like all courts it had warring factions, and I am not a courtier. I decided to adopt a bluff, open style never seeking to impose myself but to be accepted as safe by all parties. I was allowed a 'command' of fellow paratroops and arranged with General Student to receive a number of fellow Fallschirmjäger of great combat reputation for an extended 'holiday'. These rotated in and out every few months. My Führer noted that my small honour guard lacked the smartness of the Waffen-SS units but enjoyed meeting men who clearly idolised him and whose rough manners were matched with plaudits from their officers.

I had early on decided that the professional *Wehrmacht* was not going to beat the SS for the Führer's ear; their arrogance had to be seen to be believed – a British Grenadier Guards officer once commented on it to me, which rather proves my point. That I, a regular and a 'hero', treated the Waffen-SS with respect and courtesy meant much to the Waffen-SS officers and men. I was even asked to advise on forming SS Fallschirmjäger units but managed to appear helpful without attracting the wrath of my fellow Hermann – the Reichsmarschall. I rubbed by, avoiding rivalries and providing my Führer with a small pocket of quietude where he could talk to men who had fought as he had fought in the Kaiser's War – face to face. My Führer was in the habit of asking my opinion as if some incarnation of Hermann of the Cherusci. And it was this that allowed me, I say with all due modesty, to serve my country. The original Hermann had been raised with Roman culture but remained a true warrior and German. Furthermore his taking of the three Roman eagles at Teutobergerwald evinced not the brute rush of German warriors but cunning and stealth followed by savage combat. Finally, it was with great pride we noted that no Gallic tribe took Imperial Eagles. I like think Hermann would have served as a Fallschirmjäger, but regimental pride is a lying jade.

The defeat of France brought great joy to my Führer. I was there at his 'dance of joy' at Compiègne.[4] He had seen the stain on his own honour, the stain on his army's honour, and the stain on his nation's honour erased in one moment. He spoke to me of a punishment for the French, and I suggested that whatever the panzer generals said the French soldier was a good soldier. If they could only be on our side, how many Germans could they free for economic work? I cannot say I made my point well enough since he deprived

Pétain of Paris, but I was thanked by a French colonel for my efforts when I attended a levée in the sixties with Prince Bonaparte before he became Prince-President.[5]

Our thoughts now transferred to war against the Bolsheviks. Surely, we all felt, the British could not continue at war with us when such an enemy stood before us both. But the war criminal Churchill knew his countrymen better than we. I was certainly vindicated with my policy of non-partisan service at the Headquarters with the defeat of my Luftwaffe colleagues over Britain. I had suggested to my Führer that Eagle Day was to offer those Roman Eagles back to an enemy fighting on his own soil (or above it). We should, I believed, be fighting the British at sea; I'm delighted to say Admiral Raeder became an exponent of my homespun German wisdom. How easy it is to be wise when wisdom is saying what others want. Yet how many more clever men than I have failed to grasp this.

The next six months were for the Staff a rising crescendo of work. Planning for what was to be Operation BARBAROSSA was starting and that led to further strategic plans to deal with the Balkans. I must say as a Rhinelander that I found Balkans politics rather puzzling. Each nation seemed to have its own equivalent of our National Socialist movement; though in some cases they resembled more the Italian fascists. Each nation also seemed to have stolen or lost a province of two from each other and was consumed by rage about the loss or fear about retaining the booty. None of them had the slightest claim (as far as I could see) to being Aryan and which side they joined seemed based on chance and old alliances. This was in many ways the old way of war; lacking any doctrinaire element. It had been a game of princes; now it was a contest of ideas.

It was traditional among my 'Prussian' comrades to decry all of the Balkan armies as being no better than those of an old German petty principality. One staff officer rudely compared them to the world of *La Grande-Duchesse de Gerolstein* this was pretty daring as it was an operetta by the French Jew, Offenbach.[6] I had the opportunity to read a British novel called *The Prisoner of Zenda* which exactly caught the comic-opera effect of these staff officers in their mixture of uniforms. The Romanians impressed me as they still had their Hohenzollern king, and I remained loyal in some nebulous way to the old line. Yet I could see that under the world of Ruritania lay a world of massacre and hatred. These men were perfectly willing to die for Transylvania or Albania or indeed Thessalonica. And, though they did not impinge on me physically their silly arguments were to lead to our invasion of Greece.

I remember being present at a staff meeting as duty aide when it was discussed whether we should intervene in Greece to save Italian face. I loved watching the intelligence of the General Staff planners. The concern about delaying BARBAROSSA was taken up by one young officer (a keen reader on Napoleon in 1812). Another pointed out that an Allied Greece would leave open the opportunity of Yugoslavia (or Serbia as he kept calling it) remaining in the war; his father had served on attachment with the Austrians. A third (a very devious fellow) pointed out that the British push into Italy's North African colonies might be halted. I might have intervened had I known what this decision would mean for my fellow paratroopers who dropped into Crete. I am not persuaded that an intervention by me would have helped – to a General Staff officer a talking paratrooper would have been a remarkable thing.

Crete did come as a mixture of shock and pride. Clearly, pride at the victory but shock at the cost; my Führer very kindly visited my group after the battle to speak of his pride in his paratroopers. Visiting paratrooper officers made the point to me how lucky we were to win; the Tommies had been led by a very brave New Zealander, but he was not, we thought, a great general.[7] We had with us that day an officer from a mountain unit; they had suffered dreadful losses when attacked by the Royal Navy. I made a chance remark that one might almost have thought they (the Tommies) knew where we would be. I notice my Führer pause at this but nothing more was said. It set my mind in motion however. The Tommies were of course traditionally incompetent as an army, but without good German battalions to stiffen their resolve as at La Belle Alliance this was hardly to be wondered at.[8] Their navy was as piratical as ever and their air force simply too numerous. What if, though, bumbling old Tommy did know what we were doing? But I dismissed it, our intelligence services were the best in the world.

This thought I held in my mind into the summer. One day just after BARBAROSSA started I was standing watching some of the children of the staff playing a game of hide-and-seek. I forget which children, it might have been some of the young Goebbels children (now all grown up with impressive careers in service of Germany) but I cannot remember their ages.[9] Whatever, my Führer joined us to watch the game. My Führer was not the ogre that the black propaganda of the war criminal Churchill made him out to be. He was a fastidious man and a very clever one even Comrade Stalin referred to him as a very capable man. His service in the Kaiser's War was exemplary. His bitter experiences after our defeat mirrored those of my widowed mother. Yet he was not a warlord as I imagined warlords. His dislike of hunting (which the Reichsmarschall loved), especially of fox-hunting ('That British disease' he called it), and love of children reminded me of perhaps a schoolmaster of high principles.

As we watched the children playing there was one boy who seemed very adept at catching his opponents. As he passed close to me I saw why, the cloth tied around his head did not fit his face and I could see the flash of his eyes. Yet he made a very good impression of being unable to see until he suddenly pounced on his target. I remarked on this to my Führer; what if, I said, Mr Churchill was also cheating? He did not treat it as a joke but stood in silence; then after due thought he turned and said, 'Why not?' But how could Churchill be peering into Germany – spies, signal intercepts, traitors? Surely Himmler and his Gestapo had the Continent watched very carefully? I walked slowly away wondering whether it had to be any of these. What if he was simply looking at our world from a distance, not via his proxies in Europe? Like our ingenious boy using the information, but not so as to attract immediate attention? I resolved to think about the matter – it was not as if I had other weighty matters keeping my attention.

The skills of a paratrooper officer are not those of the cryptographer or the intelligence officer. But there were many of the latter passing through headquarters. I spoke to one young Waffen-SS officer on the topic. He was an interesting young man, very involved in signal interception (something that was very easy with the Russians). He recounted tales from his father's time in Russia where the enemy broadcast without code. This was clearly an area just as much full of cunning and ambush as my kind of combat, a sort of deadly chess. Given his intellectual bent, he did not fit in with the more sporty Waffen-SS officers and we found time to talk. Indeed, I wondered why he was not in the *Abwehr*; some political reason, I suspect.

He explained (simplifying matters for me) how in action one could use simple code-names and code terms. 'White Knight to White King' might be a company commander contacting his Oberst, or it might be a tank commander contacting his *Zug* leader. Without knowing who was who signal intelligence officers intercepting the call were unlikely to be able to identify who was firing or moving even if the rest of the call was in open language. Of course by diligent application one could identify some code names in time. Of course for less immediate transmission of orders a more complex coded solution could be adopted. He told me that German formations used an ENIGMA machine. This was a complex machine that worked, I think, on the basis of exchanging letters of the alphabet using a device that connected the two ciphers. Once translated from German into text the recipient could translate it back as long as he had the correct code wheels. To make things even more secure the code wheels were changed regularly. So breaking one code did not help you, you had to keep breaking it as it changed. The result of the various code wheels was to give you a very large number of combinations. It all sounded very impressive. But for some reason I pressed the issue. What if your opponent did break the code? My friend stopped and thought, and turned back to me to say, 'We would be defenceless.' It seemed difficult to conceive of how such a code could be broken but there were, he assured me, a great deal of very clever people around.[10]

Surely, I wondered, we would know if the enemy tracked our every move. He would win a series of surprise victories. Then I thought of the boy with the eye cover; he knew better than to reveal his cheating too soon, this allowed him to lull his opponents into a false sense of security. Could the Allies really be that controlled? Well, as we now know, the duplicity of the war criminal Churchill defied belief. They had broken our ENIGMA codes and were listening to our every strategic move under the code-name ULTRA.

But to two young officers discussing matters all this seemed difficult yet intriguing and we had other events to consider. The further into Russia we went the more we seemed invincible. One evening we were discussing our favourite topic (we called it Bat Ear) when my Führer appeared at the door of the mess. As always he directed us to sit and we explained our theory. He remembered the children's game and listened with interest. Although with staff officers he could be abrupt, with us he was more kindly. I pointed out that the Abwehr officers seemed to be rather too keen on preserving their power-base than in thinking the unthinkable. Yet the Romans had just as easily assumed they could not be defeated by the Cherusci. Could we, I asked, trust the Abwehr to question the competence with which they operated? My Führer was clearly not a great believer in Canaris. He took up my suggestion that it might be a good idea to use a second agency to consider the matter.

That agency was (of course) the SS. However, to give Himmler his due (he was killed soon afterwards with his loyal lieutenant, Heydrich, by Czech assassins[11]) he seldom did a job badly. A section was set up to track enemy reactions to our signal traffic. Some very unlikely cryptographers who did not appear very Aryan appeared in SS uniforms; indeed the Polish names they bore were unlikely, I thought, to be the names of their fiefs in Prussia. However, Himmler was driven on occasion by expediency rather than policy.

I would like to say that I helped the SS cryptographers to crack the ULTRA secret, but I did not. I was a Headquarters aide, not an intelligence officer. I hope my early suggestions can claim to be its birthplace, and I certainly believe that my suggestion that it was not handled by the Abwehr was important. I was not to see the fruit of this tree until 1944.

Meanwhile we struggled in Russia. The first winter was terrible; the generals wobbled, but my Führer did not. We held against the Siberians and the winter, but for the first time there appeared two parties each blaming the other. I remained outside this factionalism but loyal to my Führer. In 1942 we fought the long drive into Russia that ended so badly at Stalingrad. My Führer became more and more affected by this defeat; and for the first time even I could see this was a defeat. I do not mean that it was my military assessment but that it was my assessment of my Führer's view. 1943 beckoned with all the challenges of the Eastern front but for me June would always be associated with pain as I was involved in the infamous motor accident and left out of events.

I returned to find the Führer had cancelled ZITADELLE and had given von Manstein permission to use a flexible defensive on the Russian Front. How different from the old days this was! Speer was now given much greater powers with orders to build the Reich's industry up and to balance anti-bomber resources and the need to re-equip the East after Stalingrad. I often wondered what would have happened if ZITADELLE had gone ahead. The Waffen-SS officers were supremely confident, but the *Wehrmacht* officers were not. Infantry combat for a paratrooper in my day consisted of rifles, machine-guns and possible a mortar. But in the wilds of the East (as one panzer officer told me) one kills tanks with anti-tank guns not by deploying tanks to fight tanks. His view, for he had fought on the front rather than merely been involved in planning, was that the Russians had learned their lessons well, and ZITADELLE would have been a meat-grinder for German tanks opposing

Bolshevik PAK-fronts. He much preferred our clever Feldmarschall's solution of strong defences and a powerful panzer reserve. He also preferred the shorter lines after Stalingrad. I pointed out that this denied us the oil fields of Baku, but he was unimpressed, telling me that we lacked the numbers to hold such a line. I have never served in Russia and distance is something that is commented on by many who have served there.

The autumn and summer campaigns were a mixture of high Bolshevik hopes confounded always by the counterblows of von Manstein. The Bolsheviks gained some ground but a fearsome cost. Yet it was a fearsome cost that they seemed willing to pay. We speculated how the councils of the allies must have been affected by this. The Western Allies had landed in Sicily but had not collapsed the Italians who now fought well, though the Führer had sent one of his Luftwaffe loyalists – Kesselring – to hold the front and to keep the King of Italy under careful guard. The propaganda wing of the SS made much of the fact that the Allies in Italy included Moroccan troops with a ferocious reputation towards civilians. The Italians balanced the fear of these brutes against the fact that the British and Americans were ashore (but barely so) in the south of Italy. I also believe that the active stalemate on the Eastern Front persuaded them that Germany was still a potent force. This view I formed from a visit to my Italian paratrooper colleagues from the Nembo unit.[12]

1943 ended with the Allies in Italy, with the Ukraine red with blood, and ferocious battles over the Reich at night. A visit from my cryptographer friend for Christmas confirmed that the SS cryptographers had concluded that the Allies had broken our ENIGMA codes. I was delighted to think that I might have been instrumental in this matter, and the Führer clearly thought so as I was privately invested with the Grand Cross of the Iron Cross (I could not receive it openly for reasons of security). However, I was amazed to hear that the SS solution had been (with the Führer's agreement) to change nothing and to use the knowledge to feed false information to the Allies. Typically the *Abwehr* was not informed.

Talking among the officers at Headquarters that Christmas there was a strong belief that 1944 would have to see a final trial of strength. The new regime in the Ukraine, and a sensible policy towards guest workers (we no longer called them slave workers and sometimes fed them) had meant that the Reich was being fed and equipped by the former slaves of the Bolsheviks. The Russians would have to try and crush von Manstein this time. In the West we all expected an Allied invasion, but had been heartened by the Dieppe raid and the stalemate in Italy. Some wags compared the Allied Italian sector to Salonika in the Kaiser's War, but the more informed officers believed Italy to be good fighting terrain. Indeed, none of us was surprised when Kesselring was sent to command in northern France and Rommel took command in Italy.[13] As a man used to fighting in mountains (he had served on this front in the Kaiser's war) and with his experience with Italian troops he constituted a firm rock upon which the south could be anchored. Naturally the Führer sent him a Luftwaffe general to ensure he was more politic towards our Italian

Allies. Would the Allies strike in France or instead the Balkans? We wiled away the hours speculating.

Our answer was to come on both fronts in a single month – June 1944. The Russians had planned a large strike against Army Group Central, Operation BAGRATION, and had spent a considerable time building up their forces. On our side the Panthers and Tigers which had been introduced in late 1943 were now fully ready for combat. This would be a true clash of giants. I discussed with my Panzerwaffe comrades the status of our tanks. They were very pleased that ZITADELLE had not occurred in 1943 noting that their equipment was not yet combat ready. Now they felt these weapons were the best that there were. The Panther, they would tell me with all the enthusiasm of the zealous, was based on the Russian T34 but was one generation further forward. The Tiger was very powerful indeed but not fast and a great consumer of fuel. Both tanks had been tested in Italy and had smashed the Allied Sherman tank regularly. Indeed, even in their boastfulness the tankers admitted that they admired the bravery of the Allied tank crews that fought in these weak-armoured tanks without a suitable gun and with a reputation for bursting into flames. I remembered gliding towards Eben Emael through the small arms fire and sensed the same feeling. How odd that I should remember this now.

In the west the Allies were to land either at the Pas de Calais (the area closest to England) or in Normandy. It was clear to the SS decrypt team that the Allies were operating a 'false army' under Patton in southern England. Although the Abwehr denied this idea, this simply confirmed its accuracy to the SS. They proposed Operation ALBERICHT; in which they transmitted a lot of signal traffic using ENIGMA in which most reserve formations were located in the Pas de Calais. A series of operational plans were referred to, making it clear to the ULTRA interceptors that the Pas de Calais force was not to move in the event of an earlier landing elsewhere. The Allies clearly saw Kesselring as fixated on that area. It was intended that they take the bait and go for Normandy.

Of course, the Allies used many intelligence sources other than ULTRA, and we sought to convince them that the ENIGMA transmissions were genuine. Every German unit with transmitting traffic was actually present in the Pas de Calais – we could not attempt the outrageous fraud of Patton's Phantom Army where the Resistance was watching and waiting. However, each unit also sent Kampfgruppe on training courses. These units (like the old Reichswehr under the Versailles Treaty) were to appear as supernumeraries, often removing arm bands or assuming the identity of their host formation. The mission of these forces was to prepare equipment so that if the Allies took the bait then formations would already be in position in Normandy. Kesselring took the view that the early days were important but that the sort of naval artillery he had seen at Salerno or in Sicily meant that units would find movement difficult and forward positioning was vital.

Although we had guessed that ENIGMA was broken we could not be sure and there was considerable concern as May arrived. The Führer had decided to allow the Vichy regime to remain in power and in the months ahead Frenchmen were to fight bravely on both sides. The Resistance was only to collapse when their patrons did. And the Vichy units (supported by Italian naval formations) were to free German units from the South of France (more is the pity for my comrades for whom it would have been a sweet billet).

The dawn of 6 June 1944 saw the simultaneous launch of attacks. The Soviet Byelorussian fronts (named in hope as they were not in Byelorussia) attacked Army Group Centre behind a wall of artillery. Despite the sneers about *untermenschen*, the Soviets attacked with skill and bravery; they truly loved their Motherland. Fortunately for us the carefully husbanded forces in the East were in large numbers and facing a foe that had lost the bravest and the best in 1943. The attack forced back our lines in some areas; and our panzer reserve cut back in behind the major drives. Just as at Kharkov the Russian forward units found themselves cut off and had to retire suffering further losses. After four weeks of this the Soviet forces had advanced hardly at all and suffered even more losses. Our losses were not light either but the flexible response once more saved the day; no more Führer Orders for us! But this grinding clash of two armies was secondary to the landings in Normandy.

The Allies had stormed ashore and suffered serious losses. The British beaches on the Cotentin peninsula were comparatively easy, both invasions being supported by clever tank adaptations which were much admired by my more technical Panzerwaffe colleagues. The Americans, despite their reputation for technical innovation, did not use them on the three American beaches (IOWA, OMAHA and UTAH[14]) and suffered accordingly – failing to capture Caen. The pre-positioned German forces and Kampfgruppe were ready for action and struck towards the beaches. Especially effective were the three heavy Tiger battalions 'attached' to Ostbattalions as 'earthmoving equipment'. The tank crews had had to spend the last four weeks dressed as the lowest of the Heer. Now at last they could don their black uniforms. The Allies were trapped on the shore unable to push more than five miles inland in the American sector. Our units were exposed to savage naval bombardment but kept fighting to prevent more troops landing – our real concern was the Allied artillery units sitting out in the landing ships. Both the Americans and the British were renowned for their artillery; whatever we suffered at the hands of the American and Royal Navies was as nothing to what lay in wait for us if their gunners landed. Our lessons in Italy were that once the Allies had a hinterland their guns would act as a massive force multiplier. They might not break through but they would cause dreadful casualties.

ULTRA intercepts (we now know) showed no movement in the Pas de Calais although the local intelligence networks referred to heavy traffic. Unaware that we were feeding them false intelligence the Allied planners stuck to their guns – or perhaps they had no choice. The panzer forces in Normandy drove hard into the Americans and pressed in on their perimeter. Beach areas were coming under fire. In the west the British and Canadian were ashore but moving slowly, too slowly. I could not help but feel as I talked to our officers that the British were too stolid to act quickly, too wedded to a plan. The Americans might have functioned better there. As it was we recaptured UTAH on the eastern flank in the second week of June. With no hinterland in which to deploy supplies or (most importantly) artillery, the Americans suffered a hellish existence worse, my Nembo acquaintances said than at Salerno. A savage Channel storm in the first week of July wrecked their supply network and US units had to withdraw behind the British lines. With just two beaches left operable and the front very reduced it surprised none of us that the Allies withdrew from Normandy in mid July. A skilful operation it was true but leaving much equipment behind.

Germany had survived the first attack in the North. It was holding in Italy and in the East. Churchill rallied his people and the Americans trumpeted defiance, but their landing equipment was wrecked, and there were further losses. Even the Abwehr thought the British Army must be weakening. The reduction in bombing attacks that followed the withdrawal indicated resources being switched to the Army from Bomber Command. We were aware that the war criminal Harris was purged at this time. The official story reported a motor accident...[15]

The Führer called a conference on the next stage. There was no sign that the British or Americans would give up yet, although we had gained six months until losses were replaced.; but what of the Russians? Since Stalingrad they had suffered loss after loss for little gain. The constant losses of the most offensive formations had affected the Red Army. They had had too many battles like Operation MARS. The failure of BAGRATION was another serious blow. Could we do business with Stalin? We had done business before. Stalin's position was supported, we believed, by a police state that even the late Himmler would have admired. He would be hated if we were not hated more. Too many partisan sweeps, too much of Mother Russia was in our hands. We had improved matters in the Ukraine but not sufficiently to hold it forever. The Führer summoned his diplomats. Seek peace he said; offer the Russians the boundaries before they invaded Poland; the return of Kiev and Minsk. Molotov met our plenipotentiaries in Kursk. He hedged this answer but our intelligence was that Stalin despaired of the western allies and like Lenin in 1917 favoured peace. His desire for a Second Front had been thwarted and hope deferred maketh the heart sick.

Stalin was an odious man in many ways though oddly impressive face to face (we met in Moscow in 1947 at the Germano-Russian Games), but he was a businessman. Faced with defeat (or at best stalemate), he understood that Germany could continue to fight and might eventually be beaten but at a cost that would leave the Americans the only major power. Already he was strengthening his NKVD units ready for a backlash. Nevertheless he played the part well demanding Poland and Romania. The Führer countered by offering him the Baltic republics and the return of all prisoners. Stalin agreed in principle to this offer. He did not however want Russian prisoners returning yet, instead we were to retain all PoWs for three years, but we were to hand over all Cossacks and other Russians who served in the *Wehrmacht*. Many officers were shocked at this betrayal of comrades in arms but these men (and often their families) were handed over to certain death as traitors against the now enlarged Soviet state.[16] There was peace on the eastern front. The Soviet state turned inward into a short power struggle, after which it regained and re-educated its many prisoners returned at regular intervals by the Reich. Comrade Stalin turned some armies east to pursue war against the Japanese.

The peace in the East did not, of course, mean that such violent hatreds ended. Many divisions remained on the East but there were spare units for Occupied France (the Führer returned the Bordeaux coast to Marechal Pétain). Italy was reinforced and a grinding warfare started on what remained the only active land front. Over the Reich extra fighter units were deployed against the remaining bombing units. The Führer also announced the building of more submarines. But would all this convince the war-criminal Churchill and his stooge Roosevelt? For three months we saw little reaction. Both seemed to be unmovable in the face of a most difficult campaign. The British Army was running out of men, and the Americans running out of patience. Then in November the President died. It was (we said), echoing my Führer, the 'Miracle of the House of Hohenzollern'. The Vice-President, Truman, quickly moved towards laying out the terms of a peace. America was very far from defeated and beyond our weaponry (we did not then know of the WALKYRIE atomic weapon). The Führer wished to obtain its neutrality by carefully reducing areas of conflict. One could not (and I would argue cannot) believe the Bolsheviks.

American emissaries identified that America wanted peace but they also wanted a free hand against Japan, which the Führer conceded, and Britain to be left uninvaded. They were concerned that they could not guarantee that Britain would sign a treaty. But the Americans believed that with a shattered Army and Air Force and a Navy trying to support a lifeline of food and munitions to America, Britain would see sense. America was just as concerned to leave a bastion to watch the peace in Europe. The Führer agreed providing that the colonial empires of all powers were to be liberated (under of course American and German auspices) and who could argue that freedom was a bad thing? I met Subhas Chandra Bose[17] one day before he flew to India to form the new Government after peace was signed, what a moment that was! A bevy of new governments were to be formed. Britain had no choice but to fight on (and they still faced a Japanese army on the eastern borders of India) or to come to terms. After much blood (as we shall see) it was to choose the latter.

What clinched the deal for Truman[18] was a matter of some controversy to this day. Revisionist historians have claimed that my Führer and Himmler had planned the mass slaughter of the Jews in Germany and the Greater Reich. I found this hard to believe. The Jews were collected in work camps to protect them and to ensure that they served the Reich. This story of intended slaughter must have been a hoax; a piece of black propaganda from our

English friends perhaps. Such a mass murder would be the work, surely, of madmen. That said I was once told by a Gestapo officer to enquire no further lest it give support to enemies of the Reich. In any case Truman required that as the final price of peace the Jews of liberated Europe be given right of passage to a new Jewish homeland in Palestine overseen by the United States. The British had offered Uganda as a homeland but it was not the land of the covenant. The Führer insisted on a German Mandate in Iraq as his price, which has since proved very valuable with its oil fields, and German firms have been drilling for oil in the Saudi Arabian fields. To prevent the two states abutting Transjordan went to France. As you will be aware there was much bad blood between the Jews and Arabs of Palestine but the presence of US troops and the Marshall Plan improved the lot of both national groups.

What could the British do; abandoned by the Russians, betrayed (as they saw it) by the Americans who were pressing them to accept peace? Within two weeks Polish units, realising they had been cheated of a homeland by the two nations they most hated, launched a rising in London. Lancaster bombers of the Polish squadrons attacked St Paul's Cathedral. This quixotic people were surprised to find themselves supported by the units of the Army from the mining regions of Britain where there was healthy dislike of the war-criminal Churchill (he had apparently threatened to use force in a strike). The Americans were forced to intervene at first but then decided to pull back as the fact of defeat sank into a people victorious for centuries.

The truth that only American diplomacy defended their shores and held at bay the U-boats was a terrible thing for so proud a people. I felt a pang of sympathy for them. What if Germany had lost the war, the defeats blamed on my Führer (as the British so correctly blamed their evil fate on the bellicose Churchill) and Berlin subject to invasion? Such circumstances were of course the stuff of invention, but I could feel for them. Now the earlier offers of peace from my Führer came home to haunt Churchill. Mosley (the British Fascist leader) was released from prison and started an attempt to undermine the Government. Mosley was shot by gangster SAS units while addressing a meeting in Solihull. Churchill's car was bombed two weeks later by British Fascists and the old brute killed. Further bloodshed was cut short by Major Attlee's newly formed but short-lived Government which was to accept the peace terms. Playing (as Churchill had feared) the part of Austro-Hungary in World War I.[19] The defeat of Britain hastened the death of their King overwhelmed by ill fortune. The Fascist Government of 1948 exiled the Queen and her two daughters (the eldest Elizabeth was to become Queen of Canada, Australia and New Zealand – I met her in the sixties) and invited the Duke of Windsor to return to the throne. His was a poisoned chalice and after decades of internal troubles, England has only recently begun to achieve stability but is filled with a desire to excel, I fear we may have built a younger version of Germany. The republics of Ulster, Wales and Scotland have, however, enjoyed a much more peaceful transition to liberty. Britain retained some of its colonies but India was lost, turned into a cantonal confederacy of princely states and democratic provinces. The experiment has not been a success.

What more can we say? My role was smaller and smaller in great affairs. Peace had come; and even with Russia it held. Stalin's death and then the accession of Comrade Beria provoked further brutality until an army revolt placed a former KGB man in the Kremlin. The Russian annexation of Manchuria has turned this Asiatic empire further eastward. The American bombing of Tokyo with their new terror weapon provoked a profound reaction in Europe. How proud we were when the Reich tested its first WALKYRIE in Masuria in 1948!

Of course nothing stays as it was. The removal of the Jews as an object of contempt (the gypsies had mysteriously disappeared) reduced the fury of German politics. The war reparations flooded into Germany and, with the Allied agreement to peace, into Italy. Troops returning home were only too pleased not to have to fight again and so this great victory resulted in a much reduced armed forces. My Grand Cross (given at the behest of the SS for the ULTRA idea) ensured me a retirement on high pay and the rank of Colonel. My son is a chemist with his own company in the Ruhr, it is as if war never happened.

France regained its northern departments in 1949 (and some British colonies in 1945) but has been involved in wars with nationalists in the colonies ever since. Germany has established a Free Trade Zone or economic community to rival the customs union from which von Bismarck fashioned Germany. Even Britain may soon join. There is prosperity everywhere under the German eagle. A world divided into three camps has achieved an uneasy peace but it is a peace.

Perhaps the most intriguing change that arose from our victory was the return of the Hohenzollerns to the throne of Prussia; an idea that the Führer developed as part of his Return to Normality programme. It has borne fruit with General Franco in Spain with King Juan Carlos only recently. We feel linked to that glorious day in the Hall of Mirrors at Versailles. How proud my grandfather would have been.

However, on this day as I watched the Führer's coffin being carried into the church it was not that great man of whom I thought; a true German with his hunting and his victories as an air ace. I thought not of Hermann Goering, Führer from 1943 to 1970, but *my* Führer, Adolf Hitler, killed in that dreadful crash in 1943. I wondered for a moment, would things have worked out the same had Adolf Hitler not died, but no, on due reflection I think German victory was inevitable.

[*Translators note*: this document is stamped with a Gestapo notice that it is to be held in the State archives following the death of Colonel Sulzbach in a road accident two days after the Führer's funeral. The driver of the car was never apprehended; but a marginal note indicates no stain should attach to the holder of the Grand Cross of the Iron Cross. This is counter-signed by Chancellor Speer.]

[The papers were released under the, short-lived, Peiper Government's Freedom of Information Act in 2005 and passed to Colonel Sulzbach's son. The driver of the car, a Gestapo officer, escaped to Argentina to avoid prosecution.]

The Reality

Of course Hitler died two years too late, beating Himmler to the Styx by a short head. The Russians benefited from Kursk to recapture the Ukraine, invade the Balkans, destroy Army Group Centre and then take Berlin. After much hard fighting reminiscent of the Great War the western Allies cut into Germany united more than ever by suspicion of their Russian ally. The world became bi-polar for fifty years.

In a book of serious alternate history this chapter represents the category of 'Tall Tale'. The problem must be that for Germany to succeed someone on the Allied side must be willing to agree to a separate peace. It seemed to me that Stalin was the man most ready to do business and with the greatest distrust of his two allies. If Germany could shatter the hope of a Second Front then perhaps we could have 1917 again. There is better way to crush the hope than let the Second Front open and then close it. For Stalin the feeling of being shackled to a corpse would have been intense. Could the Germans have pinned the Allies back on the coast in Normandy? All we can say is that they would have had a better chance with the troops pinned by Patton's phantoms.

However, it takes two to tango, and even if Stalin was ready to talk he had to have a German leader with whom to converse. In my view Hitler was not that man; he was a 'True Believer' and getting more so with each year. Himmler was, at the end, ready to negotiate but I think him still too much the True Believer in the middle years of the war where I needed to generate movement. I needed someone who was intelligent but not too rigid; with Hitler and Himmler gone Goering met these conditions. Reading the views of Nüremburg prosecutors it seemed clear to me that Goering was cleverer than his colleagues even if (or perhaps because of that) less effective. A man of sybaritic tastes will always cut a deal; we had no need of the spartan Hitler and Himmler.

Would Harry Truman have cut Churchill off at the knees? Truman was a man for whom I have great respect but I did feel that the British attitudes to the Americans and the difficulties of alliances in defeat would have made Truman think of what was best for America. I could not see Japan ever getting away from American vengeance but nor could I see America fighting an unwinnable war to support the British Empire. We British were beaten by 1943, our role was to hand on the baton.

Other twistings against history include:

- The Goebbels' children were poisoned by their mother in the *Führerbunker* in 1945.

- SS-Obergruppenführer, Reinhard Heydrich was assassinated by Czech resistance fighters in 1942. The Germans launched savage reprisals and 15,000 Czechs may have died as a result. One man's resistance fighter is, of course, another's assassin. Probably the highest ranking target of such attacks was a Russian Front commander killed by partisans. Himmler was nowhere near at the time of Heydrich's death. He finally surrendered to Western Allied units in 1945.
- Kesselring remained in Italy and did not go to France, which was Rommel's post. Both were excellent builders of fortifications.
- The Allied deployment at Normandy is reversed from the historical one, requiring a third beach.
- The handing over of Cossack prisoners by the British Army occurred in 1945. These units had an unsavoury reputation from the Balkans and Warsaw. It was the subject of a celebrated libel action but not between Germans.

Notes

1   There had been five recipients of the Grand Cross in World War I; the Kaiser, von Hindenburg, Ludendorf, Prinz Maximilian Arnuf and von Mackensen. Hitler gave it to Reichsmarschall Hermann Goering.

2   The battle of Gravelotte-St Privat 1870 was a classic clash of the aggressive German forces against the more defensive French and their dreaded Chassepot rifle. The slaughter of the units is well described in Howard, 1961.

3   The attack occurred on 10 May 1940.

4   The signature of the Franco-German peace occurred in the same railway carriage as (in 1918) the Germans had surrendered to the Allies.

5   France enjoyed (in the strict sense of the word) claimants from three houses, Bourbon, Orleans and Bonaparte. In 1852 Prince Louis Napoléon became Prince-President. The Prince mentioned here is a descendant of Louis's cousin Plon-Plon, son of Jerome of Westphalia.

6   The operetta, first performed in 1867, involved the Grand-Duchess's love for Fusilier Fritz whom she creates Baron Vermuth-von-Bock-bier, Count of Pilsener-Lager von Auld-Lang-Schweinstein. The punning references to drink convey some of the contempt. Bismarck attended the first night and was not impressed with the message. His response came in 1870. Balkan rulers tended to be found from German princely families and the scion of one such house returned to power in Bulgaria recently.

7   Bernard Cyril Freyberg (1889–1963) earned the Victoria Cross for courage on the Somme in November 1916 plus a further four DSOs. Born in England but raised in New Zealand, he represents the new spirit of New Zealand as it moved away from ex-colony to full nation.

8   *La Belle Alliance* is the German name for Waterloo, see numerous books by Peter Hofschröer. It is easy to forget how much the military histories of Britain and Germany were intertwined as allies.

*9   The six children have had a varied career following the unfortunate death of their father hunting with the Führer. Probably the most famous, (the second daughter) became ambassador to the United States and married Richard M. Nixon, future President of the United States. See Hermann Goering, *Ace of Aces*, München: Stahlhelm Verlag, 1965

10   Marian Rejewski, Jerzy Rozycki and Henryk Zygalski had broken ENIGMA codes before the war at the University of Poznan. Once in Britain Alan Turing (often called the 'Father of British Computing') also worked on the decrypting.

*11   Following the slaughter of the two highest (and more dangerous) SS Officers the Germans extracted much blood from the Czechs treating them as badly as the Poles. The Waffen SS now reported directly to Adolf Hitler under Hausser, the other branches of the SS to Eichmann.

12   183° Reggimento Paracadutisti (Parachute Regiment) 'Nembo'. *See Seymour Bütz, *Uniforms and Regalia of the Allies* Manitoba: J.J. Fedorowicz, 1998.

*13   Kesselring is noted for his anti-glider installations known as Kesselring's Asparagras. He was the Reich's Ambassador to France after the war and often vacationed at Deauville, not far from the site of his greatest victory.

*14   Montgomery, the British leader was highly critical of the Americans for failing to capture Caen. See Field Marshal B. L. Montgomery, *From Normandy to the Thames*, London: 1952.

*15   See David Irving, *Bomber Harris; the case for revision*, Berlin: Potsdamer Verlag, 1996.

*16   The surrender of the Cossacks was the subject of a celebrated libel action in the seventies between two German historians. See Patrick Delaforce, *Fighting with the Canadian Resistance*, Alberta: Leo Cooper, 2000.

17   Leader of the Indian forces operating with the Japanese.

18   Truman had written articles before Pearl Harbor noting the importance of America supporting the balance of power allying with the loser effectively. American policy was clear sighted in those days and American diplomats were profoundly concerned about America being used to prop up the British Empire.

19   Germany lost comparatively little territory in 1918 but Austro-Hungary was shattered into a number of states.

Bibliography

Calvocoressi, Peter and Guy Wint, *Total War: Causes and Courses of the Second World War*, London: Allen Lane, 1972.

Howard, Michael *The Franco-Prussian War*, London: Rupert Hart-Davis, 1961.

Jenkins, Roy, *Churchill: A Biography*, London: Pan, 2002.

Kershaw, Ian, *Hitler 1936–1945: Nemesis*, New York: W. W. Norton, 2000; London: Penguin Books, 2001.

Sebag-Montefiore, Simon, *Stalin: The Court of the Red Tsar*, London: Phoenix, 2004

Tsouras, Peter, *Third Reich Victorious: Alternate Decisions of World War II*, London: Greenhill Books, 2002.

Winterbotham, F. W., *The Ultra Secret: The Inside Story of Operation Ultra, Bletchley Park and Enigma*, London: Orion, 2000.

Zaloga, Stephen, *Bagration, 1944: The Destruction of Army Group Centre*, London: Osprey, 1996.

3 The Spanish Gambit
Operation Felix
John Prados

Once the guns had fallen silent on the Western Front, Adolf Hitler had to decide what to do next. The fall of France took out one of the two major allies, that summer of 1940. Hitler wanted to end the war with England by force if not by diplomacy. Italy had entered the war also, and eyed the British protectorate in Egypt and the Suez Canal. Hitler started with Operation SEA LION, a scheme to invade Great Britain. That would require a host of preparations, not merely creating a German amphibious army, which had never existed, but an invasion fleet, which the Kriegsmarine did not have, and it made it a necessity for the Luftwaffe to destroy the Royal Air Force, winning command of the skies over the British Isles.

The prospect of SEA LION hardly excited the German military. They were well aware of the difficulties involved in an invasion of Britain. There were other ways to knock the British out of the war, and the High Command canvassed the alternatives. Action in the Mediterranean became the leading possibility. Planners turned their focus to the possibilities there. The Navy proposed an action in concert with Spain to take Gibraltar on 5 July. Colonel General Alfred Jodl, chief of the operations staff, was among the first to confront the issue of future strategy. Jodl prepared a memorandum that considered not only an invasion of Britain but action in the Mediterranean. He argued the former at much greater length than the latter, but in that section he discussed fighting England on the periphery, in the Mediterranean. That was at the end of June. A month later Jodl followed up with an appreciation of the situation in which he advised Hitler to help the Italians in North Africa, especially with panzer troops to reinforce the attack on Suez. In a further paper on 13 August Jodl extended his analysis of defeating England by other means.

Gibraltar – Gateway to the Mediterranean

With 'The Rock', the huge mountain towering over the strait that led from the Atlantic to the Mediterranean, the British were perfectly positioned to bar passage between the seas. With Gibraltar the British could run fast convoys to Egypt, avoiding the long voyage around Africa. The Rock also provided a base for shipping to Malta, the central Mediterranean island from which the British blocked Italian supplies to North Africa. Italy would never make egress to the Atlantic with the British there, even submarines – both Italian ones and German U-boats were attempting to enter the Mediterranean – would have an increasingly hard time making passage in the face of British surface patrols as long as The Rock held out under the Cross of St George. And Gibraltar could base a British task force that might act at will in either the Atlantic or Med. Spain, under the Fascist dictator Francisco Franco, wanted Gibraltar back too – the British had taken The Rock away in 1704 and held it ever since.

In Spanish hands those British advantages would evaporate. If Italy and Germany held Gibraltar, or secured basing rights there, the structure of advantage would change markedly. British supply of Malta would become tremendously more difficult. The British would lose their most important refuelling stop between Portsmouth and Capetown. Italo-German naval co-operation would become much easier. The newly activated Axis would have a potent airbase obstructing a region of the eastern Atlantic and effectively barring British operations off the North African coast. An Italian naval task force at Gibraltar could cooperate in an invasion of Britain or make forays into the Atlantic. At a minimum it would seriously distract Britain's Home Fleet, which would no longer be able to focus entirely on the Germans. There was much to commend a strategy that aimed at the capture of Gibraltar.

Field Marshal Wilhelm Keitel, General Jodl's boss as chief of the *Oberkommando der Wehrmacht* (OKW), started the ball rolling around 10 July. He called in military intelligence chief Admiral Wilhelm Canaris and asked him to investigate the feasibility of an attack on Gibraltar. Canaris's intelligence service, the *Abwehr*, had a strong operation in Spain, and indeed Canaris himself had cut his teeth as an intelligence operative on the Iberian Peninsula, including service in the Spanish Civil War, during which he became a close associate of Franco's. *Abwehr* Foreign Section director Vice-Admiral Leopold Buerkner learned immediately of Canaris's orders and felt the chief believed in the Gibraltar contingency operation.[1]

But Canaris needed hard data, not supposition. On 20 July he left for Spain. With him were confidant Colonel Hans Piekenbrock, Lieutenant Colonel Mikosch and Captain Hans-Jochen Rudloff. The latter, a special warfare expert, led the *Abwehr* survey group, which passed through Madrid, checking in with the agency's station there, headed by Captain Leissner. They went on to La Linea, the town just beneath The Rock on the Spanish side of the demarcation line, and Algeciras, the port right behind that. Rudloff's people spent two days observing Gibraltar.

On his return Admiral Canaris paused at Biarritz on the French Riviera, where on 28 July he met with Spanish armed forces Chief of Staff General Juan Vigon plus General Martinez Campos, the Spanish intelligence chief. Admiral Canaris discussed the Gibraltar contingency. The Spanish generals warned that their country, exhausted by the civil war ended barely a year earlier, could not take a serious role in an attack on The Rock. Germany and Italy would have to do what needed to be done. They advised Canaris to see Franco.

The *Abwehr* chief knew Franco well and realised someone had to talk to the Spanish leader, but that initiative had already begun. Four days earlier Adolf Hitler had brought in Luftwaffe General Wolfram von Richthofen, the Luftwaffe's close support expert, and deputised him to go to Madrid, meet with the Spanish defence ministry, and see Franco. Richthofen, who had headed the Condor Legion, the German contingent in Spain during the civil war, was also Franco's friend and, as an operational commander, better suited for this particular contact.

Richthofen also stopped at Biarritz to confer with Canaris and get a preliminary briefing on the Gibraltar survey on his way to Madrid. General Franco had his own problems. Not only had Spain been badly damaged by the civil war, there remained pro-Allied factions in the country alongside the pro-German ones. Colonel Juan Beigbeder Atienz, the foreign minister, belonged to the pro-Allied group. German heavy-handedness did not help: when Franco sent General Vigon to see Hitler in June, the Führer had kept him waiting for almost a week before according him a perfunctory forty-five-minute interview. Vigon expressed his anger to Canaris and Richthofen at Biarritz. The Luftwaffe general went to Madrid aware of the delicacy of Franco's position.

Francisco Franco was not '*El Caudillo*', the leader, for nothing. He successfully played out a balancing act between the factions. At the beginning of the year Franco had emphasised ending famine and putting the nation back on its feet in his New Year's message. In June, as General Vigon awaited Hitler's pleasure, Franco suddenly changed Spain's status in the world war from neutral to that of a 'non-belligerent', the same status Mussolini had maintained from September 1939 until Hitler's French campaign, when Italy entered the war. On 14 June Franco's troops put teeth into the more aggressive stance, taking over the international zone in Tangiers, across the strait from Gibraltar. A month later, on 18 July, Franco delivered a speech in which he reasserted Spain's claim to Gibraltar. On the other hand El Caudillo fired a general who had declared that Hitler and Mussolini should be honoured with a reception on the Spanish frontier, and he permitted the British to create an office in Madrid to study conditions in Spain and advocate Anglo-Spanish ties, effectively an outpost for the British Secret Intelligence Service (SIS). Equally significant, Franco signed a tripartite agreement with Portugal and Great Britain to facilitate trade with London's sterling bloc.

While Franco played to both sides his heart lay with the Axis. In addition, he wanted Gibraltar, or more accurately, wanted to be the leader who brought Gibraltar back to the national patrimony. Generals Franco and Von Richthofen devised a cover scheme when the Luftwaffe officer saw El Caudillo in Madrid. Franco would not commit Spanish forces to any operation and would publicly oppose an Italo-German manoeuvre, but he would lend assistance behind the scenes and would join the Axis once the operation had been successful. Richthofen got all he had hoped for.

The Axis, and even Spanish, threat to Gibraltar were logical possibilities not to be missed by London. Sir Winston Churchill took over as Prime Minister there in the midst of the debacle of the fall of France, and 'Winnie' had always had a sea-eye cocked toward the British Empire, in which Gibraltar long served as a key link. Though Churchill pursued pet projects throughout his time at Downing Street, he had his hands full with Dunkirk and the rush to prepare the British Isles to ward off invasion. He nevertheless spared some attention for The Rock.

Churchill took the measures he did despite the views of his own intelligence experts. On July 2 London's top analytical unit, the Joint Intelligence Committee (JIC), delivered a report estimating that Hitler would make some kind of peace overture (which he did), but that Germany was probably planning one or more operations, starting with an invasion of Britain but including attack on Russia, an offensive into the Balkans, headed toward the Middle East and in conjunction with initiatives in Syria and Palestine; or attack in the Mediterranean against Egypt or Gibraltar. The JIC anticipated Germany might conduct more than one operation at the same time. British sensitivities were such, however, that Hitler would try and finish Britain before moving against the Balkans, and could not act against Britain and Russia simultaneously. In the Mediterranean the danger focused on Egypt and the Suez. On balance British intelligence judged the Germans would forego an invasion of Britain (which turned out true for reasons the JIC never anticipated) and would not act against the Soviets before dispensing with Britain. In effect, that left the Balkan and Egyptian operations.[2]

Prime Minister Churchill rejected Foreign Office advice that Britain should attempt to accommodate Spain by offering to discuss Gibraltar's status after the war. That was in late June, just a week after the collapse of France. (British diplomats nevertheless made a statement to that effect to the Spanish ambassador. It cannot be established how this snafu occurred.) Instead Churchill ordered reinforcements to Gibraltar.

At The Rock there was little knowledge of these matters of high policy. General Sir Clive Liddell, the governor, laboured to put his post in defensible condition. This remained work in progress – Canaris's survey mission established that some of the defence positions at the base of the mountain appeared dilapidated, whatever the case with those higher up in The Rock. Fabled as a labyrinthine work of tunnels and bunkers to rival the Maginot Line, The Rock was initially weakly defended by just two infantry battalions (2nd The King's Regiment and 2nd Somerset Light Infantry) plus two anti-aircraft batteries (four 3-inch, four 3.7-inch, and two 40 mm guns) plus three more for coast defence (eight ancient 9.2-inch guns, seven 6-inchers and six twin 6-pounders). Under Flag Officer North Atlantic, the naval flotilla amounted to a single battleship, a cruiser, nine destroyers and some mine and patrol craft.

Gibraltar had no aircraft complement. An Anglo-Spanish diplomatic agreement in 1939 had provided that Great Britain would base no combat aircraft at Gibraltar except for those of the Fleet Air Arm or planes in training. In any case the runway of Gibraltar's air base was located in the lowland beyond The Rock, right next to La Linea, where it could not be protected from artillery fire and remained vulnerable to surprise attack. During the summer of 1940 the British occasionally sneaked a couple of Maryland bombers into Gibraltar, using them for photo reconnaissance in the Western Mediterranean, and each time this happened the high command held its breath in case the Spaniards caught them.

The British made a start at reinforcement in May, sending another infantry battalion, the 4th Devonshires. But the big augmentation came after Churchill's instructions, and with the fall of France. Some 10,000 escapees from southern French ports were funnelled through Gibraltar. A few stayed, but only those essential for the war effort: 16,000 'Gibos', as the citizens were known, were shipped out of the place. In July a fresh rifle battalion, the 4th Black Watch, came to The Rock, accompanied by major anti-aircraft forces: radar equipment, searchlights, sixteen more 3.7-inch guns with eight 40 mm Bofors. Thus shortly after the German intelligence survey the British significantly strengthened their defences. Altogether the garrison amounted to perhaps 10,000 troops, but just over 3,000 infantrymen.

Almost immediately Prime Minister Churchill pulled Gibraltar to the centre of attention, augmenting the fleet there and using this to attack the Vichy French squadron at Oran in early July. Vichy retaliated with bombing raids against The Rock and by expelling the 14,000 Gibo residents in French North Africa. They joined the others, in England, the Azores, Madeira or Jamaica. Fortunately the French air raids were desultory and the French bombs not that well aimed. The British fleet went on to raid Italian naval bases, skirmish with Mussolini's warships, and take part in the first of the vital Malta convoys, one of which conveyed a group of modern Hurricane fighters to defend the skies over that critical island. During that foray Force H served to divert attention by raiding the Italian port of Cagliari on Sardinia.

These activities served to remind Axis leaders of the dangers of Gibraltar in British hands. Mussolini was the most directly affected but the implications were not lost on the Germans. Different threads in German thinking came together at a command briefing on 31 July. Navy Leader Grand Admiral Erich Raeder cautioned that preparations for invading England were going slowly, making it necessary to secure a postponement. Hitler himself now mentioned that he wanted to bring Spain into the war and act in concert with it to seize Gibraltar. Admiral Canaris presented the results of his survey of The Rock. The Army suggested sending a pair of panzer divisions to North Africa to help the Italians there and the Führer approved that as well. Planning began to move ahead steadily.[3]

In early August the top Navy officer on the OKW operations staff briefed its chief, General Jodl, on the dangers of turning away from battle with England before the Royal Navy had been defeated. Section L of Jodl's staff comprised his most senior planners and they finished an analysis of the requirements for attacking Gibraltar on 7 August. At mid-month Jodl renewed his call for peripheral operations against England. Hitler approved the major operation on 14 August. The initial drafts of what would become Hitler's directive for attacking Gibraltar were written in July and August. On 19 August Admiral Canaris again saw Spanish staff chief General Vigon to ask the Spaniards to work at improving the roads leading to Gibraltar and prepare nearby airfields. The Spanish assented. The next day Section L briefed Jodl on an operations plan based upon its studies. Two days later the Army General Staff (OKH) was given the latest intelligence on the objective and began its detailed planning.[4]

Though Hitler was becoming increasingly preoccupied with visions of attacking Russia, Italian screams of protest at the depredations of the British fleet caught some of his attention. This was especially true because both Italy and Germany depended upon the same source for oil – Romania – and Mussolini demanded a greater share to free his fleet to combat the British. The Führer became even more incensed when top Romanian officials discussed the oil problem with him in late July. Scared of British bombing of the Ploesti oil fields, a British covert operation to sabotage them, or an attempt by the Russians to occupy them, Hitler ordered the German Army to enter Romania, protecting the oil and supporting Romanian allies. This move came early in September. Ironically concern about the Mediterranean had played a large role Germany's becoming enmeshed in the Balkans.

On 6 September a critical meeting took place at Hitler's headquarters that laid down subsequent strategies. All the top leaders attended. Navy commander Grand Admiral Erich Raeder opened, declaring his judgement that the capture of Gibraltar and Suez must be the key objectives for the next phase of the war, and needed to be achieved before the United States entered the conflict. Jodl chimed in that the moment had come for a decisive advance against Britain. Even Reichsmarschall Hermann Goering, whose Luftwaffe was busy making the invasion of England impossible by failing to neutralise the Royal Air Force, contributed a grandiose vision of three conquering columns – one through Spain to Gibraltar, another through Morocco into Africa and the third through Turkey to Suez, in combination with the Italians coming through Egypt. Senior German leaders thus all agreed on the need to take Gibraltar. General von Richthofen, sent to appraise the Spanish of the latest developments, saw Franco at San Sebastian on 9 September.

'How' became the next key question. Back in July the concept Admiral Canaris had presented had been for what amounted to a covert operation. *Abwehr* had a special unit, the Brandenburger Regiment (zbV. 800), expanded from a battalion about the time of the French campaign. Canaris envisioned a battalion of the Brandenburgers secretly positioned at Algeciras, a second aboard ships nearby, with artillery to support them and aircraft to suppress the British defences. Some engineers and more Brandenburgers would be parcelled out as assault teams to overcome The Rock's outer defences. There were many holes in this plan, among the worst of them the paucity of artillery support. Canaris had wanted heavy guns to fire across the Strait from Ceuta, the Spanish Moroccan port on the opposite shore, but that was just not practical. Finally Canaris came to the conclusion that a more conventional operations plan was necessary.

In September the *Abwehr* chief made a further visit to Spain and saw Francisco Franco. El Caudillo made his own idea known: Germany should provide huge 380 mm guns to Spain to shatter The Rock's defences, then Spanish troops would bear the brunt of the attack. The Spanish foreign minister later told Hitler that ten of the big guns were necessary. Only a few German elite troops would be needed. Hitler argued that guns were less effective than aircraft: a Stuka group (flying three sorties daily) could drop 120 2,200-lb bombs *a day*, whereas a 380-mm gun would need a new barrel after 200 rounds, and each of those shells would contain only 155–165 lb of explosives. And Franco's general staff soon convinced him the Spanish army was in no condition to assault such a fortress at Gibraltar. This concept, too, evaporated. The ball went back to Germany's court.

Hitler ordered an indefinite postponement of the British invasion, Operation SEA LION on 17 September. Some days later a modifying order to the OKW directive for SEA LION brought the first *Wehrmacht*-wide announcement of an intention to deal with Gibraltar. On 26 September Admiral Raeder met again with Hitler, not only to urge him to express definite views on the British invasion, but to re-emphasise the importance of action in the Med. Hitler needed no convincing.

Section L of the OKW staff came up with the solution. Germany would carry out the mission, codenamed Operation FELIX. The endeavour, small enough to be conducted as preparations for Russia continued, would utilise two army corps. One, a panzer corps, would guard the flank and ensure against interference from any British counterlanding on the Iberian peninsula. The force selected would be General Rudolf Schmidt's XXXIX Corps, with the16th Motorised Division, the 16th Panzer Division, and the SS Totenkopf Division. These mechanised units were necessary not only to reach their blocking positions quickly, but so as to leave Spanish railroads free to move the assault troops and their critical ammunition supplies.[5]

The actual Gibraltar assault would be the province of General Ludwig Kuebler's XLIX Corps with extensive artillery support. Kuebler was slated to have no fewer than twenty-six heavy and medium artillery battalions, two to make smoke, three observation battalions and special weapons, including 150 radio-controlled 'Goliaths', small tracked vehicles packed with explosives that could be guided to defence positions and then detonated. General von Richthofen would bring his redoubtable Luftwaffe Stukas and medium bombers to complete the fire support arrangements. Kuebler's actual assault formations amounted to little more than a single division: the Grossdeutschland Infantry Regiment, the 98th Jäger Regiment of the 1st Jäger Division, three engineer battalions and a detachment of Brandenburgers. The latter, a specially trained company, would get close to Gibraltar's breakwater hidden below decks on a merchant vessel, then seize this key position by means of a *coup de main*. German possession of the breakwater and docks would outflank the main defences in front of The Rock, enabling the Germans to get around the side of it into Gibraltar city, subsequently attacking The Rock from the rear. U-boats deployed outside the Strait would obstruct British ships trying to reach the fortress.

German forces began to prepare. The XLIX Corps was created in France toward the end of October 1940. Units began to concentrate at training bases. German supply experts started to stockpile artillery ammunition and funnel new guns to the assault formations.

This was a good plan as far as it went. One key weakness in the FELIX concept is evident in the assignment of a full army corps for a blocking role. That is, the action force would have to cross the Pyrenees mountains, move through Madrid to the frontier line around Gibraltar, almost 600 miles, and then deploy for a set-piece assault, including emplacing heavy artillery and bringing up ammunition. FELIX could not be a blitzkrieg. During the Norwegian campaign the British had demonstrated that they were perfectly capable of intervening against a German invasion operation if they knew about it, were determined to act, and had troops who could be deployed. Norway had been a choice for London. Gibraltar would be a command performance. Success for FELIX could well ride on the Germans ability to deceive the British in such fashion that British reaction forces were not available or were out of position. Hitler had one very good thing going for him: the Balkans.

When Canaris saw Franco in September they fleshed out some of the scenario the Spanish leader had spoken of in general with von Richthofen. By this time US President Franklin D. Roosevelt, acting to favour Great Britain while preserving US neutrality, had cut oil exports to Spain by half, greatly complicating Franco's position. Angry, Franco saw that his ballet of playing to both sides had not worked and decided to throw in his lot with Hitler. But Franco, too, wanted to do that quietly and preserve his freedom of action for as long as possible. He agreed with Canaris to conduct a diplomatic charade in concert with the Germans to fool London. Now Hitler had a Spanish card as well as a Balkan one.

Preparations

The next act of this intricate play began in late September. British intelligence received specific reports of German units deploying into Romania, particularly Ploesti. On 29 September Agent A-54, a Czech source now working to the Secret Intelligence Service (SIS), and a well-placed German officer who sometimes attended meetings with Field Marshal Keitel, reported that Germany would march into Romania in preparation for a thrust through

Turkey. A few days later the SIS added that the Germans had begun re-deploying divisions in Eastern Europe and had offered to station Luftwaffe squadrons in Romania. True, A-54 had also mentioned a German operation into Spain, but there were so many more indications of movement into the Balkans that those overwhelmed the other intelligence.

On 4 October Hitler and Mussolini conferred at the Brenner Pass in their first wartime summit on strategy. Mussolini, about to unleash his armies in Libya to make for the Suez, and with an offensive from Albania against Greece up his sleeve, was anxious to impress the Hitler. He had already rejected the first German offer of two panzer divisions for the Egyptian offensive. Mussolini needed something to show a measure of cooperation in the alliance. Operation FELIX was just the thing. The Axis allies agreed on the Gibraltar operation. They also agreed to put out the word that their real strategy was to attack through Turkey, which Hitler had no intention of doing, as that would drive Turkey into the hands of the British.

On 9 October, duly informed of the Brenner cover story by Spain's Anglophile foreign minister, based on briefings from the Germans, the British embassy in Madrid cabled London that the Axis would advance through the Balkans, Turkey and Syria. Ambassador Sir Samuel Hoare was confident of that information. The same day British code-breakers decrypted a Vichy French attaché message from Athens reporting Yugoslav general staff fears of imminent German action against that country and Greece. All this received major confirmation when Italy in fact invaded Greece late in October. In London, Churchill's war cabinet ordered up a study of Britain's vulnerability to attack through the Near East.

The JIC at this point issued a new appreciation of Axis potential. The Balkan danger predominated. In the 10 October JIC paper the German moves in Romania, the other intelligence, and Bulgarian accession to the Axis clearly favoured the Near East option, but British intelligence felt that danger could not become manifest until the spring of 1941. During the interim the possibilities were an intensified assault on Egypt backed by German panzers (which would have happened had not Italy rejected the assistance) and an Italian attack on Greece. The worst anticipated for Spain would be Axis political pressure. Meanwhile the cabinet vulnerability study completed at the beginning of November, relying upon the JIC intelligence, jumped upon the bandwagon of those who feared an Axis thrust through the Near East.

New intelligence on the Spanish question brought fresh warnings in October, just as Axis diplomacy swung into high gear. Hitler met Franco at Hendaye on the French border on 24 October. In late September, Franco prepared for this move by replacing Beigbeder, his foreign minister, with the pro-Axis Ramon Serrano Suñer. The new foreign minister immediately went to Berlin to coordinate the Franco meeting with German officials. He saw Hitler on 17 September and again on the 25th. Suñer then went to Rome and went over the same ground with Mussolini's minions. The German–Spanish summit took place on 23 October, Hitler having sounded out Vichy French leaders the previous day aboard his train at Montoire. Franco arrived on a personal train of his own. The arrangements had been for a short meeting followed by an early luncheon in the dining car, after which details would be left to the foreign ministers. But Franco came late and the talks stretched on until shortly before dark. El Caudillo declared that Spain would gladly fight on Germany's side. The difficulties to be overcome were known to both leaders, Franco added. He then complained that both the United States and Argentina seemed to be precisely following British orders in their commercial dealings with Madrid. Hitler argued that Germany and Spain needed to create a large front against Britain. He expressed doubts about Franco at a private dinner once the Spanish left, but at this point there was no going back.

Hitler had offered parts of French colonial territory – Morocco and the Oran department of Algeria. Vichy France would be given conquered British territories after the war to make good the losses. Franco agreed. Germany wanted bases in Morocco, about which El Caudillo was more squeamish, but he agreed in return for higher levels of German aid. Spain would enter the war in January. Operation FELIX would then go into motion. The date was set for 10 January, 1941. The day after the Hendaye conference, OKH staff chief General Franz Halder sent out the orders for the 98th Jäger Regiment, the Grossdeutschland Regiment, and the 106th Artillery Command to move to a training site at Besançon, France.

A most delicate piece of the business revolved around how to make this alliance meeting work for the deception operation. There was no way to spin Spain into a Near East scenario. The best idea was to deal directly. The Spanish put out the story that Hitler had offered Franco an alliance but that El Caudillo had *rejected* the proposition. Differences over territorial rewards, and Spain's oil and economic shortages would be made out as the reason for the rejection. The Spanish knew that former foreign minister Beigbeder had preserved his channel to the British, and it would be natural for Serrano Suñer, his brother-in-law, to tell his predecessor something of the Hendaye talks, so that would be the conduit. The Axis got only part of what they wanted – Beigbeder passed along the contrived account of Hendaye, but he also told the British he suspected the Germans might demand a right of passage through Spain. Deception remained a difficult game.

Hitler's train returned through France, stopping for a further meeting with Vichy leader Marshal Pétain. Hitler learned of Mussolini's invasion of Greece, scheduled to kick off the next day. He immediately diverted his train, by then at Aachen, and railed through Munich to see Mussolini in Florence on 28 October. As the Axis leaders met, German soldiers began arriving at the FELIX training centre at Besançon. Despite their surprise the Germans realised the Italian operation could contribute to their deception plan. Italian foreign minister Galeazzo Ciano would record in his diary, 'German solidarity has not failed us.'[6] Hitler told the Italian Duce that Franco was brave but no statesman, a contention plainly belied by El Caudillo's careful perch between the warring camps and his participation in the Gibraltar deception. But Franco could posture and pontificate with the best – Hitler recited the crack he had made to Field Marshal Keitel: 'Better to go to the dentist than have a second meeting with Franco.'[7] If the Spanish pulled back from the brink at the last minute, the Axis Powers determined to go anyway. On 2 November General Halder reported that FELIX would be ready to go on New Years Day. A full-scale briefing took place that afternoon where Major Fritz Kautschke, *Abwehr* post chief at Algeciras, presented Halder with photos, maps, and charts detailing the British defences at Gibraltar.

Hitler arrived back in Berlin on 10 November. Two days later he issued his Directive No. 18, authorising Operation FELIX. In Phase I advance parties in civilian clothes under *Abwehr* orders were to prepare the operation, including Luftwaffe men to ready airfields to receive the planes of von Richthofen's Fliegerkorps VIII. Brandenburgers would infiltrate Algeciras and La Linea to stiffen Spanish defences in case the British made any sorties out of Gibraltar. The major force troops would complete their assembly. Three weeks were allotted for this activity. FELIX would overtly begin with Phase II, in which the Luftwaffe would execute a surprise bombing of the British fleet in Gibraltar and then land at Spanish airfields, thereafter carrying out a sustained bombing of The Rock while assault forces moved into position. The attack would be Phase III, and follow-up, perhaps even to the Canary Islands, would occur in Phase IV.[8]

One element left out of Directive No. 18 was Italian participation. In fact the directive anticipated no Italian role whatever. That had already begun to change. On 11 November in a daring carrier raid, British aircraft executed a night torpedo attack on the Italian fleet at anchor in Taranto. Three battleships and a cruiser were damaged, the battleship *Cavour* badly enough to be rendered permanently inoperable. The modern battleship *Littorio* and the older *Caio Duilio* would be out of action for months. At a stroke the striking power of the Italian navy's battle line was halved. Furious, Mussolini demanded action. When, a few weeks later, the fleet sparred inconclusively with the British off Cape Teulada, his fury mounted. Italian armies were already in Egypt (though they had halted their advance toward Suez) and were then driven back by a British offensive, embarrassing Il Duce even more. Suez had been one possibility for the base for the attack on Taranto and the other was, of course, Gibraltar. The Italian high command, Commando Supremo, immediately approached OKW. If Italians could not participate in FELIX they would mount their own invasion. From the German perspective such a course would not do. Better to incorporate Mussolini's legions. Count Ciano would visit Berlin on 17–18 November to follow up on items that still needed attention. On that trip he and Spaniard Serrano Suñer together saw Hitler.

Fortunately a natural role for the Italians was obvious. The biggest flaw in FELIX remained the time interval necessary to move troops through Spain and array them around Gibraltar for the assault. There was enough time for the British to react if London was alert and moved quickly. The solution was to get London to move the wrong way. The Italians could threaten The Rock in a different way, inducing the British into a premature and misdirected response that would pull them out of position. Commando Supremo crafted a plan for an Italian cruiser force to support the landing of the Sicily-based 18th Infantry Division in the Balearic island of Ibiza. Along with the garrison, troopships would bring the two battalions of the San Marco Regiment, Italian Marines, one from Trieste, the other from Pola. Not long before, the San Marcos had been at Valona preparing for an amphibious assault on Corfu in the Adriatic. Gibraltar became the new target. Italian aircraft would then move in – four squadrons from the Servici Aerei Speciali, plus a transport group of the 3rd Squadra Aerea. The planes would make an air bridge like the one Italy and Germany had operated during the Spanish Civil War, shuttling the Marines and the Folgore Parachute Battalion, which Italy had created the previous summer, to the Spanish Moroccan port of Ceuta, barely fifteen miles from Gibraltar on the other side of the straits.

Commando Supremo's operational concept was simple. The British would learn of the occupation of the Balearics. That would be timed for about a week after FELIX crossed the Spanish border. Everything would be made to look like an Italian amphibious invasion. One week before the Gibraltar assault, the Italian task force would set sail with the troopships and some of the 18th Division troops to act the part of assault forces. If Force H, the British fleet at Gibraltar, had not already been driven away by the German bombers – which is what Hitler anticipated – it might be smoked out by the Italian manoeuvre, drawn into a killing ground of Italian submarines infesting the Straits. If British reinforcement convoys came from the Atlantic side they would have to cross a similar U-boat barrier on the approaches to The Rock. The Italian Marines and paratroopers would cross from Ceuta and actually participate in the assault.

Once Berlin accepted the inevitable preparations began in earnest. An advance staff was established at the Besançon training centre in the first week of November. Artillery units practised pinpoint fire missions. The jägers and infantry used cave entrances in the Jura mountains to rehearse tactics for attacking entrances to the British tunnel galleries, while Brandenburgers practised cutting through fences – the assignment for elements of the regiment that would be stationed at The Frontier – or assault from ships, as they would do at the mole. Engineers participated to familiarise themselves with combined arms techniques. On 20 November Hitler appointed Field Marshal Walter von Reichenau, whose Sixth Army was to have taken part in the British invasion, to overall command of the joint operation.

FELIX began with Phase I on 7 December, when Hitler ordered the advance parties into Spain. Marshal von Reichenau ordered his Sixth Army to assemble at the border. The move followed a final round of conferences – between OKW and OKH two days earlier, and that day with both the operational and higher commanders. Hitler presided over both meetings. General Kuebler used a terrain model to show how the Gibraltar attack would unfold. Admiral Canaris presented the latest intelligence on the British. Raeder discussed the naval aspects. Hitler seemed pleased. He dispatched Canaris to coordinate with Franco one more time. General Walter Warlimont of Section L handed Jodl a draft of Directive No. 19, which would be the final order for the operation. Hitler issued it on 10 December.

Winston Churchill had one last chance to avoid catastrophe in the closing months of 1940. But London remained mesmerised by the Axis deception of the Balkan–Near East ploy, as well as the Italian armies in Egypt. Churchill focused on Egypt, insisting that area commander Archibald Wavell make some counter. British intelligence nevertheless came up with certain indications of enemy action against Gibraltar. On 3 November Spain unilaterally took over Tangier, terminating the international administration of that place. London's suspicions spiked two weeks later when foreign minister Serrano Suñer returned to Berlin for further discussions. In late November London considered taking over Ceuta as a precautionary measure, missing a key opportunity when it decided against the move.

By December, when Wavell went on the offensive in Egypt – he would eventually almost throw the Italians out of North Africa – Churchill was convinced the Axis would respond in Spain. But British intelligence thought the move would take the form of a Norway-style amphibious operation against points on the Iberian coast, or else the Azores and Cape Verde islands. When photo reconnaissance planes could find no sign of invasion shipping at Brest or other German-occupied ports on the Bay of Biscay, fears began to appear groundless. Meanwhile the British chiefs of staff rejected a pre-emptive occupation of the Azores, pleading lack of troops. In a 16 December minute, Churchill argued that a German action in Spain was more likely than a Balkan offensive, but he could not move the Defence Ministry or the Foreign Office. No action resulted.

Predicting German intentions for the coming year, the Future Operations (Enemy) Section (FOES) of British intelligence held at the end of 1940 that no German move into Spain impended. Their paper, prepared for a cabinet Defence Committee meeting held on 8 January 1941, dovetailed nicely with the account of the British naval attaché in Madrid, who attended the cabinet session. The attaché still recommended preparations to support a Spanish resistance movement, opening contact with likely opponents of the Franco regime, but Embassy Madrid's reports were optimistic. British code-breakers did supply some chilling indications – in December the experts at the Government Code and Cipher School had succeeded in breaking the *Abwehr*'s book code, and some of their intercepts contained German intelligence reports on Gibraltar. But authorities dismissed these as routine German efforts to gather strategic intelligence. Then all hell broke loose.

The Rock Shudders

Friday, January 10 1941, dawned calmly at Gibraltar, which seemed a backwater to many even though it was so important. The day, like so many others in this long war, opened with the standard raising of the colours at Devil's Tower Camp, on The Rock, and at Headquarters down at Rosia Bay. Sentries shivered at their posts on the mountain. Sailors went about their business at the port. It was still dark at 6:30 a.m. when the radar post at the northern crest of The Rock began reporting a huge flight of aircraft approaching fast from the northeast, following the Spanish coast. It took a few minutes to inform the chain of command, a few to sound the alarm, and much longer for all the soldiers to reach their alert stations. General von Richthofen's planes were overhead just minutes afterwards.[9]

The Luftwaffe hit Gibraltar with a mass strike from Fliegerkorps VIII. Some 170 Ju 87 Stuka dive-bombers of StGs 1 and 77, forty-three Do 17Z twin-engine bombers of I/KG 2 and III/KG 3 made up the attack element, escorted by thirty-six Bf 110 twin-engine fighters of III/JG 77. Major Graf von Schoenborn-Wiesentheid led the formation. The Germans expected heavy opposition. Their intelligence was that Gibraltar had thirty-four fighters, nineteen bombers and thirteen scout planes. In reality there were none. Indeed, there were fewer than three dozen anti-aircraft guns to defend the base, most of them around the harbour or the airfield. The colony, 2.5 miles square, really was not defended all that well. Having learned the perils of radar in the Battle of Britain, the Luftwaffe dedicated two full Stuka squadrons just to hit the radar station, which they put out of action. The Germans also carefully cratered the runway, preventing British aerial reinforcements. Many more planes struck installations at the barracks, Devil's Tower Camp, Europa Point, and the port area.

Force H was caught at anchor. Admiral James Somerville could not even raise steam aboard his ships for hours. Fortunately much of the Luftwaffe effort was directed elsewhere. But a few Stukas, their primary targets already neutralised, peeled off to hit destroyers, and the ships *Hostile* and *Dainty* were damaged. Somerville did not know that a second wave of German aircraft, thirty-four Ju 88s of KG 30, had launched from Bordeaux and were even then winging south along the Atlantic coast of Iberia. Those planes arrived at 10:17 a.m. Somerville remained unable to steam away. This time the aircraft went straight for the warships. Without radar there was no warning. Battleship *Rodney* suffered medium damage. The cruiser *Dorsetshire*, struck by half-a-dozen bombs in tight patterns, settled in the water at her dock. Destroyer *Hasty* sank.

The British had a tough decision to make. That afternoon Admiral Somerville huddled with the Flag Officer North Atlantic, Admiral Sir Dudley North, and the governor and commander, General Sir Clive Liddell. A dispatch from London reported that Spain had declared war on Great Britain. A Spanish attack on The Rock was possible at any time. None of them knew that German troops were pouring across the border, but the Spaniards plus the Luftwaffe seemed bad enough already. Somerville bravely determined to stick it out.

Luftwaffe aircraft regrouped at Spanish airfields, most around Seville, but Stuka squadrons were forward-based at San Roque, Guadiaro, Vejer de la Frontera and Tarifa, all quite close by. Over the following days those planes were able to fly two or even three sorties a day. Bigger strikes came in at least once a day, sometimes more often. General von Richthofen's pilots flew over 1,200 sorties against Gibraltar during the first week alone.

Admiral Somerville's determination lasted just three days. Loss of the destroyer *Imperial* on 11 January shook him, but on the 13th the Luftwaffe succeeded in inflicting major damage on the *Rodney*, sinking another destroyer (*Ilex*) and scratching the escort *Vampire*. If this went on Force H would be annihilated. On the night of 13 January Somerville got his fleet under way, heading into the Atlantic. But off the Straits the Kriegsmarine had concentrated fourteen U-boats in a huge killing zone. With *Rodney's* speed reduced because of her damage, she could not clear the area before dawn. After first light the flotilla inevitably revealed itself to Luftwaffe scout planes, which summoned both the bombers and the U-boats. Submarines and bombers finished off the *Rodney* and destroyers *Defender* and *Juno*. U-boats alone accounted for the damaged *Vampire*. Of the proud Force H, only a few destroyers remained.

The Relief Attempt

Prime Minister Churchill faced hard decisions of his own. The fate of Force H showed that the Straits had become a submarine trap, and that plus the Luftwaffe threatened to make Gibraltar a Dunkirk in reverse. The British chiefs of staff pleaded lack of troops, importuned Churchill of the dangers to the Royal Navy, and assured him Gibraltar was impregnable. After all hadn't the Spanish failed to take the place in a five-year siege (1779–83)? Churchill sympathised but remained adamant. He ordered a strong relief expedition.[10]

Under Admiral Sir John Tovey, who had come from the Mediterranean to take over the Home Fleet just three months before, the Royal Navy assembled a powerful task force for the mission. The Army provided the 9th Brigade of its 3rd Infantry Division for the ground component. More troops than that just could not fit into Gibraltar, whose total land area amounts to only two and a half square miles. Tovey wore his flag in the battleship *King George V*. With him were battle cruiser *Hood*, aircraft carriers *Ark Royal* and *Victorious*, four cruisers and sixteen destroyers, five troopships with the infantry and strong anti-aircraft reinforcements, and another vessel with their guns plus new radar equipment. Carrier *Ark Royal* also embarked two-dozen Hurricane fighters from the RAF to give The Rock some air defence.

Putting this force together – no simple task – required two weeks. The fact of the relief operation also put the Royal Navy in a critical situation when, on 22 January, German battlecruisers *Scharnhorst* and *Gneisenau* sortied on a raiding operation into the Atlantic. Admiral Raeder had ordered the heavy ships into positions from which, if necessary, they could intervene in the Gibraltar fight. The British could not oppose the German breakout into the North Atlantic. The presence of German heavy ships at sea suddenly complicated the calculations of Churchill's admirals.

Tovey's transport force departed Portsmouth just after dark on 25 January, looking like any typical convoy except these were fast ships making about twelve knots, using the night to get past German patrols from occupied France. The convoy had a close escort of five destroyers and several frigates under Captain The Earl Mountbatten, commanding 5th Destroyer Flotilla from the *Jupiter*. The main body of the task force had left Scapa Flow days earlier, refuelled at Belfast, and was steaming hard down the Irish Channel to pick up the troop convoy at a rendezvous point in the Atlantic west of Brest. Admiral Tovey operated independently within about fifty miles of the convoy. Mountbatten turned the convoy into the broad Atlantic about 07:30 a.m. on 26 January. Tovey, at that point to the north-west, slowed to refuel at sea, then moved ahead of the convoy.

The expedition was already in trouble. Lieutenant Nicolai Clausen's submarine *U-37* was en route to his patrol area in the eastern Atlantic when, late in the day on the 26th, he spotted Tovey's fleet. Claussen's dispatch reporting British warships arrived too late for any action, but at first light the next day the Germans began a maximum effort to find these vessels. The Luftwaffe had concentrated most of its four-engine long-range FW-200 aircraft in one unit, I/KG 40, based at Bordeaux-Merignac to watch the sea. They found nothing – heavy cloud cover and high winds hid the British that day. But on 28 January I/KG 40 put up five planes to search every sector. Oberleutnant Bernhard Jope's plane found Mountbatten's convoy first, but briefed to look for warships, Jope kept up his search and soon saw Tovey's fleet as well. Jope's sighting reports electrified the German command.

By then the British relief expedition was halfway to Gibraltar. Admiral Tovey bent every effort to move even faster but he was limited by the speed of the convoy. Then came the British turn to be electrified. Scout planes out of Malta radioed news of a large Italian convoy with cruiser support west of Sardinia headed westwards. This marked their first inkling of the Italian manoeuvre in Operation FELIX.

The Italians had left Naples early in the morning of the previous day. British victories in North Africa, steadily driving back Mussolini's forces, and already deep into Libya, had only infuriated Il Duce more, and he had pushed even harder on Gibraltar. Fleet commander Admiral Inigo Campioni had refused to engage any of Italy's remaining battleships, but his cruiser strength was considerable and these he willingly hazarded. Huge advantages would accrue if the Axis held Gibraltar. Admiral Pellegrino Matteucci led the force, his flag in the heavy cruiser *Pola*, backed by the navy's I Division – the heavy cruisers *Zara*, *Gorizia* and *Fiume*, along with twenty destroyers or torpedo boats, either with him or the convoy. He would arrive at Ibiza in the Balearics at mid-afternoon on 30 January.

British officers could not know Metteucci's destination was Ibiza, not Gibraltar, and indeed focused completely on Gibraltar. Admiral Tovey had led one of the British fleet units in the first major battle in the Mediterranean,

Punta Stilo in July 1940. Tovey saw opportunity against the Italian fleet, balanced against the danger of losing The Rock. Winston Churchill also weighed danger against opportunity. The only way to attempt an interception of the Italian fleet was to have Tovey dash ahead with his heavy ships, leaving the reinforcement convoy to make its own way. Churchill had always been an aggressive leader, now he and Tovey agreed the chance was worth the risk.

At 21:00 hours on 28 January Tovey's fleet surged ahead at eighteen knots. He detached his two aircraft carriers with four destroyers in close escort to continue the mission of aerial reinforcement of Gibraltar. His surface action group now comprised two fast battleships, four cruisers, and a dozen destroyers. If Tovey met Matteucci the Italians were finished.

Sir John Tovey had always intended certain tactics for his passage of the Straits of Gibraltar. He was perfectly aware the U-boats would flock there. In a pinch between the U-boats and the Luftwaffe, Tovey thought submarines the greater danger. He would therefore weaken his anti-aircraft screen in order to put destroyers on anti-sub sweeps ahead of his battle group. Had Tovey been proceeding with the convoy this would also have cleared the way for Mountbatten, but with the new situation the battle force would be crossing the Straits twenty-two hours ahead of the convoy, leaving plenty of time for U-boats to get back into position. More danger thus loomed for the relief mission.

Meanwhile, the Germans learned quite quickly what had happened. Picking up the trail of the British fleet on 29 January, Captain Verlohr, squadron leader of I/KG40, spotted all three British formations and saw Tovey pulling away from the other forces. Admiral Raeder understood. He ordered Vice-Admiral Guenter Luetjens to bring his battle cruisers to the Straits area at best speed, warned the Italians, and coordinated with Admiral Karl Doenitz to get his U-boats ready. From the next day the Luftwaffe began to follow the British fleet movements using aircraft based in Spain. Starting about noon, the German air force attacked, first with Ju 88 and Do 17 bombers, then with Stukas. The concentrated air battle became fiercer even as Tovey began reconfiguring his force to transit the Straits, putting two groups of four destroyers each at ten mile intervals ahead of the battle group.

Now the British AA defence weakened, not only for the battle force but for the destroyer groups, deployed on a line of bearing and unable to support each other. Ships were picked off one after another. Destroyer *Campbell*, holed near the bow, lost speed and had to abandon her position in the first anti-submarine line. In the main force, *King George V* took three hits but was unaffected, while cruiser *Sheffield* suffered moderate damage and destroyer *Zulu* was sunk. Then came the Stukas. They wiped out the older destroyer *Vivacious* and damaged two others, while putting two bombs into the *Dorsetshire*, leaving that cruiser with her speed reduced by two knots. As the warships manoeuvred violently under air attack, submarine *U-44* found herself in position for a lucky attack and put a torpedo into the *Sheffield*. Suddenly the cruiser was dead in the water. The next wave of Stukas put her under the waves. On the plus side, three U-boats were caught in the ASW sweeps and dispatched with depth charges.

The best part of Admiral Tovey's plan was that it set him up to transit the Strait at night, when the U-boats would have the most difficulty. Dusk was fast approaching. Tovey began to breath sighs of relief. But he was too soon. The hole in his ASW line had opened the way for U-boat ace Otto Kretschmer in his *U-99*. Again a submarine got inside the screens, and Kretschmer launched a perfect spread. Three of his four torpedoes hit *King George V* in her port side. The ship was still under way, but crippled, her speed reduced to five knots. This ship could not go into a surface battle. Admiral Tovey was forced to transfer his flag to the *Hood*, first moving to a destroyer *Cossack*, which then caught up to the formation. The crippled battleship was forced to put into Gibraltar. Tovey completed the move about 06:00 hours, with his flotilla coming out of the Straits on the Mediterranean side. There a couple more U-boats and a dozen Italian submarines awaited them. Submarine *Cobalto* got past the screen and launched four torpedoes. The British evaded this early-morning attack successfully, but their frantic manoeuvres disrupted the formation at the exact moment the first air attack of the morning arrived overhead. Two more destroyers and the battlecruiser *Hood* suffered their first damage. The manoeuvres once again benefited the enemy submarines, and the Italian *Finzi* put a torpedo into the Polish destroyer *Piorun* which sank her.

Admiral Tovey pressed to the west hugging the African coast to stay as far away from the planes as possible. Late in the morning of 1 February he learned from a photo reconnaissance plane out of Malta that the Italian invasion force had entered port in the Balearics, it was not at sea at all. Already aware of the extreme distress of Mountbatten's reinforcement convoy, Tovey reluctantly decided to turn back. As the fleet headed west the sailors did not notice the formations of transport aircraft to the south of them, bound for Ceuta. The Italian air bridge had opened. Once more Tovey had to cross the submarine ground. Italian subs and German aircraft accounted for cruiser *Dorsetshire* and two more destroyers. Submarine *Otaria* got honours for sinking the British cruiser.

Earl Mountbatten was truly in dire straits. At first the detachment of the battle fleet had been to his advantage. The Germans concentrated their effort against Tovey, leaving the reinforcement convoy alone. But by the afternoon of 30 January, with the ships off the Portuguese coast, the Germans paid attention. Two dozen Stukas of I/StG 77 hit in the late afternoon, damaging two of the troopships so badly they had to put into Lisbon, and sinking the *Glen Clencampbell*, which carried the artillery and anti-aircraft equipment. With morning the German spotter planes were back and picked up the trail. But now the Germans concentrated against the aircraft carrier unit west of the convoy, again a reprieve for Mountbatten. Another strike came before dark, as the convoy approached the Straits, this time striking home, sinking destroyers *Kashmir* and *Jackal*, plus two of the corvettes. Now the U-boats closed in like true jackals. Leutnant Reinhard Hardegen in *U-201* sank transport *Rochester Castle*, while Wolfgang Schepke in *U-100* sank a corvette and put two

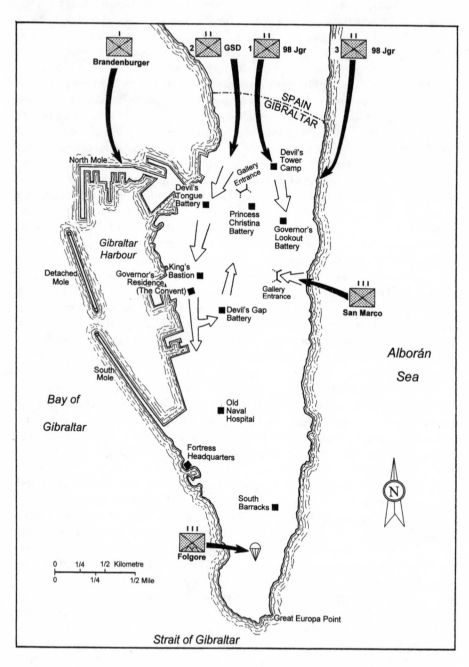

Operation FELIX

torpedoes into the *Waimarama*, leaving her heavily damaged. With the one damaged ship Earl Mountbatten could not make the anticipated 10 p.m. arrival at Gibraltar. The morning of 1 February found Mountbatten, his three remaining destroyers and the *Waimarama* still about forty miles from The Rock. The transport staggered into port late that afternoon as Admiral Tovey neared the Straits from the Mediterranean side. Mountbatten joined Tovey's escort with his remaining ships. Tovey's proud fleet had now been reduced to the *Hood*, the cruiser *Berwick*, and nine destroyers, almost half of them – and the *Hood* – damaged.

The air reinforcement of Gibraltar had its own tale to tell. Carriers *Ark Royal* and *Victorious* had sustained heavy Luftwaffe attacks on 30 January, but thanks to their armoured flight decks survived intact, except that five of the precious cargo of Hurricane fighters were destroyed by bomb hits. Escort destroyer *Jersey* had also succumbed to German bombs. Fortunately the flight decks remained in action, and on the morning of 31 January nineteen Hurricane fighters took wing for Gibraltar. Approaching The Rock they encountered Luftwaffe fighters, of which they knocked down a half dozen, losing three Hurricanes in exchange. Two more of the Hurricanes smashed up landing on the cratered runway at Gibraltar. A total of fourteen Hurricane fighters survived the harrowing reinforcement run.

Even this did not end the story of the naval battle. The carrier unit headed west into the Atlantic, attempting to put space between it and the Luftwaffe airfields. Admiral Tovey was closing up from behind. The Germans continued their attacks, but in weakening strength as they shifted back to striking Gibraltar itself. The final victim would be the destroyer *Javelin* in Tovey's force. Suddenly, on the afternoon of 2 February, lookouts on the destroyer *Eskimo* sighted masts on the horizon. Within ten minutes these resolved themselves into the superstructures of the German warships *Scharnhorst*, wearing the flag of Admiral Luetjens, and *Gneisenau*. Commodore Philip L. Vian immediately turned his ships back to the east, toward Tovey, increasing speed to maximum. The Germans began firing at long range. Luetjens had visions of the Norwegian campaign, when the same two battle cruisers had slaughtered the British carrier *Glorious* in a surface action. But this time the British were fast and help was over the horizon. Luetjens engaged in a long stern chase. Toward nightfall Tovey's fleet made its appearance. Admiral Luetjens immediately broke off and made for the open Atlantic. Tovey, relieved to have prevented further serious losses, joined up with the carriers and laid a course for home.

The Battle of Gibraltar

Day 1
The execution of FELIX became the final act in this long drama. The naval action took place just as the German troops and token Spanish forces had

completed their preparations for the attack. Field Marshal von Reichenau set 4 February for the assault, both to give the Italians time to assemble at Ceuta, and to let the British fleet exit the area without tempting them into a surface bombardment that might damage his crucial artillery. The last day before the storm passed with trepidation. The Luftwaffe made its concentrated attacks on The Rock once again, this time opposed by British fighters which exacted a heavy toll – four Bf 110s, three Bf 109s, three Do 17 bombers and four Stukas were lost on 3 February, only a couple of them to anti-aircraft, against two Hurricane fighters. The British exulted but were ignorant of what lay in store.

As the assault troops took position that night, General Liddell was taking stock of his situation. Churchill's great reinforcement operation had ended up yielding relatively little – the one damaged transport that had staggered into harbour gave him a single new battalion, the 2nd Battalion, the Lincolnshire Regiment. After losing two Hurricanes in the day's air battles, Liddell had a dozen aircraft. And the crippled battleship *King George V* sat in the harbour, her crew fighting hard to control leaks and damage that had the ship in a near-sinking condition. If the battleship could be righted and made sound, she could represent a super reinforcement, a floating battery of tremendous power. Liddell felt he had some reason for optimism.

But the British had not realised just how close they were to the great battle. Before dawn the German artillery began pounding designated targets. Here the geography of Gibraltar played to their favour: the only place suitable for an airfield in the British base was the stretch of flat land north of The Rock and immediately across the territorial boundary. The Germans had direct observation of the airfield and an easy shot. Even infantry mortars could hit it. Remaining British aircraft were almost all destroyed, and the runway itself cratered so badly none of the others could take off.

Under cover of the darkness several Spanish coasters had put out of Algeciras. Out of sight below decks were 200 Brandenburgers. The vessels headed for Gibraltar's North Mole, behind the frontier defences and west of The Rock. The mole had few defences, merely a couple of anti-aircraft gun positions and some guard posts. Beginning at 04:00 the Brandenburgers scaled the mole and quickly overwhelmed its defences. British troopers sent the alarm, of course, and the causeway that led off the mole was swiftly blocked, preventing the Brandenburgers from exiting, but that was not their purpose. Rather, the German special forces took position to snipe and harass, and bring mortar fire on British troops attempting to move along Queensway and man the position at Devil's Tongue Battery and the Customs House at the head of the outcrop of land. The Brandenburgers became a major irritant to General Liddell, for they threatened to break into Gibraltar town and outflank his northern defences if he failed to keep them sealed up.

Meanwhile, other Brandenburger troops cut through the fences sealing off the Neutral Zone, and assault parties of Germans began moving through it, approaching the defence line at the frontier. The 2nd Battalion, Somerset Light Infantry held the frontier line, on the neck of the peninsula barely half a mile wide. They were echeloned, with two lines of resistance, and well prepared, but they were facing four elite German battalions further reinforced by the Brandenburgers, and the Germans had Spanish guides to show them the most defiladed paths up to the British positions. Within thirty minutes Brandenburger observers were close enough to direct artillery fire onto the key bunkers of the defence line. With first light Luftwaffe aircraft swarmed overhead. Between the planes and the Germans on the North Mole, General Liddell found it impossible to move troops around, except those already stationed inside the mountain fortress. This there could be no reinforcements for the Somersets.

All morning the battle raged. At the police station on the border, with nearby hangars and buildings, the Somersets made a stand, inflicting heavy losses on the 2nd Battalion, Grossdeutschland Regiment (GSD), but the 1st Battalion, 98th Jägers, rushed past this position to the east, and quickly hooked in behind to capture the Air Terminal, defended by RAF ground crews, and surrounding the defenders at the border. Remaining Somersets retreated toward the barracks at Devil's Tower Camp. There came another shock. Elements of the 3rd Battalion, 98th Jägers in small boats had paddled past the frontier on that side and landed at Eastern Beach. Instead of withdrawing into a secure bastion, the Somersets found themselves embroiled in another maelstrom. By noon the Germans had captured the frontier defences, overrun most of the airfield, and were pressing hard at Devil's Tower. The police station defenders surrendered as 13:15, opening the road into Gibraltar town.

British artillery did their best to support the defenders. Three batteries were capable of firing to the north: Governor's Lookout and Prince William Batteries atop The Rock, and Devil's Tongue at the northern tip of the town. Only the mountain batteries had direct observation, however, and they were under heavy Luftwaffe attack. Devil's Tongue remained under fire from Brandenburgers on the North Mole. Thus artillery support was no better than sporadic, and proved completely unable to break up the German amphibious flanking move that threatened Devil's Tower barracks.

The fall of Devil's Tower came late in the afternoon. Liddell had sent two companies of the Black Watch out of The Rock from a sally port behind the camp to help hold the place, but no combination of service troops, anti-aircraft detachments, Black Watch and Somersets – about a thousand troops in all – could hold this position against German artillery, air and elite troops. The worst part of the action was that the Brandenburgers again succeeded in infiltrating behind the British position making retreat impossible.

Meanwhile in the harbour the sailors aboard the *King George V* lived a nightmare. Already beset by heavy damage, their ship attracted constant strikes. Probably over a hundred of the 460 sorties the Luftwaffe flew on the first day of FELIX went against the battleship. Three bombs had hit before lunch, and at 13:30 a Do 17 scored with a 1,000-lb bomb that blew the top off A Turret and ignited ready propellant charges, inflicting grievous damage that put both forward turrets out of action. Two large bombs that exploded alongside sprang new leaks at the starboard quarter. Four other bombs hit the superstructure, and one fell right down the stack, starting fires in the boiler room. By nightfall the *King George V* had begun settling in the water. All night long her crew fought the fires and leaks. Captain W. R. Patterson, increasingly desperate, strove to save his ship. Admiral North watched closely from his command post. At midnight North summoned Patterson to canvass the options. It was clear the Luftwaffe would be back with morning, and under daylight attack it would become extremely dangerous to conduct rescue operations to save the crew. Admiral North reluctantly ordered Patterson to evacuate the ship.

The ship had already suffered several hundred casualties. Getting these men off before morning, plus over a thousand sailors of the rest of the crew, proved to be an insuperable problem. Over 250 men were still aboard the ship at dawn. At that point, Brandenburgers on the North Mole also began calling artillery fire onto the *King George V*. Once the Luftwaffe returned her fate would be sealed. The battleship sank at her moorings at 09:57.

Day-2

FELIX's second day offered no good news for the British. The battle north of The Rock had already robbed General Liddell of one of his four experienced battalions and half of another. The newly arrived battalion, missing some of its equipment, terrified from the voyage to Gibraltar and completely unfamiliar with the place, was not an adequate compensation. Liddell ordered the Lincolnshires into the mountain fortress hoping to organise them into some usable unit. The 900 remaining able-bodied sailors from the battleship also went into the fortress where Captain Patterson formed them into a naval battalion, primarily to help British artillery, anti-aircraft, and service units. Meanwhile, the Black Watch fought to keep the Germans from gaining a foothold at the sally port at the north end of the fortress.

General Kuebler of XLIX Corps now moved to the second phase of his plan. He committed the fresh 1st Battalion, GSD to reinforce 2nd Battalion in a thrust along the old city wall into the centre of Gibraltar town. The Jägers would fight for the sally port of the mountain and begin scaling its face. Sir Clive Liddell used his 4th Devonshires and 2nd Battalion, The King's Regiment to defend the town. The battle seemed to go well until 14:40 that afternoon, when formations of planes approached Gibraltar from the south. These were the Italians, who used thirty SM.79 transport aircraft to lift the 500 paratroops of their Folgore battalion. The troops parachuted on to Windmill Hill Flats at the south end of The Rock and, for the first time, on to the uplands of the position. The Spur Battery and O'Hara's Battery, about 500 yards to the north, were the only defensive positions in this sector and the British had no infantry nearby. They immediately faced the necessity of forming a new front line against the Italians. This drew troops away from the Gibraltar town battle and forced Liddell to send in the Lincolnshire Battalion before they were ready for action. The Italians were pinned down on the Flats, but by night

Grossdeutschland was making steady progress in Gibraltar town, closing in on City Hall and the old King's Bastion, near which stood the crucial electric power plant. At this stage General Kuebler sent in the third battalion of the Brandenburgers and kept up the fight through the night.

By morning the Germans had secured those objectives. They turned off the electric supply to Gibraltar. Henceforward only the fortress itself, powered by its internal generators, would have electricity.

Having secured the centre of the town, the Grossdeutschland Regiment redirected its 3rd Battalion to attack up the switchback roads that led to the top of The Rock. The British resisted strongly. The King's Regiment did much of this fighting while the Devonshires contested the town. Meanwhile the 98th Jägers continued to work their way up the mountain's northern face. All the while the Luftwaffe and artillery pounded British batteries, emplacements, and bunkers. The next shock came when half-a-dozen Spanish steamers appeared off the west coast and closed in on Catalan Bay, which had a narrow beach, behind which stood oil tanks holding much of the fuel for the fortress, not to mention the Williams Way Tunnel Entrance. This area was defended only by service troops. General Liddell hurriedly dispatched some of the Naval Battalion to reinforce them.

As the Spanish steamers neared the coast, hull up over the horizon came an Italian naval force. These were Admiral Matteucci's heavy cruisers, come to deliver fire support for the San Marco Naval Regiment. The British sailors lost their way inside the fortress and never reached the Catalan Bay position. The service troops already at the bay could not hold their positions against San Marco backed by heavy fire support and withdrew to the tunnel entrance, with the Italians in pursuit. Finally the British naval infantry arrived, just in time to prevent San Marco from driving deep into the tunnels, but even so Mussolini's elite troops had made the first breach into the fortress itself.

Fighting raged in Gibraltar town throughout the night. With a frontage only 600 yards wide one of Ludwig Kuebler's biggest problems was simply what troops to put on the line. The Spanish had sent him their 15th Estremadura Infantry Regiment, with the 19th Pavia Regiment in reserve at San Roque. On the second night Kuebler committed a battalion of the Estremaduras, heavily stiffened by German pioneers, on his right flank, pulling back one of Grossdeutschland's battalions for rest. Another Spanish battalion Kuebler used to clear the Coaling Island, which it accomplished by morning. The high point of the night's action came shortly before dawn when 1st Battalion, GSD, assaulted the Devil's Gap Battery. Meanwhile, 3rd Battalion, GSD, made slow but steady progress up the switchback roads to the top of The Rock. The battalion had captured the old Castle and city walls from the rear the previous evening, and by dawn had worked its way to a point below the Princess Caroline Battery.

Day 3
Day 3 would prove decisive. General Liddell had the opposite problem to

Kuebler's. Almost all his troops were engaged one way or another, the main question was the intensity of combat. Essentially he had to fight on four fronts. The presence of the Folgore's paratroops on Windmill Hill was especially distracting. Without that extra complication Liddell could have formed a reserve of his own. He now decided on a calculated risk, pulling the Lincolnshires back into Gibraltar town, substituting the 4th Devonshires and half the 2nd Kings for an all-out counterattack to wipe out the Italians. He would defend the town with the rest of the Kings, the Lincolnshires and scratch naval troops assembled from the Gibraltar base forces.

At first all went well. The substitution of the units, a key manoeuvre and especially problematic because the Lincolnshires knew little of Gibraltar, came off without a hitch. The Devonshires' and Kings' attack on Windmill Hill started well, the Folgore paras pressed back into a tight perimeter for a last stand. But then the Luftwaffe arrived on the scene. Under tremendous aerial attack, no British could move. The Windmill Hill assault collapsed into a stalemate.

Meanwhile in Gibraltar town the lack of local knowledge on the part of the Lincolnshires proved telling. The Germans and Spanish kept up strong pressure and ground ahead. The fall of Devil's Gap Battery at 09:30 hours opened up the Europa Road, a route leading straight to the approaches to Windmill Hill, and Kuebler brought back 2nd Battalion, GSD, to attack right down the road and relieve the Italians. By noon the battalion was more than halfway to its goal, capturing Hospital Hill. In the town itself GSD's 1st Battalion ground along Rosia Road and reached Sand Hill about the same time. The last battalion of the Spanish regiment was brought in to hold the flanking line along the base of The Rock. The Spaniards of 1st Battalion, 15th Regiment, then lined up to attack toward the waterfront, capturing The Tower at 14:20. The FELIX attack forces had now cleared three quarters of Gibraltar town and were nearing the dockyard and British Headquarters at Rosia Bay.

General Liddell resorted to desperate measures. Leaving the Kings on Windmill Hill, and detaching a company of the 4th Devonshires to hold the South Barracks against the oncoming 2nd Battalion, GSD, he brought the remainder of the unit back to Gibraltar town. They arrived at 15:20, about the same time Kuebler had completed positioning a battalion of Brandenburgers for the assault into the dockyard. The Devonshires never reached the dockyard. Instead they were sucked into a fight for the Old Naval Hospital against 1st Battalion, GSD. The defences in the rest of the town were reduced to constantly shifting scratch groups, platoons and squads to do the work of full companies. By nightfall the Brandenburgers had reached the waterfront at Rosia Bay, south of Gibraltar Headquarters, trapping the remaining defenders in a pocket against the sea. The Devonshires around the Naval Hospital retreated into the fortress. Along Europa Road, 2nd Battalion, GSD, began reaching the highlands, assaulting South Barracks at 17:35. The company of Devonshires there proved overmatched and finally retreated into the galleries of the fortress. By 19:00 the Germans were attacking downhill toward the last of the Kings Regiment who were penning up the Italians. These British were surrounded in their turn and finally capitulated around midnight.

The day also brought disaster on top of The Rock. On its north face the Brandenburgers and Jägers finally reached the summit and captured Governor's Lookout Battery and the radar station. They began a sustained assault against the Upper Gallery Entrance near the Lookout. Meanwhile 3rd Battalion, GSD, took the Princess Caroline Battery. German forces now began working down the Signal Station Road and Queen's Way, along both sides of the summit. At Catalan Bay the Italian San Marco troops continued their fight in the lower galleries of the fortress, gaining only about a hundred yards that day but consolidating their penetration.

A Job Well Done

By dawn on 8 February the British in Gibraltar were in deep trouble. General Liddell had effectively lost two of his five battalions, a third was trapped in the waterfront pocket. The 4th Devonshires were severely weakened. Only two companies of the 4th Black Watch were in relatively good shape and one of these was embroiled in the fight for the Upper Gallery Entrance. Beyond that he had remnants of artillery and anti-aircraft troops, the naval infantry of the base and from *King George V*, plus service troops. The Germans, Italians, and Spanish were all over Gibraltar. The waterfront pocket was eliminated that day, Headquarters being captured shortly after noon. At 16:05 Liddell lost his last surface position when 2nd Battalion, 98th Jägers, captured Signal Hill. The situation by nightfall was that perhaps 5,000 British occupied the interior fortress in The Rock, with one penetration already inside, while the Axis held the entirety of Gibraltar town and all the surface of The Rock.

General Liddell and Admiral North believed they could go on fighting in the fortress and should do so at least until troops and ammunition were exhausted. They believed they could go on taking a toll of Axis soldiers for weeks if not months. On 9 February, however, they began to hear explosions on the east side of The Rock, and quickly learned that German pioneers were setting demolition charges in the water catchment area below Signal Hill. That day also, German troops gained entrance to the Upper Gallery, while Germans and Italians together broke into the tunnels behind the South Barracks. Brandenburgers, pioneers, and Jägers made significant progress in the Upper Galleries on 10 February, and two days later they made a junction with the San Marco Italians, for the first time controlling a significant portion of the interior of The Rock. British troops were exhausted and demoralised. General Liddell learned that water had ceased to flow into his reservoirs. Resistance had become a diminishing quantity.

On 13 February General Liddell asked Field Marshal von Reichenau for terms. The Germans accepted the surrender of Fortress Gibraltar the next day. Slightly more than 5,000 remaining Britishers marched off into captivity. In all the British had suffered 3,592 killed in action, and another 4,246 wounded. The battleships *King George V* and *Rodney*, four cruisers and seventeen destroyers had been sunk with the loss of 7,000 sailors; two troopships and 3,000 British soldiers and sailors were interned in Portugal, and Gibraltar was lost. German casualties totalled 1,196 dead, 3,220 wounded, and 397 missing, including aircrews and the sailors of four sunken U-boats. Some 69 aircraft had been lost as well. Italian losses were 174 dead and 246 wounded, about half of them in the Folgore battalion. Spanish casualties included 115 dead and 332 wounded. Hitler, Mussolini and Franco could agree that the job had been well done.

Gibraltar became a strategic disaster of the first order for Great Britain. Winston Churchill was accused of a 'New Dardanelles', a reference to his strategic error in Turkey in the World War I, and his cabinet fell. He was replaced as prime minister by Anthony Eden. British naval losses severely impacted convoy defence against German surface raiders in the North Atlantic, and for eight months the Kriegsmarine enjoyed a 'Happy Time' during which battleships, including the new *Bismarck*, and battlecruisers wreaked havoc. Convoy travel time to Egypt was increased by three weeks without the option of running ships through the Mediterranean, while the Italian fleet had the run of the Western Mediterranean. British supply of Malta was greatly complicated by Italy's ability to concentrate forces against just a single avenue of approach. Conversely, Italian supply lines to forces in North Africa were simplified. And an Italian cruiser squadron stationed at Gibraltar represented a constant threat to British convoys bound for Egypt. Spanish armies joined the Axis and increased its forces, while Vichy France moved even closer to an Axis orbit. Operation FELIX had been a brilliant success.

The Reality

An interesting feature of this alternate history is how closely it runs to reality. Unlike some alternative conceptions, in which very large differences need to be postulated to result in relatively small differences in outcome, the British loss of Gibraltar would have had quite major consequences and could have happened with relatively small tweaking of events. Except for the actual attack on Gibraltar and the specific operations at sea and in the air centred around it, almost all the events recounted here actually took place. The account of German planning is accurate. The preparation of troops also occurred. The various diplomatic meetings between Germans, Spanish and Italians really took place, and what was said at those meetings is essentially what is recounted here. Several key differences are that I postulate an effort to build a deception out of the diplomacy to mislead the British, and a determination to proceed, rather than an ambivalence on Franco's part to become involved; that I have the Vichy French cast in a more positive response to German power than was the case; that I have Mussolini exhibiting greater determination than was the case; and that I have the Germans seriously committed to FELIX rather than suspended between that operation and SEA LION. The British actually did debate a German Balkan–Near East thrust (and Hitler did consider one). Here I have the Germans taking advantage of that interest for their deception. British intelligence really did get the reports referred to here, and make the analyses cited. Only the late December debates are exaggerated to favour the alternate history. Churchill might well have refused to reinforce Gibraltar, limiting his losses and the political consequences if not the strategic ones, but I think it a fair assessment of his general posture that he would have insisted on a relief operation. In general, the Luftwaffe, the Kriegsmarine and the Italians as portrayed in this account operate within their existing capabilities. Even *Scharnhorst* and *Gneisenau* (which sortied as noted here) had the practical capability to intervene as postulated. The British garrison was as noted, less the reinforcements the alternate history gives them. The battle details are a plausible construction given terrain, the forces involved, and tactics and techniques available to the sides. The major difference in the battle account is the inclusion of Italian and Spanish roles where the Germans expected to conduct the operation unilaterally. I felt that Hitler could not reasonably have excluded a Spanish role given Franco's claims on Gibraltar, or an Italian one if Mussolini had insisted hard enough.

Notes

1   Material on Canaris is drawn from Brissaud, 1974; cf Hoehne, 1999.
2   British intelligence appreciations are drawn from Hinsley, 1979, pp. 250–9.
3   Ansel, 1960.
4   For German plans see Warlimont, 1964 and Halder, 1988.
5   Burdick, 1968.
6   Ciano, 2002, p. 391.
7   Corvaja, 2001, quoted p. 179.
8   Trevor-Roper, 1966.
9   Fighting at Gibraltar is the subject of Mueller, 1955.
10   The account of naval operations herein is based primarily on Hilton, 1987.

Bibliography

Andrews, Allen, *Proud Fortress: The Fighting Story of Gibraltar*, New York: E.P. Dutton, 1959.

Ansel, Walter, *Hitler Confronts England*, Durham NC: Duke University Press, 1960.

Bekker, Cajus (trans. and ed. Frank Ziegler), *The Luftwaffe War Diaries*, New York: Ballantine Books, 1969.

Brissaud, Andre (trans. and ed. Ian Colvin), *Canaris: The Biography of Admiral Canaris, Chief of German Military Intelligence in the Second World War*, New York: Grosset & Dunlap, 1974.

Burdick, Charles B., *Germany's Military Strategy and Spain in World War II*, New York: Syracuse University Press, 1968.

Churchill, Winston S., *Their Finest Hour*, Boston: Houghton Mifflin, 1949; New York: Bantam Books, 1964.

Ciano, Galeazzo (trans. and ed. Robert L. Miller and Dr Stanislao G. Pugliese, et al.), *Diary, 1937–1943*, New York: Enigma Books, 2002.

Cooley, Leonard S., *What Next? The German Strategy Crisis During the Summer of 1940*, Baton Rouge: Louisiana State University, MA Thesis, 2004.

Corvaja, Santi (trans. Robert L. Miller), *Hitler and Mussolini: The Secret Meetings*, New York: Enigma Books, 2001.

Giorgerini, Giorgio, *La Guerra Italiana Sul Mare: La Marine Tra Vittoria e Sconfitta, 1940–1943*, Milan: Oscar Mondadori, 2001.

Halder, Franz. *The Halder War Diary: 1939–1943* (trans. Charles Burdick and Hans-Adolf Jacobsen). Novato CA: Presidio Press, 1988.

Hilton, Ronald, *Hell at the Pillars of Hercules: Gibraltar and the Fall of Churchill*, London: Slate Books, 1987.

Hinsley, F. H., with E. E. Thomas, C. F. G. Ransom and R. C. Knight. *British Intelligence in the Second World War: Its Influence on Strategy and Operations, v. I*, New York: Cambridge University Press, 1979.

Hoehne, Heinz (trans. J. Maxwell Brownjohn), *Canaris: Hitler's Master Spy*, New York: Cooper Square Press, 1999.

Kershaw, Ian, *Hitler 1936–1945: Nemesis*, New York: W. W. Norton, 2000; London: Penguin Books, 2001.

Megargee, Geoffrey P., *Inside Hitler's High Command*, Lawrence: University Press of Kansas, 2000.

Mueller, Hans Helmut (trans. B. Smith), *The Seven Days of Gibraltar*, Hibbing MN: Lost Sons Press, 1955.

Mussolini, Benito (trans. Frances Lobb, ed. Raymond Klibansky), *Mussolini Memoirs, 1942–1943*, London: Phoenix Press, 2000.

Trevor-Roper, Hugh R. (ed.), *Hitler's War Directives, 1939–1945*, London: Pan Books, 1966.

Von Below, Nicolaus, *At Hitler's Side: The Memoirs of Hitler's Luftwaffe Adjutant, 1937–1945*, London:Greenhill 2001.

Warlimont, Walter, *Inside Hitler's Headquarters*, New York: Praeger, 1964.

4 Navigare Necesse Est, Vivere Non Est Necesse

Mussolini and the Legacy of Pompey the Great

Wade G. Dudley

In 57 BC, some ten years after his conquests of the Cilician pirates and his defeat of the navy of Mithridates, the Senate again turned to Pompey as famine stalked the streets of Rome. Into his hands they gave the *annona*, the administration of food within the city, making Pompey proconsul for five years with absolute control of all grain production in the empire as well as maritime navigation on the sea.

Gathering his trusted lieutenants, among them the orator Cicero, the great admiral attacked the problem with tremendous zeal. He did not spare himself, travelling around the Mediterranean as he visited the fields, ports, and squadrons that must perform efficiently to feed Rome's masses and preserve the empire. It was in Africa where he chanced to be in a harbour as a grain fleet prepared to sail. A sudden storm arose, and its commanders hesitated. Pompey, leaping to the deck of the lead vessel, ordered it to cast off. Glancing with disdain at the fleet's commander, Pompey's voice boomed above both wind and thunder, '*Navigare necesse est! Vivere non est necesse!*'[1]

The teacher closed his book, and captured the eyes of a student, 'Benito, do you understand the lesson and the legacy that Pompey the Great offers to you?'

The boy, his mind already aflame with visions of quinquiremes and an empire reborn, answered softly, 'Yes, sir, I do.' And those flames would only grow brighter as Benito Mussolini began his slow and painful rise to absolute power over the Italian state.[2]

Il Duce

Born in 1883 in Predappio, Italy, Benito Amilcare Andrea Mussolini was the son of schoolteacher, who saw to his education, and a blacksmith, from whom Benito imbibed the heady brew of socialism. By 1910, he had emigrated to

Switzerland, then Austria, seeking employment. Trained as an elementary schoolmaster, he subsequently became involved with journalism, where his real passion seemed to be rabble-rousing. Both Switzerland and Austria deported him, and in Italy his early years seem marked by near-constant confrontation with the police. However, his willingness to suffer for the doctrines of socialism, his charisma and his powerful oratory brought Mussolini to the attention of the state socialist party. In 1912, the young man, appointed editor of the leading socialist newspaper, *Avanti*, called for a proletariat uprising in one great *fascio* (bundle) that would beat the capitalists from power.

In July 1914, the outbreak of World War I surprised few Italians. In November, Mussolini founded a pro-war party, the *Fasci d'Azione Rivoluzionaria*, and his own activist newspaper, *Il Popolo d'Italia*. Clearly, Mussolini and his followers hoped that the strain of war would engender a massive uprising of the proletariat in Italy, and pave the way for their own rise to political power. Unfortunately, Mussolini (as with most of his followers) found himself called to the flag as Italian military misfortunes multiplied. Injured by a grenade in a training accident in 1917, Mussolini returned to his newspaper.

In early 1919, as the Italian state manoeuvred for gain in Versailles against a defeated Germany, Mussolini organised the *Fasci de Combattimento*, a national Fascist political movement. By the time of his election to parliament in 1921, Mussolini had abandoned his socialist values for the political support of traditional right wing elements of society, especially industrialists. Time and again, armed units of his Fascist Party used terror tactics to silence socialists, usually with the tacit agreement of a government that feared the anarchy sweeping Italy in the wake of the Great War. In October 1922, the king asked Mussolini to form a new, conservative cabinet to prevent the collapse of the nation.[3]

Over the next four years, Mussolini managed to rescue Italy from anarchy. The price for the Italian people was a police state – a nation in which challenging Fascism meant death at the hands of the government. Then, as a Great Depression swept the world, Mussolini used his peoples' hardships to strengthen his position. By the early 1930s, *Il Duce* – The Leader – sat at the top of a totalitarian regime that could not be toppled internally; and from that lofty perch, Il Duce dreamed of a new Roman Empire.

To Mare Nostrum

Clearly, Mussolini dreamed of rebuilding the old Roman Empire and reclaiming the Mediterranean as *Mare Nostrum* (as the Romans had termed it, 'Our Sea'). To do so meant gaining a naval superiority as great as that enjoyed by Pompey after his triumph over the pirates. With that in mind, he personally took control of the naval ministry (not unusual in and of itself as Mussolini personally controlled five to seven ministries at any given time), and well that he did as decisions in the late 1920s shaped the force that would bear the brunt of naval combat during World War II for the Axis.[4]

The Regia Marina Italiana (RMI, the Italian Royal Navy) ended the Great War as a defensive force, relying primarily on torpedo boats, submarines, and mine-layers for its destructive potential. However, RMI visionaries considered the viability of torpedo-planes as early as 1913, and actually tested the concept between 1918 and 1922. Similarly, the RMI explored the use of dedicated naval air, at least for reconnaissance, as early as 1915 with the conversion of the hydrographic vessel *Quarto* to the seaplane carrier *Europa*.[5] By the late 1920s and into the 1930s, a number of factors combined to threaten continued development of naval air power.

Among those factors was the identification by the Italian admiralty of France as the logical opponent in any future war. France's pursuit of a big-gun battleline, and its failure to commission carriers, seemed to dictate a reciprocal response by Italy. The constant increase in the operational range of land-based air coupled with the location of Italian airbases appeared to further mitigate the need for the development of carriers. Additionally, the Regia Aeronautica Italiana (RAI, the Italian Royal Air Force) – the independent and thoroughly fascist Italian air arm created in 1923 – continually pressured both the admiralty and Mussolini to consolidate all aircraft under its control. Finally, Italy's lagging industrial complex (only two per cent of the world's industrial output) and weak overall fiscal resources seemed to argue against the development of new, unproven weapon systems.[6]

Pressure from the RAI to eliminate the naval air arm peaked in September 1927. Mussolini, already scheming to expand his empire and more than cognizant of communications difficulties between branches of the services, not only vetoed the idea but ordered plans drawn for a fleet carrier. In his own words:

Though Italy itself serves admirably as a carrier in the central region of our sea, any future conflict will take our fine sailors beyond that range, and will inevitably bring the English into the fray – their regional interests are too many to hope otherwise. Though our fleet could stand gun for gun against the French, the English battle line is a different matter. True, we could stand on the defensive within our RAI's air umbrella, but to do so would surrender the military initiative as well as the resources Italy must have from the outer regions of our sea.

I envision a fleet of fast ships supported by their own air contingents from land and afloat. Their aircraft will find the enemy and weaken them with repeated air attacks before our battleships and cruisers race to smash the remnants. For this reason, I instruct the admiralty to develop plans for the construction of a carrier of 15,000 tons, with two more to follow over the next ten years. Similarly, I instruct the admiralty, with the assistance of the RAI, to develop a class of aircraft that can handle reconnaissance, pursuit, bombs, and torpedoes. Funding for these projects will be made good by eliminating planned battleship construction and various special programmes.[7]

Unfortunately for the RMI, the collapse of the global economy in 1930 forced the cancellation of Mussolini's first carrier. Across the next years, work did continue on the naval aircraft component. This led to the development of the land-based Savoia Marchetti SM 79 as a torpedo bomber by the mid-1930s, followed by the SM 84 in late 1940. Both planes featured strong defensive capabilities and could deliver their superb Italian-built torpedo (second only to the Japanese 'Long Lance' in performance in 1940) at a range of 600 miles from home base. Development of carrier aircraft also continued, but at a slower pace. By 1935, such concepts as tailhooks and folding wings were being tested.

Finally, in 1936, Italy laid the keel of its first carrier, *Roma*.[8] Launched in 1938, it featured a top speed of thirty-eight knots, light armour only over key areas but excellent compartmentalisation, six 152 mm guns in two triple turrets, and a heavy anti-aircraft armament of sixteen 90 mm guns in dual mounts supported by machine-guns. Its air wing consisted of forty-two planes, all Reggiane RE 2000 models, with eighteen configured as torpedo bombers and the remainder serving as fighters, fighter-bombers or scouts as needed.[9] Following its fitting out, *Roma*'s crew gained its first combat experience in the final stages of the Spanish Civil War – the last in a long line of conflicts involving Italy in the decade before World War II.

The aggressive nationalism of Mussolini had led his legions to Albania and Ethiopia in the 1930s. Though Il Duce opposed Germany's expansion under Hitler, Italian aggressiveness (especially an extremely active support of Spain's General Francisco Franco from 1936–9) alienated both France and Great Britain while continued persecution of Italian communists aborted any support from Stalin. By 1939, only an alliance with Germany remained feasible, and in May of that year the 'Pact of Steel' inextricably bound the two fascist nations together.

From Mussolini to the newest of sailors in the RMI, no one doubted that full-fledged war would soon explode across Europe, though Mussolini himself calculated that Italy would not be involved before 1942. The RMI needed that time desperately to increase its fuel reserves (barely enough on hand for operations for a year) and torpedo stocks (only one-and-a-half loads per vessel and two loads for aircraft on hand), and to complete its naval building programme. At the top of the list for building was the conversion of the passenger liners *Roma* and *Augustus* to aircraft carriers, a plan implemented by Il Duce only days after the formation of the Axis Alliance.[10] Italy, delinquent in sonar, radar and even specialised radios, also needed time for its infant electronics industry to reach the levels of its potential opponents.

But in September 1939, the Polish question escalated to a full-fledged conflagration that, by June 1940, saw Italy's ally extend its hold throughout northern Europe and into France. With the British beaten from the Continent and France reaching for the white flag, Mussolini declared war on France and Britain on 10 June rather than see only Germany benefit from its massive conquests. Two days later, the Italian submarine *Bagnolin* hammered a torpedo into HMS *Calypso* seventy miles south of Crete. As the cruiser sank beneath the waves, it marked the first of several hundred ships and thousands of bodies that would nourish Mussolini's *Mare Nostrum* across the coming years.[11]

Punta Stilo

On the day of Italy's declaration of war, the RMI floated two battleships (with two more completing their fitting out), one carrier, twenty-one cruisers, fifty-two destroyers, and 106 submarines for a total of 184 major warships. Over sixty torpedo-boats and ten land-based squadrons of naval air (six torpedo-bomber squadrons, two fighter-bomber squadrons, and two reconnaissance squadrons) totalling 129 aircraft supported these warships. The heavier surface ships concentrated in the harbours of Naples and Taranto, while a number of flotillas composed of lighter craft based and operated throughout the Aegean and Adriatic seas. Most available naval air assets operated from Sicily and the 'toe' of Italy, sometimes sharing bases with squadrons of the RAI. Additionally, a small force of naval vessels operated in the Red Sea, for all practical purposes abandoned by Mussolini and the admiralty, who hoped they would at least distract the British East Indies Command based in Ceylon.

The loss of France on 24 June 1940 removed ninety-five warships from the Allied order of battle in the Mediterranean. This left Britain with four battle-ships, one carrier, nine cruisers, twenty-five destroyers and ten submarines operating from bases at Alexandria and Malta. An additional ten destroyers guarded Gibraltar, for a total of fifty-nine major warships in the Mediterranean supported by a rather motley collection of land-based aircraft. Admiral Andrew Cunningham, top British naval commander in the theatre, quickly called for reinforcements, especially a first-line carrier to support his aged HMS *Eagle* (top speed of twenty-four knots and an aircraft capacity of a mere twenty-one planes – eighteen Fairey Swordfish torpedo-bombers and three Gloster Sea Gladiator fighters in June 1940). Britain could and did respond with more ships, Prime Minister Sir Winston Churchill encouraging Cunningham to be as aggressive as possible in the central Mediterranean. The British admiralty, aware that the war had more than one theatre and that the RMI outnumbered local forces, actually suggested abandoning control of the central and eastern Mediterranean by relocating the fleet to Gibraltar, at least on a temporary basis. Cunningham and Churchill vehemently opposed this option as it would cause the certain loss of Malta, the key bastion for interdicting Italian supply lines to its massive army in Libya, and possibly the Suez Canal.[12]

Cunningham's final plan called for the interdiction of Italian supply lines to the Libyan ports of Benghazi, Bardia and Tobruk, harassment of Italian coastal positions in Africa and supplying Malta as needed. Additionally, he planned to wear down the Italian navy wherever possible while minimising his own losses. This meant mounting an aggressive assault on enemy convoys and their escorts, thus pulling significant elements of the RMI into covering forces which could be isolated, overwhelmed by locally superior forces, and

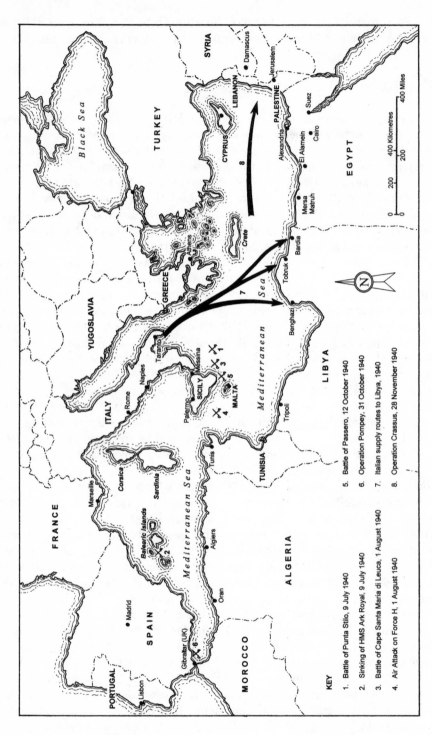

Mediterranean naval operations

destroyed. Oddly enough, Admiral Domenico Cavagnari, Italian Naval Chief of Staff, initially had the same thoughts. By keeping constant pressure on Malta from the air, a job for the RAI, the Royal Navy would be forced to replenish and reinforce the island base on a regular basis rather than see its people starve or face invasion. If the British fleet could be whittled away, and if Germany could be convinced to support Italian efforts in the Mediterranean, then other options would arise.

June saw only small skirmishes in the theatre, resulting in Italian losses of a destroyer and ten submarines. For their effort, the sailors of the RMI had removed a cruiser, a destroyer, three submarines and a sloop from the Royal Navy's list. By 4 July, Britain had neutralised the bulk of French naval forces in the region through diplomatic efforts in Alexandria and a rather sharper form of diplomacy at Oran. On 5 July, torpedo-bombers from HMS *Eagle* sank the destroyer *Zeffiro* and a merchant ship in Tobruk. Then, on 9 July, both sides attempted to push convoys through the central Mediterranean, one aimed for Malta and the other for Tobruk and Bardia. As covering forces clashed, the resulting battle of Punta Stilo proved to be one of the most decisive naval battles in modern history.

The Italian convoy consisted of five large merchantmen transporting over two thousand soldiers, vehicles and supplies, and over five thousand tons of fuel. Admiral Inigo Campioni commanded two refurbished battleships (*Giulio Cesare* and *Conte di Cavour*, both with 12.8-inch guns), the carrier *Roma*, six heavy and eight light cruisers, and sixteen destroyers as a covering force. He also had available the bulk of RMI's naval air squadrons, a cordon of eleven submarines, and the assurance of support from the RAI. Naval intelligence, relying on signal intercepts (SIGINT), advised that a major British fleet was at sea on 6 July. Air reconnaissance and submarine sightings confirmed this the following day. On 8 July, Campioni requested all available RAI bombers be put at his disposal on 9 July.

British intelligence confirmed that the Italian fleet had put to sea only on 8 July.[13] To escort his convoy of seven merchantmen, Cunningham deployed three battleships (flagship *Warspite*, *Royal Sovereign* and *Malaya*, each mounting 15-inch guns), the carrier *Eagle*, five light cruisers, and twenty-four destroyers. Force H, a recently formed British fleet under Vice-Admiral Sir James Somerville based at Gibraltar, sortied on 8 July as a diversion with three battleships (*Valiant*, *Hood* and *Resolution*), the carrier *Ark Royal*, four cruisers, and seventeen destroyers.

Cunningham stood with his lookouts on the port bridge wing of HMS *Warspite* at 1000 on 9 July. In the distant sky floated the black speck of an Italian CANT Z506 reconnaissance plane. Staying clear of any anti-aircraft fire, it had already downed one of *Eagle*'s three Gladiators. A second climbed to meet it, while the last set on the hanger deck with engine problems. One of *Eagle*'s Swordfish torpedo-bombers, doubling as a scout, had just radioed a garbled report of Italian battleships some eighty miles north of Cunningham's position and about sixty miles off Punta Stilo before dropping off the air. Now

Eagle rushed to launch its twelve remaining Swordfish. Cunningham switched his glasses to the carrier – one, two, three, then another of the lumbering bi-planes edged down the deck and clawed into the sky. He jerked his head around as a lookout called and pointed to the west. There, a dense cloud of specks floated across the horizon – fifty-eight SM.79 bombers and twenty-four escorting fighters of the RAI had been accurately vectored to his fleet by the naval scout.

As the planes approached, his ships turned to evade and opened with anti-aircraft fire. Fortunately for the Royal Navy, the RAI had loaded 250-pound and 500-pound bombs, then dropped them from high altitude. Only eight hit, and none did significant damage. Unfortunately, the RAI attack distracted lookouts and gunners from another threat – thirty-eight land-based naval torpedo-bombers bore in at low altitude from the north as the SM79s finished their run. By the time sufficient anti-aircraft fire shifted to the low-level attackers to disrupt their formation, it was too late. Following the directions of Admiral Campioni, the naval aviators concentrated on the carrier and the battleships. Three torpedoes struck *Eagle* in quick succession, leaving it dead in the water and listing to port. *Malaya* took two torpedoes, including one in the stern that destroyed its rudder and mangled its props. *Warspite* took a hit to starboard, but suffered little damage other than losing a knot of speed. *Royal Sovereign* dodged two torpedoes, but rammed a destroyer which subsequently sank.[14] In return, the Italian fliers lost two bombers and one torpedo-bomber.

Cunningham listened as the reports of damage flowed into his flagship. Now aware that none of his attackers had been carrier planes, and that the Italian surface fleet knew his exact location and would be closing rapidly, he made a snap decision. Leaving six destroyers to take *Malaya* in tow and rescue the crew from the sinking *Eagle*, Cunningham led his two damaged battle-ships, four cruisers, and a dozen destroyers (one cruiser and five destroyers provided the close escort for the convoy, now steaming for Malta as rapidly as possible) directly for the Italian fleet. At 13:53, his cruisers began exchanging long range fire with those of the Italians, who withdrew to the north after taking several non-critical hits while dispensing only one (and that one a dud). Thirty minutes later, Campioni's *Giulio Cesare* and *Conte di Cavour* ranged the pursuing British cruisers. The cruisers immediately fell back on their battle-ships, which began exchanging fire with the Italians at 15:03. For thirty minutes, both sides did little more than raise huge spouts of water. Then, in rapid succession, *Warspite* hit *Cesare*'s aft stack and a round from *Cavour* pene-trated *Royal Sovereign*'s weakened bow, driving deep into A turret's magazine. *Cesare* lost four boilers temporarily, with a drop in speed to eighteen knots, while internal explosions gutted the forward third of *Royal Sovereign*.

As the steel behemoths battled, the cruisers fought their own war, the speedy but lightly armoured Italian warships catching the worst of it. By 15:30, *Bolzano* had taken four heavy calibre rounds and coasted to a stop, its superstructure in flames and turrets hanging askew. British cruisers *Liverpool* and *Gloucester* had also been roughly handled, with numerous casualties and half their firepower gone. Fortunately, their speed had not been reduced, and they needed every knot of it at 15:40 hours when the next wave of Italian bombers, torpedo-bombers, and fighters roared into the fray. Fifty-six SM 79s of the RAI rained bombs on the struggling fleets – indiscriminately. Both sides managed to dodge the poorly executed attack and Italian anti-aircraft fire actually downed one of their own bombers. The twelve well-trained land-based naval torpedo-bombers, with their fighter escort of six Fiat CR 42s, fared much better. Three or four torpedoes struck the ill-fated *Royal Sovereign* over a two-minute period. The warship capsized less than thirty minutes later, entombing over 900 of its crew within its ruptured hull. *Warspite*, twisting and turning to the best of its ability, avoided all but one of the torpedoes aimed its way. Again, speed dropped fractionally as more water flooded its compartments. As the aircraft disengaged to return to their airfields, both sides sought to break from action, destroyer-laid smoke covering their retreat.[15] As *Warspite* and its battered fellows turned for Alexandria, a shocked Cunningham prayed for darkness to hurry and cover the movements of his shattered fleet. Still, he had time to wonder, 'Where is the Italian carrier?' The answer would be revealed in a matter of hours to another British fleet.

Force H had turned from its diversionary mission to return to Gibraltar at noon on 9 July. As sunset spread gloriously in the west, the fleet sailed sedately about thirty miles south of Majorca. Its lookouts did not spot the thirty RE.2000s winging out of the eastern gloom until minutes before they attacked. As eight fighters smashed the four plane Combat Air Patrol (CAP) above the fleet, ten bombers and twelve torpedo-bombers executed a textbook attack on one target – the aircraft carrier *Ark Royal*. Two bombs did little damage to its armoured flight deck, but a third ignited fuel in a group of Swordfish lashed along its fantail. Three torpedoes found their mark along the starboard side, while a fourth missed but struck a destroyer, breaking its back. Two RE 2000s fell to enemy aircraft fire, while another misjudged its altitude and crashed into the fighting mast of the battleship *Resolution*. *Ark Royal*, listing and aflame, would be sunk by its own destroyers later that evening, long after the victorious Italian fliers had returned to *Roma* and the task force that had split from the Italian main fleet two days earlier. Fearful of facing the vengeful battleships of Force H and having accomplished his mission of sinking any carriers with the British force, Rear-Admiral Ernesto Gavavinni turned his ships (*Roma*, two cruisers, and six destroyers) for Naples.[16]

Though Force H made Gibraltar with no additional losses, Cunningham's battered force faced three hard days of repeated attacks from the RAI, naval air squadrons, and submarines. By the time his fleet, bleeding oil and canvas-shrouded bodies, reached Alexandria, *Royal Sovereign* had been lost to the Italian submarine *Tazzoli*, two additional destroyers had succumbed to bombs and torpedoes, and *Warspite* as well as three of Cunningham's four cruisers would need months in dry dock to effect repairs. His convoy had reached Malta, but two destroyers and three of the cargo ships soon rested in the harbour mud – victims of aggressive bombing by the RAI. Total British losses for the Punta Stilo operation stood at two battleships, two carriers and five destroyers. In the mind of Cunningham, no option remained except to abandon the central Mediterranean in the face of Italian air superiority, especially from the well-coordinated torpedo-bombers of the RMI's naval air squadrons.[17]

Campioni and his ships returned to Taranto to the cheers of a grateful nation and decorations bestowed from the hands of Il Duce himself, having delivered their convoy to North Africa and bested the enemy. For the price of a single cruiser, a handful of aircraft and relatively light damage to a battleship, four cruisers, and a destroyer, Campioni had crippled British naval power in the Mediterranean. Yet beneath this outward celebration hid serious faults in the Italian infrastructure: the reserve of naval torpedoes and heavy bombs had been expended, Italian rangefinders suffered problems when ships operated at the high speed for which they had been designed (thus the few hits scored on British ships, especially by the RMI's cruisers), few planes existed in the pipeline to replace those lost (much less to create new squadrons), and only a few months of oil reserves remained. As skirmishing continued, especially in the western Mediterranean, planning began at the highest levels of both Axis and Allied commands.

Interim: The Vienna Meeting

Adolf Hitler, the man who had named his Italian allies an 'inferior race' on more than one occasion, found himself forced to re-evaluate the Mediterranean as a valid theatre of operations after the victory at Punta Stilo. On 24 July, Mussolini, Hitler and their respective high commanders met in Vienna to examine the possibilities offered by a Mediterranean strategy designed to secure the oil fields and refineries of the Middle East. Mussolini, desperately in need of torpedoes, bombs, electronic components and especially diesel oil and aviation fuel, offered the use of sixty Italian submarines on the Atlantic front, a move readily accepted by Admiral Karl Doenitz, German Chief of Submarine Operations. In return, Hitler offered political pressure in the Balkans to remove danger of a Greek attack in support of their British Ally as well as the loan of three divisions – 7th Panzer, the 5th Light Panzer, and the 29th Infantry (being motorised with captured French equipment) – and supporting air groups for an assault towards the Suez Canal and into the Middle East. Initially, Mussolini demurred the loan of the troops until Hitler offered to place them under the command of Italian Field Marshall Rodolfo Graziani as long as they operated as a unified German Corps, then sweetened the pot by offering immediate shipments of needed war materials.[18] By 30 July, once reluctant allies had reached an agreement that the conquest of the Middle East, and a 50:50 split of its oil, should begin within two months.[19] Forty-eight hours later, lines of vehicles and trainloads of material began to wind their way from France and Germany to Italian ports.

The Convoy Battles

Though the battle of Punta Stilo seemed to vindicate the British admiralty's desire to evacuate its major fleet elements from the Mediterranean, Churchill would have none of it. Instead, he ordered the planning of Operation HATS to resupply Malta and reinforce the remnants of Cunningham's fleet at Alexandria. The German all-out air offensive against the British Isles, launched on 8 July 1940, merely strengthened Churchill's resolve to fight in the Mediterranean: his people needed a victory, no matter how small.

On 30 August, a strengthened Force H left Gibraltar. Somerville commanded three battleships, two carriers (*Illustrious* and *Furious*), the anti-aircraft cruisers *Coventry* and *Calcutta*, a heavy cruiser, and twelve destroyers. It covered a convoy of three merchantmen escorted by a light cruiser and six destroyers. One day earlier, Cunningham had dispatched a convoy of two merchantmen, an oiler, two light cruisers and twelve destroyers. The plan called for both forces to rendezvous near Malta, with *Furious*, the battleship *Valiant*, and the anti-aircraft cruisers joining Cunningham's convoy escort to return to Alexandria.

Italian submarines and naval reconnaissance planes spotted both forces within hours of their departure. On 31 July, Campioni sortied from Taranto and Naples with three battleships (*Cavour*, *Vittorio Veneto* and *Littorio*), *Roma*, ten cruisers and thirty-three destroyers. He intended to smash the Alexandria element, since it lacked air cover, then turn to attack Force H after it had been weakened by land-based air attacks.

The trials of Cunningham's convoy began early on 31 July, as elements of the RAI operating from Aegean bases unleashed a hail of bombs at 08:36, crippling the flagship *Cornwall*, which remained with the convoy despite its damage. Commodore Brenton K. Blair and his staff died in the attack, leaving the convoy bereft of leadership at a key moment. Unaware of the sortie by the Italian fleet, and very much aware of the importance of the convoy's crated planes and aviation fuel to the defence of Malta, the senior captain replacing him did not consider aborting the mission, even when repeated air strikes over the next twenty-four hours cost him a destroyer and one of the merchantmen. Around noon on 1 August 1940, the convoy came in range of the Italian battleships some seventy miles off Cape Santa Maria di Leuca. Within minutes, the remaining merchantman and the oiler became flaming wrecks. Over the next six hours, the cruisers and destroyers of the RMI proved the worth of their speed as they pursued, then destroyed, each of the British escorts.

Somerville's Force H fared much better. Three poorly coordinated attacks by elements of the RAI and naval torpedo-bombers found a combination of increased CAP and two anti-aircraft cruisers to be daunting. In return for slight damage to HMS *Hood* and two destroyers, and the downing of six British fighters, the RAI lost twelve bombers, while five torpedo-bombers and three fighters of the RMI met fiery ends. Bad weather closed in late on 1 August, suspending flight operations and covering the arrival of the Force H convoy at Malta. Though the same weather pattern had encouraged Campioni to return to port, Somerville, after discovering the fate of the Alexandria convoy, opted to abandon the reinforcement mission and returned his entire force to Gibraltar.[20]

During the remainder of August, Italian dominance in the central Mediterranean went unchallenged by British capital ships. Convoys of three to five ships left Italian ports for North Africa every two days, each escorted by destroyers and the occasional cruiser. Twice, destroyers operating from Alexandria (itself bereft of anything larger) engaged convoys. Two other attempted sorties had been disrupted by Axis air power, including the first German Ju 87 bombers shipped to Libya and operating from airfields near Tobruk. Infrequently, the RAF, operating from fields in Egypt, attempted to bomb convoys, but usually found itself overwhelmed by Italian fighters. During these actions, the RMI lost two destroyers to three for the Royal Navy. Not a single merchantman or tanker suffered damage.[21]

On 12 September, after gentle prodding from Hitler and a major tongue-lashing from Il Duce, Marshall Graziani at last crossed the wire and invaded Egypt. Behind his Italian infantry, an impatient Rommel continued to organise his DAK. Most of 5th Light and elements of 7th Panzer had arrived by early September, but the Sahara offered challenges to men and machines quite different from the green fields of Poland and France. Thus a necessary period of acclimatisation for the men and desert-proofing of equipment kept him from joining the advance immediately.[22]

As the Italians began their invasion of Egypt, Malta continued to suffer under constant air attack. By mid-September, its defenders found themselves with only four functional fighters, low ammunition stocks, and less than four weeks of food on full rations. Between 8 and 12 October, Somerville attempted to ram a convoy of four merchantmen through using five battleships, two carriers (with fifty-four planes, mostly fighters), six cruisers (including two anti-aircraft cruisers), and sixteen destroyers. With Force H covered by a weather front and under strict radio silence, the Italians never realised it had sailed until a force of torpedo boats and destroyers engaged four British destroyers and a heavy cruiser off Cape Passero, Sicily. The RMI lost two torpedo-boats, and the destroyer *Artigliere* when it returned to the area to rescue survivors. In this engagement, the RMI faced radar-equipped British warships. The advantage allowed the British by this new technology was not lost on the Italian admiralty, which, lacking radar of their own, continued to stress the avoidance of night actions.[23]

Operations POMPEY *and* CRASSUS

By mid-October, Mussolini had reasons to be quite happy with the course of the war to date. His army in East Africa, despite its isolation, had captured British Somaliland, while elements of the RMI continued to aggressively harass British convoys in the Red Sea, disrupting the flow of supplies to Egypt via the Suez. In the Mediterranean, the RMI and RAI controlled the vital sea routes to Libya, daily convoying the remaining elements of DAK and a constant supply of munitions and fuel to Graziani's army, which was slowly (very slowly) plodding closer to Alexandria. Finally, the rapid conversion of the liner *Roma* to the carrier *Aquila* had been completed in record time.[24] Already, its air squadrons, equipped with the proven RE 2000 and a few of the new RE 2001 fighter-bombers, were conducting final training off Sicily.

On the other hand, fuel consumption had not been offset by Hitler's stingy release of German oil, which did not promise to increase even after the German Army occupied Romania – and its refinery complex at Ploesti – on 9 October. Mussolini's admiralty felt that remaining stocks would allow normal operations for no more then three months, after which sorties of the RMI would be severely curtailed. They suggested a quick seizure of the British refineries at Haifa by amphibious assault coupled with a more vigorous move on the Suez by Graziani's 10th Army. However, they also warned that the increasing strength of Force H in Gibraltar, especially after the successful reinforcement of Malta and the battle off Cape Passero, signalled a potential return of major fleet elements to Alexandria. In response, Mussolini requested two plans: one, which would be known as CRASSUS, for an amphibious invasion of Palestine to secure Haifa, and the second, Operation POMPEY, to neutralise the British force at Gibraltar. For the invasion, he designated units of the 9th Army, then garrisoning Albania, as the main landing force to be supported by armoured elements of the *Ariete* Division. He also requested that no German units be involved. Let Hitler have his Romanian oil; Il Duce would take the oilfields of the Middle East!

Operation CRASSUS would strain the limits of the RMI, which had never conducted an amphibious invasion larger than brigade strength. The final plan, set for the last week of November 1940, called for two task forces, each centred on a carrier and two battleships. One task force would blockade Alexandria (and screen Port Said at the mouth of the Suez) to prevent interference from light British naval units harbouring there. The other would support the landing at Haifa of a full division of infantry, though it would take better than two weeks to transport and land that entire force. During those weeks, the demand on cruisers and destroyers would be extensive, so extensive that virtually the entire RMI would be needed in the eastern Mediterranean, and would not be available to counter any thrusts from Gibraltar. Operation CRASSUS would also be a 'do or die' situation – it would exhaust Italian oil reserves, thus the capture of the Middle East's refineries and oilfields must occur. Mussolini agreed, dependent upon the success of the admiralty's second plan, the audacious Operation POMPEY.[25]

On 28 October, carriers *Roma* and *Aquila*, under the command of Admiral Angelo Iachino, and escorted by six cruisers and sixteen destroyers, left Naples under cover of darkness and heavy weather. As the sun set in a rapidly clearing sky on 31 October, the captains of both carriers read the following message to their assembled aircrews:

Warriors of the new Roman Empire, I salute you. It is a time of great danger, a time of great need by your country. Once in the old empire, a man stood on a rolling deck and said, '*Navigare necesse est, vivere non est necesse.*' Now, as you reach the objective of the operation which bears his name, I say the same to you. Survive if you can, but fly you must – for your love of home, for the honour of your navy, and for the glory of Italy! *Il Duce*[26]

Then, with a cheer, the men ran to their waiting planes. As night fell across a wine-dark sea, thirty-four torpedo-bombers, twenty-four fighter-bombers, and twelve fighters formed and winged their way for the Spanish coast. Forty miles inland, they turned ninety degrees to port over three immense bonfires lit in a triangle, then, a little over one hundred miles further west, similar fires signalled another turn to port.[27] Twenty minutes later, the torpedo-bombers dipped into the sleeping harbour at Gibraltar, while the fighter-bombers, each carrying a single thousand pound armour-piercing bomb circled briefly to identify their assigned targets. *Illustrious* and *Furious* never had a chance, as each took three torpedoes and two bomb hits. Gutted, they settled into the mud. *Valiant*, victim of four torpedoes, foundered as its crew dove over the side. Most of them died from concussion when *Hood*, its forward magazine penetrated by a single bomb, exploded, immolating all but three of its own crew. Two other battleships and a cruiser received hits that left them afloat – barely. Perhaps the most important damage occurred when a wayward torpedo struck a docked and partially laden oiler. Fumes ignited and the resultant explosion destroyed much of the fuel storage and transfer capacity at Gibraltar.

Fifteen minutes after the first torpedo hit the water, the last planes of the RMI headed to sea, their crewmen gaping in disbelief at the flaming port behind them. Their only losses came when an inexperienced torpedo-bomber squadron from *Aquila* managed to lose its way and land in Oran. They would regret their internment for the remainder of their lives, as it kept them from a celebration the like of which Italy had not seen since the days of the Caesars.[28]

The destruction of the heart of Force H left the Royal Navy crippled almost beyond recovery. It simply had nothing else to give to the struggle in the Mediterranean – its remaining ships needed to be conserved for the convoy war in the Atlantic and a potential struggle for the Channel itself. With heavy heart, Churchill ordered the evacuation of as much material from Malta as feasible without committing additional assets, then gave its garrison permission to surrender when food ran short. He also gave Western Desert Force, facing the advancing Italians in Egypt, permission to fall back to the Nile river if absolutely necessary.

Retreat became a moot point on 9 November when Rommel, his concentration of DAK almost complete, passed around the right flank of the Italian Army. Using his 29th Motorised Infantry to smash through screening elements of the 7th Armored Division, he exploited the breakthrough with 7th

Panzer and 5th Light. Three days later, his reconnaissance elements took Mersa Matruh, cutting the coast road and isolating 7th Armored and 4th Indian Divisions. As the British reversed their forces to dislodge Rommel from their supply route, additional German units filtered into Mersa Matruh. Building a defensive line of infantry and anti-tank units, Rommel quickly dispatched a mobile force to seize the bottleneck at El Alamein to delay any relief from the direction of Alexandria. Over 13 and 14 November, British armour and Indian infantry threw themselves heroically against the German line – great heroism, but little coordination allowed weaker German forces to hold on. Finally, Graziani (spurred by orders and threats from Il Duce) pressed his divisions to pursue the British. Crushed by heavier forces and devoid of supplies, the remnants surrendered on 17 November. As Graziani paused to rest and celebrate a great victory, Rommel pushed his tired troops to join the thin defensive line at El Alamein – a line now under considerable pressure from the 7th Australian and 4th New Zealand Divisions.[29]

On 26 November, Rommel received some unexpected help as the Italian First Fleet under Admiral Capioni appeared off the Egyptian coast. The battleships *Cesare* and *Cavour* pounded the 7th Australian's brigade entrenched along the coastal road as the fleet's cruisers and destroyers blockaded Alexandria under air cover provided by *Roma*. Never one to let an opportunity pass, Rommel quickly organised an attack by 7th Panzer that crumpled the coastal flank of the British position, then swept behind it as his reconnaissance elements headed for Alexandria. That evening, a final sortie by the last six British destroyers in the Mediterranean met total destruction at the guns of six veteran Italian cruisers.

The execution of Operation CRASSUS on 28 November was almost anti-climatic. The Middle Eastern Command had been stripped of troops, tanks, and aircraft for a new line along the Nile river. Local militia and a single battalion of British regulars defended all of Palestine. The Italian *Brescia* Division secured the port and its invaluable refineries with minimal casualties, and quickly began to expand its bridgehead, supported by the guns of Admiral Iachino's Italian Second Fleet and *Aquila*'s now veteran aircrews. Two weeks later, the first Italian tanker left Haifa for Taranto – the same day that the remaining British forces in Alexandria surrendered to Rommel and a guard of Italian marines.[30]

The Price of Peace

On 20 December, around a table in Madrid sat three men, all flanked by aides. As they debated, bombs rained on British cities, Malta starved, hulks in Gibraltar bled oil, and soldiers still bled into the dusty soil of Africa. In the Atlantic, Axis submarines sent ship after ship to the depths, while across occupied Europe men and women had merely began their suffering under the German yoke.

Winston Churchill knew the war was lost. Without American aid – and that quickly – there was no hope. Roosevelt had told him that it would come, but he could not risk the call for war unless Axis forces directly threatened the United States. Yet, Churchill was determined to hang on to as much as possible. After all, how many wars had it taken to defeat Napoleon?

Hitler, his eyes already turning toward the east, demanded little except an end to war, demilitarisation of the English Channel, and reparations (to be specified later). Mussolini, however, claimed all the Middle East, Egypt, and Malta. Further, Gibraltar would at last be returned to Spain. In return, he offered the immediate return of over 150,000 prisoners of war (of great importance to the Commonwealth nations that had supplied them) at the expense of Italy, if necessary. Finally, he offered to restore trade with Britain and its remaining possessions, including allowing British merchantmen into the Mediterranean. Churchill at last agreed, and on 24 December 1940, all parties signed the Treaty of Madrid, and the European War of 1939–40 came to an end.[31]

Hitler crowed over the victory. Mussolini waxed bombastic over the New Roman Empire. The men of the RMI, the true victors of the war, simply painted the following inscription on the quarterdeck of every vessel: '*Navigare necesse est! Vivere non est necesse!*'

The Reality

The Italian Navy of World War II has frequently been underrated by historians, amateur and professional alike. Its handicaps notwithstanding (and there were many), it gave as good as it received until the surrender of Italy, and even then many units gave selfless service to the Allies after 1943. In combat within the Mediterranean until its surrender, the RMI lost 151 warships and torpedo boats (including sixty-two submarines) to losses of 107 warships (including forty-one submarines) by the British. Certainly the RMI did not suffer a catastrophic defeat.[32]

Design quibbles aside (and the faster but less armoured Italian ships frequently benefited from their speed), the RMI suffered from three major problems: shortage of fuel, lack of radar (and sound electronics in general), and no naval air wing. The first two of these problems were less of a handicap in 1940 than one might think. The fuel issue would have been solved by a successful campaign leading to the capture of the oil-rich Middle East, including the British refinery complex at Haifa (a campaign actually planned, but poorly executed and supported). The lack of radar, in its infancy in 1940, became a problem only after the development of reliable naval sets by the British and their whole-hearted introduction into the fleet beginning in late 1940. In both cases, however, the longer the war lasted, the less the oil poor and fiscally lacking fascist state could do about it.

The third problem – the lack of naval air – was a killer from the first day of war. The decision in 1927 to centralise almost all aircraft under the RAI (truly a bastion of fascist loyalists) and the inability of the Italian admiralty to fight that decision, meant no effective air reconnaissance, the virtual abandonment of the second best naval torpedo program in the world, and no carriers. When war arrived, the RAI proved itself unable to effectively find British ships, unable to effectively sink British ships (also unable to sink the Italian ships that it all too frequently bombed – and yes, Italian anti-aircraft guns did down their own fliers), and behind the curve on aircraft development.[33]

Thus the RMI, able to engage effectively only during daylight hours because it lacked radar, also lacked the long-range air units needed to find British naval assets during the day. More importantly, without carriers it could not effectively operate outside the central Mediterranean (as it tried to do at Cape Matapan). Even within reach of Italian airbases, it had its problems, as the RAI had its own chain of command and frequently confused or ignored requests for support from the RMI. Did Mussolini realise that he had erred in concentrating on battleships, submarines, and torpedo boats? You betcha! Effective use of the (less than effectively designed) British carriers and naval air convinced Il Duce very quickly to begin conversion of a merchant vessel to the carrier *Aquila*. Too little, too late says it all.

What is missing? Oh yes, X Flotilla MAS. It was lost in the budget changes surrounding the building of *Roma*. That seemed appropriate, as the experimental weapons of the unit were a 'poor man's approach' to war, defensive war at that, and not in keeping with the aggressive spirit of – well – Pompey the Great.

Notes

1   'It is necessary to sail! It is not necessary to live!'
2   It is the lessons of youth that shape us. Had young Benito Mussolini been moulded by the stories of Pompey and his navies instead of those of the Caesarean legions, the history of the Mediterranean basin may, indeed, have changed.
3   Bosworth, 2002, pp. 37–217. See Bosworth for a detailed account of the early life and rise to power of Mussolini.
4   Sadkovich, 1994, pp. 1–44. See chapter 1 of Sadkovich for the best discussion of the development of the Regia Marina Italiana available.
5   Bragadin, 1957, p. 10.
6   Sadkovich, 1994, pp. 3–6.
*7   Alonzo A. Palmeri, *Collected Writings of Il Duce*, ten vols, Alexandria, Italia Minora: Tobruk Press, 1983–2004, 3: p. 106. This is the pivotal moment, as Mussolini realises the importance of naval air to expansion while acknowledging that Great Britain will be involved in any future conflict. In actuality, the Italian admiralty surrendered control of air power to the RAI, Mussolini kept his vision on the French, and Italy eventually lost a war.
*8   The building of *Roma* and a new emphasis on naval air power placed constraints on other construction. Two battleships originally scheduled to be laid down in 1937

would never be built, and delays – though not substantially affecting the coming war – were felt in all naval construction.

9   Regia Marina Italiana, http://www.regiamarina.net/. This carrier is based on the actual 1936 design. Note that the RE2000 came into service a tad later, and saw far more service by other countries than by Italy. Fortunately, in this counter-historical world, Mussolini sponsored a design contest in 1935 which expedited Regia Aeronautica's efforts, and encouraged them to develop the RE2000 (and its successor, the RE2001) on a more rapid schedule and primarily for use by the RMI.

*10   The conversions took the place of four cruisers in planning for 1939. Of six additional cruisers with keels laid in 1939, two would be completed in 1942, two in late 1943 as anti-aircraft cruisers, and two would be converted to light carriers in 1945 and eventually sold to Argentina.

11   Roskill, 1960, p. 103.

12   Roskill, 1978, pp. 150–1.

13   Sadkovich, 1994, pp. 55–7. Note that British Intelligence had considerable difficulty predicting the sailing of the Italian navy as the RMI relied heavily on landlines to its bases, and the upper echelons seldom micromanaged forces at sea by radio. Once Germany entered the Mediterranean in force, however, sloppy German radio procedures and an ever-present element of micromanagement coupled with the breaking of the ENIGMA code by British Intelligence, too frequently led to problems for the Italians.

*14   John F. K. Drake, *Punta Stilo: Turning Point in the Med*, London: Gladiator Press, 1952, 52–87. Drake, the pilot of the second Gladiator, engaged the SM79s of the RAI as they approached. Their machine-guns riddled his antique crate. His crash landing gave him an excellent, if somewhat damp, view of the torpedo attack by the RMI's SM79s as he clung to his seat cushion. His book speaks with great admiration of the organisation and skill of the Italian fliers, especially the fighter pilots who made short work of the *Eagle*'s Swordfish.

*15   Marco Palmarini (ed.), *RMI War Dairy, 1940–43*, 5 vols, Rome: Pizzeria Press, 1963, 1: pp. 238–69.

*16   Somerville, Admiral Sir James. *The Battles that Doomed Europe*, Plymouth, UK: Hawkins Press, 1951, pp. 87–103.

*17   Cunningham to Admiralty, July 15, 1940. LS, UkLPR, Adm. 14/505, pp. 87–90.

*18   The force would quickly be given the catchy title of *Das Afrika Korps* (DAK) and be commanded by the veteran German general, Erwin Rommel.

*19   Pieter von Ranken, *Amazing Alliance: Men and Supermen*, Berlin: Schlitz Press, 1962, pp. 102–68.

*20   Somerville, 1951, 148–180.

*21   Marcus A. Lucca, *Navigare Necesse Est!* Florence: Machiavelli Press, 1954, pp. 38-150.

*22   Manfried Paulus, *Panzers to the Front: To Suez with Rommel*, New York: Battlefront Press, 1989, pp. 25–8.

*23   Somerville, 1951, p. 208. (Note that both convoy and battle are based on actual events. See Sadkovich, 1994, pp. 87–9.)

*24   At the expense of the second carrier conversion – *Sparviero* remained months away from completion. *Aquila* had a top speed of thirty knots, little armour, strong anti-aircraft protection, and carried a maximum load of fifty-one planes.

*25   Palmarini, 1963, 1: pp. 400–48.

*26   Palmeri, 1983–2004, 3: p. 18.

*27 Neutral Spain never offered help to the Axis – veterans of the Spanish Civil War, however, especially those once supported by the aircraft of the *Roma*, were another matter entirely.

*28 Adm. I. A. Iluzzia (RMI Ret.), *The Wrong Way Boys: Torpedo Squadron 87 at Gibraltar*, trans. Jarrad Self, Naples: Three Flavour Press, 1993, pp. 24–96.

*29 Paulus, 1989, pp. 53–87. Though complimentary to Italian troops, both Paulus and Rommel had little good to say about the Italian Army's Graziani officer corps.

*30 Palmarini, 1963, 2: p. 169

*31 Winston Thatcher, *The Price of Peace*, London: Lessthan Press, 2004, pp. 75–150.

32 Sadkovich, 1994, p. 332.

33 Ibid., pp. 3–13.

Bibliography

Avalanche Press, *Bomb Alley: The Mediterranean War, 1940–43*, 2000 (Simulation).

Bosworth, R. J. B., *Mussolini*, New York: Oxford University Press, 2002.

Bragadin, Commander Marc' Antonio, *The Italian Navy in World War II*, Annapolis, MD: Naval Institute, 1957.

Regia Marina Italiana, http://www.regiamarina.net/.

Roskill, Captain S. W., *White Ensign: The British Navy at War, 1939–1945*, Annapolis, MD: Naval Institute1960.

Roskill, Captain S. W., *Churchill and the Admirals*, New York: William Morrow, 1978.

Rutter, Owen, *The British Navy's Air Arm: The Official Story of the British Navy's Air Operations*, New York: Penguin Books, 1944.

Sadkovich, James J., *The Italian Navy in World War II*, Westport, CT: Greenwood, 1994.

Schofield, Vice Admiral B. B., *The Attack on Taranto*, Annapolis, MD: Naval Institute, 1973.

5 The Health of the State

Italy and the Global War

David C. Isby

Victory smiles upon those who anticipate changes in the character of war, not upon those who wait to adapt themselves after the changes occur. *General Guilio Douhet*

War is the health of the state. It was said, with much irony, in the cafes and backrooms where Italy's remaining anarchists would gather, viewing Europe's slide towards war in the late 1930s. The same phrase, without the irony, was also a common view among Italy's fascist leadership. Italy's *Duce* (leader), prime minister Benito Mussolini, had shifted from a vague approval of war as an effective policy tool to a realisation that if Italy was ever to achieve its emerging strategic goal of becoming a world power, anchored in a regional Mediterranean base where it had uncontested domination, it would have to be as a result of the existing order being smashed and reformed in the fires of another European War. Increasingly, from 1936 on, Mussolini turned away from an earlier strategy based largely on opportunistic aggrandisement to one intended to assure that when war did come, Italy would be in a position to benefit from its results.

The reality undercut the rhetoric, as even the leadership perceived in their rare moments of clarity, awaking from their fantasies of glory like a charming drunk encountering ugly sobriety. The whole edifice of late 1930s Italy, government, party, society, church, industrial base, armed forces and diplomacy alike, was unlikely to survive the audit of war if it turned out to be anything more than a triumphal procession. It was easier to explain away these limitations than put in place policies that addressed them. Indeed, the Italian government – like its British and German counterparts – was often guilty of looking no further than blaming dismissive comic stereotypes of the Italian population and its behaviour rather than taking the results of this allegedly racially determined behaviour seriously.

As the European crisis of the 1930s entered its terminal stages, a range of constraints limited Italy's ability to play a role in it. Some of these constraints were shared with most of the other participants, such as a failure to produce significant numbers of modern weapons and, more important, train the armed forces in their appropriate use. Other limitations were unique to Italy. The monarchy, traditional ruling classes, papacy and armed forces alike, while all Mussolini's internal allies, functioned, each in a different way, as a check on the Duce's inclination to be at Germany's side from the start of a conflict. The regime's internal allies shared Mussolini's expansionist goals but not his tolerance for risk. Even the Italian masses could be roused to share Mussolini's ambitions and goals, as no less an expert on mass political behaviour than Adolf Hitler repeatedly stated.[1] But each of these power sources shared the dissatisfaction with Italy's place in the European and world orders. The accession of Italy to great power status, marked by the creation of a *spazio vitale* (vital space) based in a Mediterranean basin that was truly *mare nostrum* (our sea) was Mussolini's goal. That Britain, France and their colonies, protectorates, possessions and allies were literally in the way of achieving this is primarily is what led him to bet on a German military victory as the way to achieve these goals, which were largely shared by the other major figures of the fascist regime. Italy's occupation of Albania in April 1939 and the reawakening of the confrontation with Greece, simmering since the occupation of Corfu in 1923, met, if not with widespread approval, than at least with acquiescence.

Mussolini saw war as the health of the state. War would allow him to centralise power and clear away the other players in the politics of fascist Italy. Indeed, the Italian people would be forged anew in the white heat of total war, emerging as something quite different from the universally accepted perceptions. Mussolini, not least because he had been minister for each of the armed services since 1936, understood little of modern war. He did not see that the gap in military capability between Italy and the great powers of Europe that had been substantial in the Great War had increased since then. The former political journalist ended up believing his own press releases, and there was no one he trusted to set him straight. If war was to be the health of the state, this one was to transform not only state but most importantly, transport him personally and his people into a central – no longer peripheral – role in the world.

The key issue was whether Italy's national security – which could only be assured by a position as a great power in a Europe in which little fish were swallowed – could be assured by participation in the war on the winning side. Even the moderates largely accepted this. But the support for war – outside Mussolini and his immediate circle – was limited. It was generally accepted that Italy needed to be on the winning side, and that was going to be the side of Germany. But when it became evident that Mussolini would not lead the country into war over Poland, even key pro-war figures such as the then-Fascist party secretary Archille Starace appeared relieved.[2] Starace, along with a number of old-time fascists, was to lose his job in a 23 October cabinet reshuffle that also brought to power moderate associates of Mussolini's son-in-law, the pragmatic yet urbane foreign minister Count Ciano. Hitler accepted this, on 23 November telling his generals that he was sure about Italy, 'so long as the Duce lives'.

A Balancing Strategy

Despite the post-*Anschluss* (May 1939) 'Pact of Steel' alliance with Germany and the general recognition as to where Italy's allegiance should lie, the invasion of Poland led not to Italy coming into the European war at Germany's side, but, rather, it initiated a new phase in Italian strategy. Italy's neutrality, more than simple waiting for the right moment to join or looking for a suitable opportunity, sought to keep engaged and balance the now-combatant powers. While it was a reactive strategy, it was more than simple opportunism.

Neutrality only became acceptable because Mussolini did not turn against it. There was no top-down advocacy for an immediate conflict. This was especially the case with the military. Well aware of the limitations in Italy's armed forces, the military leadership hoped that a balancing strategy would provide access to resources that could be incorporated in the near terms. This meant weapons and equipment as well as the coal and steel, the lack of which had pushed Italy into junior partner status in coalitions since the nineteenth century. Mussolini had personally handed in a lengthy list of military and resource requirements to the Germans. The German ambassador in Rome had encouraged the Italians to be as comprehensive as possible, both to get their needs on the records and – his true unstated purpose – to provide evidence in Berlin how useless the Italian armed forces might become in the event of a prolonged conflict.[3] The German General Staff treated the Italian requests with disdain. It was to be, after all, a short, victorious war and, with Germany aiming to avoid the costs of full mobilisation, providing resources for Italy was not going to be a priority. Germany was not going to fight a coalition war except on its own terms, whatever the strategic advantage.

A balancing strategy takes, by definition, two or more forces. The British and French, after their tensions with Italy over Ethiopia and Spain and the failure to put together a workable policy even where there were shared interests in preventing the *Anschluss*, were far from ideal partners to balance against Germany. They had already tried to engage with Italy and failed. They had little respect for the Italian leadership, government, or war-making potential, which tended to be dismissed without limited serious analysis of its capabilities.

Perhaps most to the point, they could not give Italy what it wanted, an increased role in a European power structure that was becoming less able to direct worldwide power relationships. The political crises of the late 1930s had repeatedly shown the importance of the Soviet Union and the United States – even in the absence of direct engagement – and the relative impotence of the British and French in creating a viable security situation. The British and the French could not offer Italy the keys to Gibraltar, Tunisia, Malta and the Suez Canal, which Italy saw as confining it and keeping if from the world stage.

Nor could they realistically redraw the map by allowing Italy to annex Nice and Corsica. They could, more substantially, offer hard currency and resources, but both of these were in short supply in both Britain and especially France, where there was less of a desire or capability to mobilise. Nor were Britain or France able to supply the weapons and equipment that Germany was being difficult about providing. They had few enough of the same types of modern weapons that Italy lacked. The British offered to buy modern Italian aircraft and weapons, but the Italians needed every one of the few of these they could produce and Mussolini, to assuage Berlin, limited the types to 'non-combatant' or 'defensive' systems. The main British sanction was a negative one: non-interference with the German coal being shipped to Italy via Rotterdam.

Tensions with Berlin

The months after Poland, with Germany perceiving itself as secure in its partnership with the Soviet Union and opposed only by a weak-willed Britain and France, were a critical window of opportunity to turn the Pact of Steel into a real military alliance, addressing the concerns that had led to Italy's non-belligerency over Poland and align the Italian concepts of 'parallel war' and a 'balancing strategy' with Berlin's needs. This did not happen. Neither Hitler nor Mussolini saw this as a priority. Little concrete was done. As Marshal Pietro Badogolio recorded: 'As frequently happened in similar crises he [Mussolini] assumed the mantle of a prophet and solemnly announced that everything must be done and possibly done more quickly than was anticipated.'[4] This reflected both internal Italian weakness and suspicion of German policies. In the wake of the fall of Poland, Italy was concerned about the emergence of a formal Russo-German alliance and that this would lead to the Pact of Steel losing importance in Berlin. In response, Italy had aimed at creating a bloc of neutrals to be under Italian political hegemony.[5] This reflected Mussolini's distrust of Hitler that had been initiated by each backing opposing sides in the 1938 'Little Entente' conflict, which saw Italy supporting Hungary and Germany its rump Czechoslovakian and Romanian opponents. Italy's new policies had the effect of combating German goals in Yugoslavia, Hungary, and, to a lesser extent, Romania. It also allowed time for British initiatives to try and bring these governments into line to oppose Germany (and Russia). These actions increased the tensions between Berlin and Rome.

The most explosive question in Italo-German relations, the Alto Adige – the German-speaking areas of south Tyrol Italy annexed after 1918 – came to a head in late fall 1939. Ciano – pragmatic enough to see that any issue that kept Mussolini from joining with Berlin was a good thing – exploited this issue. He aimed to use it to drive a wedge between Berlin and Rome while striking a nationalist theme that would resonate with other Italians.

On 21 October 1939 Hitler and Mussolini agreed on the Germans of the

South Tyrol having until 31 December to choose between remaining in Italy (and losing all minority rights), or emigrating to the Third Reich (as some eighty-five to ninety per cent did). Mussolini had originally looked away from this issue, but the actions of a range of low-level German officials increased tensions. Many Germans made suggestions that it was the Alto Adige itself that would 'return to the Reich'. Pro-Nazi organisations aimed to 'turn this [issue over the Alto Adige] into an effective pro-German plebiscite.'[6] By early November, Mussolini was reported to be highly anti-German in private. He hearkened back to earlier post-*Anschluss* statements he had made about 'changing sides' and that as a result 'Germany would be crushed for at least two centuries.'[7] Ciano noted that if the British and French were 'on the ball' they could exploit this division over the Alto Adige.[8] The British and French governments of November 1939 were many things; 'on the ball' was certainly not one of them. In this period Mussolini had been willing to talk with Britain, to look towards a tactical détente (providing re-insurance against a German negotiated peace) to isolate the French, building on the remaining links of the April 1938 Anglo-Italian agreement.

By late 1939, there was little indication that the balancing strategy would lead to anything other than a move towards war with Italy on the side of Germany. But the Alto Adige crisis soured even the Duce. Within a fortnight, Mussolini was reinforcing troops in the region, telling Ciano that the situation in the Alto Adige was a serious one that could lead to war with Germany.[9] Later in the month, Ciano recorded 'the German star is beginning to pale even in the Duce's mind.'[10] Ciano then set to using his limited political capital to try and solidify this position. At the meeting of the largely rubber-stamping Grand Council of Fascism meeting on 7 December, Ciano justified Italy's neutrality and had his views approved by a subsequent Mussolini address. Despite German attempts to smooth over the issue, a speech by a German official suggesting that the Alps were part of the natural Reich led to the recall of the German ambassador from Rome. The Italians started sharing their intelligence on German offensive plans in the west with the Netherlands and Belgian embassies in Rome.[11] In mid-December, the Italian ambassador in Tokyo was directed to encourage anti-German resentment. The Alto Adige and the Yugoslavia and Balkans issues became sticking points in transforming the relationship between the two countries. But Berlin's rough treatment of Italy in the Alto Adige and Yugoslavia issues in 1939, was not going to turn away Mussolini from his fundamental support of Hitler or, more important, from his belief that only through participation in a victorious war could Italy – nation and people – achieve greatness.

What changed was, initially, German treatment of Italian concerns. German mishandling of the relationship with Italy was considered to be of no account in Berlin. However much Italy might resent the way the Germans acted to achieve their policy goals, they were going to shape the future rather than try and preserve an unsatisfactory status quo. Berlin, looking at the personal relationship between Mussolini and Hitler, where Italy's coal was coming from, and the fundamental incompatibility of Italy's revisionist strategic goals and the necessity for maintaining the status quo by Britain and France, basically assumed Italy was not going to re-align itself and that these crises could be best addressed by ignoring them and pressing on with plans to win the war through offensive action in the west in 1940.

New Players for the Italian Game

Graveyards are said to be full of indispensable men. When Mussolini perished in an airplane crash on New Year's Eve of 1939, it represented a break with previous policies and opened up Italy to a range of strategic options even though its basic dilemma remained unchanged.

The death of Mussolini led to a reshuffling of the Italian government. The commitment to war as the best way to advance Italy's interests was not limited to him, but the weak, highly bureaucratised institutions of state power were open to influence by the monarchy and others – including Ciano – interested in achieving neutrality. Ciano emerged as prime minister. His personal loyalty to Mussolini, his lack of a substantial independent power base within the regime and his inability to formulate and, above all, implement a policy alternative to Mussolini had made him the candidate of continuity. He was not the first team player and understudy to be thrust forward into a role that would have tried Cesare Borgia.

The roots of change in Rome's alignment were in the resources shortages Italy faced during the 'Phoney War' period with no assurance from Germany as to how they would be met. Foreign exchange reserves were down to under 3,000 million lira. Despite the Pact of Steel, there was no indication how the twelve million tonnes of coal required in 1940 would be obtained. The army and the air force had fuel reserves for perhaps a month of sustained combat. The Soviets halted the delivery of fuel oil already contracted. Mussolini had been unconcerned. Many of those close to him had not shared the same attitude.[12]

Fundamentally changing the security situation for Italy was the emergence of a potential ally in an unanticipated quarter. The US had seen, as with the rest of the participants, that Italy was peripheral in the European security crises of the late 1930s. Any willingness to give Mussolini and his regime consideration was gone after the failure of Italy to work against the *Anschluss*. There was little sympathy for Mussolini anywhere in the US, expect for ethnic and religious fringe groups. But with limited resources and leverage, the State department aimed to 'neutralise' Italy.[13] The US acted in Italy's favour on 14 December 1939, when it challenged the Royal Navy blockade plan whereby neutral ships were diverted to British and French control bases for inspection for contraband. This was seen in Italy as a challenge especially to their German coal lifeline.

At this point, President Franklin D. Roosevelt took a personal interest in the

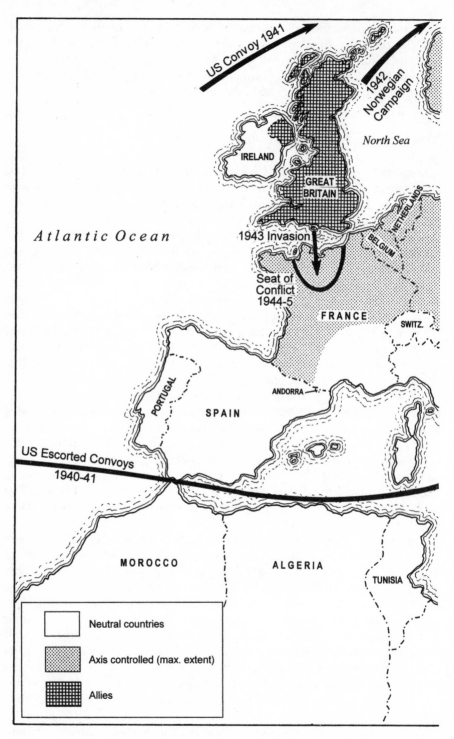

US Convoy 1941

1942
Norwegian
Campaign

North Sea

IRELAND

GREAT
BRITAIN

Atlantic Ocean

1943 Invasion

NETHERLANDS

BELGIUM

Seat of
Conflict
1944-5

FRANCE

SWITZ.

PORTUGAL

ANDORRA

SPAIN

US Escorted Convoys
1940-41

MOROCCO

ALGERIA

TUNISIA

	Neutral countries
	Axis controlled (max. extent)
	Allies

Italy and the global war

US–Italian relations that had been a low priority since 1938. The death of Mussolini now gave an opening, removing a key part of the stigma from still-fascist Italy. It was also a move that would prove popular among Italian-Americans in an election year. He dispatched Sumner Welles, Under-secretary of State, to Europe. Roosevelt personally gave him a difficult task: certainly gather intelligence, but if at all possible, split the Axis.[14]

Welles' first stop was Rome. He hit it off with Ciano in their initial meetings on 26 February. Ciano thought Welles to be '*un signore*' and talked of his antagonism towards Hitler. The meetings coincided with the start of a British embargo on the maritime shipment of German coal to Italy. The Bank of Italy had but 2,300 million lire in gold in reserve to cover market alternatives.

Welles wired back that this was a potential opportunity made possible by the death of Mussolini. Roosevelt responded. He authorised the supply of US coal – at a level designed to limit potential re-export to Germany and with assurances and safeguards intended to assuage British concerns – on credit as long as Italy remained neutral.[15] At the same time, Hitler offered one million tons a month by rail. The Ciano government went with the US offer.

The Roosevelt administration's decision to make support to post-Mussolini Italy, a major part of its 1940–41 policy, was unprecedented. The relationship with Italy lacked the importance of that with Britain, the long standing of that with China, or even the appeal of that with emerging regional partners such as Brazil. The details would be worked out, but included US naval escorts for US-flag coal ships through the Mediterranean – also serving as escorts against U-boats – to ensure the principles of neutral-to-neutral trade.

The European War Becomes a World War

Italy's balancing strategy had, with Mussolini's death, become something more than a way to best pick the time of joining the Axis at war. With the potential for an effective US relationship, there was now something concrete for the Italian balancing strategy of 1939–40 to effectively offset the relationship with Germany. The Ciano government, without Mussolini driving it to war and with the hope of the US relationship, did not declare war even as France was collapsing in June 1940. Without the personal relationships of the dictators, a more realistic appreciation of Germany's long-term strategic vulnerabilities and Italy's unreadiness to fight a modern war had led those that mattered – including the military leadership – to support neutrality, as pro-war generals were swiftly retired or sent to unimportant commands.

Hitler's reaction was one of fury. The Pact of Steel had rusted away through Italian weakness. Italy had, so far, proven to be a weak ally, failing to declare war on Germany's enemies. He had counted on Italy, in the Mediterranean, to open a second front against Britain that would force a negotiated peace. Still, this was a secondary setback. Hitler saw no reason to change his basic strategy of relying on air and sea action against Britain until next year's campaign – the conquest of the Soviet Union – would allow him the ability to force British concessions at his leisure. While plans were made to invade Italy to open up a Mediterranean front, Hitler generally treated a neutral Italy as a larger version of Franco's ungrateful, neutral, Spain rather than a missing strategic linchpin. This was a war to decide the future of Europe, the world, and its racial future. Italy would come to heel soon enough once the issue was settled. German intrigues in Yugoslavia, especially Croatia, took on an ant-Italian direction.

Hitler moved on to what he saw as his greatest challenge and the one action that would allow him to shape the future. The German invasion of the USSR, Operation BARBAROSSA, started in April 1941 as planned, without Balkan distractions or the need to divert air or ground forces to the Mediterranean. The German's invasion devastated the forward deployed Soviet units. There had been less time to prepare fortifications and shift forces from interior military districts, so while resistance was less, there was also not as large a bag of prisoners as might have been hoped. The most significant limitation from the early start was that the initial advance had to counter with the spring mud as the Germans advanced. Hitler soon found that there was a reason why Napoleon had waited until June before invading Russia. Stalin's 1941 demands for a second front reflected not only the desperate military situation faced by the Soviet Union but his fears that Britain was colluding with Hitler. Stalin saw the British not engaged in land combat with the Germans anywhere and, despite the losses of the Norwegian campaign and Dunkirk, with most of the Royal Navy still intact, this fuelled his suspicions that Britain was playing a long-term game against him.

The early start of Operation BARBAROSSA did ensure that, despite hard-fought defensive battles, the impetus of the German invasion did get them to Moscow. Even the failing and improvised German logistics held together long enough for them to be able to surround the city and collapse the resistance. But the act of raising the swastika over the Kremlin and seizing key elements of the governmental and transportation infrastructure did not stop the impact of Russian mobilisation and had only a limited effect in assuaging the German limits in force structure, logistics, and ability to operate in the Russian winter.[16] The Soviet winter counter-attack of 1941 forced a line-shortening German withdrawal from Moscow. An early start had not been decisive.

The German invasion of the Soviet Union presented Britain with a strategic quandary. While promising aid to the Soviet Union, Britain had limited options to fight Germany while avoiding a direct decisive land battle in north-west Europe that, even if Britain won, would impose losses and costs that would end it as a world power. The bomber offensive remained in an embryonic form, killing more RAF aircrew than Germans living in its targets. Churchill's first response was to try and use the US connection and, indeed, every diplomatic asset he had available to try and bring Italy as an ally into the war against Hitler. Churchill's proposed 1941 strategy of the 'soft underbelly' was based on a southern front including Yugoslavia, Greece and Turkey, joining with Italy, providing the ground forces and bases for British supplies and air power in a northwards advance. But implementing such a strategy proved to be unworkable. The armed forces of these countries were unlikely to overcome the Germans in decisive battle, and their leadership was reluctant to join against the Germans as they were seemingly unstoppable.

Britain had the flexibility to commit its few strategic reserves – after Dunkirk – to the war against Hitler at a time and place of its choosing, but this proved to be less of an advantage than it had been hoped. Germany's success against the Soviet Union meant that there was a need for a strong home defence force against a renewed invasion threat. Britain lacked the landing craft and specialist organisations for effective large-scale amphibious operations. The shadow of Norway 1940 was added to that of Gallipoli to undercut the confidence of the British military leadership that such operations could be carried out in modern war. The resources available for implementing an offensive strategy against Germany in 1941 were limited; in addition to home defence, Britain still had to keep strong garrisons in the Mediterranean against potential German and Vichy French moves and in India and the Far East against the Japanese. Italy was included in Lend-Lease when the US implemented the programme. While never at the same priority as Britain or the Soviet Union, the Italian military started to receive a trickle of US-designed hardware. The users preferred their own national designs.

In early 1942, Stalin made, through a number of channels, secret overtures for a separate peace with Germany. Despite the evidence – through intelligence sources and scenes of atrocities in recaptured Moscow – that Hitler was not open to compromise in a racially based war of extermination, Stalin saw that, with the British (and now the Americans) disengaged, this was his war. What prevented a separate peace was the simple fact that, by 1942, Hitler was not interested in a separate peace or on any resolution that would leave the east under Stalin and intact while there was every likelihood that the Anglo-Americans would continue the conflict. As in 1941, Italy's 'betrayal' – Hitler convinced himself that 'the martyred Duce' would never have so let him, down – was a source of frustration, but it was not seen as a strategic problem. This would be a war about the future of Europe, of all humanity, in the eyes of Hitler. Control of Italy and the Balkans, like Spain and other neutrals, could be decided at leisure by the winners. Churchill, aware of this through signal intercepts, feared a return to the Hitler-Stalin pact. This made implementing a peripheral British strategy in 1942 – before US deployments made such a thing impossible – a high priority.

Still a World War

The fall of Moscow and the German successes caused by the early 1941 campaign in Russia had made it appear, to Japan, that the northern rather than the southern direction would be the most productive, arguing for a war against the Soviet Union rather than the US and the western allies. But the failure of the Soviet Union to collapse or successfully make a negotiated peace with Germany despite the successes made possible by an early start of BARBAROSSA did not create the vacuum the Japanese had wanted to the north. Japan was left with its long-standing strategic dilemmas. As it had to Mussolini before his demise, war appeared the only way for Japan to overturn a world and regional situation that seemed designed to perpetuate its second-class status.

The US Navy, with the commitments to Italy as well as the North Atlantic routes to Britain, found itself escorting convoys entering the Mediterranean by 1941. This made fewer US ships available for the Pacific even as the situation there deteriorated. The Royal Navy was heavily engaged in sending hard-fought convoys through to Russia as well as the battle of the Atlantic. The absence of a Mediterranean war meant that Anglo-American planning to defend against Japanese moves to the south were more substantive than they might have been otherwise, but these plans, with their increasing emphasis on a forward defence of Hong Kong and the Philippines made possible by air power reinforcements, was pre-empted by the Japanese occupation of French Indochina. Britain could devote more resources to guard against the increasing likelihood of a war against Japan. The Royal Navy was able to dispatch a reinforced naval force to Singapore in the months before the Japanese struck in December 1941. The defences of the base had also been reinforced, with additional fighter squadrons and infantry divisions – to the extent that the limited infrastructure of Singapore and Malaya would allow – but this had the effect of outing more forces in harm's way without the ability to defeat a more proficient if numerically inferior enemy in Malaya, Singapore and the Netherlands East Indies.

The lack of a Mediterranean conflict did not provide the means to address the unreality in British preparation for a war against Japan. The qualitative problems remained. The failure of the Indian government to mobilise effectively for a modern war, the lack of realistic training for the infantry divisions deployed to Malaya, and the inability to set up an integrated air defence system that would help defend Singapore were questions of operational competence rather than resource allocation. The basic flaws in British strategy and their ability to implement it at the operational level meant that even having more resources available could not save Malaya, Singapore, and the Netherlands East Indies. It slowed the Japanese advance in Burma, but control of the air and more effective ground tactics allowed them to advance towards the Indian border during 1942.

No Soft Underbelly

Neither British diplomacy nor military action could turn Hitler's 'soft underbelly' into reality rather than Churchillian rhetoric. Churchill was challenged both by Stalin's demands for a second front and the Americans who, led by General George Marshall, wanted a direct invasion of France in 1942. The result was a new Norwegian campaign in the spring and summer of that year.[17] Intended to seize German air and naval bases that threatened the northern convoys, the campaign ended unhappily – with evacuations and the loss of landed brigades – despite several British naval victories The Germans could divert more air power from the eastern front to attack the British lodgements than the British could bring up to sustain them. As this campaign was not part of the overall Anglo-American strategy planned before the US entry into the war, the US refused to commit more than limited forces. This led to much bitterness, with Churchill convinced ever after that a large-scale US commitment would have led to the liberation of Norway.

The role of junior partner in the alliance hit London early and hard. In the wake of the Norwegian campaign, in meetings with their US counterparts, the British high command found that their views failed to have much weight with their US counterparts. The British peripheral approach to strategy had been tried and failed. The British had no offensive victories, however hard-won, to legitimate their competence at war-making. With the US increasingly sustaining the Allied war effort – including buying and paying for Italian neutrality – it was difficult to counter the US emphasis on an invasion of France.

Despite the deep misgivings of the British, Operation BOLERO, the Allied invasion of Europe, started in July 1943 with the invasion of Normandy.[18] In the fighting that followed, it became apparent that the German forces had one tremendous existential advantage. They had been able to learn to conduct modern war at an operational level against weaker opponents.[19] The 1943 fighting in France allowed the Germans to demonstrate this capability to the fullest. By invading France in 1943, the Allies had also struck while the Combined Bomber Offensive had little time to make an impact on German production or remove the Luftwaffe from the battlefields.[20] The Allied invasion of France led to much bloody fighting and it was only after a number of setbacks in 1943 and static fighting over the winter of 1943-44 that Allied material superiority finally told and forced the Germans back to the German borders in mid-1944.[21]

The decisive battles of World War II were largely those fought between the Volga and the Vistula. By this time, the advancing Soviet armies had started to come up against the borders of neutral Yugoslavia and Greece. Stalin considered treating them as he had nominally neutral Bulgaria and issuing an ultimatum, but instead decided to rely on his internal allies in each country, now each bordered by pro-Soviet territory.

The real prize, however, remained Italy. The Ciano government had held on to power throughout the war. The Communists and their allies had, after 1941, not wanted to violate a state of neutrality that was keeping resources away from Germany. With Italy effectively dependent on US economic and lend-lease aid, Roosevelt's constant pressure to ameliorate at least the more repressive elements of the fascist regime could not be ignored. The more restrictive policies (including anti-Jewish policies) put into place in the 1930s were quietly removed. But the revolutionary fascist zeal of the 1920s did not return. Instead, Italy was gradually transformed to an authoritarian state, fascist in nominal ideology but actually a repressive police state concerned with its own security, with the different stakeholders each trying to maintain their interests against the inevitable reckoning.

It was spring 1945 before Soviet troops reached the Italian border as Austria was liberated. With the end of the war in Europe in June 1945, Italy was finally about to go to war, offering a US-equipped corps and a naval task force for operations in the Pacific. The atomic bombs ended the war before they could deploy.

The end of the war and the death of President Roosevelt – who had considered the relationship with Italy to be a personal one, created and nurtured by him while the military and diplomatic establishments considered it peripheral – cast the future of the Ciano government in doubt. The abrupt end of US Lend-Lease and economic aid under the incoming Truman administration brought about a major political crisis. Without US security guarantees, Italy felt compelled to evacuate Albania, which immediately collapsed into civil war. Ciano himself fell. The successor regime found it needed to broaden its base with nationalist appeals. New governments officially or tactically recognised more opposition groups and allowed them effective participation in a state drifting further from its Mussolini-era roots. Attempts to co-opt emerging opposition proved problematic. To the great dismay of the government, their emerging base-broadening alliances proved volatile as the divisions of pre-1922 Italian politics started to re-emerge.

The military and their allies, now the strongest forces in the government, made plans for internal repression and imposition of martial law. However, renewed importance for the relationship with the US prevented these moves. Fortunately, Italy was included in both the Marshall plan and US security relations with southern Europe that started in 1947. The US security relationship grew with the Cold War, as Italy's Communists were looking towards turning the control of the country over to Stalin by whatever means possible.

The Italian Communists attempts at fomenting unrest did not receive the support they had hoped for from Stalin. Italy was seen as peripheral and Communist success was seen as likely to provoke a strong western response. Moscow was a day late and a rouble short in its political penetration of Italy. It was not until 1948 that Yugoslavia fell to a pro-Moscow Communist coup. In Greece, a pro-Moscow insurrection supported from over the border in Bulgaria was not successful. The Soviet Union faced the problems of being an empire but with parts of Europe that did not constitute a vacuum for post-war expansion. Confronted with the neutral elements of Balkans and southern Europe that had resulted from Italian neutrality, the Soviets did not try and cross the border into Yugoslavia, Greece or Turkey.

Italy's status as a neutral reflected in its delayed joining of the UN and NATO, but – again reflecting the US relationship – in the 1950s became a key member of both groups. Because of its neutral wartime status and resentment over its fascist roots, Italy was not included in the initial membership of the

European Coal and Steel and Economic communities. This had the effect of deferring Italian 'integration into Europe' until the 1970s.

Victory from the Margins

There are few second-place winners in total war. Italy was certainly the biggest winner of its decision to stay neutral. The limitations of Italian arms, economy and society were spared the 'audit of war' that would have found them all wanting. Its industries were undestroyed, its infrastructure unbombed, and it was a beneficiary in the elimination of the Nazi threat to Europe just as much as the countries that had expended tremendous amounts of blood and resources in the cause.

Italy was a fortunate country. It had, through neutrality, shifted tying its fortunes from Hitler and National Socialism to Washington as it started its rise to world power. By doing this, Italy made a decisive change in its preferred means of changing the European status quo from military conquest (as junior partner to Berlin) to taking part – albeit passively – in a coalition led by an emerging superpower that would accept that Italy's internal political problems would take decades to gradually resolve themselves. Italy, literally accidentally, was on the winning side, anticipating, through good fortune if not by clever strategy or insightful thinking, the changing nature of the twentieth century. The future belonged not to the Führer and Berlin, but to a transatlantic relationship underpinned by shared values. Italy anticipated these changes not only in avoiding entering a romantic war of conquest and colonial-territorial aggrandisement but set itself up to participate effectively in the remainder of the twentieth century by not following the spirit of Mussolini into an alliance with totalitarian dictatorship. Rather, Italy linked itself to the US, anticipating the end of the Europe-centric world power system that led all of its major pre-1939 participants to end up aligned with either the US or the Soviet Union post-war.

Italy had anticipated the change in the nature of the power system and benefited from it. It also anticipated this change in its internal perception of what it needed to improve its own position. Again, by default and chance rather than brilliant strategy, Italy's post-Mussolini leadership turned away from the Duce's vision that required the *tricolori* to fly over Gibraltar, Tunis, Suez and more distant shores. Rather than the old-style zero-sum world revolving around colonies and chokepoint occupation, Italy was able to avoid destruction and be present at the birth of a new system based on trade, increasing political openness and, in the end the long-term coalitions that would, eventually, win the Cold War.

If the effects of Italian neutrality were, not unsurprisingly, almost totally beneficial at home, its effects on Britain were mixed. Britain benefited from there being no need for a long and costly war in the Mediterranean that would have drained limited resources and showed the shortfalls in British war-fighting capability that had resulted from the policies pursued after 1918. But there were also fewer all-British victories. The Battle of Britain and the lone stand against Hitler in 1940–41 receded into memory. Britain's claim to great power status was seriously undercut; the diplomatic capital gained from the Battle of Britain only stretched so far, and by the end of the war, even Roosevelt was using Britain's dependence on the US for leverage. His anti-imperial views had free range as Britain ended up not as the victor of the North African war, but as junior partner and failure at peripheral warfare. With the increased US wartime relationship with Italy proving decisive for that country, the special relationship with Britain was, in effect, balanced with another pillar. While the British Empire and Commonwealth remained strong post-war, the effects of Singapore and economic disruption through wartime mobilisation could not be undone. The British increased their place in the western coalition post-war, as they could make distant bases available to their US allies. The British Empire was whittled down, under US pressure, over the following decades. The US found they would rather deal with indigenous governments rather than seen as being the successors of imperial power. As the Italians had discovered by accident, the practice of operating as part of a coalition, for all its frustrations, beats that of operating as an empire.

Mussolini, for once, was right. War did come, and Italy did benefit.

The Reality

The scenario above follows reality closely to the end of 1939 and, to a lesser extent, in the months running up to Italy's fateful decision to join a war that then seemed all but won. Italy did try and keep a balancing situation going between its allies in the Pact of Steel and the Anglo-French alliance. Everything on the Italian side is historical up to the death of Mussolini and on the US side up to the results of the Welles mission.

In reality, the fundamental strategic reality perceived by Mussolini and shared by most of those that mattered in 1940 Italy was that Italy needed to expand its control to remain a viable power and that such expansion could only come at the expense of the status quo powers, France and Britain. This perception emerged gradually as Mussolini's regime transformed and was confirmed in its course by Franco-British policies following the conquest of Ethiopia, the Spanish Civil War and the *Anschluss*. This scenario identifies some of the ways – both in discrediting the inevitability of alignment with Germany and in providing a (US-provided) alternative – this perception could have been altered even in 1939–40. This included the tensions with Germany over the Alto Adige and Yugoslavia in that time-frame. These were, in reality, dealt with in the course of Axis relations, though the resentments and suspicions remained to contribute to the poisonous nature of those relations throughout the war. Here, in the way that such issues do, they became more important, not only because they can take on a life of their own, but because there were those in the Italian leadership who, while sharing the desire to increase Italian power, were reluctant to do so as co-belligerents of Hitler.

The major change that allows this reluctance to become more than the stuff of diary entries and regrets in this scenario is the combination of a *deus ex machina* to remove Mussolini from the stage and a lifeline – a major intervention by a non status quo power, in the case the US (the other alternative, Stalin's USSR, is less likely to have been seen as a viable partner for 1939–40 Italy especially given the role of the Hitler–Stalin pact in increasing suspicions of Berlin). When it became apparent, as a result of Italy's 1939–40 'balancing' policy, that Britain could provide only a little of what Italy desired, that effectively left the US as the only alternative to Germany. Here, the US came through and was accepted. In reality, Mussolini was not interested in alternatives to the Axis.

The projected US policy towards post-Mussolini Italy postulated here includes elements of Roosevelt's policies towards 1940 Britain, Brazil and China.[22] The US–Italy rapprochement in this scenario is based on the actual Welles mission. This did not lead to any significant changes, but it could have, especially if leaders on both sides were to have put their weight behind it. However, Mussolini had too much invested in his policies even for an optimal deal with the US to lead to a fundamental change in his policies. For this scenario to work, Mussolini had to be removed. With few in a position to do so having the will to act to remove him, this became the result of chance.

One of the values of the counterfactual approach is that is requires setting out what conditions would have been needed for alternative outcomes to materialise. In this case, however much one might have looked to sources of tension with Hitler, it was apparent that a neutral Italy was not going to happen if Mussolini was in power. This explicit, personal commitment has been discussed by Knox and others in the standard English-language works on the subject. For this counterfactual, it required either a coup – which was unlikely except in a time of extreme political crisis – or an outside force to remove him. An air accident is certainly not far-fetched. Even though only one head of state – Poland's Sikorsky – actually perished this way during the war, each of the major Allied conferences was marked by at least one crash with high-ranking casualties. Getting Mussolini out of the picture was a necessary condition for examining the idea of what impact a neutral Italy would have on the course of the war. An air crash seemed the most logical way of achieving that condition.

Notes

1   Trevor Roper, 1953, see no. 132 (31.1.1942) and no. 268 (24.7.42) for examples.
2   Ciano, 2002, volume II, 1.9. 1939.
3   Ibid, volume I, p. 265.
4   Badogolio, 1948, p. 12.
5   See generally Marzari, 1970.

6   Ciano 2002, volume I, 7.12.39.
7   Smith, 1981, pp. 218–19.
8   Ciano 2002, volume II, 11.11.39.
9   Ibid., 21.11.39.
10   Ibid., 26.11.1939.
11   Ibid., 26.12.1939.
12   Ibid., 11.2.1940.
13   Schmitz, 1988, pp. 218–19.
14   Israel, 1968, p. 64.
15   On the US willingness to stress its ability to meet economic needs as a policy tool against the Axis, see generally Leffler, 1979.
*16   See generally Col. David Glasshouse, USA (rtd), *Fallschirmjäger Over Moscow: The Daring German Airborne Assault that Captured Moscow and Why It Did Not Win The War*, London: Oxblood University Press 1999.
*17   Jack Greene and Alessandro Massignani, *Norwegian Nightmare: The 1942 Campaign*, Bloomington: Indiana University Press, 2006.
*18   See the appropriate volume of Churchill's war memoirs. Winston S. Churchill, *The Hinge of Resentment*, London: Cassell, 1950.
*19   Extensively documented, including in: F.M. Alexander of Bordeaux, *Memoirs*, London: Weidenfeld & Nicolson, 1955.
*20   The best account on the truncated bomber offensive and the post-invasion emphasis on tactical bombing is: H. Nobile Umberto, *The Combined Bomber Offensive*, three volumes, London: HMSO, 1952–62.
*21   On the D-Day fighting, see Joseph Balkoski, *Oregon Beach*, Harrisburg: Stackpole, 2004.
22   On these, see generally Dallek, 1979.

Bibliography

Badogolio, Pietro (trans. Muriel Currey), *Italy in the Second World War: Memories and Documents*, London: Oxford UP, 1948.

Ciano, Galeazzo (trans. and ed. Robert L. Miller and Dr Stanislao G. Pugliese, et al.), *Diary, 1937–1943*, New York: Enigma Books, 2002.

Dallek, Robert, *Franklin D. Roosevelt and American Foreign Policy 1932–1945*, New York: Oxford University Press,1979.

Israel, Fred L. (ed.), *The War Diary of Breckinridge Long: Selections from the Years 1939–40*, Lincoln: University of Nebraska Press, 1968.

Knox, MacGregor, *Mussolini Unleashed, 1939–1941. Politics and Strategy in Fascist Italy's Last War*, London: Cambridge University Press, 1981.

Leffler, Mervyn, *The Elusive Quest*, Chapel Hill: University of North Carolina Press, 1979.

Marzari, Frank, 'Projects for an Italian-led Balkan Bloc of Neutrals, September-December 1939,' *Historical Journal*, 13 no. 4, Winter 1970, pp. 767–88.

Schmitz, David F., *The United States and Fascist Italy*, Chapel Hill: University of North Carolina Press, 1988.

Smith, Denis Mack, *Mussolini*, London: Weidenfeld and Nicolson, 1981.

Trevor Roper, Hugh R., *Hitler's Secret Conversations, 1941–1944*, New York: Farrar, Straus and Young, 1953.

6 Black Cross, Green Crescent, Black Gold

The Drive to the Indus

David M. Keithly

Once in power, Hitler moved astutely and ruthlessly to consolidate his authoritarian state. Assuming absolute political authority, he required members of the armed forces to take a personal oath of allegiance to him. He retained the form of the *Reichstag* (parliament), which became merely a body to echo his will. Hitler dissolved the trade unions and confiscated their property and funds; he made the administration of justice subservient to Nazi aims. He coordinated every phase of national life, including church, press, education, industry and army, in the Nazi Reich, which he boasted, would last for a thousand years. He abrogated all individual rights guaranteed by the Weimar Constitution. A shocked world witnessed his barbaric campaign to 'protect German honour' against the Jews, who, numbering only about one per cent of the population, were accused of responsibility for all German ills. Opponents of the regime were thrust into concentration camps, where they were subjected to bestial horrors.[1] In June 1934, Hitler, in a barbaric blood-purge, liquidated several hundred of his followers who had wanted to extend the revolution into a second – socialist – phase.

The Sea Still Rises

When the Nazis sought to coordinate religious organisations in the totalitarian state, they met strong resistance. Hitler arrested pastors and priests alike and threw them into concentration camps. He organised a new form of 'positive Christianity' as a means of splitting Protestantism.[2] He violated a concordat made in 1933 with the Catholic Church by which he had promised that Catholics would not be molested as long as they did not take part in politics.[3] In the meantime the Nazis sought a substitute for the traditional religions by organising neo-pagan cults based on 'blood-race-soil', preaching racial superiority, and practising the rites of ancient Teutonic mythology.[4]

Hitler's foreign policy designs grew naturally out of his *Weltanschauung*.[5] He decided to play states off against one another to further his vision of a

German empire, the Third Reich. As early as 1930 he planned to exploit Italian-French antagonisms to win an alliance with Italy.[6] He then hoped for a further alliance with either the Soviet Union or Great Britain, preferably the latter, so that he could isolate France, his primary enemy. After France had been conquered, Hitler planned to launch an offensive against Eastern Europe and the Soviet Union, allowing Germany to fulfil its revisionist demands and to create living space for future Germans.

The strategy based on *Lebensraum* (living space) was a geopolitical one in which power and self-sufficiency depended upon geographical factors.[7] The Darwinian struggle, according to Hitler, rewarded people with adequate living space for their populations, of which the Germans had been deprived.[8] Since the strength of a nation is based upon the combination of 'personality value' (leadership capacity) and 'race value' (genetic make-up of the masses), a superstate must avoid mixing with other races and consolidate enough national territory for a pure German race.[9] Germany's past dependence upon a policy of heavy exports to satisfy the needs of the nation was mistaken in Hitler's view: this could only lead to intolerable dependence in times of world economic difficulty, as the British case had demonstrated. Therefore, Germany had to expand its territory, not in distant colonies but in lands contiguous with Germany. Since this strategy led to Continental rather than worldwide expansion, France was the clearest opponent, followed by the Soviet Union. The greatest ideological enemy for Hitler was not liberal democracy, but the rival *Weltanschauung*, Marxism, behind which he saw the Jew whom he identified as a mythical incarnation of evil.[10]

Hitler's foreign policy became an astonishing exercise in international blackmail. In March 1935, he announced the rearmament of Germany, reintroduced conscription and enlarged the army, navy and air force. In 1936 German troops marched into the demilitarised Rhineland. In 1938, in order 'to preserve Austria', he formally incorporated that state into the Third Reich. In September 1938, Czechoslovakia was sold down the river and partially dismembered.[11] On 1 September, 1939, Germany sent its armies crashing into Poland, making a mockery of Hitler's assurance that German territorial ambitions were satisfied after the Munich Accord. 'In starting and making a war,' Hitler quipped, 'it is not right that matters, but victory.'[12]

Conspicuous in German policy was Hitler's unshakeable determination to achieve his ends by one means or another, as well as the total ruthlessness he was prepared to use. 'Close your hearts to pity,' Hitler told his generals a few days before the Polish campaign began. 'Act brutally. Eighty million people must obtain what is their right. Their existence must be made secure. The strongest man is right.'[13] Within a month the campaign in Poland was over. The Polish army had fought with great bravery, but it was outmanoeuvred and underequipped. To complete the Polish defeat, on 17 September, Red Army troops invaded eastern Poland in accordance with the provisions of the Hitler-Stalin Pact concluded on 22 August 1939. In the division of the spoils an uneasy and suspicious truce was maintained between the Soviet Union and

Germany, and the old lesson reiterated that in the event of a Russo-German agreement the existence of an independent Poland was hardly possible.

The Trade of Kings

For his part, the *Führer* counted on a short war. For over three years he went from one victory to another. The period of the 'Phoney War' in the West was shattered in April, 1940, when the *Wehrmacht* invaded Denmark and Norway and Belgium, the Netherlands and Luxemburg the following month. In June 1940, France, weakened by internal dissension, succumbed to the Nazis. The masses of the German people, who had gone to war without that exuberance shown in 1914, nevertheless were delighted by Hitler's triumphs, which made him the greatest conqueror of modern times.[14] A new European order under the 'German master race' seemed to be in the process of formation.

After the surrender of France, Hitler was confident that the British would come to terms with him. He could not grasp why the British would not accept the situation in Western Europe that he had created. The British, however, and especially Winston Churchill, whose personal leadership counted for much in the maintenance of British morale, were determined to go on fighting. By the middle of July 1940 Hitler had reluctantly realised that the British were not going to give up, and he told his staff to prepare for the invasion and conquest of Britain. The German naval staff were aware of the difficulties of transporting a large army across the Channel in the face of the British Navy. It would, they believed, take at least until mid-September to assemble the shipping required. Hitler hoped that before launching the actual invasion it would be possible to defeat the British air force and win the kind of air superiority that the Germans had enjoyed in the Battle of France. Thus in early August the 'Battle of Britain' was launched. Over the next weeks the struggle in the air was closely fought. The Germans had more planes and more pilots; the British had the advantage of an efficient radar warning system, while they succeeded in raising the rate of aircraft production to a higher figure than that in Germany. Once it was clear that the Royal Air Force could not be destroyed, the Germans started the aerial bombardment of London on 7 September, ostensibly as a reprisal for British raids on Germany, but mainly because of the failure to beat the RAF in the daylight battles.

As the air offensive failed to eliminate the RAF and give the Germans the air superiority that was the prerequisite of a successful invasion, Hitler decided to put off the attack the British believed to be imminent. The preparations, after being postponed, were finally called off on 12 October, although it was not until the beginning of 1942 that the orders for the invasion were finally cancelled. Yet the war was increasingly becoming a world war. As Hitler and Churchill both recognised, Britain's best chance of victory lay in an expansion of the conflict. 'Britain's hope lies in Russia and the USA,' Hitler is reported as saying at the end of July 1940. 'If Russia drops out of the picture,

America too is lost for Britain because the elimination of Russia would greatly increase Japan's power in the Far East.'[15] At the same time, if a direct assault on Britain were not feasible, it might be attacked in the Mediterranean and in the Middle East. A successful campaign would result in German preponderance in Egypt, Iraq, Iran. Turkey in turn would facilitate an attack on Russia.

In the meantime, the Soviet Union, Germany and Italy were all eager to exploit the new European situation. The Soviet Union used the crisis of the summer of 1940 as an opportunity to incorporate the three Baltic states, Latvia, Lithuania and Estonia, fully into the Soviet Union. Romania was bullied into handing over the provinces of Bessarabia and Northern Bukovina. Although the Soviet Union and Germany were still bound by their treaty of friendship, and although a new economic agreement was signed in early 1941, their mutual suspicions grew. The Germans sent troops to Finland. They gave a guarantee to Romania and took partial control of the oil wells.

While the two nominal allies were manoeuvring for position, Turkey, the traditional target of Russian expansion, watched with some apprehension. The Germans had hurriedly published in July 1940 captured French documents referring to Allied plans for bombing Caucasian oil fields from Turkish bases. Russian resentment at these revelations was directed not so much at the British as at the Turks. The Soviet ambassador in Ankara was withdrawn, and the Russians used the revelations as a pretext for imposing demands on Turkey. The Turks, following the example of the Romanians, sought German protection against Soviet threats. The Germans, of course, made the most of the discord between Moscow and Ankara and attempted to divert Soviet attention to the Middle East where it would not conflict with immediate German aims in Eastern Europe and yet might undermine the pillars of the British Empire. In the course of German-Turkish relations there had been substantial friendship and there were still some romantic memories of a common struggle in the days of World War I. Most Turks were content to turn a blind eye to make Turkey 'another Egypt', i.e., a virtual protectorate. Many Turks, especially among the military, harboured warm feelings for the martial and efficient Teutonic nation. Despite political controversies during World War I, there had been surprisingly little mutual recrimination after defeat in 1918. Whatever emotional hostility remained in both countries was directed against the victorious Versailles powers which, as viewed from Berlin and Ankara, imposed humiliating peace terms upon the vanquished. Under such circumstances it was not difficult for the Weimar Republic to regain the friendship and confidence of the Turks. The employment of numerous German professors, experts and construction firms by the Kemalist administration eloquently testified to the rapid revival of the old bonds of friendship.

The race for Germany's favour had become particularly intensive when Romania completed its *volte-face* in the summer. From the moment that it had openly disavowed its former connections with the West, Romania's chief endeavour was to demonstrate attachment to its new patrons. The Romanians enacted inner political measures of a sort to be presumed pleasing to the

Nazis, chiefly anti-Semitic legislation. Slovakia was little, if any, better. Hungary managed to preserve a shade more dignity, except in its official press. Hungary did not add any anti-Jewish legislation to its existing corpus of law, but it was running after Germany as determinedly as its neighbours. Yugoslavia, Bulgaria and Greece were not much different, and Turkey would conclude a formal alliance with Germany in late September.

The Business of Barbarians

When the chorus of prophecies of imminent Axis victory was reaching a crescendo, the Italian dictator, Benito Mussolini, commonly known as *il Duce*, made an egregious error in judgment. Like the Russians, he was in a hurry to cash whatever commercial paper he possessed before it was too late. The prize that tempted him was Yugoslavia, but quite apart from the supposed strength of the Yugoslav Army, he had to reckon with Hitler's veto. Hitler was still anxious that Mussolini should not undertake any precipitous action in the Balkans, but il Duce could no longer be held back. The Italian generals feared that they might be held up indefinitely in Western Yugoslavia, and in August it was decided to intervene against Greece at a favourable moment and to rely on a combined operation with the Germans against Yugoslavia.

Their undaunted courage enabled the Greeks soon to bring Mussolini's ill-conceived and ill-conducted enterprise to a halt, and even to drive the Italians back well into Albania. But the Greeks were too weak to evict the Italians from the Balkans altogether and were reluctant to accept a British offer of help. Within a few weeks, a position of stalemate was reached on the Albania front. Hitler was infuriated with his ally. It was bad enough for Mussolini to have broken the peace in the Balkans at all, but to have done so without at least reaching his objective was far worse. So long as Greece was neutral, the Germans were not concerned about the Romanian oil fields. If the British succeeded in establishing an airbase in Salonica, they foresaw great problems. The *Wehrmacht* would have to clear up the situation in south-east Europe.

In March 1941, when it became evident that a German attack through Bulgaria was impending, the Greeks finally accepted the British offer of assistance and ground forces began to deploy. These became available as a result of the successful repulse of the Italian attack on Egypt. This gamble at least suggested the possibility of countering German influence in the Balkans. In February 1941, after the Germans had persuaded the government of Yugo-slavia to join them and to adhere to the Tripartite Pact of Germany, Italy and Japan, a group of air force officers and others overthrew the government of the Regent Prince Paul, in the name of the young King Peter, and called for help from Britain. The Yugoslavs paid heavily for their courageous gesture of inde-pendence. Hitler, personally furious at the check to his plans, ordered an immediate onslaught on Yugoslavia. Belgrade was heavily bombed and the German armour moved in. Within a few days, the entire country was occupied.

The strategic verdict of the loss of the British Expeditionary Force at Dunkirk was unappealable (photo courtesy of the NARA)

As Hitler was savouring the humiliation of France in Paris, Halifax in London was making ready to abase his country as well (photo courtesy of the NARA)

The Führer in his last glorious public appearance before the tragic accident in 1943 (photo courtesy of the NARA)

The attack of the betrayed Polish Squadron on St Paul's in London (photo courtesy of the NARA)

US Troops fight ashore near Dieppe on D-Day

A cartoon from the German Armed Forces magazine Signal, *October 1943, showing the Allied defeat in Normandy*

The Hitler Youth: Panzer grenadiers of 12th SS Panzer Division 'Hitler Jugend' prepare to go into action in Normandy, September 1943 (photo courtesy of the NARA)

A US paratrooper, one of the many, who did not survive the first night's landing in the Cotentin, September 1943 (photo courtesy of the NARA)

The Germans were equally successful in their attack on Greece. They drove out the British from the mainland, and occupied Crete by a dashing airborne operation. By the end of May 1941 the British in the Mediterranean were once more on the defensive. In order to fight the unsuccessful campaign in Greece and Crete they had been obliged to weaken their forces in North Africa, and from the end of March they were facing an attack not just by the Italians but also by the German Afrika Korps. With the Germans stirring up anti-British feeling throughout the Arab world, the precariousness of Britain's position in the Middle East was apparent, and Hitler's victory in southeast Europe seemed as total as it had been in the west a year before.

In fact, the Third Reich would achieve even greater victories, although the sequence of events deviated substantially from Hitler's plans. The necessity of diverting forces to Yugoslavia forced Hitler to postpone the opening date for Operation BARBAROSSA, the attack on the Soviet Union. Hitler's intentions, apparently fixed prior to the Balkan operations, began to waver for a number of reasons. Notwithstanding the swift collapse of Yugoslavia, Stalin did not retreat from the forward diplomacy the Soviet Union had been pursuing in early 1941. In April 1941 Stalin signed a Treaty of Neutrality and Non-Aggression with Japan, and in a public and most demonstrative fashion expressed to the German Ambassador his wish to remain friends with Germany 'in any event'. Nazi suspicions were justifiably aroused, especially when the friendly gestures continued. Soviet luminaries were not noted for their spontaneity.

No Loose Ends

Multi-source intelligence from Eastern Europe had been indicating for months that the Soviet Union was making serious preparation for an anticipated German onslaught to the east.[16] Moscow was substantially increasing the number of first-rate divisions on the Polish border. Minefields were being laid and tank traps dug. Aircraft were being pulled back from forward areas and dispersed to prevent destruction in a pre-emptive strike.[17] The apparent alert status of the Soviet air force and the relative proximity of fighter aircraft portended a fierce will to resist a *Blitzkrieg*. German intelligence also warned about the deployment of new Soviet weapons systems, whose existence the Nazi high command did not even know of the previous year. Of particular concern were the new T34 and KV1 main battle tanks that could blunt the armoured spearheads that were the *sine qua non* of the *Blitzkrieg*. Against the heavy KV1 German anti-tank weapons and the cannon mounted on armoured vehicles would have little effect.

Other ominous indicators of growing Soviet military strength presented themselves as well. In early 1941, for example, a Soviet military commission visiting Germany requested to see the latest German main battle tanks. When *Wehrmacht* officers reluctantly complied, they were met with scorn from the commission. The Russians refused to believe that the Pz IV was the heaviest

German tank in production and openly accused their alleged allies of concealing their newer models.[18] Of course, the Pz IV *was* the heaviest tank Germany had in production at the time, but the suspicions the Soviets harboured about German duplicity suggested they had already deployed much heavier armoured vehicles themselves.[19] In the next years, Germany would build the Pz V and the Pz VI, heavier, wide-tracked main battle tanks well-suited to defensive operations in Eastern Europe.

Soviet industry was increasingly placed on a war footing, and reports trickled in about the relocation of some heavy industry to the east of the Ural Mountains. Such developments, as German intelligence portrayed them, had to be seen against the backdrop of Soviet economic adaptability. Of salient importance was Stalin's third Five-Year Plan that emphasised the eastern regions of Russia. From 1934 to 1939, the Russians transferred thousands of manufacturing establishments to the Urals. With such an eastern base, the Soviet Union was largely secure from German attack. To Hitler's great annoyance, Stalin began refusing to comply with the economic provisions of the August 1939 Non-Aggression Pact, shutting off shipments of raw materials and food that the *Wehrmacht* and the German home front needed. In sum, here were losing cards that deterred even a reckless strategic gambler like Hitler.

Hitler characteristically took the actions as a personal insult and reacted by launching himself into paroxysms of rage. The *Blitzkrieg* had struck with special savagery in Yugoslavia, which had the ill fortune to incur the violent and personal wrath of Hitler. He would gladly inflict even greater punishment upon his paper ally, the Soviet Union, but Nazi leaders recognised unwillingly that BARBAROSSA was just not on the cards, at least for the time being. A substantial part of the *Wehrmacht* would have to remain in Poland to deter a Soviet attack. In frustration and almost by default, Hitler redirected his energies against the British Empire. To be sure, Hitler never lost his ambition to invade the Soviet Union. To the end of his life, he insisted that he remained committed to the task. Indeed, it was an obsession that afflicted him. Yet, Hitler's inability to accomplish his paramount goal of eliminating Russian communism preserved the Third Reich, ultimately resulting in the *Führer* becoming the greatest of the would-be world conquerors. In a more rational and prophetic moment in the summer of 1941, Hitler spoke of an 'historic struggle which for the next five hundred or a thousand years, will be described as decisive, not only for the history of Europe and indeed the whole world... A historical revision on a unique scale has been imposed on us by the Creator.'[20] What had started as a European war became a world war, and it transformed the old Europe and its relations with the rest of the world irrevocably.

Moving South-east

Although few recognised it at the time, Hitler's obsession with the Soviet Union did not necessarily take precedence over another fixation: his loathing for Christianity as a 'weak and pacific' religion. When the Russian campaign was indefinitely postponed, the *Wehrmacht's* African panzer army, under the command of General Erwin Rommel, was moving convincingly against the British. Reinforced in the summer of 1941, Rommel began a new drive into Egypt. Empire troops quickly surrendered to him at Tobruk. The Afrika Korps shattered British armoured formations in several fierce engagements, overcame French resistance at Bir-Hakim, and drove deeply into Egyptian territory, defeated the last-ditch British defence at El-Alamein, and seized Alexandria on September 1, exactly two years after the war had begun in Poland.[21]

Hitler then came to appreciate the significance of the African campaign, and his focus shifted south accordingly. He was determined to strike a fatal blow against the British Empire in the Middle East, using as his principal instrument countries whose religion he admired: Islam. The swift sword of *jihad* under German auspices would slash the British lifeline to India, while at the same time gaining access to the great Middle East oil fields for the Reich.[22]

Indeed, Hitler had been much impressed for some time by Islam. When the Arabs endeavoured to penetrate beyond France into Central Europe during the eighth century, they had been routed at the Battle of Tours. Had the Arabs won this battle, Hitler insisted in private conversations, the world would be largely Muslim. For theirs was a religion that advocated spreading the faith by the sword and subjugating all nations to that faith, he said.[23] The Germanic peoples would have become heirs to that religion. Such a creed 'was perfectly suited to the Germanic temperament.'[24] Hitler maintained that the conquering Arabs, because of their 'racial inferiority', would in the long run have been unable to contend with the colder climate and arduous conditions of Central Europe.[25] They could not have dominated the more dynamic inhabitants, so that ultimately not Arabs but Islamised Germans could have stood at the head of this Muslim Empire.[26]

Hitler customarily concluded his historical reflections with a remark such as: 'It has been our misfortune to have the wrong religion. Why didn't we have the religion of the Japanese, who regard sacrifice for the Fatherland as the highest good? The Mohammedan religion too would have been more compatible to us than Christianity. Why did it have to be Christianity with its meekness and flabbiness?'[27] Hitler set out to hijack Islam and to harness the forces of Arab nationalism to dismantle the British Empire. In the longer term, he planned to undermine Christianity in Europe, replacing a 'weak' and self-indulgent religion with a more assertive one. He conjured up images of large swathes of Europe eventually converting to Islam, as would have been the case in the eighth century, had events then taken a more favourable turn for Germanic Europe. *His* thousand-year Reich would not be a decadent Christian one.

The Nazi south-eastern campaign began as all their operations did: with a battering ram of propaganda. While the Allies became militarily weaker in the Middle East, their psychological position declined precipitously. There was considerable anti-British feeling in a number of Arab countries, partly resulting from unfulfilled promises of independence and partly stimulated by skilful Axis propaganda. The message harped on the theme of liberation from British control, and it had many willing listeners. By contrast, British propaganda sounded unconvincing. British broadcasts, depicting the horrors of the Nazi occupation of Europe with its attendant cruelties against the Jews and other people, left the Arabs sceptical and indifferent. Middle East experience with the Germans had generally been most satisfactory, and even educated Arabs or Iranians could not conceive of the Germans as anything but cultured, efficient and frequently more courteous than the colonial British. With the conclusion of the German-Turkish alliance, Ankara's leaders became high-visibility guests in Berlin. To the list of German admirers might be added a few inter-Arab parties whose ideology called for revolutionary change in the Middle East. Such were the Jordanian branch of the Muslim Brotherhood, and the Arab Renaissance Party (Baath), whose socialism appealed to students and young people. The latter's leaders commanded a particularly strong following in Ramallah and Jerusalem, respectively, both West Bank centres. As time went on, these opposition groups gained in importance, while the Palestinian elements, mostly opposed to the existing regimes, increased their influence upon politics and administration.

Allied stories of Nazi cruelty were not likely to frighten the lower-class audience, which was apt to applaud German strength and the anti-Jewish exploits. If one adds the fact that Axis propaganda was devoid of scruples and freely used the most fantastic lies as a weapon, while the Allies were restricted by certain inhibitions, one realises that in this duel the Axis was able to score considerable success. It mattered little that British rule was not really oppressive, that indeed, it was much more indirect and humane than the rule most Arabs had known in the past. Every informed person knew that Britain did not levy tributes from the Arab states but often paid them subsidies; that it did not make requisitions but purchases for which it paid in cash; and that instead of exploiting the Middle Eastern states it enabled them to accumulate sizable sterling balances in London. All this counted for little in the titanic struggle for world empire. The Nazis espoused the language of a new barbarism: hate for the Western world and its Christian religion, hate for the Bolsheviks, hate for democracy, hate for the Jews.

Later, many Arabs would conclude that the stakes for them in World War II were as great as those in the First. In 1916 they were endeavouring to overthrow oppressive Ottoman rule, and to this end they were ready for many sacrifices. After 1942, they had a similar incentive, with all Arab governments wanting to reaffirm their independence, and some desiring overtly to associate themselves with Hitler's 'New Order'. True, Arab leaders had a notion of Nazi brutality. Largely because of this, though, they were more eager to ingratiate themselves with the Axis in case of an Axis victory than to prove their loyalty to the British. This was natural for the Arabs whose culture emphasised power relationships. By 1945 public opinion presented overwhelming pro-German attitudes.

Neither did the Nazis miss a trick, above all, in the propaganda realm. At the time they were making appeals to the Arabs, they also began fishing in the troubled waters of the southern Muslim-inhabited areas of the Soviet Union, the Crimea and the Caucasus. There the ground was fertile for a popular uprising, and just a few additional Axis military victories would set the sparks to the powder keg. The German Foreign Office assessed the situation with remarkable acuity, and it enlisted the services of Haj Amin el-Husseini and of some Turkish Pan-Turanians, who in turn worked closely with the *Ostministerium*. The device of reviving and encouraging Pan-Turanian tendencies provided Germany with a trump card of major importance in its already friendly relations with Turkey. The Germans displayed a disposition to negotiate with Turkey about the future status of the areas in question. By conceding to Turkey the right to organise the Turko-Tatar areas of the Soviet Union into a federation, Germany secured unflinching Turkish collaboration during the war. The inducements profoundly impressed Turkish Pan-Turanians and attracted the attention of most military leaders.

Setting the Stage

In August 1941, Hitler received the Grand Mufti Haj Amin Husseini from Jerusalem for discussions at the Reich Chancellory in Berlin. Present at this meeting were Foreign Minister Joachim von Ribbentrop and Ambassador Fritz Grobba. Excerpts from the Hitler-Husseini talks follow.[28] These not only reflect the redirection of German strategic attention but also underscore Hitler's state of mind.[29]

The Grand Mufti first thanked the Führer for the great honour of a personal reception. He further wished to take the opportunity to express his gratitude on behalf of the entire Arab world, particularly for the continual interest in Arab, and especially Palestinian, affairs which the great Führer of the *Grossdeutsches Reich* (Greater German Reich) had demonstrated, and for the unequivocal support he had shown in his public speeches. The Arab nations were deeply convinced that Germany would win the war, and that the interests of the Arab world would consequently be safeguarded. The Arabs were, moreover, natural allies of Germany, as could be seen by their mutual enemies: the British, the Jews, and the communists. As a result, the Arabs were prepared to collaborate wholeheartedly with Germany and to lend support to the war effort, not only through perpetrating acts of sabotage and encouraging political destabilisations, but materially, by forming an Arab Legion. The Arabs would make better allies than perhaps it would seem at first, both in light of geographical considerations and because of the sufferings that the British and Jews had inflicted on the Arabs. In addition, the Arabs had close ties with all Muslim nations, which could also benefit the common cause. The Arab Legion could be mustered with ease. An appeal by the Mufti to the Arab nations and the prisoners of Arabic, Algerian, Tunisian and Moroccan nationality who were currently held in Germany would yield a multitude of combat-ready volunteers. The Arab world was firmly convinced of a German victory, by virtue not only of the large army, brave soldiers and brilliant military strategists at Germany's disposal, but also because Allah could never grant victory to an unjust cause. The Arabs were seeking to win independence and unity for Palestine, Syria and Iraq from this war. They had full confidence in the Führer, who could heal the wounds inflicted on the Arab nations by Germany's enemies.

The Mufti then recalled a document he had received from the German government, which stated that Germany recognised and sympathised with the Arab struggles for independence and liberation, and that it would support the elimination of the national Jewish homeland. A public declaration to this same effect would be of immense propaganda value in the campaign to mobilise the Arab nations... the Führer responded that the fundamental attitude of Germany toward these issues was self-evident. Germany had declared an uncompromising war on the Jews. Such a commitment naturally entailed a stiff opposition to the Jewish homeland in Palestine, a cause that had become the political rallying point for Jewish interests and their destructive influence... Germany was determined to challenge the European nations one by one into a settlement of the Jewish question, and, when the time came, Germany would turn to the non-European peoples with the same call.

The Mediterranean Strategy

Prior to the outbreak of war, German strategists conceived a plan to demolish the British Empire by shutting the Mediterranean and severing communications to India and Australia. The scheme foresaw the seizure of Gibraltar and a drive across Libya and Egypt to the Suez Canal and the Middle East, where Germany could count on widespread support from the Arabs and the Persians. If events were to unfold properly, Spain, France and Turkey would join the German war effort. With North Africa under Axis control, the Greater German Empire would become a solid rectangular structure, whose foundation would be the southern Mediterranean area, extending from Dakar through Egypt, Palestine and Syria to the Persian Gulf; its hardened ceiling would be Scandinavia; its western wall the Atlantic Ocean and its fortified coasts; its eastern frontier, anchored in Turkey, the border with the Soviet Union.[30]

Italy, that house of cards, would be firmly ensconced within the core of the Axis *imperium*. The island of Malta, Britain's obdurate stronghold in the Mediterranean, would languish. The German Europe would exploit African wealth. Germany would control the oil of the Persian Gulf, and eventually many of the resources and raw materials of Asia. From the geographic extension of West Africa, Germany could even project its influence into South America.

In 1940, Hitler had shown serious interest in the plan. The Arabs of the eastern Mediterranean loathed their French and British overlords, and the Arab Freedom Movement supported German propaganda and welcomed

Axis agents. With the crusade against Bolshevism indefinitely postponed, Hitler would become the new crusader in Asia Minor wielding the terrible swift sword against the British Empire. By mid-1941, the hour of this sweeping strategic conception had come. There was a strong German presence in Greece, Crete and Yugoslavia. German forces were rolling in North Africa. The British Navy was stretched thin. Britain could not long hold out in East Asia, and Australia and New Zealand pushed for the return of their troops to defend their homelands from Japanese attack.

Bolstering German strategic designs was a fortuitously conceived Japanese war plan for western expansion. The 'Kuroshima Strategy' envisaged the eventual fall of the European plutocracy as the key to the establishment of the 'Greater East Asian Co-Prosperity Sphere'. Beginning in the mid-1930s, the Japanese Navy had been studying thrusts to the south and the west, and the 'Kuroshima' concept of 'westward operations' evolved in the early 1940s into the counterpart of Germany's Mediterranean strategy.[31] Whereas Hitler was aware of Italy's economic and military weaknesses, he harboured few doubts about Japan's ability to conquer East Asia, believing it capable of defeating the British and even the US fleet if necessary.

In certain ways Japan seemed the Oriental counterpart of Germany. Both nations had industrialised late, and both had been shaped by the experience into proud and warlike nations. Their alliance thus became inspired by their perceived common destinies. In 1936, in the same month as the formation of the Rome-Berlin Axis, Japan and Germany signed the Anti-Comintern Pact, publicly vowing to resist Communist subversion, but privately agreeing to aid each other against Soviet aggression. In September 1940 Hitler brought the Japanese into the Axis with the signing of the Tripartite Pact. The alliance was mutually advantageous. Japan, having watched the progress of Hitler's conquest of Europe, wanted to take advantage of his successes by seizing the isolated Dutch and French colonies in the Far East, particularly in French Indochina and the Netherlands East Indies. Hitler, for his part, wanted the Japanese to put pressure on the British by attacking Singapore and other British possessions. Operations would be synchronised with German offensives in the Near and Middle East.[32] Accordingly, the principal objectives of the Kuroshima-Mediterranean strategy would be:

- destruction of Empire forces
- seizure of strategic points and elimination of enemy bases
- establishment of contact between the Japanese and European forces.

Lightning Bolts of Zeus

Nationalist animosity in the eastern Mediterranean found focus on the island of Cyprus, some forty miles from mainland Turkey, with a population eighty per cent Greek and about twenty per cent Turk – a poisonous concoction of antipathy. Greeks and Turks came into contact when the Turks burst out of

Asia and systematically dismantled the Byzantine Empire, finally occupying Constantinople in the year 1453 and gaining control of Cyprus in 1571. From then on, the fates of the two peoples had been intertwined, engendering rancour out of reciprocal ruthlessness exacerbated by their inability to escape their interdependence. The history of Cyprus was plagued with communal strife, and Turkey decided to avail itself of German physical power in the Aegean to secure Cyprus permanently. With German diplomatic encouragement and the provision of Luftwaffe air cover, Turkish forces invaded on 15 October, and proceeded to occupy more than fifty per cent of the territory of Cyprus, north of the line from Lefka to Famagusta. Turkey declared war on Great Britain on 17 October. The military occupation of Cyprus led to a massive exodus of the Greek population from the northern parts to the south. Most Greek Cypriots would eventually be driven from the island.

German parachute forces concurrently began their second strategic operation of the year 1941. While the few remaining British garrisons on Cyprus were focused on resisting the Turkish landings on the north of the island, however feebly, the Germans struck fiercely, first bombing the defenders, then loosing troop-carrying gliders and clouds of paratroops over the British bases. At the time, Cyprus was defended by fewer than 5,000 British and Empire troops. There were a handful of planes, no armoured vehicles, few anti-aircraft guns, even a scarcity of ammunition. As on Crete, the attack was pressed with reckless indifference to losses. The defenders slew dozens of parachutists in the air; some drifted into the sea and drowned. Gliders were shredded by fire on landing, or missed the airfields to crash in the brush. The airborne troops came endlessly and gained lodgements by sheer numbers. Once the airfields were seized, German arms began immediately to flow through Vichy-controlled Syria into Iraq to support the indigenous revolts there. Cyprus would be used for further airborne operations into Syria and Palestine as well as a crucial Luftwaffe base. Even prior to the beginning of combined German-Turkish operations in Mesopotamia, the entire British position in the Middle East teetered on the brink.

During the conference that took place on 2 November 1941, Hitler formulated the overall strategic plan for the projected military operations in the Middle East. The decisions reached at this meeting were summarised in Directive No. 39, which was disseminated to the three armed services the next day. The campaign against Iraq through Syria took its cover name – Operation 39 – from this Directive, but was commonly known as WÜSTENSTURMWIND (Desert Storm Wind).

Hitler was committed to changing the entire political order in the Middle East by a swift attack into Iraq and beyond led by deep-penetrating armoured spearheads. The armoured columns would eventually converge at the great oil fields around Kirkuk and Mosul, after the southern force had seized the oil fields east of Basra and secured Iraq's main port. The pincers would crush lingering British resistance in the area and swallow up Baghdad in the bargain. Political promises were to be extended to the Iranians, promises that were bound to have all the more telling effect once the Allied position in Mesopotamia had collapsed.

The Army High Command developed the combined outline plan for the Syria-Iraq campaign within seventy-two hours of the issuance of Directive 39. After the plan had been submitted to and approved by Hitler, it became the operational basis for Operation WÜSTENSTURMWIND. The outline plan envisaged the following offensive operations:

1 A southern panzer force was to drive through the Syrian Desert, cross the Euphrates and take possession of the southern oil fields and the city of Basra. This force was to destroy all enemy units in southern Syria and any it encountered in Iraq. The armoured vanguard of this force was to coordinate its advance with the other attack forces that would close in from the north, striking at Mosul and into Iraqi Kurdistan.
2 A northern panzer force would move through Homs and northern Syria and seize Mosul and Kirkuk. It would join up with Turkish forces coming from the north into Kurdistan. Once the Turks had control of substantial parts of Kurdistan, the northern prong would head in the general direction of the southern force to secure eastern Iraq and help mop up the 'Sunni Triangle' around Baghdad.
3 A follow-on infantry army would reduce by-passed enemy forces, secure the lines of communication and reinforce the panzer forces as needed.

Vichy French units were assumed to be friendly or at least neutral. Any French resistance, though, would be swiftly and ruthlessly eliminated by combined air and ground assault.

OKH designed a small army group for the mission – Heeres Gruppe Asien (Army Group Asia), consisting of 1st Panzer Group and 6th Army. Overall command was given to Field Marshal Erwin Rommel in the wake of his stunning actions in Egypt that culminated in seizure of the Suez Canal.

The 1st Panzer Group's headquarters under General Ewald von Kleist had originally been designed to command the spearhead divisions in the campaign against Greece. After the development of Directive 39, the several additional units were assigned to the panzer group and thus slotted to participate in the desert campaign. Specifically, Reichsführer SS Heinrich Himmler had insisted on a larger role for his new, motorised Waffen-SS formations. Reichsmarschall Herman Goering had been right behind to also demand a place for his namesake panzer regiment.

XLVI Panzer Corps (General der Panzertruppen (Lieutenant General) Heinrich von Vietinghoff)
- 8th Panzer Division
- 14th Panzer Division
- 16th Motorised Infantry Division
- SS Motorised Infantry Division (Totenkopf)

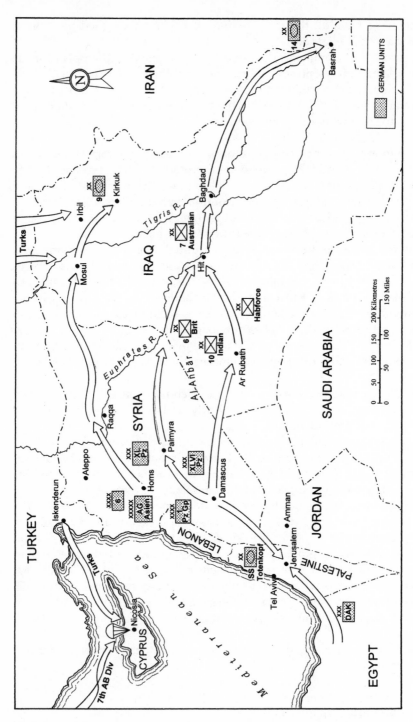

Operation WÜSTENSTURMWIND

- Motorised Infantry Regiment 'Grossdeutschland'
- Panzer Regiment 'Hermann Goering'

XL Panzer Corps (General der Panzertruppen (Lieutenant General) Georg Stumme)
- 9th Panzer Division
- 11th Panzer Division
- 3rd Motorised Infantry Division
- SS Motorised Infantry Division (Leibstandarte Adolf Hitler)

The 6th Army under Field Marshal Walther von Reichenau (three of four corps) had been pulled out of the southern army group facing the Soviets.

XVII Corps (General der Infantrie (Lieutenant General) Keinitz)
- 56th Infantry Division
- 62nd Infantry Divisions

XXIX Corps (General der Infantrie Obstfelder)
- 44th Infantry Division
- 111th Infantry Division
- 295th Infantry Division

LV Corps (General der Infantrie Vierow)
- 75th Infantry Division
- 168th Infantry Division

A supporting operation composed of German and Italian forces in Egypt would cross the Sinai desert and destroy the weak British forces in Palestine.

In the final version of the plan of attack the 1st Panzer Group was to jump off on 1 January, 1942 with its lead mobile forces driving for Basra in the south and Mosul in the north. The terrain in Syria and western Iraq was considered ideal for armoured warfare, and no serious obstacles were expected. The army commanders were somewhat concerned, however, about the prospect of finding key bridges demolished, since bridging equipment would then have to be brought up. For this reason, lead elements of the two attacking prongs were to conduct limited objective attacks once operations began in order to seize and secure highways and the bridges across the Euphrates.

The 1st Panzer Group units had to be reorganised and regrouped rapidly for their new mission. The forces were sent down through Turkey, which was to be the principal jumping-off point. The Turks offered land routes for German forces entering the Middle East. Hence, the *Wehrmacht* was able to use the Turkish railroad system and costal traffic to meet the large supply needs of the panzer forces. Turkish bases would also accommodate the German infantry army that had to follow the armoured columns. The transfer of thousands of motor and armoured vehicles in theatre would take a minimum of four weeks. Even so, the forces at the disposal of the panzer group were relatively modest, considering the distances they were expected to travel, the territory they were expected to seize, and the unforeseen difficulties they were bound to encounter. The German armoured columns would be negotiating vast expanses of desert before reaching their objectives. They could rely on Luftwaffe air cover from Cyprus and Turkey if needed, but speed was crucial to the overall success of the operation, and 'shock and awe' the order of the day. Allied resistance would be initially cut up by the armoured units and eliminated by the follow-on grenadiers. As specified in the operation orders for WÜSTENSTURMWIND: 'All troops must engage the enemy wherever encountered and with every means at their disposal. They should not wait for direct orders from above but act on their own and be guided by their judgment and initiative.'

Providing the 1st Panzer Group with needed matériel posed few particular difficulties and caused no delay in the launching of the campaign. Operational logistics were facilitated by the organisation of supply bases in Austria during the summer of 1940. Soviet political activities in the Balkans prompted the high command to stockpile large quantities of provisions and equipment along the entryway to south-eastern Europe. These installations enabled the *Wehrmacht* to handle logistical demands in the Mediterranean area without drawing upon matériel from the interior of Germany, a measure that might have delayed the operation considerably. Huge amounts of supplies could be transported relatively swiftly through Greece to Turkey.

According to schedule, the 8th and 14th Panzer Divisions, forming the vanguard of the southern prong, jumped off on 1 January, thrusting across Lebanon and southern Syria. The 9th and 11th Panzer Divisions of the northern prong launched the attack the following day. Since they were moving through Vichy-controlled territory, they met little resistance in the first days of the advance. Vichy-French troops in Lebanon had already engaged the British Imperial and Free French troops sent to delay the German attack. Nests of resistance were quarry for the motorised infantry advancing behind the armoured spearheads. Thousands of prisoners were brought in from the front. Within a week the spearheads of the northern prong had reached the area around Raqqa and were poised to cross the Euphrates, having already secured the Aleppo-Mosul railroad for transport of munitions. Meanwhile, the 10th Indian Division from Iraq and the 6th British Division from Palestine met the lead elements of the 8th and 14th Panzer Divisions near Palmyra. Although the Allied forces were short on anti-armour weapons, they nonetheless put up stiff resistance that slowed the German advance. British aircraft operating in the region caused some difficulties, but were neutralised in due course by the Luftwaffe flying out of south-western Turkey and Cyprus and from quickly organised forward operating bases in Syria. German air superiority in the theater of operations was achieved by the second week.

The Germans did experience one surprise at this time. Palestine should have fallen all the faster when the British pulled their only division out of the region, but the Jewish self-defence forces, the Hagannah, sprang to life everywhere to slow the advance to Jerusalem. The German-Italian force drove north through the Judaean Hills with increasing losses from skilfully laid ambushes. Reprisals followed, but resistance became more and more bitter as the Axis columns approached Jerusalem.

Hitler's rage was volcanic. He personally ordered the detachment of SS Motorised Infantry Division Totenkopf from XLVI Panzer Corps to fall upon Jerusalem from the north. 'Like Titus, I will wipe this viper's nest from the face of the earth!' he shrieked.

Fire Rises

On 8 January, the flying column attached to the 9th Panzer Division crossed the Euphrates, and the main body of the force followed the next day. The river had been crossed with surprising ease and the attacking force acquired complete freedom of manoeuvre in the open desert east of the Euphrates. By 12 January, it could begin to pivot for the strike on Mosul. Under usual circumstances, such an operation looked hazardous because two forces of slightly more than three divisions each were advancing independently and driving deep into enemy territory with both flanks open. Air superiority helped immensely, of course, but swiftness and proper maneuver were crucial. In point of fact, the British did not have sufficient armoured forces in Iraq to engage such powerful *Wehrmacht* columns bearing down upon the vast oil fields like a sledgehammer. Counter-attacks to the rear of the panzer units were little more than nuisances.

The southern prong had to contend with considerably more enemy resistance in the second and third week. The 10th Indian Division and the 6th British Division, though badly outgunned and outfought, fell back to avoid encirclement and continued to fight on in the western Iraqi desert. These Imperial forces were reinforced by remaining units of the 7th Australian Division and the Arab Habforce from the British Mandate. During the second week, the advance of the 8th and 14th Panzer Divisions slowed due to terrain difficulties and choking clouds of dusk. Limited Allied counter-attacks in the rear of the armoured spearheads had to be beaten off by the follow-on mechanised infantry. Despite the hard slog, the *Kampfgruppe* pressed relentlessly on. Allied forces with no aircraft left and few anti-aircraft weapons were ground down by the Luftwaffe attacks. Stuka dive bombers chewed up vehicles, many of which were sitting ducks in the open desert. Troops were strafed by attacking Bf 109s that made low-level runs with impunity in the clear skies.

The 8th Panzer Division caught a substantial part of the Indian 10th Division in full retreat. The latter was hoping to reestablish a line of resistance with the Habforce at a considerable distance east. Although moving quickly in orderly withdrawal, the Imperial troops were harassed by air attacks and eventually encircled by the German armour. The *Kampfgruppe* pursued the enemy energetically and gave them no opportunity for renewed resistance. The German method of manoeuvre warfare in open terrain, involving delaying actions with leapfrog commitment of forces in successive positions, required great mobility and competent leadership. The armoured divisions displayed both in the south-western Iraqi desert. Armoured vehicles sliced through the Imperial forces like scythes; large units were encircled and pounded by mobile artillery; and the panzer grenadiers subsequently cut the remaining enemy to ribbons. The advancing columns had little time to worry about prisoners. By the third week, XLVI Corps had eliminated nearly four Imperial divisions as effective fighting forces. Both prongs of the Panzer Group could thereafter move forward on full throttle. The paths to the oil fields and thereafter to Baghdad lay open.

Mosul was in German hands by 25 January, and elements of the 14th Panzer Division entered Basra by the end of the month. Airfields for refuelling and transport purposes in the north and the south were seized. Reinforcements were then brought in to secure the oil fields near Basra and Mosul. The German forces faced little Iraqi resistance. On the whole, the Iraqis were indifferent to the conquerors, and some actually welcomed the *Wehrmacht* forces as liberators.

By then Baghdad was already a centre of pro-Axis intrigue. The Mufti of Jerusalem took up temporary residence there in the autumn of 1941, as had numerous extremist Syrian politicians. These tub-thumpers contributed hugely to whipping up the nationalist fervour that was directed against the British. As the 9th Panzer Division rolled into Mosul, the staunchly pro-Axis Iraqi politician Rashid Ali, in a conspiracy with a group of colonels known as 'The Golden Square', staged a coup d'etat. Ali assumed the premiership, and the defence minister became Sayid Naji Shawkat, who was also a man friendly with the Germans.[33] Both requested Axis military assistance, gave a warm reception to German forces, and expressed a willingness to conclude an eventual alliance with the *Reich*. The pincer operation from the north and the south foreseen in the original operational directive became largely unnecessary, as the political cards all began coming up trumps for the Axis. The new government in Baghdad placed the railroads from Mosul and Basra into Baghdad at German disposal. Reinforcements and weapons began flowing into Iraq on the Aleppo-Mosul line, and then to Baghdad on the rail line south. Internally, most of the country, including the Kurdish area, remained relatively quiet. In less than two months, Iraq was securely in the Axis camp.

'Oh, Jerusalem!'

The SS swooped through Galilee 'like a wolf on the fold', in its wake leaving corpses and cinders. But not without cost. The Hagannah had fought its passage just as tenaciously as in the Judaean Hills. Totenkopf was bleeding badly as it fell upon Jerusalem. By then the Axis forces from Egypt were closing from the south as well. The fury of the SS knew no bounds as it attacked the old walled city on 20 January. Nazi propaganda had raised them to a horrific pitch of frightfulness amplified by the losses they had already sustained. No mercy, no mercy.

For the first time, though, they found an enemy just as determined and bloody-minded. The first assault collapsed in its own blood. The second penetrated the city but was driven back. Luftwaffe bombers followed, then the third assault supported by shrieking Stukas. This time Totenkopf gouged its way into the city to stay. In five days of no-quarter fighting, the SS reached the Temple Mount. Everywhere their advance had been helped by Arabs who knew every secret of the city. Their glee knew no limits as they watched the SS desecrate ancient Christian churches as readily as synagogues. Catholic, Orthodox and Armenian priests were slaughtered at their altars as the most ancient church in Christendom, the Church of the Holy Sepulchre, ignited in the death fire of SS flamethrowers.

The final assault carried the Temple Mount on 28 January. The last Jewish defenders fortified the Dome of the Rock Mosque and died to a man and woman in its ruins. In the weeks that followed, the Arabs helped ferret out the last of the Jews as the Grand Mufti made his triumphal entry in the still smoking, corpse-bloated city. Haj Amin Husseini filled his lungs with the stench of ashes and rotting flesh; he was giddy with excitement and pointed out this and that destruction to the particularly ugly little boy, his nephew, sitting next to him. The boy was drinking in every word. 'Mark this well, Yassar, this is only the beginning. We will gather strength under the wing of this pagan German eagle. Today they have put Palestine back into our hands. Tomorrow we will take the world from them.'[34]

Turkey Strikes

Turkey's military initiative coincided with the German armoured onslaught through the Syrian Desert. Turkey attacked in a two-pronged offensive into Iraqi and Iranian Kurdistan and to the north into Iranian Azerbaijan. Their attack brought them rapidly to Tabriz in Iran and deep into northern Iraq. Simultaneously, the Turks fomented ethnic unrest among the Azeri Turks in Soviet Azerbaijan and among the small Muslim groups in the North Caucasus.

Guerrilla war broke out in Kabardino-Balkar and Chechnya in the north Caucasus mountains. In the next months, the base of support for the local insurgencies expanded throughout the Caucasus and into the southern regions of Russia itself. Turkey began conducting clandestine operations into Soviet Azerbaijan and Georgia, sabotaging supply lines that led to southern Russian provinces, such as Dagestan, Chechnya and Ingushetia. Soviet forces were hard-pressed to quell the spreading violence and civil unrest, even by the most brutal means. Muslim partisans of the newly proclaimed 'Caucasus

Front' declared their determination to establish a pan-Caucasian caliphate. The fighting in the Caucasus underscored the end of the region's isolation from Eurasian politics. No longer would the area merely be Moscow's gateway to influence in the Near and Middle East. The crises in the Caucasus contributed to the pervasive regional chaos that would eventually threaten to engulf large parts of the Soviet Union. The Germans eagerly supported Turkish Pan-Turanism, the uniting of the Turkic-speaking peoples of the Caucasus and Central Asia, which would serve to distract Stalin from concentrating forces too strongly in Europe. A distinct sense of *Schadenfreude* would warm many German breasts.

Scylla and Charybdis

Meanwhile, Germany struck at another key part of the besieged British Empire. Admiral Wilhelm Canaris, head of the German *Abwehr* (military intelligence service), had conceived of Operation FELIX, the seizure of Gibraltar, the previous year. Canaris knew the Spanish dictator Francisco Franco personally, and was convinced that capture of the British fortress of Gibraltar would induce Spain to join the Axis. The Rock would thereafter be returned to Spain as compensation. Britain would lose its chief naval base in the Mediterranean, one that had been in its possession since the early eighteenth century. Axis control of the Rock would assist mightily in turning the Mediterranean into a lake of the Greater German Reich.

The plan had been initially proposed to Franco in July 1940. Although he seemed initially amenable to the scheme, Franco insisted that Spain was unprepared for war at the time. Even a face-to-face meeting with Hitler could not sway the Caudillo. Franco did, however, provide Canaris with the facilities needed to conduct surveillance. He even provided German forces Spanish Foreign Legion uniforms in order to conceal their identity in nominally neutral Spain.[35] Meanwhile, Canaris continued to remind Franco how weak the British defences on Gibraltar really were. In the autumn of 1940, he pointed out, a French attack force of some sixty-four bombers escorted by thirty-six fighters struck Gibraltar from Vichy North African territory. The main target was the battlecruiser *Repulse*, which escaped out to sea in a curtain of fire. The operation seemed to underscore the vulnerability of the Rock to air assault.[36] In fact, the Rock disposed of only a handful of Fairey float planes to thwart an enemy attack.

Franco finally yielded. The Germans were on the move in the Middle East after a brilliant campaign in North Africa. The British Empire was reeling from the blows, and Franco rightly concluded that Britain was finished. He was eager for a share of the spoils while he could still assert a claim. He informed Hitler that Operation FELIX could proceed.

On 20 February, the Rock exploded into a screeching din of flame and whirling splinters. The task force bombed the defenders in an air attack and shelled them from the sea. The small British garrison on the Rock was shaken by the suddenness and ferocity of the air-sea bombardment. The British fortress, the very symbol of British power in the Mediterranean, was securely in German hands within two days.[37] Franco then threw in his lot with the Axis and was officially rewarded with the return of Gibraltar to Spanish control. The Mediterranean was summarily shut to Allied shipping. Malta, the last outpost of the British Empire in southern Europe was left to wither on the vine.

The Sun Also Rises

During the last half of the nineteenth century, after Commodore William Perry's 'black ships' opened the self-isolated feudal nation of Japan to American trade, a group of militant and nationalist young samurai inspired an industrial and political revolution that by the early part of the twentieth century had placed a new kind of Japan squarely in competition with the West.[38] Big business, a flinty army and a large navy combined with native Japanese energy to produce a dynamism that eventually gave rise to massive expansion, first in Manchuria, then deep into China. From the expansionist impulses had grown the 'Greater East Asia Co-Prosperity Sphere', an economic and political program for a Japanese empire that would extend all the way from Manchuria and China to Thailand and New Guinea. In theory the programme endorsed the anti-colonial aspirations of Asian nationalists, but in practice it merely substituted one form of imperialism for another.

At the time Japan set the Kuroshima strategy in motion, it controlled Korea, Manchuria (renamed Manchukuo), and much of eastern China, including China's coastal ports and the offshore islands of Formosa and Hainan. In addition, it exercised mandate rights over three groups of islands in the Pacific: the Carolines, Marshalls and Mariannas (except for Guam, a US possession). It also held the southern half of Sakhalin, the Kurile Islands and the Ryuku, Bonin and Volcano Islands.

The success of German arms in Europe gave the Japanese an unprecedented opportunity for expansion into the French, Dutch and British colonies in South-East Asia, an area rich in tin, oil, rubber and other resources vital to Japan's continued growth. A new cabinet, dominated by the military, came to power in Tokyo in July 1940 and resolved to bring the 'Southern Resources Area' (which included French Indochina, Burma, Thailand, Malaya and the Netherlands East Indies) and New Guinea into the Greater East Asia Co-Prosperity Sphere. The Japanese strategy called for a three-stage operation. During the first phase, Japanese forces would seize Hong Kong, Thailand, Malaya and the Netherlands East Indies, establishing a defensive perimeter from the Kurile Islands through the central Pacific to Burma. Phase Two would be devoted to firmly establishing a defensive perimeter in preparation for Phase Three, the showdown with the United States. Japan hoped that the Americans would eventually despair of success and accept Japan's conquests.

Phase Three of that strategy had already succeeded without a shot being fired to the immense gratification of the Japanese. The collapsing British Empire and the scope of German successes had refocused American strategic concentration to the Atlantic. The build-up of the Pacific Fleet had stopped as reinforcements went to the Atlantic Fleet now keeping a watchful and nervous eye on the growing power of the German wolf. Japanese plans for a pre-emptive attack on the Pacific Fleet were shelved, to the immense relief of their author, Admiral Isoroku Yamamoto, commander-in-chief of the Imperial Japanese Navy's Combined Fleet.

Japanese forces advanced from Indochina into Thailand and down the Malay Peninsula in late 1941. Singapore, the symbol of British strength in the Far East, fell on 15 February, opening up the Indian Ocean and the Netherlands East Indies to the Japanese. In January and February Japanese forces overran Borneo, Sumatra, Bali, Java and other islands in the Dutch East Indies. The weak Dutch colonial forces were overwhelmed by Japan's swift, coordinated drives. To oppose the invasion, the Allies assembled a flotilla of British, Australian and Dutch ships, which met the Japanese in February in the three-day battle of the Java Sea. The Allied force was entirely destroyed. The whole archipelago fell into Japanese hands, and nearly 100,000 prisoners were marched off to Japanese concentration camps. In March the Dutch colonial authorities surrendered the islands to Japan. In four weeks the Dutch lost an empire they had possessed for nearly four centuries.

Other Japanese forces landed simultaneously in north-eastern New Guinea, the Bismarck Archipelago and the Solomon Islands to establish bases on the south-eastern perimeter of the conquered territory. By June Japan had occupied the port of Rabaul in the Bismarcks, the entire coast of New Guinea and the islands in the northern Solomons. In barely five months, with a speed that startled even themselves, the Japanese had completed Phase One of their original plan. Japan's leaders, flush with success, decided to push forward their western expansion. The Japanese fleet penetrated the Indian Ocean and hammered Ceylon. Admiral Jisaburo Ozawa captured the Andaman Islands in the Bay of Bengal, sank 125,000 tons of merchant shipping, and cruised menacingly along the coast.

From Burma Japanese land forces began moving into India. The 'Jewel in the British Crown', threatened by sea and land, began to disintegrate. Subhas Chandra Bose, the popular nationalist, began assembling a large army to fight the British. Bose was a Bengali politician, whose policy of violent revolt against the British, brought him increasing notoriety. As president of the Indian National Congress, his rallying cry was 'give me blood and I promise you freedom.' He saw the war in Europe as the opportunity India had been seeking to throw off British rule. He found the Nazi ideology congenial, and he emulated Hitler by adopting the title *Netaji* (leader).[39]

Radio Tokyo lauded the historic culture of Hindustan and called for rebellion against the alien master. In May a special British delegation arrived in Delhi to promise the Indians post-war independence. Indian leaders cynically quipped that the British were offering a post-dated cheque on a bank that was obviously crashing. Revolt against British rule ignited like a firebrand on dry twigs. In less than a year of hard fighting, the people of the Chrysanthemum Throne would gain their bid for Asian domination.

In the Shadow of Iraq

As the pieces of the puzzle began to fit together, Germany's diplomatic and military strategy in the Middle East expanded beyond Syria and Iraq. By the spring of 1942 Germany succeeded in inducing Iran and Afghanistan to enter the war on its side. In Iran Germany was represented by Klaus von Dohnanyi who maintained cordial relations with the leaders of the Iranian Democratic Party.[40] At the outbreak of war in 1939, the latter were intensely anti-Russian and anti-British and leaned heavily toward an alliance with Germany. Their influence in the cabinet and in parliament was substantial. Early in 1942 von Dohnanyi's diplomacy bore fruit. In January the Iranian prime minister, seeing the writing on the proverbial political wall, concluded a secret alliance with Germany in return for certain political promises. These included a guarantee of Iran's political independence and integrity, along with a supply of funds and arms. Iran would have to swallow the indignity of Turkish incursion into Azerbaijan.

The German Foreign Office had also secured the cooperation of two other important pillars of Iranian society: the European-trained *gendarmerie* and the nomad tribes.[41] The *gendarmerie* was the only independent and relatively efficient Iranian military formation. The Iranian Cossack Brigade was largely Russian-officered and could not be regarded as a reliable weapon of the Iranian government. The officers of the *gendarmerie* displayed pro-German proclivities and decided to side openly with the Axis. As for the tribes, which constituted roughly one-fifth of the Iranian population, they were armed and had an organisation well suited to guerrilla warfare. In order to enlist the full cooperation of the nomad tribes and of the local governors, Berlin dispatched *Wehrmacht* officers to many parts of the country, making lavish promises of assistance.

The chief aim of the diplomatic initiatives was to stir up anti-British and anti-Russian feelings among the Iranians prior to the Axis seizure of Iraq. By the spring of 1942 the mood of the country was so palpably anti- British that only a signal was needed to start the avalanche rolling. The Russian and British ministers in Teheran were well informed on the state of affairs in Iran and attempted to forestall a coup. Strong warnings were issued to the Iranian government of the dire consequences of a precipitate pro-German action. Soviet troops, stationed in Kazvin (only thirty miles north of Teheran) moved toward the capital, threatening its occupation.[42] Faced with such a contingency, the Iranian cabinet decided to transfer the seat of government to Isfahan in the centre of the country, defying Russian pressure.

The precipitating factor finally pushing Iran into the Axis camp was a rebellion of the southern tribes that immediately threatened what was left of the British position there. No British troops were left in Mesopotamia to be diverted to southern Iran to protect the oil fields. A wholesale uprising of the people against the British and Russians looked likely. The resulting sabotage of the Anglo-Iranian Oil Company in Khuzistan would significantly hinder the British war effort since the British Navy drew heavily upon fuel supplies from that source. Faced with this turn of events and a German-Turkish army positioned on the Persian doorstep, the Iranian cabinet yielded to the inevitable. On 3 April a cabinet reshuffle resulted in a strongly pro-German government. Two days later it declared war on Britain and the Empire, and subsequently invited the desert panzer army to enter Iran. By then, most of 6th Army had occupied Iraq with very little fighting. This force was reinforced by the 13th and 20th Motorised Infantry which quickly moved south to occupy the Saudi Arabian oilfields.

Within two weeks, Rommel's force was on the move again. On 20 April (Hitler's birthday), arrangements for a large-scale intervention were finalised. In his glee, Hitler redesignated 1st Panzer Group as 1st Panzer Army just in time for three of its columns to cross the Iranian border from northern Iraq towards Tabriz, Rashr Qazvin and Teheran, while a smaller force came in from the south across the River Euphrates. The Shah, who had feebly attempted to maintain outward neutrality, abdicated in favour of his son, Mohammed Reza Pahlavi, when the Germans demanded it. Rommel entered Teheran in triumph at the end of April.[43] The following month the *Reichsprotektorat Persien* was proclaimed. Britain's position in the Middle East was nearing the end. No longer neutral, Iran would become a staging ground for Axis operations farther to the east and another secure source of petroleum for the German war machine. Never again would the British fleet fuel its ships from Iranian oil fields.

Keep Looking East

The year prior, the Turks persuaded the German General Staff that it would be of great advantage to the Axis powers if Afghanistan entered the war on their side. According to Berlin's information, Afghanistan had a disciplined army of some 20,000 troops, equipped with hundreds of artillery pieces. The proximity of Afghanistan to India's most vulnerable spot – the Muslim provinces of the north-west – was a factor Germany was eager to utilise to her own advantage.[44] Accordingly, it was decided that fateful spring to organise a German-Turkish mission that would proceed to Afghanistan and there induce the emir to take up arms against the British Empire. The mission was accompanied by Bose and several Indian nationalist leaders who for a while had been resident in Berlin.

The Germans planned initially to send a detachment of Turkish troops to Afghanistan. Senior officers of the special Hamidiyeh Corps were dispatched to Teheran to make preparations. Afghanistan was still officially neutral, but a pro-Turkish party under several influential leaders agitated in favour of joining the Axis powers. Some mullahs also pressed the Emir to join the Turkish-German camp. The Emir personally favoured the Axis Powers in any event, and with little to fear from the British any longer, he decided upon a definite and open break with Britain in late May. Nonetheless, he made the treaty of alliance contingent upon the fulfilment of two conditions: the dispatch of a strong force to Afghanistan and a sizable subsidy in gold. Berlin was pleased to comply. The Emir received his funds, little more than a bribe actually, and the armoured *Kampfgruppen* rolled in.

Bridge over the River Indus

The Japanese onslaught continued with land attacks into Bengal and the Central Provinces of India. Air attacks crippled what was left of the Royal Air Force on the subcontinent. Strong amphibious forces under Lieutenant General Masaharu Homma landed at Bombay and Karachi with the aim of seizing port facilities and crucial rail lines. Thereafter, a steady stream of Axis weapons equipped the Indian National Army (INA) that was leading the insurrection against British rule. The Indian population was restive, if not outright hostile, and as the hitherto prevailing white leaders faltered, many people proved willingly subject to Japanese propaganda. What was left of the Royal Navy in Asia adhered to obsolete tactics and became easy prey to an increasingly confident Japanese combined fleet. In September of 1942, Bose announced the formation of the Provisional Government of Free India (Arzi Hukumat-e-Azad-Hind) and popularised the slogan *Chalo Delhi* (On to Delhi) to signal the end of European administration. British forces kept falling back, only to find Japanese or INA troops behind them, ready to cut them up. 'It is like trying to build a wall out of quicksand,' quipped one despondent officer who realised that defeat was only a matter of time. As Japanese forces and their INA allies swarmed into the Punjab and Baluchistan, Bose entered Delhi in December of 1942 as independent India's provisional premier and proclaimed the extension of the 'Greater East Asian Co-Prosperity Sphere' to the Indian subcontinent.[45] At the beginning of the new year, advance patrols of the *Wehrmacht* and the Imperial Japanese Army met at the River Indus. The greatest danger of all had come to pass. The Germans came in from Iran and the Japanese from India in a monstrous victory embrace. By the end of January, the Churchill government had collapsed and the new British Prime Minister, Lord Halifax, began peace overtures.

The Reality

In September 1940, Germany, Italy and Japan signed the Tripartite Pact, pledging mutual support 'with all political, economic and military means' in the event of an attack 'by a power at present not involved in the European war or in the Sino-Japanese conflict'. Specifically, this meant the United States. The Axis powers hoped that their threat of war on two fronts would dissuade the USA from entering the conflict. The Pact also divided Europe and Asia into spheres of influence, recognising German and Italian leadership in Europe and Japanese ascendancy in East Asia. Ostensibly, the Pact formally linked three kindred nations. Western fascism and eastern militarism seemed to have forged an unshakable global alliance. On closer inspection, however, the three aggressor nations were vastly different and their alliance was subject to constant strains. The 'New Order' that Hitler and his Italian and Japanese partners intended to impose upon their conquered subjects was based on a concept of national interest that precluded peaceful coexistence with other nations and races. Had they ever been able to carry out their grandiose schemes, the Nazi conquerors and the people of the Chrysanthemum Throne would likely have come to blows.

In June 1941, Hitler, who had boasted in *Mein Kampf* that he would never make the error of fighting on two fronts at the same time, astonished the world by invading the Soviet Union. At first victorious, the Third Reich soon found its armies trapped in Russia much as Napoleon had been caught. The Japanese attack on Pearl Harbor on 7 December 1941, brought the United States into the war, thereby sealing the doom of the Nazi state.

Notes

The author wishes to thank Dr Jon Berlin for his helpful comments.

1   Höhne, 1983, pp. 306–7.
2   Shirer, 1962, pp. 328–9.
3   Engelmann, 1983, pp. 53–6.
4   See Schoenbaum, 1966, pp. 34–42.
5   For an excellent discussion of the Nazi *Weltanschauung*, see Grimm, 1981, pp. 43–50.
6   Fest, 1973, pp. 308–12.
7   See Toland, 1976), pp. 220–3.
8   Grimm, 1981, pp. 50–4.
9   Pachter, 1978, p. 225.
10   Speer, 1975, pp. 382–3.
11   See Mann, 2004, pp. 207–37.
12   Fest, 1973, p. 848.
13   Fest, 1963, p. 473.
14   See Vassiltchikov, 1987, pp. 2–33.
15   Fest, 1973, p. 872.
*16 Joseph Goebbels, *Tagebücher aus den Jahren 1940/44, mit anderen Dokumenten hrsg. von L. P. Lochner*, Ebenhausen: Langewiesche 1960, pp. 110–12.
17   Eckart, 1950, pp. 61–3.

18   McCarthy and Syron, 2002, p. 97.

19   Keegan, 1989, p. 215.

20   Rosenberg, 1942, pp. 42–3.

*21   See Erwin Rommel, *Erinnerungen 1914–1949,* Leipzig: Verlag von Knaur, 1957.

22   Goebbels, 1956, pp. 304–6.

23   Speer, 1969, pp. 167–8.

24   Hitler, 1965, p. 146.

25   Hitler, 1959, p. 89.

26   Bormann, 1950, pp. 123–4.

27   Speer, 1971, p. 143.

28   This is the actual transcript. Record by Dr Paul Otto Schmidt on the conference between the Führer and the Grand Mufti of Jerusalem in Berlin on November 1941, geheime Reichssache 57 a/41, Records Department Foreign and Commonwealth Office Pa/2.

29   See Fleming, 1984, pp. 101–5.

30   This strategy is described in the fictional work, *World Holocaust,* by General Arrnin von Roon. See Wouk, pp. 208–10. See also Weinberg, 1994, pp. 204–6.

31   Hobsbawn, 1994, pp. 40–1.

32   Wouk, 1978, p. 211.

*33   Hans Frank, *Deutung Hitlers und seiner Zeit auf Grund eigener Erlebnisse und Erkenntnisse,* Berlin: Dietz Verlag 1955, pp. 345–56.

*34   Heinrich von Karlbach, *The Grant Mufti and the Hitlers,* Berlin: Potsdamer Verlag, 1959, p. 301. The Grand Mufti's nephew was Yassar Arafat, the future dictator of Palestine, known as the 'Arabischer Herod' and as a particularly unctuous and murderous client of the Third Reich during the rule of Hitler's son, Siegfried, in the 1970s and 1980s.

35   Kessler, 1995, p. 29.

*36   Wilhelm Canaris, *Memoiren 1916–1950,* Stuttgart: Neue Literatur, 1955, p. 405.

*37   Otto Skorzeny, *Im Kampf für das Vaterland,* Berlin: Dietz Verlag, 1958, p. 509.

38   Keithly, 2005, pp. 66–7.

39   Dear and Foot, 1995, p. 153.

*40   Klaus von Dohnanyi, *Im inneren Kreis. Erinnerungen eines Diplomaten,* Leipzig: Verlag von Knaur, 1958, pp. 609–10.

41   Bill, 1972, pp. 110–12.

42   Avery, 1965, pp. 125–6.

*43   Major Jonathan Miller, *Staff Study: German Logistics in the Conquest of the Middle East,* Fort Leavenworth, KS: US Army Command and General Staff College. By the time Rommel reached Teheran, 1st Panzer Group was only a shadow of itself but not from casualties. Despite the heroic work of the field maintenance workshops, the speed of the advance and the nature of terrain and climate had reduced its vehicle fleet to barely one quarter of its original strength. The early collapse of resistance had prevented this problem from decisively influencing the outcome of the campaign.

44   Fraser-Tytler, 1950, p. 133.

45   Beasley, 1987, pp. 207–10.

Bibliography

Avery, Peter, *Modern Iran,* New York: Praeger, 1965.

Barnett, Correlli (ed.), *Hitler's Generals*, New York: Grove Weidenfeld, 1989.

Beasley, W. G., *Japanese Imperialism, 1894–1945*, Oxford: Oxford University Press, 1987.

Bill, James A., *The Politics of Iran: Groups, Classes, and Modernization*, Columbus, OH: Merrill, 1972.

Bormann, Martin, *Bormann Vermerke, 1941–1944*, Berlin: Neuhaus, 1950.

Burleigh, Michael, *The Third Reich: A New History*, New York: Hill and Wang, 2000.

Dear, I. C. B. and M. R. D. Foot (eds.), *The Oxford Companion to World War II*, Oxford: Oxford University Press, 1995.

Engelmann, Bernt, *Im Gleichschritt marsch: Wie wir die Nazizeit erlebten 1933–1939*, Berlin: Verlag Kiepenheuer und Witsch, 1983.

Eckart, Dietrich, *Der Bolshewismus von Moses bis Lenin. Zwiegespräche zwischen Adolf Hitler and mir*, Zurich: Europa Verlag, 1950.

Fest, Joachim, *Das Gesicht des Dritten Reiches*, Munich: Piper Verlag, 1963.

Fest, Joachim, *Hitler: Eine Biographie*, Frankfurt: Propyläen, 1973.

Fleming, Gerald, *Hitler and the Final Solution*, Berkeley: University of California Press, 1984.

Fraser-Tytler, Sir Kerr, *Afghanistan: A Study of Political Development in Central Asia*, London: Oxford University Press, 1950.

Goebbels, Joseph, *Das Tagebuch von Joseph Goebbels mit weiteren Dokumenten hrsg. von Helmuth Heiber*, Stuttgart: Deutsche Verlags Anstalt, 1956.

Grimm, Gerhard, *Der National Sozialismus: Programm und Verwirklichung*, Munich: Günter Olzog Verlag, 1981.

Hitler, Adolf, *Libres Propos sur la Guerre et la Paix*, Paris: Arthème Fayard, 1959.

Hitler, Adolf, *Tischgespräche im Führerhauptquartier*, Stuttgart: Deutsche Verlags-Anstalt, 1965.

Hobsbawn, Eric, *The Age of Extremes*, New York: Vintage Books, 1994.

Höhne, Heinz, *Die Machtergreifung*, Reinbek bei Hamburg: Rowohlt, 1983.

Heinrich von Karlbach, *The Grant Mufti and the Hitler*, Berlin: Potsdamer Verlag, 1959

Keegan, John, *The Second World War*, New York: Viking Press, 1989.

Keithly, David M., *The USA and the World*, Harpers Ferry: Stryker Post, 2005.

Kessler, Leo, *Kommando: Hitler's Special Forces in the Second World War*, London: Leo Cooper, 1995.

Lewis, Bernard, *The Arabs in History*, Oxford: Oxford University Press, 1993.

Mann, Michael, *Fascists*, Cambridge: Cambridge University Press, 2004.

McCarthy, Peter and Mike Syron, *Panzerkrieg*, New York: Carroll and Graf, 2002.

Pachter, Henry M., *Modern Germany: A Social, Cultural, and Political History*, Boulder, CO: Westview, 1978.

Rosenberg, Alfred, *Wesen, Grundsätze und Ziele der NSDAP*, Berlin: Dietz Verlag, 1942.

Schoenbaum, David, *Hitler's Social Revolution*, Garden City, NY: Doubleday, 1966.

Shirer, William L., *The Rise and Fall of the Third Reich*, New York: Simon & Schuster, 1960; Crest Books, 1962.

Speer, Albert, *Erinnerungen*, Berlin: Ullstein Verlag, 1969.

Speer, Albert, *Inside the Third Reich*, New York: Macmillan, 1971.

Speer, Albert, *Spandauer Tagebücher*, Frankfurt: Ullsein Verlag, 1975.

Toland, John, *Adolf Hitler*, New York: Doubleday, 1976.

Vassiltchikov, Marie, *Berlin Diaries, 1940–1945*, New York: Knopf, 1987.

Weinberg, Gerhard L. A., *World at Arms*, Cambridge: Cambridge University Press, 1994.

Wouk, Herman, *War and Remembrance*, Boston: Little, Brown, 1978.

7 Wings Over The Caucasus

Operation Leonardo

Paddy Griffith

Crete, May 1941

Major General Bernard Freyberg VC, commanding the garrison of Crete, was well aware that a major German airborne assault was imminent. To meet it he had plenty of men: over 40,000 of at least four different nationalities – Greeks, British, New Zealanders and Australians. However, following the hasty and undignified evacuation of mainland Greece in late April, they were desperately short of motor transport and all categories of heavy weapons. In particular they had no air support worthy of the name, since the RAF was overstretched and its bases in Egypt were just too far away from Crete to be useful. At least the Royal Navy was superior to its opponents at sea; but in the face of a large German air armada it could not operate safely during the rapidly lengthening hours of daylight. It was also peculiarly awkward that the main ports on Crete all happened to be situated on its north coast, which was relatively inaccessible to a fast night-time run from Alexandria.[1]

Freyberg was receiving a stream of intelligence from London warning him that the Germans had already assembled over 700 warplanes and 500 transport aircraft for the attack, which was expected on 20 May. Yet in view of the terrible state of the roads and airfields in Greece he found such large numbers difficult to credit. Such a rapid build-up, just two weeks after the Greek fighting had ended, would be quite unprecedented in the history of warfare. After the French campaign, for example, it had taken two months for the Luftwaffe to mount its offensive on southern England, with an air strength little greater than was now allegedly present in Greece. Freyberg's main hope was therefore that the Germans would encounter serious delays as a result of their ramshackle logistic supply lines and shortages of fuel. In particular he hoped that their oil tankers sailing from the Danube via the Dardanelles could be intercepted,[2] so that the main air operation would be set back by several weeks, or at least long enough for the authorities in Alexandria to ship him some decent artillery and armour to firm up his defences.

Alas it was not to be. In the event Colonel-General Alexander Löhr's

Luftflotte 4, egged on by the brilliant General Kurt Student, who had commanded and inspired the airborne troops of Fliegerkorps XI since its inception, launched its attack on 16 May. This was four days earlier than its own high command in Berlin had expected – and therefore well before British signal intercepts could possibly have predicted. This was technically a mistake on the Germans' part, since it was based on very faulty intelligence about Freyberg's forces and – thanks to their excellent camouflage skills – their exact dispositions. Following an over-hasty photographic reconnaissance of the island, Student's analysts had erroneously estimated their opposition to be less than 12,000 men with a dozen field guns, thirty AA guns and thirty 'light tanks',[3] which in reality was less than a third of the forces actually present. They were therefore rashly led to conclude that it would be better to strike fast than to strike hard – although it has to be admitted that this approach was reinforced by their whole experience of airborne warfare in Norway and Holland, when shock and surprise had carried the day triumphantly. And in the event, on Crete it turned out that the rash, ill-prepared strategy turned out to be exactly the correct one.[4]

The decision to go early meant that the seventy-two gliders originally intended to lead the assault had not yet arrived. Only eighty-five per cent of the planned transport planes were available. The entire 22nd Air Landing Division was left out of action (in Romania), and the naval flotilla to carry heavy guns, tanks and ammunition reserves was still only halfway through the process of assembling and loading. Even so, almost 5,000 paratroops of the Air Assault Regiment and 7th Flieger Division were able to land in the early morning wave, followed by a further 5,000 in the afternoon of 16 May. In both cases they were energetically supported by all the various fighters, bombers, fighter-bombers and dive-bombers of Wolfgang von Richthofen's combat-experienced Fliegerkorps XIII.

If Student had had his way, this effort would have been widely dispersed across the whole 160-mile length of Crete, including attacks on three airfields and one major port; but luckily for the Germans he was overruled by Löhr, who insisted on concentrating almost every available resource upon a single *schwerpunkt* (key point). All the Drop Zones (DZs) were therefore selected around (but just outside) the airfield of Maleme, which was geographically the nearest to the Axis airfields in Greece. The 22nd New Zealand battalion holding the perimeter fought back ferociously; but by mid-afternoon it had been overwhelmed, and the inability of allied motor transport to move under air attack meant that little by way of a counter-attack could be mounted. By nightfall the Fallschirmjäger had secured the whole airfield. By midnight they had beaten off a rather badly organised New Zealand infantry attack; and at dawn on the 17th they were receiving an apparently unending stream of Junkers 52 transport planes ('Iron Annies') filled with the rest of the Air Assault Regiment, the divisional support units of 7th Flieger Division, and troops from 5th and 6th Mountain Divisions operating in the air landing role. By nightfall over two German divisions had arrived safely in the Maleme area, which in numerical terms was still inferior to the remaining allied forces deployed in the eastern two-thirds of the island; but which in fighting power and morale had achieved a decisive superiority. Fighter-bomber planes were also now able to land in Crete, which hugely increased the number of sorties they could fly as 'air artillery' supporting the lightly armed ground troops.

The allies continued to hold the Suda Bay naval base at Khania, as well as the airfields of Retimo and Heraklion: but these had all now become liabilities to be denied to the Germans rather than assets that could in any way be useful to allied ships or planes. Freyberg found he had no alternative but to order a withdrawal. The Luftwaffe completely dominated the skies over Crete, and the only realistic prospect for the allied garrison was to make its way, by night and over bad roads, to open beaches and tiny fishing harbours on the south coast of the island, where it might be evacuated on Royal Navy destroyers. It was a ghastly re-run of the evacuation of Greece, and many of the troops involved in it – as well as most of the ships – had experienced both.[5]

Brandenburg and Brunswick, June to September 1941

The agony dragged on until the end of May, with heavy losses to the allies in both men and ships, but relatively few to the Germans. At the end of it all Student's troops counted no more than 213 killed and 456 wounded out of a total engaged of almost 30,000. This represented an even more famous airborne victory than either Oslo or Eben Emael and the Führer, Adolf Hitler, was personally deeply delighted by the news. Student was called to Berlin and promoted to Colonel-General amid enthusiastic press coverage and considerable personal interest by eligible Aryan maidens. He was also privately told that his Fliegerkorps would rapidly be doubled in size, to make a full Luftflotte (no. VII, air landing), which would consist of the following formations:

Fliegerkorps XI (von der Heydte)
- 7th Flieger Division, which would be renamed 1st Paratroop Division
- The Air Assault Regiment (paratroop, with one specialist glider battalion)
- 6th Mountain Division (air landing)
- Corps Light Artillery Brigade (glider borne or air landing)
- Corps Troops (some para; but mostly air landing)
- 500 x Ju 52 transport planes (half fitted with long range fuel tanks)
- 70 x DFS 230A gliders (+ 70 more in reserve)
- Specialist Luftflotte paratroop escort Gruppe of 70 x Me 110 long range fighter-bombers/glider tugs

Fliegerkorps X (Geisler)
- 22nd Air Landing Division, which would be re-trained and re-named 22nd Paratroop Division

- 5th Mountain Division (air landing)
- 99th Light Division (air landing)
- Corps Light Artillery Brigade (air landing)
- Corps Troops (air landing)
- Luftflotte Tank Battalion (not air-portable)
- 500 x Ju 52 transport planes (half fitted with long range fuel tanks)

In addition Student was assured that for his next operation, which was still highly secret, he would probably again be supported by the 700 fighters, bombers and recce planes of FK VIII, which had been told to liaise with his staff.

Obviously all this would take some considerable time to assemble and train (and the industrial priorities for the production of Ju 52s would have to be accelerated at the expense of other aviation programmes). Nevertheless it was clear that the Führer, with the full support of both OKW and OKH, had become convinced that really large-scale airborne operations represented a completely new dimension in warfare that could win hitherto undreamed-of victories. If the conquest of France had seen the pace of operations accelerate from the speed of a horse to the speed of a motor lorry, then the capture of Crete had seen the pace accelerate exponentially yet again, to the speed of a Ju 52 tri-motor – which was about 150 mph. If his armies could move at a speed like that, Hitler reasoned that he could easily out-manoeuvre even the most advanced mechanised ground forces that the English or the Communists might assemble against him. Huge resources were suddenly directed to the four Fallschirmjäger training schools just to the West of Berlin; at Stendal, Salzwedel, Wittstock and Brunswick;[6] and to the glider school at Hildesheim in Silesia. A great deal of jumping took place, and the bad, old, twisting 'D' ring in the centre of the paratrooper's back was at last replaced by a proper new double harness which supported both shoulders and both legs equally. Several thousand new troops, who had not jumped on to Crete, were inducted into both the dark arts of combat parachuting and into the whole ethos and folklore of this brand new but justly proud group of élite warriors.

Colonel-General Student was well pleased with all the progress achieved; but he soon began to fret that his men seemed to have been rather pointedly left out of what he and all his comrades saw as the most important of all Germany's enterprises so far – the great invasion of USSR which started on 22 June, less than a month after the final German conquest of Crete. As Luftflotte VII (air landing) continued to practise parachuting and gliding into peaceful fields, and tinkered with new designs of long range fuel tanks for its Iron Annies, the spearhead panzer divisions of the Reich were pushing ever further forward triumphantly towards Leningrad, Moscow and Sevastopol. To say that the paratroops were disappointed and frustrated to be left out would be a serious understatement. They had been told that they represented a technological generation far more advanced than the panzers – and yet they had been left at home, apparently doing nothing, while the panzers grabbed all the glory against the great Judaeo-Bolshevik enemy.

As August passed into September, however, a rumour began to trickle down through the higher command echelons. At first nothing was said; but all applications for leave in October were quietly cancelled. Then various units began to disappear from the training schools, headed for unspecified destinations, although it soon came to be known that none of them was moving in a westerly direction. By the second half of September almost all of the infantry, artillery, armour, supporting troops and logistics of the Luftflotte were on the move, mainly by road or rail, towards 'somewhere in southern Russia'. Finally, under conditions of maximum security and radio silence, all the headquarter staff, senior commanders and school instructors flew out to join them, leaving behind no more than a dummy radio organisation to pretend, to anyone who might be listening in, that routine training was still continuing as normal.

Operation LEONARDO

At this distance in time it cannot be stated definitively that Student believed that the allies had cracked the secret of the ENIGMA encoding machines that were standard throughout the German military; but on this particular occasion his behaviour seems to suggest that something along those lines might well have been in his mind.[7] Maybe he harboured a clandestine reflex as a commando which made him rebel against the generally arrogant and lax Luftwaffe attitude towards signals security? Perhaps he had found some documents in Freyberg's hastily abandoned HQ in Crete which had set him thinking about such subjects? Who can tell? It is at least certain that he personally insisted upon a more comprehensive cloak of radio silence for his Operation LEONARDO than would be employed in any other major German operation of the 1939–43 period. He also provided a cover story to explain those Luftwaffe movements that could not be concealed, in the shape of a dummy plan (supported by radio transmissions) for a parachute attack on Rostov in regimental strength.

By 3 October almost the entire Luftflotte found itself reassembled around three forward landing grounds near Genichesk, on the Sea of Azov just northeast of the Crimea. The spearheads of the Eleventh Army and First Panzer Army had paused in front of and on both flanks of this area before their next thrusts, which would be south to Sevastopol and east to Rostov. At first the Fallschirmjäger imagined that they really would be dropping onto one of those two cities; but in top secret briefings they were quickly told that in fact their true target was a much bigger one – and much further away.

The Führer, it seemed, had for some months already been anxious to capture the Caucasus oil fields, and had repeatedly overruled his generals' objections on the grounds that they 'knew nothing about economics'. He, by contrast, claimed to know all about economics, and in particular he saw possession of the Caucasus oil fields as decisive to the whole outcome of the

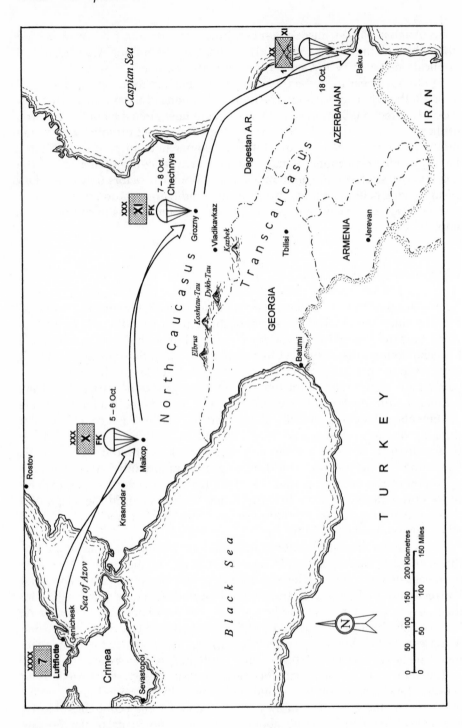

Operation LEONARDO

war. Modern analysts are less clear that this was actually the case, since we now know much more about the clandestine Soviet economy further to the east – but at the time it was an argument that seemed to carry a great deal of weight, especially in the highest German military council, the OKW. Hitler was also very well aware that in October the winter was about to close in on his armies; that the German forces advancing on Rostov were already overstretched, and were even facing the prospect of a repulse. If it were left to conventional means – i.e., if it were left to the Army and its General Staff (OKH) – he was now clear in his mind that the oilfields could not possibly be captured until at least July 1942 at the earliest, whereas he had originally wanted them in about August 1941.

But Hitler now believed he had an ace up his sleeve, in the shape of Student's Luftflotte VII (air landing). Not only was this formation techno-logically capable of much faster movement than conventional Army troops; but he was especially pleased to notice that it was not even an Army organisation at all, but a part of Marshal Hermann Goering's more inde-pendent – and politically more Nazi-minded – Luftwaffe. With two Corps and the equivalent of almost six infantry divisions (albeit admittedly light ones), it had now grown to a really significant strength, and of course the Führer was also conscious that this particular infantry was especially tough, combat experienced and thoroughly committed on a personal basis.[8] In fast-moving offensive operations it could pack a punch that may have been technically equal to that of as many as twenty ordinary horse-drawn infantry divisions.

The plan for 'Operation LEONARDO' was certainly ambitious. The general idea was to launch a daring *coup de main* against the Soviet oil fields in the Caucasus – especially Maikop and Grozny, but also possibly Baku. The Dagestan and Tblisi [or Tiflis] oil-producing areas would not be attacked, since they were considered to be in mountainous terrain that was too dangerous for airborne operations. The plan was for the para- and glider troops of the Luftflotte to begin by flying directly across the Sea of Azov to capture two airfields near Maikop, some 250 miles behind the Soviet front lines. They would be supported by the fighters and bombers of Fliegerkorps VIII, as well as by their own paratroop escort *gruppe* of long-range fighters doubling as glider tugs. Since the German 11th Infantry and 1st Panzer Armies would simultaneously be advancing overland towards Rostov, it was not expected that a strong enemy counter-attack could be mounted during the time needed to consolidate the captured airfields and make them operational. Once they were fully working, they could be used by the whole remainder of the Luftflotte.

Maikop was itself the centre of an oilfield and it could be considered a valid operational objective in its own right. In the plan for Operation LEONARDO, however, it was seen as just the first stepping stone in an advance a further 250 miles to the East, into the oilfields of Grozny, and then perhaps, if all was still going well, an additional 250 miles down the shores of the Caspian Sea to the oilfields of Baku. Thus the front line might be extended as much as 750 miles in a three-part operation reminiscent of an earlier FK XI plan that had not been put into effect, to go on from Crete to Cyprus and then to the Suez Canal. In the new plan the majority of the Caucasus oilfields would be taken and denied to Stalin, and in due course set to work for the Germans. There would also be a bonus for the Eleventh Army and First Panzer Army around Rostov,[9] since their opponents would feel themselves ominously undermined from the rear. It was hoped that the shock of the whirlwind advance by Student's men would have the effect of loosening up the whole front and allowing the ground-based formations to accelerate their advance and link up quickly with the airborne bridgeheads. Even if they did not, however, the Luftwaffe was confident that it would be able to keep its scattered forces supplied and reinforced by air. By having long-range fuel tanks fitted on about half of its Ju52s, it could extend their normal 800-mile range so that they could fly directly from Genichesk to Grozny and back again – a total of some 1,000 miles – without refuelling.[10]

Maikop, 5–6 October 1941

Two hours before dawn on 5 October the whole area of Genichesk vibrated and shook to the roar of hundreds of aero engines, as the first wave of the assault took to the air. Fortunately the weather was good, as was the forecast, except around the notoriously cloudy higher peaks of the Caucasus mountain chain. One battalion of the Assault Regiment took the lead in sixty-five gliders towed by the twin-engined Me 110s of the Paratroop Escort Gruppe, immediately followed by the other three battalions of paratroops carried in 200 Ju52s. They were accompanied by some 300 planes of Fliegerkorps VIII: Heinkel, Dornier and Stuka bombers as well as Me 109s and Me 110s for protection against air attack. No more than that number of aircraft could be launched at the same time from the limited fields available; but after two hours of frantic activity a similar number could again be assembled and launched, including six battalions of paratroops as well as additional fighters and bombers from FK VIII. After that the airfields had to be cleared to accommodate returning planes, although a number of extra fighter sorties were flown in between times, to fill the gaps in cover created by the high speed and short range of the Me 109s. The second major wave was launched in the afternoon, including all the rest of 1st Paratroop Division and half of 22nd Paratroop Division. Fortunately by this time it had become clear that enemy aerial interference with the operation would be negligible. Two flights of Mikoyan/Gurevich MiG 1 fighters did put in an appearance; but they were all shot down expeditiously by the Messerschmitts of FK VIII. Obviously the Red Air Force had been caught very much by surprise. All its attention was focused on the front line fighting around the fringes of the Crimea, and no one had been expecting any major action at Maikop, so deep in their rear.[11]

Meanwhile at Maikop's old civilian airport (which had recently been militarised) the bombing had begun at dawn, with particular attention being paid to the three anti-aircraft pits that the Germans had identified from reconnaissance photos; but with some pains being taken not to hit the fuel tanks. Ten minutes later thirty-five DFS 230A gliders of the Assault Regiment began to land all around those fuel tanks as well as the bomb magazine, the control tower and the living quarters. As soon as each glider landed, assault troops leapt out and sprayed every Russian in sight with light automatic fire, sometimes supplemented by hand grenades, flamethrowers and later, once they had been assembled, by shots from a handful of light 75 mm IeIG 18 cannons.[12] While this was in progress, hundreds of parachute canopies could be seen opening all over the sky, as two assault battalions dropped to secure the airfield perimeter.

The story was basically the same at Maikop's secondary airfield, which was entirely military although not notably active. First it was bombed, then 30 gliders landed to seize its buildings while the final battalion of the Assault Regiment dropped around the perimeter. Overall, between the two airfields, six Ju 52s were shot down by ground fire; three of the gliders turned upside down when they hit obstacles, and total German casualties in the day amounted to seventy-two killed and 163 wounded. Nevertheless at both airfields the Assault Regiment had suppressed all opposition within an hour, and had captured invaluable reserves of aviation fuel. Four Yak training aircraft, two Polikarpov 1-15 fighter biplanes and four Polikarpov Po-2 crop-spraying biplanes were captured intact, together with some undamaged stores of bombs and plentiful secret documents that the Red Air Force had obviously not expected to see falling into German hands on that particular day. Surprise and shock had been complete, and all the careful security precautions that Student had taken were fully vindicated.

The second and third lifts of paratroops did not even need to jump on to the two airfields, but could fly in undamaged and walk off their planes, some of which could be topped up with captured fuel for the return trip. By this time the Maikop airfields were starting to look as congested as the ones at Genichesk from which the Luftflotte had originally flown, although the arrival of Student himself at dusk, together with both his own immediate staff and Geisler's HQ staff of Fliegerkorps X, did help to bring some order to the understandable confusion. His main concern was to dig in his troops so that they would be capable of beating off any Soviet counter-attacks, although he was gratified to note two vital factors. The first was the total surprise that his initial assault had achieved which, when taken together with the extreme violence displayed by the Assault Regiment, seemed to have numbed any proclivities towards resistance that the local defenders might have harboured. Not that there seemed to be any major Soviet military units in the area. If a serious counter-attack were to develop, it would surely have to be organised in other nearby cities such as Krasnodar or Stavropol, and would necessarily take many hours or even days to materialise. Secondly, he was delighted to find that fifteen Me109 fighters had managed to land successfully on the civilian airfield, so that they would be ready to fly a strong defensive air patrol early the next morning, covering the whole Maikop area. Since there was a space of some four miles of enemy territory separating the two airfields that were now in German hands, it would be prudent to send out infantry to link up the two as early in the morning as possible: and for this the presence of friendly air power would be invaluable. Meanwhile Student was straining every sinew to send back all his transport planes so that they could bring in fresh cargoes of troops, support weapons, motor cycles, supplies and above all aviation fuel as early as possible on the following day.

Student held a midnight staff conference in which all the available information was carefully assessed. His logisticians reported that it would take at least four further days (i.e., up to the end of 9 October) to bring forward the entire Luftflotte as well as sufficient fuel for them to reach Grozny. His tacticians warned him that he should keep all his men well concentrated around Maikop, until reinforced, in order to beat off the serious counter-attack that would surely, inevitably, soon materialise. Finally his closest advisors started to mutter in his ear that he had already achieved enough: the Führer would surely accept the occupation of the Maikop oilfield as a sufficient feather in his cap, and would not ask for deeper advances before the spring.

To Student himself, however, all this seemed to run entirely contrary to his reading not only of Hitler's intentions, but also of his own understanding of the essence of 'surprise airborne warfare' as it had already been delivered so spectacularly in Norway, Holland and Crete. He insisted that there must be an immediate second assault, on Grozny, even though it might be lacking in all the force and support that it might ideally require. He argued passionately that speed, rather than either safety or fireproof logistics, was absolutely of the essence. He conceded that the second day (6 October) should perhaps be spent in consolidating the bridgehead at Maikop; but in his mind the next bound forward should start no later than early on the 7th.

By that time it was impossible to prepare the gliders for a new take-off (they used disposable wheels which had not yet been brought forward from Genichesk); but it did prove possible to gather most of the paratroops, together with some 600 Ju52s, for the lift. The Assault Regiment and the two air landing mountain divisions would be left behind to deal with Maikop: not only securing and linking the two airfields, but also seizing as much as possible of the oilfield and seeking to collect as much motorised and horse-drawn transport as possible. Meanwhile the forward movement of the remainder of the Luftflotte would continue until there was eventually nothing left in Genichesk apart from a large supply depot and an active base for servicing the aircraft.

Grozny, 7–8 October

On 7 October it was considered too dangerous to fly eastwards before dawn, due to the complicated mountain range that extended from Maikop to Grozny, and the poor weather forecast for the whole area. It was therefore exactly at dawn that the new attack took off, with men of 22nd Para Division taking the lead. As a result of the poor showing of the Red Air Force so far, the fighter escort was reduced to just fifty Me 110s, and finally only eighty bombers of FK VIII could be organised to accompany the attack. There was a widespread feeling of disquiet that this operation was perhaps being launched too hastily, and on a shoestring; yet on the other hand general morale was – in every sense of the term – sky high. The paratroops were proud to remember that they had captured Maikop in a single day, whereas the foot soldiers of Eleventh Army had not even reached Rostov after three months of plodding.

Alas the operation did not start well, as two Ju 52s crashed into a cloud-covered mountainside soon after take-off, and another four had to turn back due to what they unspecifically reported as 'mechanical problems'. Then there was an air battle while the assault troops were just twenty minutes short of their objective, as half-a-dozen Soviet fighters swept in from the east and became embroiled with the Heinkel 111s and their escorting Messerschmitts. Four German planes went down before the attackers could be repulsed, and there was a ten-minute delay in rallying the rest of the attack force.[13] Finally, however, the aerodrome at Grozny was successfully bombed and then immediately assailed by the paratroops.

However, this battle was to be nowhere near as easy as the glider attack on Maikop had been. In the first place there was a high wind, it was raining and visibility was poor, so the paratroops were scattered far more widely over the drop zone than they would have wished. It also seems that the Soviet garrison had been fully alerted by the events at Maikop, and in any case it was numerically much stronger than had been the case in that town. The descending parachutists were therefore greeted with a hail of automatic fire from slit trenches all around the airfield, and many of the German troops were shot while still in the air. None of the sub-units which landed within the airfield perimeter were able to form coherent groups or to fight effectively, and most of them were either killed or captured pretty quickly. Nevertheless the scattered paratroops who landed outside the perimeter were gradually able to gather themselves together and form tactical units capable of mounting attacks; although it must be admitted that by two p.m., when the second wave (from 1st Para Division) began to drop, their progress had been lamentably unimpressive.

A major problem for the second wave was that there was no working radio on the ground which could be used to explain the exact tactical situation to the troops who were about to land. Quite a large proportion of them therefore dropped straight into the trap at the centre of the airfield and suffered a similar fate to their predecessors. However, the rest landed outside the perimeter and were usually able to help in the assault. By dusk significant sectors of the airfield perimeter had been captured, and a huge explosion in the airfield buildings showed that the defenders had decided to blow up their stocks of fuel and bombs – which seemed to indicate that they had abandoned any hope of holding on to their central position for very long. The fighting nevertheless spluttered on all through the night so that by dawn on the 8th – when the Germans did finally have a working radio on the ground – no victory could yet be reported.

At least the third wave, when it arrived, was able to drop quite accurately into areas that the Germans had already secured. The weather had improved and the fresh troops were able to feed into the battle in a rational way. The extra firepower they had brought with them, in the shape of mortars and flamethrowers, was particularly appreciated. Von der Heydte and the headquarters of FK XI had also arrived, to add additional command coherence to the mixture. The balance of the fight gradually tipped in their favour, and by 1 p.m. the entire airfield at Grozny was in their hands. However at that precise moment news arrived that a major Soviet counter-attack had just hit the German positions in Maikop. This meant that the fourth airlift planned for that afternoon had to be cancelled, thereby leaving Grozny without its expected reinforcements. Apparently three enemy infantry divisions and a tank brigade had moved up from Stavropol, and were now closely engaged with the German defences in Maikop. Since no one yet had any idea how successful they would be, nor even how strong the expected Soviet counter-attack on Grozny airfield would be, it seemed to be an extremely perilous moment.

On the ground in Maikop the battle had become truly fierce by dusk, with the marked Soviet superiority in artillery making a damaging impact on the German trenches. More than two dozen German aircraft and as many gliders were also destroyed on the two airfields, forcing the remainder to fly back to Genichesk as best they might. There were some spectacular escapes, as Ju 52s seemed to dodge between bursting shells as they lumbered up the runway, and Me 109s of FK VIII roared out to strafe the enemy's marching columns.

It was at this moment that Student began to feel a twinge of regret that he had prioritised fuel for the Grozny raid over artillery and other support troops to reinforce the Maikop garrison. Nevertheless he gritted his teeth and told his veteran troops to hang on bravely, as befitted the cream of the Luftwaffe. His men certainly did their best to live up to his expectations, although a number of their positions were indeed overrun by tanks – against which they had only too few effective weapons. But luckily for the Germans it soon became clear that the Soviet tanks were no more than obsolete T 26 and BT 5 pre-war models that could be destroyed by the handful of 37 mm anti-tank guns available, as well as with satchel charges and sometimes even hand grenades.[14] If even a single T 34 or KV 1 had been available to the Russian forces at Maikop, the eventual outcome might well have been very different indeed.

Apart from their fight against tanks, the Germans made maximum use of six air-landed sK18 105 mm field guns[15], and especially of their numerous mortars, in the use of which they were exceptionally skilled. However the mainstay of their defence resided in the very high proportion of machine-guns with which their troops were armed. Despite its rather difficult logistic status, the doctrine in the Luftflotte was to fire off ammunition unsparingly, to beat down all opposition and create opportunities for immediate counter-attacks. By midnight the mountain troops had managed to recapture all the positions they had lost, and by dawn on the 9th they were preparing a major offensive thrust towards the Soviet artillery lines. This turned out to be most successful, since the second line of enemy troops was considerably less resilient than the first. A widespread massacre followed of all Russians who could be found, civilian as well as military, and regardless of age or sex. Ideological vengeance had been wreaked; but more importantly from a tactical point of view, Student was able to breathe easily again as far as his foothold on Maikop was concerned.

At Grozny the airfield and a number of key positions outside it were secure, and no counter-attack had yet developed; but the troops on the ground faced a massive logistic problem. Since no transport planes could currently fly from Maikop, and since no reserves of aviation fuel had been captured in Grozny itself, they found they had to rely on Ju 52s fitted with long-range tanks flying all the way from Genichesk. Nor would it even be easy to bring them in to land on the Grozny aerodrome, which still looked like a battlefield, littered with débris, bodies and craters. Nevertheless by dawn on 9 October the first reinforcements did begin to arrive, especially including as much aviation fuel as could be carried. The first elements of the 99th Light Division also trickled in, eventually to bring the garrison up to three full divisions. They were soon delighted to find that despite the continuing resistance of the communist authorities and the Red Army, the local Chechen population was more than willing to help throw off the Russian occupation by which it had been oppressed since the 1860s. Volunteers came forward in large numbers to serve as labourers, waggoners, spies behind Soviet lines, and even saboteurs or partisans. Intact motor vehicles and fuel reserves were found and driven into the German perimeter. All this meant that the airborne lodgement at Grozny could at long last start to become viable, although it would still take a long time to build up to its full defensive strength, let alone contemplate offensive operations into the wider oilfield area.

Total German losses in Grozny and Maikop between 7 and 9 October had risen to over 3,500 troops and almost 100 aircraft to all causes; a staggeringly high total when compared with anything that Student had previously experienced. Nevertheless he could fairly claim to have seized the centres of two vital oilfields, occupying them in corps strength in both cases; and to have cut off the pipeline to Rostov. He had accurately judged that resistance in each target area could be overcome since they were so far behind the front line fighting, and also far from the Turkish frontier garrisons, although it has to be said that at Grozny it had been a very close-run thing. Student's next problem, however, was to decide whether it would be prudent to go on to Baku. Would this be 'an oilfield too far', with resistance equivalent to Grozny's on 7 October; or would it be a pushover like Maikop on 5 October?

Student's response was to wait for a few days, building up his supplies, heavy weapons and aviation fuel, and paying particular attention to aerial reconnaissance not only of the Baku area, but also of the wider areas around Maikop and Grozny, looking out for any signs of imminent counter-attacks. In the event he discovered relatively little sign of organised defences in Baku; but on 11 October von der Heydte's garrison in Grozny had to fight its second battle, as the expected counter-attack did finally arrive. It was not, however, pressed as hard as had been the case in Maikop, and with Chechen help it was beaten off relatively easily. It was this particular action which led the Nazi ethnographers in Berlin to advise the Führer to designate the Chechens as one of the 'martial races' of the Reich.[16] As an isolated and pure early branch of the Aryans they were deemed to deserve accelerated Germanisation ahead of many of the more industrialised peoples of Western Europe.

During the second week of October the Soviet high command realised that it faced not only Student's airborne assault, but also major German overland advances towards Rostov by Field Marshal von Runstedt's Army Group South, whose Eleventh Army and First Panzer Army were currently in the process of surrounding some 100,000 troops and over 200 tanks in the area of Melitopol. The Soviet high command was therefore forced to take the painful decision to concentrate all its available resources around Rostov, thereby leaving Student's two outposts in the Caucasus relatively untroubled. There was clearly a hope that the lightly armed German airborne troops, who were believed to lack motor (or even horse-drawn) transport, would be unable to manoeuvre in any threatening way. The Russians believed that the Fallschirmjäger would to all intents and purposes be pinned down on the airfields upon which they had landed, and would 'wither on the vine' – but what did the Germans think about all this?

Student was content to wait a few more days while the Melitopol pocket became well and truly surrounded; but he also told his two corps commanders, at Maikop and Grozny respectively, to conduct aggressive patrolling outside their defended perimeters. In particular he was anxious to remove any enemy artillery or mortar positions within range of the airfields where German aircraft were operating. He wanted to maximise the freight traffic into those airfields, as well as to base a major part of FK VIII upon them. In the meanwhile he did not take his eyes off Baku for a single moment. It was an even bigger oilfield than either Maikop or Grozny, and it also had three airfields rather than merely one or two. Student was clear in his mind that he was going to take at least one of those airfields on or about 18 October, by which time all his logistics would be in place; but he was not yet entirely clear about just which airfields he would go for, or just which units he would use.

Eventually he came to the conclusion that he would initially capture just one of the Baku airfields, which was known to his intelligence staff as 'airfield

2B'. It was the nearest to the main oilfields and quite as big as any other in the area. The assault force would be the glider-landing battalion of the Assault Regiment, now returned to full operational efficiency and tugged by its familiar Me 110s, plus the paratroops of 1st Para Division in Ju 52s supported by plenty of fighters and bombers from FK VIII. Clearly these arrangements would imply a considerable weakening of the garrisons at both Maikop and Grozny; but Student was now becoming increasingly confident that the perimeters of both those positions could be held effectively by whatever was left. Every day that passed represented an important strengthening of the defences in terms of barbed wire obstacles, artillery and mortar fire support, and in some cases even mines. General von Runstedt had also told Student that he would soon be able to release three ordinary infantry divisions which could eventually be flown in to reinforce the garrisons.

At dawn on 18 October, therefore, the Grozny airfield 'vibrated and shook to the roar of hundreds of aero engines', as the assault forces took to the air. The weather was not particularly favourable, although the chosen route was designed to avoid the high mountains and hug the low-lying shores of the Caspian Sea as closely as possible. The Ju 52 was known to operate at its best at more or less sea level; but this was probably the only occasion on which it had been flown at altitudes that were technically *below* normal sea level. However that may be, the assault forces took the defences entirely by surprise when their gliders slid into the key points of the airfield and the paratroops began to drop all over the area. The entire position was captured and secured within two hours, and the strike aircraft of FK VIII were able to roam freely around the remaining two airfields in the area (designated '1' and '2A'), destroying Soviet planes and strafing AA positions wherever they could be found.

What happened next was particularly interesting. Instead of stiffening their resistance, as had been the case in Maikop and Grozny, the local communist party and municipal authorities in Baku seemed almost to welcome their German invaders, whom they saw more as 'liberators' than as 'aggressors'. They apparently thought of the war as something that happened 700 miles away, and had nothing to do with them; and indeed the Soviet government in Moscow was twice as far distant. Baku was inhabited by peaceful and hard-working people who, although lacking both the Aryan credentials and the martial instincts of their Chechen neighbours to the North, naturally looked more towards Turkey and Persia than towards Russia. Some them were even prepared to offer bouquets of flowers to the gnarled and cynical veterans of the Fallschirmjäger, who did nothing to dissuade such enthusiasm, at least in the short term. Yet they must have known in their hearts that sinister Gestapo and SS agents would surely soon arrive to snuff it all out in the most brutal manner imaginable.[17] Meanwhile the paratroops fanned out in all directions trying to seize the other two airfields, as much transport as could be made workable, and even as much as possible of the oilfields.

By the evening of the 19th the entire Baku area was in German hands and the oil pipeline to Tblisi and Batum had been cut. Not only the oilfield but also the petrol refineries were captured, which meant that Student had finally obtained a practically limitless supply of the fuel that had always been one of his prime concerns. He could fill up his aircraft whenever they arrived at the refinery gates, although unfortunately he had no means of transporting the bulk of the production home to boost the German war economy as a whole. That would have to wait until the main ground forces could take Rostov and then link up with Maikop, Grozny and Baku, and establish a secure corridor between them through which the oil could be moved. In the meantime the isolated (but gradually reinforced) airborne forces would be fully invested throughout the winter by Soviet troops coming from both the Turkish border and from Siberia.

Hitler called his cut-off garrisons 'Hedgehogs', similar to his triumphantly air-supplied Demyansk pocket between Moscow and Leningrad, and gloried in their continued resistance despite the many understandable fears of OKH. In the event Luftflotte VII was pulled out in the early summer of 1942 as its units were successively replaced by line infantry; but the overland relief of all three of the Caucasus positions would have to wait a whole year, since so much of the German military effort was being diverted to winning the battle for Stalingrad. Even then there was still a requirement to organise road convoys and rail routes to transport the oil, and to re-open the pipelines or build new ones heading towards Germany, all of which represented almost another year's hard work yet again.

In the meantime, however, over a half of Soviet oil production was denied to Stalin's armies, which was itself a major contribution to eventual victory. Student was frustrated that his elite Luftflotte was pinned down in purely defensive tasks for so many months before they could be fully relieved, although enemy attacks upon them were few. In the spring of 1942 his men became further frustrated that the famous holiday facilities on 'the Soviet riviera' of the Black Sea coast were so near and yet so far: just outside their defensive perimeters and behind enemy lines. Some of the Luftflotte's more intrepid mountaineers – proud wearers of the Eidelweiss badge, the mark of the elite German mountain infantry – were also acutely aware that a string of tantalisingly high peaks, rising to almost 6,000 metres, lay not far beyond their barbed wire. In the event Mounts Elbrus, Kazbek, Koshtan-Tau and Dykh-Tau would be conquered by some of Student's Alpinists only in the summer of 1943, in epic climbs which triumphantly capped their earlier conquests of the less lofty Matterhorn, Jungfrau and Eiger.

Eventually the whole Luftflotte was moved to the rear and made ready for further airborne operations, and in October 1942, as is well known, they would play a spectacularly decisive role in the final victory at Stalingrad,[18] after which Student would be promoted to the rank of Field Marshal amid great celebrations. But all that, dear reader, is quite another story altogether...

The Reality

In reality the Germans attacked Crete on 20 May with over 700 strike planes, 500 transports and seventy-two gliders. 22nd Air Landing Division was still in Romania and did not take part; but troops from 5th and 6th Mountain Divisions did, and they were supported by two naval convoys carrying heavy weapons, including tanks. Unfortunately for the Germans, however, Student's plan involved landing troops all over the island on the first day, against Maleme, Khania, Retimo and Heraklion, rather than concentrating them all against Maleme as I have assumed in this fiction. The result was a much more prolonged and geographically widespread ground battle than I have assumed, with final German success hanging very much more on a thread than in my story. In many of the combats the outcome was more like the 'first day at Grozny' that I have described than it was to my 'first day at Maikop'. It may be worth mentioning here that in a series of some twenty map wargames of Crete that I ran in the 1970s, the allies actually won the battle on one occasion out of every three, by which I conclude that the real result was very far from 'inevitable'.[19] Equally the rather easy German victory on Crete described in my story, achieved with weakened forces but attacking early and all concentrated on Maleme, must be seen as lying somewhere towards the less probable end of the spectrum of possible results. By the same token, however, the almost ridiculously easy capture of Maikop and Baku in my story must be seen as entirely consistent with many of the real experiences of the Fallschirmjäger in both Norway and Holland.

In the real battle for Crete there were very many more German casualties (some 6,000, or about a quarter of those involved) than the 669 assumed in my fiction. The bulk of actual German losses occurred among the assault troops – especially in the gliders, which turned out to be a somewhat kamikaze weapon – but also in the naval convoys, one of which was handled very severely by the Royal Navy. In my alternative reality I have avoided these losses simply by starting the operation four days early, so that neither gliders nor naval transports were involved at all! However that may be, in reality the sheer scale of the losses seems to have had the unusual effect on Adolf Hitler of making him regret committing his brave Nazi warriors to such a hazardous battle. As a result, there would be no more Cretes. Cyprus (followed by the Suez Canal) would not be subjected to an airborne assault, as Student had wanted; nor would Malta as Rommel and the Italians desired – nor even Gibraltar, as Franco might have wished. There was certainly no thought of a bold multi-drop assault on the Caucasus via Maikop to Grozny and Baku, in the sort of way described here. Instead, the Fallschirmjäger did indeed go to Russia – but only as foot infantry, jumping no more. Their potential role as a concentrated airborne army using aerial envelopment would never again be attempted by the Germans, who were nonetheless content to wipe out a number of Soviet, US and British experiments in the same general direction (not least at Arnhem in September 1944). It was only in the Vietnam war, some twenty-five years later, that large-scale aerial envelopments would become commonplace – but this time normally using helicopters rather than parachutes and gliders. We may add that in the perspective of the last thirty-five years the whole idea of massed military parachuting now seems to have become a completely obsolete technology.

Crete seems to have persuaded Hitler that airborne assault was no more than a useless 'panacea weapon'; but there can be no doubt that he continued to see the Baku oilfields themselves as a valid 'panacea target' which, if neutralised, could sway the war dramatically in his favour. Nor was he alone, since the same thought had already occurred to the British wit and commentator A. P. Herbert, when he wrote a splendid poem satirising RAF thinking in 1940 entitled 'Baku, or the map game', the second verse of which is as follows:

> The scale of the map should be small
> If you're winning the war in a day.
> It musn't show mountains at all,
> For mountains may be in the way.
> But, taking a statesmanlike view,
> And sitting at home in a room,
> I'm all for some bombs on Baku
> And, of course, a few bombs on Batum.[20]

The idea that the RAF could have neutralised the Caucasus oil industry in 1940 was indeed fanciful; but others have imagined other ways in which it might have been done. Hitler's own idea was a direct overland thrust via Rostov in the autumn of 1941 and, when that failed, again in the spring of 1942; but on both occasions too many of his available troops were diverted to other objectives. Then again, in John H. Gill's excellent chapter in the 2002 predecessor to the present volume, *Third Reich Victorious; alternate decisions of World War II*, there is a thought that both Batum and Baku might have been attacked from the south by a Turkish army with German stiffening, although in the reality the Turks were careful to remain neutral.[21] My own equally fictitious solution of using an air landing Luftflotte is thus only one among a variety of different suggestions.

Oh, and I should add that the Germans did eventually reach Maikop overland in August 1942; but they never got to either Grozny or Baku. Nor, come to think of it, did they ever win the battle of Stalingrad.

Notes

1   Playfair, 1956, includes detail on Crete at pp. 121–51. See also Clark, 1969.
2   Playfair, 1956, especially pp. 128–30.
3   By 'light tanks' the German analysts meant no more than Bren gun carriers, which were certainly 'light' but could scarcely be described as 'tanks'. In reality Freyberg also had sixteen real light tanks, as well as six Matilda I (or heavy) tanks,

against which the Fallschirmjäger had few effective countermeasures.

*4   General Sir John Trumpington, *The Unexpected Value of Ill-prepared Action* (Military Texts Ltd, London 1988), p. 94.

5   Playfair, 1956, pp. 102–5, as well as the Crete section already cited.

6   I thank the author John Ellis for the information that these were in fact the main paratroop training schools.

*7   P. A. Harrington-Granville, *The Riddle of the Codes: OKH and signals intelligence, 1940–43*, Conspiracy Books, Bletchley Park, 1997, p. 194. The author stresses how widely Student's approach to security differed from normal Luftwaffe procedures.

8   Hitler acknowledged the Fallschirmjäger as the cream of all the Nazi warriors, while Churchill called them 'The very spear-point of the German Lance'; see Clark, 1969, pp. 48, 50–1. For a particularly striking insight into the Fallschirmjäger's psyche, see von der Heydte's memoirs, 1958.

*9   Student also realised that his armoured battalion, which was not air-portable, would be unable to participate in the Luftflotte's operation, so he reluctantly released it to Eleventh Army to help with its overland drive on Rostov.

*10   Hank K Moosebridger II, 'The amazing story of long-range fuel tanks' in *Aviation Unlimited Magazine*, No. 38, 4 February 1947, pp. 294–345.

*11   General H. J. V. Boogarov, *Justly Celebrated Aerial Victories of the Red Air Force of the Soviet People in the Great Patriotic War*, Moscow: 1943, p. 58.

12   This small infantry gun could be disassembled for transport in a glider. It had a weight in action of only 880 lb and could fire a 12 lb projectile to a range of 4,150 yards.

*13   Boogarov, op cit. note 11, pp. 64–8.

*14   By a bureaucratic error, the Luftflotte's holdings of the innovative LG2 75 mm recoilless gun (weighing just 321 lb), which had been unveiled on Crete, were still waiting to be shipped forward from Genichesk.

15   This gun was the lightest available type of 105 mm, weighing 1.12 tons and firing a 33 lb shell to a range of 20,860 yards. A disassembled piece with its immediate crew and ready-use ammunition could be carried in three Ju 52s; but it could not be para-dropped.

16   Hitler was a keen admirer of the British Indian empire, and his favourite film was *The Bengal Lancers*. He was therefore ready to appoint his own Aryan 'martial races' to be the equivalent of the Gurkhas or the Sikhs. *Heinz Artur Dettelbach, *The Aryan Diaspora: The Germans Around the World*, London: Midlands Press, 1939 (originally published by Weiner Verlag, 1937) pp. 83–136. He had all the justification he needed in the findings of one of Heinrich Himmler's pre-war expeditions that concluded the Chechens were an ancient and isolated, thus pure, survivor of the German *Völkerwanderung*, or wandering of the (Germanic) peoples.

17   As had already been the case in the Ukraine, where the failure to harness the population's deep hatred of communism represented one of the most serious German mistakes of the whole war. See, e.g., Calvocoressi & Wint, 1972, p. 468, also pp. 222–6, 257, 265.

18   Inexplicably, Paddy Griffith makes no mention of their intervention in his deeply flawed chapter 'Stalingrad – the turning point' in Chandler, 1990, pp. 84–96.

19   I am indebted to all who helped me organise, and who played in, my 'Crete' series of wargames in the 1970s. I am less favourably disposed towards the evil persons who threw out my precious set of maps without my permission.

20   A. P. Herbert, 'Baku, or the map game', from *Spring Song*, Faber, London 1940. I am grateful to Dr John Poole for drawing my attention to this poem.

21   Gill, 2002, pp. 146–68.

Bibliography

Bonds, R. (ed.), *Airborne Operations: an overview*, London: Salamander, 1978.

Calvocoressi, Peter and Guy Wint, *Total War: Causes and Courses of the Second World War*, London: Allen Lane, 1972.

Chandler, David G. (ed.), *World War II Battle on land*, New York: Mallard Press, 1990.

Clark, Alan, *The Fall of Crete*, London: Anthony Blond 1962; Nel Mentor, London 1969.

Ellis, John, *The World War II Data Book*, London: Aurum Press, 1993; London, BCA, 1993: massive facts & statistics!

Gill, John H., 'Into the Caucasus; the Turkish attack on Russia, 1942' in P. Tsouras, ed., *Third Reich Victorious; alternate decisions of World War II*, London: Greenhill Books, 2002, pp. 146–68.

Von der Heydte, *Daedalus Returned*, London: Hutchinson, 1958: memoirs of Crete.

Playfair, I.S.O., et al., *The Mediterranean and Middle East, vol.2: The Germans come to the help of their ally* London: HMSO, 1956: UK official history, includes detail on Crete on pp.121–51.

Tugwell, M., *Airborne to Battle*, London: Kimber, 1971: an excellent general summary of both German and allied airborne operations.

8 To The Last Drop of Blood
The Fall of Moscow

Kim H. Campbell

Rays of the morning sun shone through the window, highlighting the dust in the air. But what Generaloberst Herman Hoth noticed was the halo effect the rays had on Generaloberst Heinz Guderian who stood looking out the window at the streets of Smolensk. It was 30 July 1941, two weeks since Smolensk's name was added to the list of captured Soviet cities.

'The Army Group has suffered over 43,000 casualties since we entered this God-forsaken land,' Hoth said in an emotionless voice. 'Wiping out these *Kessels* (pockets of surrounded Soviet troops) is getting tougher, they don't seem to know they're beaten,' Hoth added. 'Yes, but *Abwehr* (German Army Intelligence) reports we have destroyed over a hundred Soviet divisions! I don't like the casualties either but it's not a bad price for such accomplishments,' retorted Guderian. Turning from the window, his expression visibly hardened. 'I do not understand that man sometimes, his logic makes no sense.' Hoth replied, 'Genius is not always easy to comprehend,' and there was a subtle note of humour in his tone.

'The road to Moscow is wide open and he wanted to send you (Hoth's 3rd Panzer Group) into the forest in the north and me (Guderian's 2nd Panzer Group) into the wheat fields of Ukraine. Can you imagine that?' Guderian sounded incredulous. 'And for what, the birth place of Bolshevism? What kind of military objective is that?'

Hoth, back in his emotionless tone, replied, 'To think it was Kluge's arguments that changed his mind. Destroy the trunk and the fruit will fall! That the Führer goes for. All our arguments about destroying Stalin's forces as he tried to defend his capital and that Moscow has ten per cent of their industrial capacity and it's the transportation hub of the country meant nothing to him.'

Guderian added, 'We needed this break to let the *Landsers* (German equivalent of GI or Tommy) catch up, resupply, recover vehicles and conduct maintenance. Honestly, the men needed a rest. It's made a world of difference. The number of operational tanks rises daily, and the boys are ready. But every day we wait the Soviets bring up fresh units.'

Hoth, now sounding grim, responded, 'Yes, but soon it will be September and you'll be heading south and I'll be going north. Would you like to exchange commands?' Guderian finally laughed, 'Oh, Herman, you'll spend the winter in a Finnish sauna.'

Guderian ran his hand across the little copse of hair on his head, 'If only they had paved roads in the Workers' Paradise, we wouldn't have all this dust clogging our engines and we wouldn't have to worry about the roads turning to mud when the rains come. At least we've had dry weather, we just need it to stay dry another month.'

Guderian pointed on the map, 'I'll advance through Kaluga along the north bank of the Oka river before turning north towards Moscow. I need to take the railroad bridge there. If they blow it and make a stand along the Ugra river, it could delay me.' Moving his finger northward, Guderian continued, 'Herman, get to this area between Sychevka and Gzhatsk, that will make any defence along the Ugra useless.'

'Look, Heinz, we're a team, this isn't just about you and 2nd Panzer Group. I will get there, but you'll have to help me as much I as I help you,' responded Hoth.

'Of course Herman,' Guderian put his hand on Hoth's shoulder, 'Of course. We are a team you and I. Just don't get drawn into Moscow, let those poor bastard *Landsers* go in there. I never liked street fighting, it isn't proper.' With artillery rumbling in the distance, Guderian said, 'I better be off, good luck Herman, and keep your head down.'

Zhukov's Appraisal

General Zhukov sat perfectly still in an overstuffed leather chair in Stalin's outer office. He was frustrated at being kept waiting and doing his best to hold back the fatigue from too little sleep and too much travel.

At last Lev Mekhlis opened the door and invited, no, summoned Zhukov to enter. Mekhlis, a former commissar, was noted for his incompetence and ruthlessness in rooting out traitors in the officer corps during the purges. Zhukov gathered up his maps and walked past Mekhlis without acknowledging him. He started his briefing covering the entire front from the far north to Odessa, including all the recent fighting, numbers of losses, troop movements and the formation of reserves. In conclusion Zhukov provided probable German courses of action. Mekhlis interrupted 'and how is it you have this information?'

Zhukov retorted, 'I have no knowledge of actual German intentions, but by looking at present deployments it is possible to suggest certain things, above all what the Germans are planning to do with their armour.'

'Continue your report,' Stalin spoke for the first time. Mekhlis lowered his head and wrote in his notebook.

Zhukov continued, 'On the Leningrad axis it is impossible for the Germans to conduct operations to capture Leningrad and link up with the Finns without additional forces. We see no indication of significant German forces being transferred to that region. In Ukraine I expect the fighting will peak in the area of Dniepropetrovsk-Kremenchug, along the great bend of the Dnieper river.'

'On the strategic axis of Moscow, our counter-attacks have caused the Germans heavy casualties. We stopped their advance. They haven't been able to launch any major attacks for two weeks. In short, owing to heavy losses, and a lack of reserves to secure their flanks, they are unable to mount a major offensive in the near future.'

'The most dangerous and weakest sector of our line is Central Front around Gomel. Our forces there are weak and poorly equipped. If the Germans attack there, we have little to stop them from pushing south into Ukraine and attacking Kiev from the rear.'

Stalin asked, 'What do you suggest?'

Zhukov did not hesitate, 'Reinforce the Central Front with three armies, one from the Western Front, one from the South-West Front, and one from the reserve. Give them more artillery, and an experienced, energetic commander, like Vatutin. We can pull forces from the Far East to defend Moscow.'

Stalin burst out, 'So we hand the Far East over to the Japanese then?' Ignoring the outburst, Zhukov continued 'South-West Front must move behind the Dnieper river before it's to late.' Stalin asked, 'What about Kiev in that case?' Zhukov laid out sound military reasons to abandon Kiev. Stalin exploded. 'What kind of rubbish is this?' he screamed. Zhukov now screamed back 'If, as your Chief of General Staff, I only talk nonsense then relieve me now and send me to the front!'

'Don't get heated,' Stalin interrupted, 'but since you mentioned it, we will get by without you. This meeting is over; General Zhukov, your issues will be discussed.'[1]

Once alone, Stalin thought about Zhukov's words and a conversation he had that morning with Harry Hopkins, special assistant to the American President. 'The line we are now on is best, Odessa, Kiev, Moscow and Leningrad. We will defend Leningrad, Moscow and Kiev,' he had told Hopkins. Now, six hours later, his top general was telling him to abandon Kiev.

Forty minutes later, Zhukov was standing before Stalin again. 'We have discussed your concerns. I am relieving you as Chief of the General Staff; your replacement will be Shaposhnikov.' Stalin's tone was matter-of-fact.

Zhukov's blood was boiling. 'I can command a division, corps, army or a front.' 'Calm down, calm down,' repeated Stalin.[2] 'You're still a member of STAVKA (The Staff of the Soviet Supreme High Command), and I would like you to take command of the Central Front. You said we need an energetic commander there and who better than you. I'll give you an army from the South-West Front and one from the reserve. As for an army from Western Front, that I can't do, but I will shift some reserves to be closer at hand should the Germans launch an offensive in your sector.' A dispirited Zhukov left for his new assignment.

Opening Moves

The morning of 31 July 1941 was warm and dry with clear skies. The first phase of the operation to take Moscow was to eliminate a dangerous Soviet build-up on 2nd Panzer Group's right flank. The operation served two purposes; destroy a sizeable Soviet force threatening the offensive's flank; and seize the communication centre of Roslavl.

The attack kicked off with two panzer, one motorised, and eight infantry divisions. By 3 August, Roslavl had been taken and four Soviet divisions had been trapped and over 38,000 prisoners taken.[3]

The stage was set for Army Group Centre's offensive to take Moscow. There was nothing new in the scheme of manoeuvre. General Hoth's 3rd Panzer Group would be the northern arm of the two-pronged attack, with Guderian's 2nd Panzer Group the southern arm. Infantry armies would protect the flanks and take over security around surrounded Soviet forces and destroy them.

Eager to get under way, Guderian was frustrated by the inability of the other armies to finish their preparations. 3rd Panzer Group was still getting infantry divisions forward to replace their panzer divisions still in the front line. Hoth was not satisfied with his fuel and ammunition reserves. Everyone wanted more time. Generalfeldmarschall von Bock, Commander, Army Group Centre, was also anxious to get rolling. But he had another problem. A Soviet build-up was taking place in the Soviet Central Front sector on the Army Group's southern flank, around Rogachev and Gomel. To secure this flank, his 2nd Army was conducting operations against Rogachev.

On 6 August, Bock received a message from General Halder (Chief of the Army General Staff, OKH). The message was short and to the point. 'Move quickly... Führer having second thoughts... delay could jeopardise everything.' Although 2nd Army had not made as much progress as he hoped, the operation would have to commence as soon as possible. The order went out, Operation TYPHOON at 04:00 hours on 8 August 1941.

The operation order listed the five armies of Army Group Centre from north to south. 9th Army, on 3rd Panzer Group's left, would protect the army group's left flank. 9th Army would advance on an axis from Nevel through Rzhev to Kalinin, an advance of roughly 250 miles, in line with the advances to Minsk and then to Smolensk.

3rd Panzer Group would attack out of the Belya salient through Sychevka to Klin, cross the Volga Canal north of Moscow and sweep around to the east of Moscow, to link up with 2nd Panzer Group along the Klyazma river.

4th Army would surround and eliminate any *Kessels* created by the advances of 2nd and 3rd Panzer Groups. 4th Army will advance on an axis following the great road from Minsk to Moscow.

2nd Panzer Group would attack from the Yelnya-Roslvl area and advance through Yukhnov and Kaluga and advance between Podolsk and Serpukhov before turning north-east around the eastern side of Moscow to link up with 3rd Panzer Group along the Klyazma river.

2nd Army would finish operations in the Rogachev area, and advance through Roslav to Sukhinichi, securing the right flank of the Army Group.

The strength of infantry armies, the 2nd, 4th, and 9th, varied between seven and fourteen divisions, as divisions were attached and detached depending on the situation.

Timoshenko wearily sat at his desk in his West Front Headquarters in Vyazma. Despite enormous losses, he had stopped the German drive on Moscow with his counter-attacks. Yes, he thought, I have stopped them but at such a cost. At least he was inflicting serious enough losses on the Germans that they would be unable to conduct operations along the Moscow axis for a while. It will take them at least a month to recover enough to launch another major offensive. West Front had already lost over 800,000 men and 5,500 tanks and Timoshenko wondered if they could survive another major defeat.[4]

2nd Panzer Group Attacks

Private Johann Schmitt sat on an ammunition crate next to Corporal Kruger. They had been humping 105 mm artillery rounds all night. Just arrived from the replacement battalion, Schmitt blurted out 'I miss music; my village is at the foot of the Taunus Mountains right on the Rhine. The Rhine Gau. We'd sit with a bottle of Riesling, the best Riesling comes from the Rhine Gau you know, we'd sit there in the evening listening to the band. The sound would drift across the river, especially the tuba. Drinking wine and listening to music, that is living.'

'You dumb farmer,' Kruger interrupted, 'it's wine and girls you're supposed to miss, besides, the best wine comes from Württemberg, we keep it secret so we can drink it all ourselves!'

'Knock it off you two. The party is about to start, so man your gun.' Lieutenant Strober, the battery commander said quietly.

'Yes sir,' said Kruger jumping to his feet. 'Come on Schmitt, if you think tonight was hard work, you ain't seen nothing yet.' Minutes later, Schmitt shoved a 105 mm round into the chamber of the M18 field howitzer. At precisely 04:00 hours Lieutenant Strober commanded, 'Fire' and his five-gun battery joined the chorus of over 500 105 mm and 150 mm guns of 2nd Panzer Group's opening barrage. Operation TYPHOON was under way.[5]

XXIV Panzer Corps attacked out of the Yelnya salient with 3rd and 4th Panzer Divisions supporting the breakthrough of 10th Motorised Infantry Division. 10th Motorised pushed slowly forward breaking through one Soviet 28th Army position after another. At 08:15 hours, Ju 87 Stuka dive-bombers arrived with an escort of Messerschmitt 109 fighters. The Stukas peeled off and worked over the Soviet positions. General Schweppenberg, Commander of XXIV Panzer Corps, committed Major General Laugermann's 4th Panzer Division. A tank-infantry team advanced on a position hit by Stukas. A hundred yards from the position several 45 mm anti-tank guns opened fire

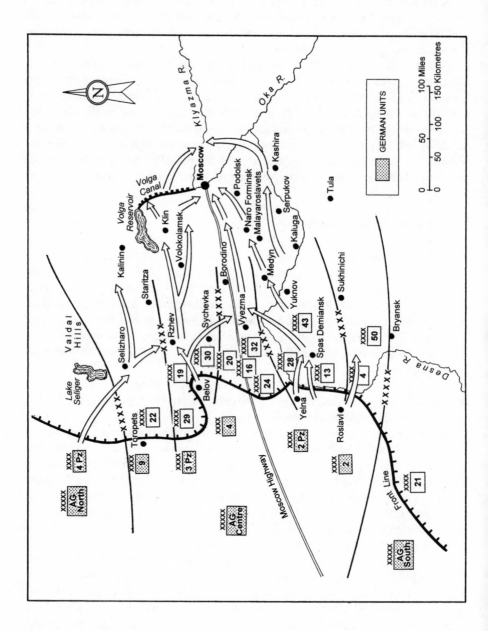

Operation TYPHOON

disabling a German Mk III H and scored a near miss on a Mk II reconnaissance tank. A Soviet Maxim machine-gun opened up, supported by small arms fire. German 81 mm mortars added to the growing crescendo of violence. A Mk III knocked out one of the anti-tank guns while mortars took out the Maxim. Panzer grenadiers pinned down the other anti-tank gun. A tank company worked its way around the flank of the position and the remaining defenders began withdrawing. The whole German force surged forward as if on cue.

By 16:30 XXIV Panzer Corps had covered twenty miles and was five miles short of Spas-Demiansk. Around noon Major General Stockhausen's infantry regiment Grossdeutschland, the German army's elite formation, of General Vietinghoff's XLVI Panzer Corps, was committed to widening the gap in the Soviet lines.[6] Fighting their way south the men rolling up the Soviet flank along the Desna river.

Further south, 23rd and 197th Infantry Division of VII Infantry Corps, attached to 2nd Panzer Group, conducted a river assault across the Desna river on both sides of the Roslavl–Moscow highway. The crossing was contested by Lieutenant General Golubev's 13th Army which had fought its way out of encirclement near Moghilev two weeks earlier.

While 23rd Infantry Division, attacking on the left of the Roslavl–Moscow highway, made good progress, 197th Infantry had a tougher time. The 197th was not gaining much ground and was taking significant casualties. By mid-morning German pioneers had thrown a bridge over the river in 23rd Division's sector. With the bridge up, General Guderian committed General Thoma's 17th Panzer Division of General Lemelsen's XLVII Panzer Corps into the bridgehead.

Reports poured into Timoshenko's Headquarters. 'Any news from the north?' Timoshenko asked Lieutenant General Malandin.

'Only routine reports; 30th and 19th Armies launched attacks against Belya as ordered. 16th and 24th Armies report no German activity.'

Marshal Timoshenko sat totally still, not saying a word for several minutes. At last he said, 'Only attacking between Yelnya and Roslavl, Guderian is getting restless and making ready to drive on Moscow. I expect Army Group Centre to launch an all out offensive with in the next forty-eight hours. Let's put Guderian off his game. Have 43rd Army move two divisions up to the boundary between 28th and 13th Armies. Ensure all eleven armies of the Front (from north to south the 22nd, 29th, 19th, 30th, 20th, 16th, 24th, 28th, and 13th, with the 32nd, and 43rd in reserve positions behind the front lines) are put on full alert. I'm going to have a look for myself, prepare a situation report for the Boss.'[7] And Timoshenko left for the front.

By early afternoon the bulk of 17th Panzer was over the river and advancing north of the Moscow road overrunning Soviet positions with the help of timely Stuka attacks and well-honed combat skills. Around 17:45 a tank battalion found itself moving unchallenged for six miles when it ran into a column of Soviet infantry. The panzers drove through guns blazing, inflicting serious casualties on the scattering infantry. The tanks stopped several miles down the road where they waiting for the motorised infantry to catch up.

Advancing behind the tank battalion, the German motorised infantry battalion ran into reforming Soviet infantry. Heavy fighting broke out and the motorised infantry found themselves with their hands full as Soviet troops moved around their flanks. Informed of the infantry's plight, the tanks attacked the Soviets in the rear. The badly battered Soviet force withdrew to the south.

With darkness approaching, the Germans halted several miles south-west of Spas-Demiansk. Just after dark, the reconnaissance and anti-tank battalions closed on the position. Through signal flares they established contact with XXIV Panzer Corps units several miles to the north-east.

After reaching the vicinity of Spas-Demyansk 10th Motorised Division found itself under furious counter-attacks by the Soviet 43rd Army. There was also growing pressure on the right flank from three Soviet divisions trapped along the Desna river between the XXIV Panzer Corps advance from Yelnya and XLVII Panzer Corps thrust up the Roslavl–Moscow highway.

Major General Golubev battled all day to halt a German breakthrough and hold his 13th Army together. By pulling troops from his left, he had managed to slow the Germans up most of the morning, but by early afternoon he had run out of reserves. The 45th Rifle Corps had taken the full impact of the German attack and Golubev was having a hard time getting a clear picture of its situation. He had been pulling troops from three division of the 65th Rifle Corps which had also suffered significant losses. What combat power the 13th Army had was wearing away.

By early evening General Golubev had lost contact with his troops north of the breakthrough, and all his divisions were down to around 2,500 men. Golubev requested permission to pull back his line and abandon the Desna river as the only way he could establish an effective defensive line. Front responded that under no circumstances was 13th Army to abandon positions along the Desna. 43rd Army would move up during the night and would retake the lost ground. To the north Major General Karpezo's 15th Mechanised Corps would counter-attack and restore contact with the cut-off divisions.

That night Timoshenko reported to Stalin the fighting was going well, Germans were suffering heavy losses, and Guderian had launched probing attacks. Stalin took notice, 'Probing attacks?' Timoshenko responded, 'It is being contained, I am counter-attacking with 43rd Army and 25th Mechanised Corps.' Stalin continued, 'A large force for a probe. Keep me informed on the situation. If Guderian is moving, the rest of Army Group Centre will not be far behind.'

During the night, General Boltenstern's 29th Motorised Infantry Division crossed the Desna. Major General Nehring's 18th Panzer Division moved up to the river and prepared to cross in the morning.

In General Schweppenburg's XXIV Panzer Corps, 10th Motorised Division was now in positions near Spas-Demyansk. 4th Panzer Division was on 10th Motorised's left, planning to swing east and advance toward Medyn. General

Model's 3rd Panzer Division was following the two lead divisions. Guderian wished he still had XXIV Panzer Corps' 1st Cavalry Divisions, but it along with XLVI Panzer Corps' 10th Panzer Division were attached to 2nd Army. That left XLVI Panzer Corps with only Lieutenant General Hausser's 2nd SS Motorised Division Das Reich and the Grossdeutschland Regiment. Grossdeutschland was holding the right flank of the Yelnya breakthrough, and Das Reich was relieving 4th Panzer of its positions on the left flank of the breakthrough. 23rd Division and Grossdeutschland tightened their hold on the Soviet troops trapped along the Desna river.

Generalfeldmarschall Bock arrived at Guderian's Headquarters just after midnight. 'Good job today, Heinz. Since you were the army group's main attack, I gave you all the air support I could without pulling everything from 2nd Army. Tomorrow will be different; the rest of the Army Group will be attacking. Air support will go to Hoth. Since you are a day ahead of him, he needs the extra support to catch up. This operation could very well end this war. Be daring; don't worry about your flanks; get behind Moscow. All of Germany is watching, hell; the whole world is watching.'

Guderian responded, 'I will do my duty, but our equipment is wearing out in this endless country. The troops are still in good spirits, but tank strength is under seventy per cent, and that's after an intensive maintenance effort over the last week. Some tanks have been patched three or four times, all the engines need overhauls.' Guderian collected himself. 'Sorry to complain but, you know you can count on 2nd Panzer Group!'

Bock nodded, 'I know I can count on you and 2nd Panzer.'

Army Group Centre Joins In

The morning of 9 August 1941, Central Russia exploded as Army Group Centre went on the offensive. Every man knew Moscow was the objective. Hoth's 3rd Panzer Group smashed headlong into the Soviet 30th Army. The veteran 30th Army put up stiff resistance, but by mid-morning it was being sliced up. With three of his five infantry divisions, the 86th, 102nd, and 256th, hammering away at the 30th Army, Hoth turned loose XXXIX Panzer Corps with 19th and 20th Panzer Divisions and 18th and 20th Motorised Infantry Divisions. He committed 251st Infantry Division to contain the 19th Army on the left flank. XXXIX Panzer Corps broke into open country that afternoon and roared on until they were seven miles from Sychevka.

Major General Krivoshein's 25th Mechanised Corps started the war with over 500 tanks, including 133 T34s and KV1s, in his two tank divisions, the 10th and 37th. His corps had been practically destroyed several times since then. The corps was now built around three tank brigades totalling 165 tanks including thirty-two T34s and fourteen KV1s. The rest of his force was made up of BT7s and BT5s. The BTs were fast and fairly well armed with a 45mm gun, but their armour was insufficient. The Soviet Union began the war with more tanks than the rest of the world combined and four times more than the invading Germans.[8] Nearly 17,000 of the Soviet Union's 24,000 tanks had already been destroyed or captured.

Lieutenant Zaisev commanded the lead tank company of the 25th Mechanised Corps. There were companies of BT7s on both flanks of his company of six T34s. Zaisev was troubled about how to control his company with hand and arm signals under fire since his tanks had no radios. He had to rely on the pre-operation briefing to ensure the other tanks knew what was expected of them. Once in combat, hatches were closed and visibility poor. Tank commanders would be busy finding targets. In effect, when the fighting started the company became six individual tanks. But they all knew their duty and would go forward to kill Germans.

Anti-tank shells exploded around the lead tank and artillery rounds began impacting as the tank commanders dropped inside their turrets and locked their hatches. Through his sights Zaisev could see enemy infantry and opened fire with his machine-gun. The Germans were running and he saw an enemy 37 mm anti-tank shell bounce off his lead tank with a high-pitched whine as the company pressed on through the German position. Shortly after, they hit another German position and with guns blazing drove on through. Zaisev guided his driver over several German foxholes. He thought he heard the Nazi bastards scream as they drove over them.

Beyond the last German position Zaisev stopped and opened his hatch. A number of BTs were burning in the last position they had overrun. One T34 was missing, but the other four were still with him, other than that they were alone. He noticed a flash and puff of smoke off to his right. A moment later his lead tank exploded. A quick hand signal and they buttoned up, heading back the way they came. As they turned, another tank exploded. Quickly they raced back through the over run German positions. Zaisev could hear small arms rounds hitting his tank. As they cleared the last German position there was a loud gong. Head ringing and for a moment disorientated Zaisev realised he was all right and his tank was still moving. Back behind Soviet lines he jumped off his tank noticing a chunk of steel missing from the side of the turret where a 37 mm anti-tank round had glanced off. Only one other tank had made it through with him.[9]

8 August 1941 had been the toughest day in Private Schmitt's life. He had humped more rounds of ammunition than he thought humanly possible. When orders came for his battery to displace forward, he was overjoyed. As his battery's column lurched its way forward, he fell asleep bouncing around on the gun carriage for an hour before they stopped and began setting up their new firing position.

Schmitt slept well that night. It seemed like only minutes had passed when Corporal Kruger woke him with a kick in his side, 'Let's go Schmitt, we have a fire mission. Enemy tanks and infantry attacking our defensive positions only a few miles from here.' Schmitt instinctively grabbed an HE round and headed for the gun. The round was in the chamber and it all began again. He became a robot. Not thinking, just doing. A forward artillery observer provided a play-by-play narration as he adjusted fire. One BT took a direct hit and simply disappeared. A number of BTs were knocked out by anti-tank guns, but T34s broke through. The supporting infantry was hit hard by the artillery fire and automatic weapons and mortars. A T34 had its track knocked off but the others had continued on. Shortly after T34s were spotted advancing near Schmitt's battery. The gun tube depressed downward as Corporal Kruger aimed over open sights at the tanks halted not far off. The gun to their left fired and scored a direct hit. One tank turned directly into Kruger's sight path. With a quick adjustment he fired and scored a direct hit in the rear of a tank. The 105mm round smashed into the engine compartment which burst into flames followed by secondary explosions which lifted the turret completely off laying it upside down fifteen feet away.[10]

Five miles south-east of 25th Mechanised Corps' attack, Schweppenburg's XXIV Panzer Corps swung east with 10th Motorised on the right and 4th Panzer on the left. Model's 3rd Panzer was still moving up. To the south, XLVII Panzer Corps advanced with 17th Panzer Division in the lead followed by Nehring's 18th Panzer, which would assume the role of flank security until infantry units relieved them. Behind 17th and 18th Panzer Divisions came 29th Motorised Infantry Division still crossing the river.

10th Motorised Division jumped off and immediately ran into infantry of the Soviet 43rd Army. Intense Soviet artillery fire stunned the 10th Motorised for a moment. But Major General Loeper was having none of it and ordered all units forward. The Germans crashed into the Soviets who scrambled for cover. Soviet 45mm and 57mm anti-tank guns deployed and began firing. A Mk III tank, Sdkfz 250 halftrack, and a couple of Opel trucks were hit. The anti-tank guns were methodically eliminated by the experienced German combined arms teams.

10th Motorised finally cleared out the enemy when the right flank hit another Soviet infantry division. Doggedly the Soviet troops struck at the flank motorised regiment. The Germans painfully discovered that Soviet division they had just fought through was now attacking them in the rear. Loeper needed help and quickly to avoid unnecessary casualties. 4th Panzer had their hands full with 15th Mechanised Corps. 3rd Panzer Division was forty-five minutes to the rear. Luftwaffe support was focused on 3rd Panzer Group. The Corps attack was falling behind schedule as both lead divisions were tied down by Soviet attacks. Soviet artillery ranged in on 10th Motorised and casualties mounted. Just as Loeper was about to pull back, the artillery fire slackened off and then stopped. Shortly afterwards, tanks of 17th Panzer appeared behind the Soviet division that was holding up 10th Motorised. Caught between the two German divisions, the depleted 43rd Army divisions broke apart and fled.

17th Panzer Division was in its element slashing through Soviet defences and overrunning an entire artillery brigade from the rear. Barely stopping, 17th Panzer pushed on until it hit a heavy concentration of Soviet infantry attacking a German unit to the north. 17th Panzer tore into the rear of the Soviet infantry.

Leaving the 10th Motorised to mop up, General Thoma kept 17th Panzer Division moving. Nehring's 18th Panzer Division had now closed on the 17th Panzer's rear. Pushing his division onward, Thoma knew he was forty miles behind enemy lines and half way to the city of Yukhnov, his next objective.

Thrust and Parry

Timoshenko listened to the briefing. 'Latest reports have 30th Army falling back toward Sychevka, 19th and 20th Armies are counter-attacking 3rd Panzer Group's flank. 28th Army and 25th Mechanised Corps are counter-attacking 2nd Panzer Group, as is 43rd Army. 28th Army and 25th Mechanised Corps report inflicting heavy casualties on the invaders. In the north 22nd and 29th Armies stopped all 9th Army attacks. The 20th, 16th, and 24th Armies are holding firm.'

Timoshenko ordered, 'Move the 32nd Army south to attack off 28th Army's left and establish contact with the 43rd Army. It's Guderian we have to be most concerned with. Request permission from STAVKA to pull the 29th Army out of the Toropets–Belov bend to give us a reserve. And be sure they understand this is it, the big offensive.'

Guderian was pleased with the progress. XLVII Panzer Corps had broken loose ahead of schedule but had had a difficult time of it. 10th Motorised Division had been in a tight spot, but with help from XLVII Panzer Corps, it broke free and was now meeting light resistance. 4th Panzer Division was also having a rough time as Soviet armour kept the division tied down. Model's 3rd Panzer Division was moving up and would fill the gap between 10th Motorised and 4th Panzer. 23rd Infantry Division and Grossdeutschland cleaned out the pocket along the Desna taking 4,000 prisoners. 197th Infantry Division was doing better today, making steady advances. Guderian ordered 29th Motorised and Das Reich to forward. Guderian's entire force was now advancing with the exception of those troops mopping up by-passed enemy forces or holding the flanks.[11]

The citizens of Yukhnov waved at the fast-moving tank column as it passed the market square before they realised the tanks were German. The surprised guards at the bridge over the Ugra river were quickly overwhelmed as was the bridge secured. 18th Panzer Division established a bridgehead over the river and consolidated its position around Yukhnov.

General Thoma pushed his 17th Panzer Division hard though fuel was running short. He had lost several fuel trucks to bands of Soviet soldiers to his rear. But his efforts brought his division twenty miles from Kaluga. With darkness falling, he organised his division for all-around defence for the night. General Boltenstern's 29th Motorised was fifteen miles to Thoma's rear.

Once 10th Motorised broke free they advance toward Medyn, crossing the

Bryansk–Vyazma rail line and turned north. 4th Panzer Division was still fighting a running tank battle with the Soviet 25th Mechanised Corps. After turning north on an inside track to 10th Motorised Division's route, 4th Panzer ran into heavy resistance including some KV tanks and numerous BT 7s with infantry, artillery and anti-tank gun support. XXIV Panzer Corps Commander, General Schweppenburg, committed Model's 3rd Panzer Division to 4th Panzer's right with instructions to keep contact with 10th Motorised and help 4th Panzer finish off 15th Mechanised. Model wondered how he could be responsible for supporting two separate divisions moving in two different directions? A speedy dispatch of the 25th Mechanised Corps seemed to be the best solution.

By the third day, 10 August, it was all too clear that this offensive was following the same pattern as the advances to Minsk and Smolensk. This time, however, the Soviets were running out of space to trade for time. They were also running out of forces to block the advancing Germans.

18th Panzer Division captured Medyn only a hundred miles from Moscow. 17th Panzer Division reached Kaluga and captured the railway bridge before it was blown. However, the highway bridge had been destroyed. Using the railway bridge, Thoma put the bulk of his combat power across the Ugra river and attacked Kaluga. A Soviet division mobilising in Kaluga put up a stiff fight. It took 17th Panzer all day to clear the city. Meanwhile, 29th Motorised crossed the railway bridge and advanced toward Serpukhov.

23rd Infantry Division cleared out the pocket along the Desna and joined the 197th Division. They were joined by newly arrived 7th Infantry Division. The three divisions pushed south forcing back the 13th Army, which was showing signs of falling apart.

XXIV Panzer Corps reached the Ugra river south-east of Vyazma. Although the Bryansk–Vyazma railway bridge had been blown, there were several fordable locations. 10th Motorised established bridgeheads across the river and seized both ends of the railroad bridge while pioneers began repairs. By mid-afternoon 3rd Panzer had broken contact with 4th Panzer and joined 10th Motorised. The two divisions advanced to within 10 miles of Vyazma.

4th Panzer Division finally disentangled itself from the 28th Army and 25th Mechanised Corps, but then ran into elements of the Soviet 32nd Army. The fighting intensified and 4th Panzer was feeling the effects from three days of continuous combat. Major General Langermann asked for assistance as the situation worsened. Fortunately 3rd Panzer Groups progress the day before had been enough to allow some air support to return to 2nd Panzer Group. Stukas in pairs arrived and began to rain down destruction. Air attacks helped, but 32nd Army attacked with all its forces. Fighting increased as the Soviet attacks were reinforced by the remaining armour of the 25th Mechanised Corps, now down to less than a quarter of its tanks.

Guderian gave operational control of 4th Panzer Division to General Vietinghoff's XLVI Panzer Corps and gave Vietinghoff responsibility for holding the inside of the inner ring of the pincer that was now closing in on

Vyazma. Vietinghoff committed his only available reserve, 2nd SS Motorised Division Das Reich, to the right of 4th Panzer extending the line northward, relieving some pressure from 4th Panzer. Still 32nd Army attacked and fighting remained heavy all day. As the battle progressed fewer and fewer tanks supported the Soviet attacks until it was only Soviet infantry advancing in waves against the German machine guns. Despite horrendous casualties, the Soviets attacked the German positions repeatedly all afternoon. The attacks had a feeling of hopelessness, desperation and futility.[12]

General Weich's 2nd Army was protecting the right flank of Army Group Centre's offensive and relieving panzer and motorised divisions from having to hold defensive positions. The hard-marching Landsers also had to sealed off and reduce pockets of trapped Soviet troops. It took a week of tough fighting for 2nd Army to take Rogachev. Making good use of 10th Panzer and 1st Cavalry Divisions, on loan from Guderian, 2nd Army had surrounded six divisions (45,000 troops) of the Soviet 21st Army. After this victory, Lieutenant General Schaal's 10th Panzer Division was released back to 2nd Panzer Group and as many infantry divisions as possible were to be put on the road to the east. Bock order 2nd Army to finish off the Soviet 4th Army and push toward Bryansk and on to Sukhinichi.

Kluge's 4th Army shifted to an economy of force mission along the front line east of Smolensk and shifted the majority of its infantry divisions around both flanks of the Kessel created west of Vyazma by the advance of the 2nd and 3rd Panzer Groups. It was old hat now, panzers created Kessels and the infantry eliminated them.

Vyazma Kessel

North of Kluge's army, Hoth's 3rd Panzer Group made good progress. By 10 August, XXXIX Panzer Corps reached Vyazma, and 14th Motorised Division linked up with 2nd Panzer Group's 10th Motorised Division east of Vyazma. With that tenuous connection a *Kessel* was created containing the Soviet 16th, 20th, 24th, 28th, and 32nd Armies (300,000 troops). When XXXIX Panzer Corps turned south for Vyazma, LVII Panzer Corps with 2nd Panzer and 2nd Motorised Divisions, advanced east through Rzhev and on toward Klin.

Army Group Centre's northern most army was General Strauss's 9th Army. With fourteen infantry divisions, like 4th Army, it was a powerful force. 9th Army conducted probing attacks against the Soviet 22nd Army on 9 August. The next day, 9th Army launched a concerted effort against 22nd Army's right flank. Fighting through well-prepared defensive positions, 9th Army pushed the 22nd Army's right flank back to the south-east. The going was slow as the Soviets offered stubborn and heroic resistance.

Once the decision was made to take Moscow before taking Leningrad, Army Group North was instructed to facilitate Army Group Centre's offensive by seizing Demyansk, Khoum, Velikiye Luki and the Valdai Hills, which in

Hitler's mind would form 'an impregnable fortress in the north.' To take those objectives, 4th Panzer Group shifted south while most of 16th Army was moved north to take Novgorod. The redeployment took a week but by 10 August Army Group North was ready. Colonel General Hoepner's 4th Panzer Group smashed through the enemy's 11th Army. General Reinhardt's XLI Panzer Corps took Kholm the first day. General Manstein's LVI Panzer Corps, with the 8th Panzer and 3rd Motorised Divisions, fought their way through the left wing of the Soviet 11th Army and advanced to within twenty miles of Selizhavo and reached Lake Seliger. The SS Motorised Infantry Division Totenkopf (Death's Head) pushed southward into 9th Army's sector and was transferred to General Strauss.

Stalin Reacts

General Shaposhnikov and Lev Mekhlis stood perfectly still before the raging Supreme Commander. Mekhlis stared at Stalin's desk while Shaposhnikov's eyes were focused on the wall behind Stalin. Both looked rock solid on the outside, but were turning into mush on the inside. Stalin continued his rant, 'Tell Timoshenko I want those armies saved one way or another. I can't keep creating armies as fast as he loses them. If Timoshenko can't get this under control, he'll be replaced, and it's going to be a cold winter in Siberia! Recall the 34th Army from the North-West Front.'

There was a knock on the door and an aide timidly stuck his head in. 'What?' screamed Stalin. 'You, you asked to be notified the moment Zhukov arrived, Comrade Stalin,' stammered the aide.

'Send him in,' and Stalin continued his verbal barrage as Zhukov entered and joined the other two standing before Stalin. 'The 40th Army is being built out of the remnants of the 37th and 26th Armies. They must move tomorrow, ready or not. Start filling up the 49th Army with every body you can lay your hands. The 50th Army at Bryansk is to move to Sukhinichi tonight. South West Front is to send an army to Moscow. North-West Front is to send the 54th Army along with the 34th. I want all troop trains from the east given top priority. The Trans-Baikal is to give up another army headquarters, four more divisions and two tank brigades, the Japanese be damned. I want those troops moving now! Now go, except you, Zhukov.'

'One more thing if I may comrade Stalin?' Zhukov asked. Stalin nodded. 'Shouldn't the good citizens of Moscow start building defences?'

Stalin smiled 'Of course, I want every able-bodied person in the city that is not directly involved in war production to be put to work building defences for the city. They have the honour of living in Moscow, they can have the honour of building its defences.' Looking directly at Shaposhnikov and Mekhlis, Stalin growled, 'Make it so.' The two turned and left.

Stalin looked at Zhukov and his demeanour softened. 'Zhukov, my friend, please sit.' Stalin pulled out his pipe. Performing his pipe-filling ritual he began to talk. 'Well, I'm sure you are aware of what's going on. You heard the forces I am pulling in. Six armies on the way, it will take several weeks to get the troops from Trans-Baikal here as you well know; you made that trip enough times.'

'What do we have to defend Moscow?' Zhukov asked. Smoke flowed from Stalin's mouth and hung in the stale air above his head.

'Timoshenko still has seven armies not cut off and I am counting on him getting some of the trapped armies out.'

'What do we have to defend Moscow?' Zhukov repeated his question.

Stalin eyed Zhukov warily, 'I've got eight divisions around the city; a couple of them are militia. A couple of tank battalions with T34s are forming up, and I have a cavalry corps with three full-strength divisions near Podolsk. With service troops, air defence forces and anti-tank units, 150,000 troops altogether.' Stalin finished.

'What do you want me to do?' Zhukov asked bluntly. 'The Central Front can barely defend itself, especially now that you have taken the 50th Army from me,' Zhukov added.

Tapping his pipe on his palm, Stalin leaned back in his chair, 'I want you to take over defence of Moscow. You have the West, Central and Reserve Fronts. I will give you all the forces I can, except my garrison in the city. I need you to stop the Germans like you did at Leningrad. More importantly I want you to destroy that villain Guderian. For air support I have built up a Reserve Aviation Front with 190 fighters, 60 ground-attack aircraft, and 155 bombers. That's over 400 aircraft at your disposal.'

Zhukov rose, 'Comrade Supreme Commander, I have much to attend to if I am to accomplish all you have directed. May I be dismissed?'

'Yes of course,' Stalin agreed, adding, 'It's good to have you back.' As Zhukov neared the door, Stalin threw in one more item, 'I'm having 25,000 replacements sent to you. They haven't been trained, but they can shoot, or so I have been told.' 'Thank you comrade' Zhukov responded as he passed through the door.

The Advance Continues

General Weich massed his XII Infantry Corps along the boundary of the Soviet 13th and 4th Armies. Weich had 1st Cavalry Division and an infantry division as his exploitation force. Attacking on 11 August, despite spirited resistance, they drove a wedge twelve miles wide and nine miles deep between the two sorely tried Soviet armies. Weich would commit his exploitation forces the following day.

The 13th Army's battles with 2nd Panzer Group had left it with a strength of less than two full-strength divisions. Most of the 13th's strength was facing north fighting the 197th and 7th Divisions. The Soviet 4th Army, weak to start with, had sent two divisions off to reinforce the 50th Army. The fact that the two

Soviet armies contained 2nd Army at all was a surprise to them. During the night, 13th Army pulled back, quietly disengaging from the 197th and 7th Divisions to the north and tying itself as firmly as possible into the right flank of the 4th Army. In so doing it extended the 4th Army's flank eastwards.

Guderian, pleased with 2nd Army's success, put 23rd and 7th Infantry Divisions on the road toward Kaluga. 197th Infantry remained, maintaining contact with 2nd Army. After its initial burst, XLVII Panzer Corps was slowed by supply difficulties. The 29th Motorised took Serpukhov on 12 August. On 13 August, General Boltenstern had pushed his forces out in two directions. One regiment advanced eighteen miles up the rail line toward Moscow, and a second regiment drove fifteen miles east towards Kashira. The rest of the division consolidated its hold on Serpukhov.

17th Panzer Division left one regiment at Kaluga until infantry relieved them. The rest of the division advanced north-east on 29th Motorised's left reaching a point half-way between Maloyaroslavets and Serpukhov by 13 August where the division stopped to refuel.

On 11 August 18th Panzer Division captured Maloyaroslavets, but on 12 August they were pushed out by a Soviet counter-attack backed by strong air support. Fighting was bitter all day as more German forces arrived. On 13 August the town changed hands twice before the Germans gained uncontested control of the ruins. By then 18th Panzer halted to regroup and resupply. On 13 August, XLVII Panzer Corps had its three divisions on a line between Maloyaroslavets and Serpukhov.

4th Panzer and Das Reich were relieved by 4th Army infantry. 4th Panzer reverted to XXIV Panzer Corps. Das Reich moved to Medyn to wait for 10th Panzer returning from 2nd Army. Grossdeutschland also headed for Medyn to rejoin Vietinghoff's reconstituted XLVI Panzer Corps.

4th Panzer Division crossed the Ugra river and relieved the hard-pressed 10th Motorised which had been fighting in two directions, holding the Soviet forces in the Vyazma Kessel and keeping relief forces from linking up with those surrounded. 4th Panzer concentrated on reducing the Kessel while 10th Motorised focused on defeating the relief attempts. 3rd Panzer Division was relieved by 4th Army and moved east to the south of 10th Motorised and prepared to resume offensive operations on 14 August south of the Minsk-Moscow highway.

4th Army relieved the mobile divisions securing the Vyazma *Kessel* with the exception of 4th Panzer and 14th Motorised Divisions. Kluge's Army began eliminating the Vyazma *Kessel*. Large numbers of Soviet troops began surrendering. By 14 August over 40,000 prisoners had been taken. A larger number were killed or wounded trying breakout.

3rd Panzer Group's XXXIX Panzer Corps had its hands full trying to maintain its hold on the north and north-east side of the Vyazma *Kessel*. 11 and 12 August saw desperate fighting and what in German reports were termed 'deadly losses' for the Soviets. Although not as high, German losses were heavy as well. Especially hard hit was 7th Panzer Division whose primary tanks, the Czech-built Pz Kw 38t, were having a tough time against Soviet 45mm anti-tank guns and a number of BT 7s. By 13 August the Soviet attacks lost their intensity and 4th Army infantry relieved 7th Panzer which redeployed north behind 14th Motorised Division. 12th Panzer was relieved the following day.

Hoth Moves East

3rd Panzer Group's other corps, LVII Panzer, seized Volokolamsk on 12 August. 18th Motorised took the town off the march. 20th Panzer advanced on 18th Motorised's left, advancing twenty-five miles short of Klin. Here both divisions waited for fuel on 13 August. The two other divisions of LVII Panzer Corps advanced against light resistance. 19th Panzer passed ten miles south of Staritsa while 20th Motorised kept abreast. By 13 August the two divisions were twenty miles north of 20th Panzer's forward positions and reaching the western edge of the Volga Reservoir.

The SS Totenkopf Division linked up with 9th Army's spearhead fifteen miles south of Selizharo on 13 August. Totenkopf led 9th Army's attack which by 15 August reached Rzhev along the Volga where an SS regiment linked up with elements of the LVII Corps which already occupied the city. With this connection, the Soviet 22nd, 29th, and 19th Armies (85,000 troops) were caught in the triangle between Toropets, Rzhev and Belya.

North of 9th Army, 4th Panzer Group drove east against weak resistance. Swinging north around Lake Seliger, General Reinhardt's XLI Panzer Corps seized Demyansk and pushed into the Valdai Hill country. Meanwhile, General Manstein's LVI Panzer Corps took Selizharovo and attacked south of Lake Seliger into the Valdai Hills. The reconnaissance battalion of 3rd Motorised advanced east cutting the Moscow–Leningrad rail line.

Zhukov Fights Back

Zhukov tried to establish a defensive line running from the Volga Reservoir south through Mozhaysk down to Kaluga. But the Germans had compromised the line before he even issued the orders. Now he could only pin his hopes on the defensive rings being built around the city by 150,000 Muscovites, mostly women and old men. Zhukov's only option was to concentrate his forces against the German forces that were threatening to encircle the city.

The 34th Army made it to Klin just before the rail line was cut. 54th Army, following the 34th, did not get through. Zhukov knew 2nd and 3rd Panzer Groups were attempting to encircle Moscow. 34th Army was to stop the northern pincer while he gathered forces to stop Guderian's southern pincer. He had to buy enough time to allow the troops from the east to arrive. 'If only we were closer to winter,' he thought.

In front of Moscow, Zhukov patched together a line with units fighting their way out of the Vyazma pocket. Timoshenko formed five divisions out of 34,000 men who had slipped out. Zhukov concentrated his forces against the encircling pincers while using the Moscow garrison as the centre of his line. He ordered the 49th Army which was forming up in Moscow to move to Podolsk.

To the south, 50th Army moved north out of Sukhinichi. Reinforced with two divisions from 4th Army, two under-strength tank brigades and the remnants of the 43rd Army, 50th Army was a formidable force nearly 60,000 strong with seventy tanks. On 13 August the 50th attacked toward Yukhnov making steady advances against German screening forces. Ten miles short of Yukhnov they ran into the 23rd Infantry Division which was on its way to Kaluga. 7th Infantry joined the 23rd the next day, and 197th came up the day after that. The three infantry divisions brought 50th Army's advance to a halt.

Guderian Keeps Up the Pressure

Creating the Vyazma *Kessel* had spread out his several corps, so Guderian set about to concentrate his Panzer Group on 15 August. XLVII Panzer Corps advanced north-east to cross the Moskva river south-east of Moscow. 29th Motorised Division attacked east cut the Moscow–Kashira rail line and seized the railroad bridge over the Oka river north of Kashira. Leaving a regiment to defend the river, the rest of the division continued towards the Moskva river. 17th Panzer Division minus a regiment left at Kaluga attacked on the left of 29th Motorised, crossing the rail line from Serpukhov to Moscow about half way between Serpukhov and Podolsk and then swung north-east staying on 29th Motorised's left flank. 18th Panzer Division attacked out of Maloyaroslavets directly for Podolsk.

The 10th Panzer Division and Das Reich of the reformed XLVI Panzer Corps, moved out of Medyn to Maloyaroslavets on 15 August. Grossdeutschland followed on 16 August. The entire corps moved behind the XLVII Panzer Corps to form 2nd Panzer Group's reserve.

Guderian's third corps, the XXIV Panzer, attacked with the 3rd Panzer and 10th Motorised Divisions from south-east of Vyazma towards Naro-Forminsk following an axis south of the Minsk–Moscow road. From Naro-Forminsk, they were to push east to link up with 18th Panzer near Podolsk. 4th Panzer Division would follow when relieved of its blocking duties at Vyazma.

Stalin called an emergency session of the State Defence Committee (GKO) on 16 August after reports that German forces were only forty miles south of the city and that there was heavy fighting in the Klin area. All Stalin could offer Zhukov was two regiments of rocket-launchers and news that he was transferring eight divisions from the Soviet Far East. As for relocating the government, Stalin announced that many functions had already been move to 'less threatened areas' and that in any case he was the government and he had no intention of leaving. 'Moscow will be defended to the last drop of blood,' had been his final statement of the meeting.

Lieutenant Zaisev had three tanks shot out from under him in two days and was sent to Moscow to pick up more tanks. He had barely escaped being trapped in the Vyazma pocket. At the T34 factory he was informed that he was promoted to captain and now commanded a battalion in a newly formed tank brigade. Captain Zaisev led his six new tanks south through the streets of the city to where his other twelve tanks were waiting.[13]

The Battle of Podolsk

On 17 August, 29th Motorised Division crossed the Moskva river against no resistance. Using captured river barges they ferried forces over while the pioneers built a bridge. By noon half the division was across. 17th Panzer Division, minus the regiment left at Kaluga, was attacked by Soviet cavalry. The initial attack was easily beaten back, but the fast-moving cavalry attacked again sweeping around 17th Panzer's flank and deployed horse-drawn anti-tank guns. The exposed panzers were forced to pull back and counter-attacked only to be beaten back. The fighting grew fierce along 17th Panzer's entire front. General Thoma's short-handed division battled three cavalry divisions one of which was working its way to his rear. Getting around 17th Panzer, the Soviet cavalry division attacked the 29th Motorised's rear echelon units a mile from the bridging site. General Boltenstern inflicting horrendous casualties on the charging Soviet horsemen using air defence guns and artillery firing point blank into the mass of riders. By 18:00 hours the fighting ended and tank/infantry teams from 17th Panzer policed the area, taking over 3,000 mostly wounded prisoners. The three cavalry divisions were practically destroyed.

In their advance to Podolsk 18th Panzer Division encountered freshly dug fighting positions and anti-tank ditches, but few were manned or covered by fire. This was the outermost of the three defensive rings being constructed around Moscow. 18th Panzer quickly destroyed the understrength Soviet regiment defending this portion of the line. While the three Soviet cavalry divisions were performing their death dance some thirty miles to the south-east, 18th Panzer smashed through the outer defence line and assaulted Podolsk.

The assault force was pushed out of Podolsk by a recently mobilised division. 18th Panzer attacked again while Stukas worked over Soviet artillery positions north of the town. In desperate fighting, panzer grenadier teams cleared the town house by house. General Nehring sent one panzer battalion north of the town to cut off reinforcements, trap the defenders and take out the supporting artillery. In this manoeuvre the panzers encountered Soviet armour.[14]

Captain Zaisev led his eighteen tanks forward against German tanks north of Podolsk. The Germans were almost in effective range. At his signal, ten of his tanks fired scoring one hit. The Germans turned to face the threat and

Zaisev's remaining eight tanks fired. Two more hits were registered, including his shot which knocked the drive sprocket off a Mk III. German tanks began to return fire rapidly and accurately scoring a number of hits, but at this range the German 50 mm guns were not penetrating the T 34's frontal armour. All his tanks were now firing and had scored hits on seven German tanks. One of his tanks had its track blown off and another had taken several hits in the turret ring knocking the turret off kilter. He aimed his 76 mm main gun and fired, hitting another German tank which burst into flames. The Germans pulled back as their artillery laid down smoke. The tank on Zaisev's left exploded. He heard a now familiar screeching sound and ordered his driver to turn around at full speed. The tank swung around as large explosion blossomed just missing them. He frantically signalled his tanks to head for a stand of tree several hundreds yards away. He could see the Stukas circling for another run. Eleven tanks made it to the trees. They had knocked out at least as many German tanks as they had lost and from Zaisev's experience, that was a good exchange rate.[15]

18th Panzer Division finally secured Podolsk and established contact with 17th Panzer. Nehring's division had broken the outer ring of Moscow's defences and seized Podolsk, but it had been costly.

The Battle of Klin

On 16 August, 3rd Panzer Group's LVII Panzer Corps advance three division abreast from north to south, 20th Motorised, 20th Panzer, and 18th Motorised Divisions. 19th Panzer Division, pulled in from the left flank, followed 20th Panzer. Ten miles from Klin they met stiff resistance.

General Berzarin deployed four of his five rifle divisions west of Klin leaving his fifth rifle division in the city. He had one cavalry division north of and one south of Klin. 34th Army was supported by four artillery regiments and two armoured trains. One train ran along the rail line north to Kalinin. The other patrolled the line south to Moscow.

Fighting spread along 34th Army's position as LVII Panzer Corps probed for weaknesses. Eventually 18th Motorised identified 34th Army's left flank. 19th Panzer Division attacked the flank. Soviet aircraft appeared, mostly PE 2 bombers which dropped their bombs from too high causing no damage. Several Il 2 Sturmoviks came in low hitting a StuG Ausf B assault gun. MiG 3 fighters made strafing runs inflicting additional losses.

Despite the Soviet air attacks, 19th Panzer's attack quickly unravelled 34th Army's line. Counter-attacking with his cavalry divisions, Berzarin bought enough time to refuse his left flank and reinforce it with infantry from Klin. His southern armoured train arrived adding its firepower to the battle which continued into the night.

On 17 August the clear morning sky was filled with Luftwaffe aircraft. Several Red Air Force formations appeared but were driven off by Me 109 fighters. Ju 88 bombers blasted Soviet artillery positions while Stukas knocked out strong points and pummelled the armoured train. Inconclusive fighting south of Klin continued all morning. North of Klin 20th Motorised split apart 34th Army's two northern most divisions. 20th Motorised, joined by 20th Panzer Division over ran most of the defensive positions as Soviet troops broke and ran.

In pursuit, 20th Motorised Division came under fire from the northern armoured train. Accurate tank and artillery fire left the train a smouldering wreck. Berzarin's two rifle divisions still holding the line were attacked in the rear by 20th Panzer and cut to pieces. What was left of the cavalry divisions withdrew to the south-east as German armour overran 34th Army's artillery. Berzarin gathered what forces he could to defend Klin which fell by the end of the day.

18th Motorised Division took 12,000 prisoners in Klin. 20th Motorised cleared the area from Klin north to the Volga Reservoir and east to the Volga Canal. 20th Panzer advanced to the Volga Canal and affected several crossings. 19th Panzer advanced thirty miles south-east and ran into Moscow's outer defensive line.

4th Army spent 14 and 15 August tightening its grip on the Soviet forces surrounded near Vyazma and relieved the remaining mobile division. The number of Soviet troops captured reached 150,000. Kluge began putting some of his divisions on the road to Moscow.

9th Army eliminated the Soviet 29th, 22nd and 19th Armies north-west of Belya taking 30,000 prisoners. General Strauss released Totenkopf back to 4th Panzer Group. General Hoepner ordered the division to Kalinin to link up with Manstein's XVI Panzer Corps.

Destruction of 54th Army

54th Army followed 34th Army on the rail line to Moscow. On 15 August, Marshal Kulik, 54th Army Commander, deployed a rifle regiment of his lead division to clear a force blocking the line and another regiment to protect his western flank. Although offering spirited resistance, the reconnaissance battalion of 3rd Motorised Division was forced back by the Soviet attack.

3rd Motorised counter-attacked, driving the Soviets back. Both sides committed additional forces. With trains loaded with equipment and troops beginning to pile up behind him, Marshal Kulik was considering unloading more heavy weapons when his flank regiment reported sighting German tanks.

8th Panzer Division had faced light resistance as they advanced east to the north of the 3rd Motorised Division. Hearing the rumble of battle to the south-east all morning, it picked up the pace of its advance. Reconnaissance units reported the Moscow–Leningrad rail line to be backed up with trains loaded with military equipment. Von Manstein, seeing a golden opportunity, deployed 8th Panzer accordingly. Hurrying his artillery into place he attacked with two panzer battalions in the lead supported by a panzer grenadier regiment. Shock and well-placed artillery fire quickly smashed the Soviet rifle regiment facing 8th Panzer. Chaos reigned in the Soviet position as German artillery struck among the packed trains. Soviet infantry tried to counter-attack, but the attacks were disjointed and lacking heavy weapons. As 8th Panzer's Mk IIIs and a couple of Mk IVs began shooting up rail cars, Stukas made an appearance and rained destruction from above. The 54th Army was doomed as the remnants began retreating to the east, leaving the train cars with their most of their equipment and supplies to the Germans.

Moscow Surrounded

4th Army relieved 2nd and 3rd Panzer Groups of responsibility for the Vyazma Kessel, releasing their two tied-down panzer corps which quickly re-deployed to continue offensive operations on 16 August. XXIV Panzer Corps swept east on between Mozhaisk and Naro-Forminsk with 3rd Panzer on the left, 10th Motorised on the right and 4th Panzer following. XXXIX Panzer Corps attacked north-east on an axis half way between Volokolamsk and Borodino with 14th Motorised and 12th Panzer leading and 7th Panzer in the rear. Both corps advanced against moderate resistance as the Soviets units conducted a fighting withdrawal back to the Moscow defences.

On 18 August XLVI Panzer Corp's 10th Panzer and Das Reich Divisions relieved XLVII Panzer Corp's 17th and 18th Panzer Divisions. 17th Panzer crossed the Moskva river and joined the 29th Motorised whose lead elements had cut the Moscow–Gorki rail line. By 19 August units of the 29th Motorised were closing on the Klyazma river east of Moscow.

North of Moscow the 20th Panzer Division expanded its bridgehead over the Volga Canal on 19 August but determined Soviet resistance kept it from becoming a general advance. The 20th Motorised screened the Volga Reservoir and affected a crossing of the canal near the reservoir. 19th Panzer continued probing the northern defences of Moscow. 18th Motorised crossed the canal and joined the 20th Panzer. On 20 August the two divisions finally broke through the Soviet defences cutting the rail line to Vologda, the last open rail link to Moscow. On 21 August, advance forces of the 18th Motorised made contact with 29th Motorised along the Klyazma. Moscow was surrounded.

Stalin Takes His Leave

On 19 August Stalin finally agreed to leave Moscow. Fifteen miles east of the city was an airfield where a plane waited. Stalin's personal guard detail consisted of a thirty-six-man NKVD platoon. They filled two trucks, one before and one after Stalin's Zil. There were also four armoured cars, three light BA 20s and one heavy BA 32 mounting a 45 mm gun. One BA 20 led the way followed by the BA 32. The others brought up the rear. Mekhlis rode with Stalin along with a driver and a plain-clothes NKVD guard. They ran into a roadblock manned by a small company of Red Army troops, several miles from the airfield. The major commanding Stalin's guard detachment came running back to ZIL. Mekhlis got out, but before the major could speak, Stalin was also out of the car. 'You will make your report to me, major.' Stalin's demanded.

'Comrade Stalin, these troops are part of a larger unit that came up from Ukraine several days ago. Their captain said several companies of their battalion are holding the airfield but there are Germans between us and the airfield. The Germans have several machine-guns and an armoured car, but he is sure together we can clear the road.'

Stalin told the major to make it so. The major barked orders, and the four armoured cars moved forward as the NKVD troops dismounted the trucks. Thirty of them joined fifty Red Army troops spread out along the road. The captain and major organised their force and began advancing toward the airfield.

Stalin sat back in the car leaving his door open as did Mekhlis. The six remaining NKVD soldiers took up positions around the remaining vehicles. Four Red Army soldiers remained at the roadblock.

Shortly after, the 45 mm gun could clearly be heard along with the rapid staccato of German MG 34 machine-guns. 'Sounds like the Germans only have machine-guns,' Mekhlis said, looking toward the sound of the firing.

A couple of shots rang out nearby. One NKVD soldier with the convoy was firing. Mekhlis told the bodyguard to find out what was going on. The guard returned, reporting one of the soldiers had seen four or five Germans. Mekhlis told the guard to get the PPsh sub-machine guns out of the trunk. While two NKVD men fired at the Germans, Mekhlis called the other four over along with the four Red Army soldiers. The eight men gathered around Mekhlis and the bodyguard. The Red Army soldiers were stunned when they saw Stalin sitting in the car.

Mekhlis instructed two NKVD troops to join the two already firing and keep the Germans pinned down. He took the last NKVD men, four Red Army soldiers and the bodyguard and outflanked the Germans. He instructed the driver to stay alert and with Stalin. Mekhlis led his improvised group off. In minutes a firefight broke out. The driver scanned in the direction of the firing. Suddenly, he staggered and fell. One of the Red Army soldiers came running up.

'What's going on out there?' Stalin demanded.

'Have you ever watched someone starve to death?' the soldier asked.

Paying no attention, Stalin repeated his question, 'I asked you what's going on out there!'

The soldier levelled his rifle at Stalin and spoke again, 'I watched my mother and sister die. We had a good harvest; your people took it all, left us nothing. My father tried to stop them, they shot him. With no food we couldn't make it through the winter, I watched them starve to death.'

'Mekhlis!' Stalin called out, then to the soldier, 'I'll have you sent to Siberia.'

The soldier looked Stalin in the eye, 'No more Ukrainians will starve because of you,' and he pulled the trigger. Stalin fell back on the seat of his bulletproof ZIL, a small hole in his forehead. As his vacant eyes stared at the cloth-covered ceiling a pool of blood formed on the leather seat. The soldier turned and walked away.[16]

Zhukov Takes Control

Zhukov heard about Stalin's 'execution' the next day. The official announcement that the Supreme Commander died defending Moscow, was still days away. Mekhlis formed alliances, including with Beria, head of the NKVD. But the Red Army was one hundred per cent behind Zhukov who announced he was taking control until the Supreme Soviet chose a new leader. There was a minor skirmish between NKVD and Red Army troops when the latter arrested Beria. No one defended Mekhlis.

After consolidating power, Zhukov put the Red Army in motion to the east to preserve as much of its combat capability as possible. Moscow and Kiev were abandoned. Leningrad would have to fight on as best it could with its own resources. With the loss of Moscow there was no rail connection with Leningrad. The new defensive line was the Volga river with strong forces in strategic areas west of the river.

The Germans, making their final thrust of the year had taken Gorky, destroying any hope of building a rail connection between Murmansk and Kuibyshev.

Captain Zaisev led a force of over 500 men who slipped through the still porous cordon around Moscow. He survived the war and was the youngest Colonel in the Red Army at the end of the war.

Private Schmitt was wounded by counter-battery fire during the battle of Kazan in July 1942, and was evacuated to a hospital in Germany. He was discharged from the army in September 1943.

Zhukov salvaged 600,000 troops out of the Ukraine. Mobilisation continued but the most populous regions had been lost. Equipment was in short supply. Supplies and equipment started arriving from the United Kingdom and to a lesser extent the United States. They came via Iran and Vladivostok. The Vladivostok route closed in December when Japan entered the war. Then there were the reinforcements already coming from the Urals, Trans-Baikal, and the Far East. These troops were well equipped and fully trained. In early October Zhukov had had definite information that Japan would not attack the Soviet Far East and instead would be attacking in South-East Asia and the United States. This allowed the transfer of even more forces to west.

The conventional Soviet-German War dragged on for two more years before degenerating into guerrilla warfare. The victory in the 1941 campaign season allowed the Germans to transfer additional forces to the Mediterranean theatre. The strengthened Luftwaffe dominated the central Mediterranean allowing troops and supplies uninterrupted flow to the German-Italian army in North Africa which seized Egypt and the Suez Canal. The loss of Egypt coupled with the clear inevitability of the defeat of the Soviet Union, convinced the Anglo-American Powers to begin peace negotiations with Germany that finally resulted in a fragile treaty in the summer of 1943.

Reality

Germany's best chance and arguably only chance of defeating the Soviet Union was to do it in 1941. In June and July 1941, Army Group Centre demonstrated that it could defeat the best forces the Soviets could put against it. From 22 June to 3 July 1941, Army Group Centre advance roughly 200 miles destroying the Soviet frontier armies, capturing 324,000 prisoners and 2,500 tanks. From 3 July to 16 July 1941, Army Group Centre advanced roughly another 200 miles past Smolensk surrounding the new array of Soviet armies deployed to stop them. By 4 August these armies had been eliminated with another 100,000 prisoners taken. By 13 August Army Group Centre was prepared to resume offensive operations and viewed Moscow, now only 250 miles away, as their next objective. There can be little doubt that with the good weather of August 1941, Army Group Centre would have no trouble destroying the weak and disorganised Soviet forces between them and Moscow. Having advanced roughly 200 miles to Minsk in two weeks and then roughly 200 miles to Smolensk in two weeks and in both cases against more powerful Soviet forces, it is reasonably to assume that Army Group Centre would have advanced 250 miles to Moscow in August.

However, Hitler had other plans. First, he vacillated about what the next objective was for nearly month, during which time Army Group Centre for the most part sat idle fending off Soviet counter-attacks. Second, when Hitler finally made his decision he sent 2nd Panzer Group and 2nd Army south into Ukraine instead of sending the entire army group on to Moscow.

When Army Group Centre was reunited and finally ordered to advance on to Moscow it was 2 October before they were prepared to begin. During that time, the Soviets had a full two months to assemble powerful new forces and prepare defensive positions. Yet even then Army Group Centre was able to destroy the better part of eight Soviet Armies between 2 and 17 October, taking over 650,000 prisoners. But on 10 October the autumn rains began nonstop for the rest of the month soaking the unpaved roads and countryside making them impassable until they froze in mid-November. This gave the Soviets another month to rebuild and prepare their forces. With the knowledge in early October that Japan would not be attacking the Soviet Far East, troops were now pulled from there wholesale. In crippling blizzards, Army Group Centre was finally stopped on the outskirts of Moscow.

Notes

1   Erickson, 1975, p. 178.
2   Ibid., p. 179.
3   Stolfi, 1991, p. 140.
4   Ibid., p. 136
*5   Keegan Campbell and Karl Campbell, *The Private War of Private Schmitt*, Fairfax: Silverbrook Publishing, 2003, p. 163.
6   Infantry Regiment Grossdeutschland was formed from German Army's elite *Wach* (Watch) Regiment Berlin in April 1939 and in June was renamed *Grossdeutschland* (Greater Germany) at Hitler's direction. It would later become a panzer grenadier division with the highest priority for personnel and equipment replacements, even ahead of the SS.
7   'The Boss' is a colloquial translation of the Russian word, *Vozd*, which means 'great war leader'.
8   Ogorkiewicz, 1970, p. 227.
*9   Ekatrina Zaiseva, *My Grandfather the Hero: The Stories He Told*, Cheljabinsk,: Great Patriotic War Press, 2002, p. 87.
*10   Keegan Campbell and Karl Campbell, op. cit, note 5, p. 195.
*11   Heinz Guderian, *Panzers to the Pacific: The March Across Asia*, Berlin: Goering Publishing House GmbH, 1954, p. 263.
*12   Ibid, p. 265.
*13   Zaiseva, op. cit., note 5, p. 186.
*14   Guderian, op. cit., note 11, p. 336.
*15   Ibid, p. 206
*16   Peter Menne, *Deposing a Dictator: The Assassination of Stalin*, Annapolis: Annapolis Press, 1998.

Bibliography

Bullock, Alan, *Hitler and Stalin: Parallel Lives*, New York: Alfred A. Knopf, 1992.

Carruthers, Bob and Erickson, John, *The Russian Front 1941–1945*, London: Cassell & Co., 1999.

Erickson, John, *The Road To Stalingrad: Stalin's War with Germany Volume 1*, New York: Harper & Row, 1975.

Fowler, Will, *The Atlas of Eastern Front Battles*, New York: The Military Book Club, 2002.

Guderian, Heinz, *Panzer Leader*, New York: E.P. Dutton & Co., Inc, 1952.

Ogorkiewicz, Richard, *Armoured Forces: A History Of Armoured Forces and their Vehicles*, New York: ARCO Publishing, 1970.

Stolfi, R. H. S., *Hitler's Panzers East: World War II Reinterpreted*, Norman, OK: University of Oklahoma Press, 1991.

Tsouras, Peter, *The Great Patriotic War: An Illustrated History of Total War: the Soviet Union and Germany, 1941–1945*, London: Greenhill Books, 1992.

von Manstein, Erich, *Lost Victories*, Chicago: Henry Regnery Company, 1958.

Ziemke, Earl and Magna Bauer, *Moscow to Stalingrad: Decision in the East*, Washington: Center of Military History United States Army, 1987.

9 The Stalingrad Breakout
'Raus Pulls You Through'

Peter G. Tsouras

Gumrak, Headquarters, 6th Army

26 November 1942

Colonel-General Friedrich Paulus' facial twitch was getting worse. He slumped in his chair as he read the letter from his senior and most capable corps commander.

Colonel-General Walther von Seydlitz-Kurzbach certainly did not pull any punches. 'The Army is faced with a decisive either/or; break-out to the south-west in the general direction of Kotelnikovo or destruction within a few days.'

He then looked again at the cable bearing the Führer decision, 'Sixth Army stand firm in spite of danger of temporary encirclement.'[1]

Paulus was a man pulled in two directions at once, and he did not have the character to stand the strain. A meticulous if not brilliant staff officer, he had been rated earlier in his career as not having the decisiveness to command. Nevertheless, he had risen steadily under the patronage of the Army chief of staff, Colonel-General Franz Halder. His planning for the invasion of the Soviet Union had brought him to the attention of Hitler. At the request of Field Marshal von Reichenau, commanding Army Group South, Paulus was appointed to command the 6th Army in early January 1942. He had handled the command competently but a little too lethargically for his army group commander. But fate pulled him forward to the Don and across towards Stalingrad.

Hitler wanted the city of his nemesis ground to dust and Paulus eagerly obliged. What should have fallen to 6th Army and its neighbouring 4th Panzer Army by manoeuvre had come to cost 20,000 casualties a week in the most brutal close fighting since Verdun in 1916. Again and again Paulus drove his divisions into the long, thin city clinging to the Volga bank. Here and there they broke through only to be driven back by Soviet reinforcements ferried across the river at great cost.

Victory hung there tantalisingly within grasp – until the Soviets had brilliantly turned the tables on their German tormentors. On 19 November, in Operation URANUS, carefully husbanded Soviet reserves attacked the weak

Romanian armies north and south Stalingrad and encircled the 6th Army and a good part of 4th Panzer Army within the new Stalingrad pocket or *Kessel*.

What to do? Obey orders, of course. For a man of a Paulus' character there was simply no other choice. Besides, he had experience a few months earlier of Hitler's all-knowing genius when the Führer had backed an ambitious counter-attack plan against Timoshenko's May offensive that had led to the destruction of two Soviet armies and the taking of almost a quarter of a million prisoners. For his part, Paulus had thought the best plan was to give ground and fall back. The experience had indelibly convinced him that Hitler's judgment was better than his own. And now to the surrounded 6th Army and its commander, Hitler commanded that they hold out. He would rescue them. For Paulus that had been enough.[2]

But not for von Seydlitz. The commander of LI Corps was certainly the most able of Paulus' generals and the most famous. He had commanded the 12th Infantry Division in the French campaign of 1940 and had been slated to take the division into the invasion of England. But his great moment in the sun had been as the leader of the special corps that relieved the corps trapped in the Demyansk pocket in early May. For that deed Hitler had given him command of LI Corps in 6th Army a few days latter. He joined just in time for the attack that would carry the army across the Don and into the charnel house of Stalingrad. He continued to shine and was even in line to succeed Paulus as 6th Army Commander when it seemed the latter was being nominated to replace Field Marshal Alfred Jodl, Chief of Staff of the *Wehrmacht* high command (*Oberkommando der Wehrmacht* – OKW). But Jodl kept his post and so did everyone else. Still, Hitler maintained a favourable impression of von Seydlitz as a determined and hard fighter.

Ability as well as independent thinking ran in the family. His ancestor, Friedrich Wilhem von Seydlitz (1721–73), Frederick the Great's distinguished cavalry general, had delivered a famous retort to the king who was micro-managing the battle of Zorndorf, 'Tell the king that after the battle my head is at his disposal, but meantime I hope he will permit me to exercise it in his service.'[3] The story had become part of the lore of the German army, typifying the concepts of initiative and delegation of authority that the General Staff system had so successfully inculcated into German military culture.

Needless to say, these concepts were taking a beating from an increasingly megalomaniac Hitler who greedily hoarded decisions, even to division tactics, to himself. Senior officers seethed and occasionally argued but to no avail. Persistent arguing quickly earned the independent soul a long leave or early retirement.

But there were exceptions. Field Marshal Erich von Manstein, fresh from his conquest of Crimea and its citadel of Sevastopol, had been given command of Army Group Don as soon as the Soviet pincers closed on the Stalingrad *Kessel*. Manstein's previous victories, including his authorship of the attack through the Ardennes in May 1940 that brought proud France crashing to her knees, had laid up a very large stock of authority which he did not hesitate to use to bluntly tell Hitler that 6th Army must break out of the *Kessel*. He did not flinch from telling Hitler that he should separate himself from direct conduct of the war. Normally, such effrontery would have landed von Manstein on the retired list, but Hitler needed the man. He may have needed him, but that did not mean he had to listen to him. Rather Hitler thought that a man of von Manstein's ability should be able to translate a Führer order into reality.

For Hitler, the prestige of destroying Stalin's city came to override all military logic. He adorned it with pseudo-logic, arguing that it would be the Verdun of 1942 in which the last reserves of the Soviet armies would be consumed. That argument must have caused more than a few eyes to widen in disbelief, for the German strategy of attrition meant to bleed the French white had been equally lethal to the Germans. The decision had been reinforced by Reichmarschall Goering's lunatic pledge to resupply the *Kessel* by air. The almost 290,000 men in the *Kessel* needed a minimum of 300 tons of resupply a day. The Luftwaffe in a good week would be lucky to bring in 300 tons.

A matter never raised with OKW was the large number of Russian volunteers (*Hilfswillige* or *Hiwis*) that were filling out the depleted German ranks. In the middle of November 6th Army's ration strength had listed 51,700 *Hiwis*. The *Hiwis* were among the most determined troops in 6th Army, imbued with a deep hatred of the Communists and steeled by the knowledge of what would happen to them if captured.[4]

Von Manstein vehemently disagreed with the Führer order. He could see clearly that the parallel German lunge into the Caucasus with Army Group A was untenable. The German Army simply did not have the strength to execute all of Hitler's plans. Unless 6th Army was freed to be employed elsewhere to protect the flank of Army Group A, it was only a matter of time before the Soviets lopped off the entire army group by striking at its weak hinge at Rostov on Don.[5] His arguments got him nowhere, but Hitler did promise forces strong enough to break into the *Kessel*. That promise would bring another strong personality to the battle.

6th Panzer Division to the Rescue

The news of 6th Army's danger immediately ended the ideal posting of two veteran Russian Front divisions resting and rebuilding in France, including Hitler's elite bodyguard formation, Panzer grenadier Division SS Leibstandarte Adolf Hitler, and 6th Panzer Division.[6] Panzer grenadier Division Grossdeutschland, the German Army's elite formation, currently on the Eastern Front in the area of Rhzev, was also alerted.[7]

6th Panzer was stationed in comfortable old French barracks in Brittany, where the living and the girls were easy. The division's new mission electrified everyone – 'Liberate Stalingrad' and the 300,000 men within the *Kessel*. Within days the division was loaded on to seventy-eight trains and sent hurtling east.

The 6th Panzer would be no stranger to Russia. This Rhineland–

Westphalian division had fought brilliantly in the drives on Leningrad and Moscow and had ridden out the great Soviet counter-attacks that rumbled on almost through the spring of 1942 under the command of General-Major Erhard Raus.

An Austrian, Raus had served in World War I as a *Jäger* (mountain soldier) on battlefields that demanded the most of good training, boldness, and initiative – lessons he learned well. After the war, he spent considerable time in the training establishment of the Austrian Army. On Austria's *Anschluss* (union) with Germany, he was serving as military attaché to Rome. When Austria's army was incorporated into the German Army he changed uniforms as well.

Raus brought a Jäger's sense of initiative and boldness to command. Instinctively aggressive he trained his officers and men to meet the most severe demands of fighting in Russia as 6th Panzer was rebuilt and rearmed between May and November. Clausewitz almost seemed to be anticipating Raus in his description of the qualities of the great captains:

> The right appreciation of their opponents... the audacity to leave for a short space of time, a small force before them, energy in forced marches, boldness in sudden attacks, the intensified activity which great souls acquire in the moment of danger – these are the ground of such victories.[8]

OKH (*Oberkommando des Heeres*, the German Army's General Staff) had anticipated just such a mission for 6th Panzer when it rebuilt it to ten to twenty per cent over strength in men and equipment.[9] Its 11th Panzer Regiment boasted 160 new Mark IVs with its long-barrelled, high-velocity 75 mm guns. This mailed fist was commanded by a Prussian warrior of the highest calibre, Colonel Walter von Hünnersdorf. An assault gun battalion had also been added, but its vehicles were promised on arrival at the front.

Raus began the journey of his division as he meant to go on – ready for a fight. He defied the logisticians' careful but non-tactical railcar loading regulations designed to carry the maximum in men and equipment. He directed that every train be organised for immediate entry into combat. The men went with their equipment. Artillery, flak and machine-guns were loaded to be employed from their flatbed cars. The reason became clear as soon the trains penetrated into Ukraine and Russia. Partisan bands came after them like moths to the flame – and were badly burned each time they attacked, leaving 6th Panzer almost unscathed but alerted for tough times ahead.

All Eyes on Kotelnikovo

Moscow, 25 November 1942
The success of Operation URANUS had left the Stalingrad *Kessel* girdled with Soviet armies in two rings. The inner ring held the *Kessel* in its tightening grip.

Its mission was to keep the trapped Germans in. The mission of those in the outer ring was to keep any relieving force out. It was clear to local commanders as well as the war leaders of both sides that the only direction from which a relief expedition could be launched was to the south-west of Stalingrad in the direction of the small railroad junction of Kotelnikovo, the very objective of a breakout that von Seydlitz had pointed out to Paulus in his letter of 25 November.

General Georgi Zhukov knew when Stalin was nervous. The Chief of the Soviet General Staff also knew that within bounds, he could deal with that nervousness. That nervousness was generated by the prize that lay beckoning inside the *Kessel* – the destruction of a major German force for the first time in the war. More importantly, it held the opportunity to completely turn around the direction of the war by seizing the initiative and sending the broken Germans reeling back and back until the Red Army could pursue them into their own den. Stalin was increasingly listening to good advice after the self-inflicted disasters of the first year of the war. He was also showing an increasingly good strategic sense.

Zhukov pointed to the critical south-west direction. 'Comrade Stalin, 57th Army holds the south-western gate out of Stalingrad. It has suffered heavy casualties in its attacks on the Germans. The ground is frozen and near impossible to dig entrenchments, and the enemy artillery and air attacks have inflicted serious losses. Nevertheless, 57th Army remains strong enough to keep the Germans in if supported by front reserves. The enemy shows no signs of preparations for a breakout.'

Stalin just puffed on his pipe and said, 'Continue.'

Zhukov's pointer moved south-west from 57th Army's positions about 100 km to the rail junction of Kotelnikovo. 'Any German relief force must use this junction as a jumping off point and base of supply. We have the 51st Army covering the front in this direction. I recommend we forestall the Germans and seize the junction.'

'What is the strength of the 51st Army? Is it up to the task?'

'Yes, Comrade Stalin. 51st Army is both mobile and strong. It consists of 4th Cavalry Corps, 13th Mechanised Corps, and four rifle divisions.'

'Trufanov commands, does he not? Are you confident of his ability?'

Zhukov knew that Stalin was setting him up for a scapegoat should Trufanov fail. The only one who never failed was the *Vozd* (Stalin) himself.[10]

Zhukov did not flinch, 'Trufanov did well in the encirclement operation. He will succeed, and I will make sure of it.'

'Then take Kotelnikovo.'

Headquarters, 4th Panzer Army

26 November 1942
'Well, Raus, you've arrived into one hell of a witch's brew!' Hermann Hoth's

dire greeting to Raus was followed by a wry smile from the 4th Panzer Army Commander. 'Glad to have you. Not a moment too soon. My God, man, now that 6th Panzer has arrived, I legitimately command a panzer army again.' He brought Raus over to the map and waved his hand at the disaster that was plain to any soldier. 'I'm assigning you to Kirchner's LVII Panzer Corps. I'm afraid to say that 6th Panzer IS the LVII Panzer Corps. 17th and 23rd Panzer Divisions round out the order of battle, but the Führer took away the 17th recently, and the 23rd is down to 20 tanks. Until you came, I commanded 20 tanks and a few terrified Romanians. Like I said, glad to have you.'

Raus asked to the point, 'What is the last railroad station it is still possible to reach?'

Hoth's bony knuckle rapped on the map. 'As of this morning, it is still Kotelnikovo.'

'What am I facing?'

'More bad news. I won't hide it from you. 3rd Tank Army, and they're good.' General Trufanov, commanding 51st Army, would, no doubt, have been amused at his transfer to an elite all tank formation by way of a German military intelligence breakdown.

The men of 6th Panzer, however, had already felt the chill as they approached the front. Raus described it:

A cold wind blew through the monotonous brown steppe, driving before it innumerable balls of tumbleweed. They resembled greyhounds chasing game at top speed, moving forward in great leaps. A few camel riders moved alongside the train on steppe trails, trying to reach their solitary huts before darkness fell.

At every siding and every halt, the men of 6th Panzer asked those Germans in the evacuation trains heading in the opposite direction the same question Raus had asked Hoth – and got the same answer. 'It is still Kotelnikovo.'[11]

Kotelnikovo, 27 November 1942

The men of the 4th Panzer grenadier Regiment aboard the first train to approach Kotelnikovo had no reason to expect anything more than a comfortable break at this pleasant little railway town, bisected by the Aksay river, after weeks of torment rattling around inside their railway cars. But even before the train had come to a stop, the Soviets attacked. Advance elements of the Soviet 61st Cavalry Division (4th Cavalry Corps) had won the race to Kotelnikovo. They had just slipped into the rail yards moments ahead of the German train and poured fire into it from both sides, then charged with shouts of 'Hurrah!'.

German battle-drill and Raus' combat loading allowed the 6th to counterpunch right off. Machine-guns and flak on top the cars and on flatbeds immediately returned fire. The panzer grenadiers with a shout leapt from their cars and, led personally by the regimental commander, met the attacking Russians in the bitterest hand-to-hand combat amid the cars and yard buildings. Bayonet and rifle butt decided the issue as the Germans cleared the station within less than an hour.

But the Soviets were not done. Artillery fire raked the yards, threatening to grind the regiment to bits. Amid the chaos, a German cavalry officer, Lieutenant Colonel von Panwitz, had happened to be at the German tank repair unit on the edge of the town. He organised the mechanics as tank crews for the half-dozen battle-worthy tanks they had repaired, and led them in a dashing sweep around the town. They came up on line behind the two unsuspecting batteries – and charged. Tank and machine-gun fire cut down the horses standing at their limbers and slaughtered the gun crews as they stood by their guns. It was over in moments as the tanks drove over the smashed batteries.

The day had begun with the Soviets getting to Kotelnikovo ahead of the Germans by a hair, but they lost it in the face of German training and determination to retain the initiative. By evening Raus had assembled a *Kampfgruppe* (battle group) of the advance elements of 6th Panzer as the Soviet 61st Cavalry Division limped away to lick its wounds.

Headquarters, 4th Panzer Army

3 December 1942

Hoth was at the airfield to greet von Manstein. The acerbic field marshal did not waste time on pleasantries as they drove back to 4th Panzer Army headquarters.

'I have failed to convince the Führer to authorise the breakout of 6th Army. We've already missed the best chance to extricate 6th Army. Paulus requested permission to breakout on 24 November. Asked permission, he did – asked permission when he should have taken the bit in his teeth and just done it. At that time, 6th Army could have broken out by itself. We then would have a strong manoeuvre force to teach the Russians a lesson.' He paused.

'Operation THUNDERCLAP, the breakout, should follow on the heels of the relief mission, WINTER STORM, but...,' his voiced trailed off, then his face grew hard, 'this *Gröfaz* (Greatest Officer of All Time) interferes, this amateur playing with the fate of hundreds of thousands of irreplaceable men. I tell you, Hoth, we could lose this war if 6th Army is not withdrawn. And it cannot be withdrawn if we follow the Führer's orders. So...,' he paused and fixed a cold, blue eye on the 4th Panzer Army commander.

Hoth was not going to touch that opening with a ten-foot pole. He had heard how frank von Manstein was among his inner circle. He supposed it was a compliment to now be included.

Von Manstein read the strained pause for what it was and went on. 'Führer

Headquarters has worked closely with my staff on WINTER STORM. You can be thankful for the major miracle that the reinforcements I originally asked for were promptly approved. At first, if you can believe it, Hitler was only going to dispatch 6th Panzer from France...' He paused to say, 'Arrived just in the nick of time, didn't they. Raus will be a man to watch.' Then he went on, 'but he did an about face and agreed to Grossdeutschland and Leibstandarte as well. Now, how do you propose to use them?'

Hoth was on happier ground now. 'I propose to liberate Stalingrad by a two-pronged attack. My main thrust will be with LVII Panzer Corps – 6th and 23rd Panzer Divisions, supported by remnants of two Luftwaffe ground divisions, driving north-east from Kotelnikovo. LVII Panzer Corps faces the weakest part of the Soviet forces surrounding Stalingrad although it has to fight across 100 kilometres.'

'My secondary thrust will be by XXXXVIII Panzer Corps along the Chir river only sixty kilometres from the western edge of the *Kessel*, but it faces the toughest opposition, the heavily reinforced 5th Tank Army. I wasn't sure XXXXVIII Panzer Corps could hold against its repeated strong attacks much less attack. With Grossdeutschland and Leibstandarte reinforcing the XXXXVIII, I can pin down the enemy's 5th Tank Army and attract most of the enemy's reserves away from the Kotelnikovo front.'

Von Manstein was pleased. 'We will have to be careful not to let *Gröfaz* switch the direction of main effort to his babies in Leibstandarte. I think he will be more interested in seeing how that battalion of new Tiger tanks he has directed be given to LVII works out. The man does love his toys.'

Still, he was uneasy. Deep in his heart, he knew 6th Army was doomed. Even should Hoth work wonders, the map was working against him. They were setting themselves up for a replay of the fate of 6th Army which had been forced to ignore the danger to its flanks. And that had led to its encirclement. Now Army Group Don's flanks were dangerously undermanned while the counter-attack would be pressing toward Stalingrad in the centre. All Zhukov had to do was smash the flanks, and the relieving force itself would be enveloped. He had been musing over this dilemma in battlefield space. Perhaps, he should rebalance this with the dimension of battlefield time.

Headquarters, 6th Army

5 December 1942

Von Seydlitz was beside himself with anger and frustration. 'What don't you understand, Paulus?' he said as he leaned over the table poking his face at the 6th Army commander. Paulus physically recoiled from von Seydlitz's overpowering physical presence especially since the corps commander had dropped the pretence of good manners. For his part, Seydlitz was appalled at Paulus' advanced bodily and mental disintegration. The facial twitch was becoming grotesque.

He tore himself away from the wreck of the man and back to his argument. 'The men are on reduced rations already. We will shortly pass the point of no return. Even if the *Kessel* is relieved, the men will take months of rest and reconditioning to recover from this physical and mental ordeal.' He straightened up and struck one fist into the other open hand for emphasis. 'This army has only enough energy for one more effort, and even that will dissipate if we do not act soon to break out.'

'Don't worry, Seydlitz. The Führer has promised he will relieve 6th Army. He has never failed us. The Plan, WINTER STORM, has already been approved, and...'

Von Seydlitz cut him off with a wave of his arm. 'Then we must help it along by attacking toward the relieving forces to catch the Russians between two fires. It is simple common sense.'

'No, the Führer does not want 6th Army to divert effort from its vital role of holding down large enemy forces.' Paulus had completely surrendered his professional judgement to his childlike faith in Hitler.[12]

The Cannae of Poklebin

5–6 December 1942

At this point, General Trufanov gave General Raus the priceless gift of inactivity. The severe handling of his cavalry division had suddenly afflicted him with a sense of extreme caution. One should not forget at that stage of the war how much in awe so many Soviet commanders still held the Germans. He pulled back to concentrate his forces for another try. Raus also concentrated 6th Panzer and argued successfully with his army and corps commanders to align his units in a twenty-by-ten-kilometre box rather than string them out to cover a long front along the Aksay river. He reasoned that Kotelnikovo was the Soviet objective and he would meet strength with strength at the decisive spot.

Unfortunately, for Trufanov, Raus was ready and waiting when the Soviet commander ordered his 4th Cavalry Corps (61st and 81st (Turkestan) Cavalry Divisions, reinforced with a tank brigade and a camel brigade) to attack from the north-west and seize Kotelnikovo. Trufanov also placed an infantry corps north of Kotelnikovo to support the cavalry attack. Plainly, Trufanov outnumbered Raus, but he was up against a master. The cavalry corps he was committing to battle had only recently been transferred from duty on the Afghan border and would be going into combat for the first time. Even so, sheer mass if well coordinated would have put Raus in a difficult position. Nevertheless, Raus was in a race for time. Although he had concentrated much of his division, the vital panzer regiment had been held up by partisan attacks and was only just approaching the area of operations.

On the morning of 5 December the 4th Cavalry Corps pushed out strongly from the north-west towards Kotelnikovo led by the tank brigade and the dismounted 61st Cavalry Division. Clumsy Soviet reconnaissance had altered Raus of the enemy's intent to drive forward through the defile leading to the village of Poklebin and then rush westward towards Kotelnikovo.

But Raus had put a cork in the bottle at Poklebin – a reinforced panzer grenadier company and an anti-tank platoon. Smoke from knocked-out Soviet tanks at the head of the column drifted skyward as the stalled Soviet column marked time in the defile. German artillery found them and worked up and down the packed roadway. A panzer grenadier battalion counter-attacked and poured more fire into the defile. Still, the Soviet mass lurched forward, grinding through the village as the shrinking anti-tank platoon killed one tank after another. The surviving panzer grenadiers were forced out of the village and the flanking battalion also forced back as the surviving tanks and the rest of the 61st Cavalry flooded through Poklebin south into the flood plain of the Askay river. The tanks headed west and ran into another German strongpoint at the village of Sakarov where a number were destroyed by the defenders. The Soviets attempted to manoeuvre around but were struck by the timely arrival of two panzer companies. Now badly shaken, the Soviet tanks lurched away to fall into swampy holes and be pounded by German artillery. The masses of dismounted Soviet cavalry were pursued by German artillery wherever they went inflicting heavy losses.

The next morning the Soviet cavalry corps commander committed his 81st Cavalry Division to the battle and sent it down the Poklebin defile, determined to continue the advance to Kotelnikovo. Trufanov assisted him by also committing the infantry corps positioned north of Kotelnikovo. Raus had been even busier, bending every effort to bring the rest of 11th Panzer Regiment to the battle. Trains bearing the tanks were unloaded at three stations before Kotelnikovo and marched overland through the night. Other trains were halted on the tracks and unloaded from special ramps Raus had had the foresight to bring along. In the process, he threw just about every German Army regulation out the window, but the tanks got there just as the Soviets were funnelling through the defile.

The first anyone in the 81st Cavalry knew of their approach was the sight of the wave of 200 German armoured vehicles topping the rise overlooking the packed defile. Then the slaughter began as 300 German machine-guns and scores of tank guns poured their file into the Soviets. 'Godsent Panic seized them, comrade of bloodcurdling Rout,' as Homer sang so long ago. All order broke down as many of the survivors fled to cross the Aksay river only to have the thin ice break under them. Those at the end of the column tried to bolt to the rear only to be mowed down by the blocking force that had slipped around them. The fate of the 4th Cavalry Corps had been sealed by 10:00 hours, but much hard fighting remained to wipe out the remnants and throw back every attempt to break out of the *Kessel*.

As the firing finally subsided, the Germans were dumbstruck to witness the final breakout attempt. The camel brigade made a dash westward through the smoke of the battlefield. Concentrated German fire cut down the first waves of the ungainly beasts, and the rest scattered to flee in the opposite direction. The German tanks pursued, but the camels were nimble and could slip across the marshy ground that stopped tanks. The survivors outran the tanks, forded the Aksay, and got away.

Raus instantly termed the victory, 'The Cannae of Poklebin' after Hannibal's crushing encirclement of the Romans at that battle in 216 BC. He had every right. Most of two Soviet cavalry divisions and a tank brigade had been wiped out. The 4th Cavalry Corps had almost ceased to exist.[13] Stalingrad beckoned.

Stalingrad Front

8 December 1942

Zhukov radiated menace. General N. I. Trufanov had to summon every ounce of self-control to not go to pieces. He knew it was not just a rumour that Zhukov had personally shot generals who had failed in the first six months of the war. The gutting of his 4th Cavalry Corps two days ago was not exactly a success. 'Yes, Comrade Zhukov, I know the consequences of failure.'

'Let us hope you do. I have personally vouched for your conduct to the *Vozd*. Stalin has his eye on 51st Army and on you. And if you disappoint the *Vozd*, you won't have to worry too much about disappointing me.'

'Yes, I am aware, Comrade Zhukov.'

'Just to make sure you are, Trufanov, if the enemy penetrates your front, I have no doubt that you will be resting along the valiant dead of your army.' He paused only briefly, 'Dismissed.'

As he left, Trufanov's mind was working overtime in trying to deploy his remaining forces to stop the Fascists' should they attack. By the time he got back to his headquarters, he ordered a reinforcement for the remnant of 4th Cavalry Corps huddled off the German left flank. He wanted them to feel the threat of this force when they moved north against his four rifle divisions which he had deployed along the northern arm of the Aksay river. Behind the rifle divisions he would mass his trump, 13th Mechanised Corps, itself the strength of a German panzer division. They would not get through.

Zhukov, in the meantime, was thinking on a much grander scale. He had as acute a grasp of the possibilities presented by the dispositions of both sides as had von Manstein. As he had already pointed out to Stalin, the main German thrust for any relief effort would come from the direction of Kotelnikovo. That prophecy had seemed to come true in the last few days with the thrashing of a good part of 51st Army. But that was not entirely a bad thing. The more the enemy pressed toward Stalingrad, the deeper he would go into a potential trap. Operation LITTLE SATURN, scheduled for 19 December, was just such a trap. A great mass of Soviet reserves, three armies, was concentrating north of the enemy's left flank, ready to roll like an avalanche right over the 8th Italian Army and all the way to Rostov on Don and cut off not only Army Group Don but Army Group A still in the Caucasus. The front would be irreparably torn open. The Germans could not recover from such a blow.

Führer Headquarters, East Prussia

8 December 1942

As Zhukov was putting the fear of the *Vozd* into General Trufanov, the staff duty officer at the Wolf's Lair, Hitler's headquarters in an East Prussian pinewood, jumped up from his desk when handed a message from Army Group Don. He ran down the hallways to pass the message directly to Field Marshal Alfred Jodl, chief of the OKW. Jodl's reaction was as swift as he personally handed Hitler the message form.

'Mein Führer, Paulus has suffered a nervous collapse. 6th Army's chief physician thinks it may be a stroke as well. Von Manstein has put von Seydlitz in temporary command, pending your approval.'

'Well, Jodl, we were going to make that change in September.'

Jodl bristled ever so slightly. It was Jodl whose expected departure would have triggered the moveable chairs reassignment. Hitler briefly regretted that comment. He could be considerate of those slavishly loyal to him.' He went on. 'I like the man, a fighter. He knows how to handle a difficult situation and showed that at Demyansk. Signal von Manstein that the appointment is confirmed.'

He was pleased with the new possibilities Fate had just presented to him. Paulus had been a disappointment. He should have taken Stalingrad in September. A fighter like von Seydlitz would have done just that. The seeming hand of destiny had favoured him again, and it made him feel generous. He turned to Jodl, 'I must do something to strengthen the hand of this fighter. Signal von Manstein that I release Wiking and 7th Panzer Divisions to him for WINTER STORM. Let's see if we can pry Das Reich (2nd SS Panzer Division Das Reich) loose as well.'[14]

Had he known the content of the message carried by von Manstein's intelligence officer flying into the *Kessel's* only surviving airfield just then, his mood of generosity would have flared into rage.

Major Eismann was lucky to get into the *Kessel* alive. His transport was shredded by Soviet flak, chased by Soviet fighters, then bounced down the frozen runway at Pitnomnik airfield dodging the steady stream of Ju 52 transports taxing to take off, not to mention the burned-out carcasses of aircraft littering the field.

Eismann's orders were to sound out von Seydlitz on a breakout attempt. Von Manstein had literally not wasted a moment when informed of Paulus' collapse. After ordering von Seydlitz to replace Paulus, he turned to Eismann and said, 'Arrange to get into Stalingrad today.'

Von Manstein had prepared Eismann to expect a conversation of indirection. He did not know von Seydlitz personally, though he had heard the man was a decisive commander. So Eisman was more than surprised when von Seydlitz leaped to his feat at the mention of THUNDERCLAP.

'By damn, at last, someone with a brain! Yes, 6th Army will do its part, more than its part to get out of this rattrap.' He walked over to the situation map on the wall and pointed to the south-west part of the perimeter and then ran his finger down to Kotelnikovo. 'Just as I suggested. The only real way out.'

His chief of staff was already red-faced at the turn of the conversation. General Arthur Schmidt had dominated Paulus' weak personality and re-inforced his instincts to obey the Führer order. Schimdt was not well liked at 6th Army. He saw strong personalities as a threat, and in particular, he did not like von Seydlitz. 'We cannot disobey a Führer order,' he said in the tone that had never failed to cow Paulus. Bad choice. But he just kept making it worse.

The two stared at each other like two dogs ready to fight. Schmidt almost literally snarled, 'We must not retreat. It is the expression of fulfilment of our duty to Germany which dictates our position – even if the army is destroyed, the war can be and has to be won. We do this by holding out for a long time, occupying Russian forces...'[15]

Von Seydlitz said evenly, 'Suicide is an idiot's strategy, Schmidt. He knew a challenge to his authority when he saw it, but he would give Schmidt one last chance to back down.

'Schmidt, do you remember the story about the major and the Crown Prince in the 1870 War?' He did not pause for the man to answer. 'The major was sent off on a mission, and in accomplishing that mission, he ignored a far, far more important opportunity.'

Schmidt tried to interrupt, but von Seydlitz waved him to silence. 'Quite rightly, the Prince took the major to task. The major defended himself that His Majesty had made him an officer to obey his orders. The prince shot back that His Majesty had made him an officer to know when to *disobey* his orders.'

'That means, Schmidt,' as von Seydlitz closed the distance between them to invade Schmidt's personal space, 'I take full responsibility for this decision. I will save this army to fight another day.'

Schmidt's body language immediately told von Seydlitz that his chief of staff had backed down. 'Now this is how we will do our part in THUNDERCLAP.'[16]

Before the Battle

11 December 1942
Von Manstein now could only wait. Two days ago on 10 December he sent out the order for WINTER STORM. He reviewed the situation in his mind once more.

Hoth had two critical battles to fight. Along the River Chir sixty kilometres from the western end of the *Kessel*, ad hoc units of 6th Army (that had not been caught at Stalingrad) under Paulus' adjutant, Colonel Adam, had done more than miracles to hold on to a bridgehead north of the river. The arrival of reinforcements (11th Panzer, 336th Infantry, and 7th Luftwaffe Ground Divisions) had enabled XXXXVIII Panzer Corps to clear the foothills south-west of the Chir a week ago. With that flank secured the corps had crossed the Chir into the bridgehead. Leibstandarte and Grossdeutschland under II SS Panzer Corps, were concentrating to pass across the river as well. The two corps would then attack due east towards Stalingrad.

He hoped that they attracted Soviet reserves like a magnet. Already, 5th Tank Army and 5th Shock Army, two of the toughest Soviet formations were concentrated around the bridgehead and had renewed their attacks as soon as XXXXVIII Panzer Corps arrived.

The main blow would come from LVII Panzer Corps (6th and 23rd Panzer Divisions and parts of two Luftwaffe ground divisions) concentrated in the area of Kotelnikovo. They had some 250 tanks between them. He was encouraged by Raus' brilliant crushing of the enemy's cavalry corps the week before.

He worried less about 4th Panzer Army's two attacks than 6th Army's breakout efforts. Von Seydlitz had moved energetically to concentrate his XIV Panzer Corps (16th, 24th Panzer and 60th Motorised Infantry Divisions) and its 120 remaining tanks for the breakout on the south-western edge of the *Kessel*. He had withdrawn all tanks from fighting to defend the *Kessel* in order to spare them and their fuel for the breakout.

Von Seydlitz had been ruthless in preparing 6th Army for the breakout. He had clamped down on all signal communications from 6th Army to higher headquarters as well as within the army itself. No mention was to be made of the breakout in any signal communications. All instructions and reports would be in writing or by word of mouth with the intention of keeping OKW as much in the dark as the Soviets.

He had also ordered that all foodstuffs were to be expended with the breakout in mind. The men had to have the energy for this supreme effort. Nothing was to be hoarded. This battle would be as much about calories as the weight of artillery. A week of sufficient rations would give them a vital edge.

Most of the artillery had also either been moved or reorientated to support the breakout as well. There was also a thinning out of the defensive positions all around the perimeter as the shrunken divisions prepared to follow XIV Panzer Corps out of the pocket. Strong outposts would hold the perimeter long enough for the rest of the army to escape and then follow.

The logistics of this operation alone made it the trickiest of the entire battle. The Luftwaffe's air resupply was limited now to fuel and ammunition as food stocks were sufficient now that nothing had to be stored beyond the breakout date. Right behind LVII Panzer Corps 'were a mass of vehicles of every kind, trucks, of French, Czech and Russian manufacture, English Bedfords and American GMCs captured during the summer, agricultural tractors towing carts and limbers – were pressed into service by the resourceful Colonel Finkh – waited with 3,000 tons of supplies which were to be run through the corridor' to resupply 6th Army's depleted stocks as it made its way out of the *Kessel*.[17] Within the *Kessel*, surviving motor and horse-drawn transport were also being readied to follow the break out of the XIV Panzer Corps with the ten thousand wounded and 4,000 tons of carrying capacity.

Everything was to be abandoned but heavy weapons and hard-to-replace equipment. Space in trucks and wagons not needed for ammunition or the wounded would carry troops. 6th Army's own resources were to be expended completely in the breakout. Those resources would take XIV Panzer Corps thirty kilometres and perhaps a bit more. The rest of 6th Army would come to a halt behind it. It was, therefore, vital that XLVII Panzer Corps cut through to wherever 6th Army ground to a halt and immediately pushed its resupply column forward to revitalise the breakout force and get it going again.

Army Group Don staff and commander had held its breath in the first week of the month when the Soviets had launched determined attacks to split the *Kessel*. But the crisis had passed before von Seydlitz had begun his preparations for the breakout.

Everything was set except for the commitment of Wiking and 7th Panzer Divisions which were moving north from Army Group A. They would be available to either of Hoth's efforts, but the army group commander had retained them as front reserve to be allocated as the battle progressed. From now on he could only wait as events unfolded. He had only that one other major task and that was the major responsibility of any commander in battle – the allocation of the reserve that would decided the battle. One other thought hung constantly at the back of his mind, and one he had posed to Hitler. 'I ask that it be considered how the battle would develop if we commanded on the other side.'[18]

Zhukov was having similar thoughts in his own headquarters, although, unlike von Seydlitz, he never considered cutting off communications to Stalin. The Soviets had not missed the large German concentrations nor some of the movement within the trapped 6th Army. But what alarmed Stalin most was the arrival of II SS Panzer Corps near the Chir bridgehead. Instinctively, he believed that the arrival of this premier SS formation, Hitler's bodyguard division itself, as well as the redoubtable Grossdeutschland, was a clear sign of the main effort. Soviet intelligence also was reporting that 2nd SS Panzer Division Das Reich was also on the way to the front.[19]

His attention shifted from the threat coming from Kotelnikovo to the danger from the forces building up in the Chir bridgehead. Behind 5th Tank and 5th Shock Armies he ordered the concentration of the best fighting force in the Red Army and his prize STAVKA reserve – 2nd Guards Army. Had he known, General Trufanov would have breathed an immense sigh of relief to know the eye of the *Vozd* had wandered away from his 51st Army.

Zhukov, despite his misgivings over Stalin's conclusions, was confident that Operation LITTLE SATURN, scheduled for 19 December would simply scoop up these German reinforcements as they pressed deeper into its trap.

WINTER STORM *Begins*

12 December

Before dawn on 12 December, 6th Panzer Division lay closely concentrated in its Kotelnikovo bridgehead over the southern arm of the Aksay river. Its immediate objective to secure a bridgehead over the northern arm of the river sixty kilometres to the north. Its right flank would be guarded by 23rd Panzer Division. 'A sunny winter day dawned. The officers looked at their watches. They and their men were fully conscious of the significance of the approaching hour.'

Out of dawn's half-light the German artillery thundered at the Soviet rifle divisions strung out across the panzer corps' front, 'the signal for the Witches' Sabbath which followed.' So powerful and accurate had been the blow of the German artillery that the enemy's command and control was paralysed. As the Soviets reeled from the blow, 11th Panzer Regiment's tanks which had penetrated their front swung around and overran the enemy's gun batteries from the rear before they had fired an accurate shot. They first had savaged the horse-drawn limbers coming up to support their guns. Raus drove over the wreckage and left a vivid description of 11th Panzer's crushing attack:

Horse-drawn limbers and ammunition carriers, which had overturned, continued to lie about for hours afterwards. Horses which had survived were nibbling at the frozen steppe grass while standing in teams together with the bodies of those which had bled to death in the fire. Here and there, horse teams dragged a dead horse along. Blood on the snow marked their paths. The remnants of the Russian infantry had been scattered and had disappeared in the tall steppe grass as if they had been whisked away by a gust of wind.[20]

When 6th Panzer struck, it had hit the weakest part of any defence, the point where two enemy flanks join. That morning he had it between the already badly wounded 61st Cavalry Division and the 320th Rifle Division. By early morning 6th Panzer had driven forward thirty kilometres and overrun both the 302nd's and rifle corps headquarters. On its flank 23rd Panzer had penetrated eighteen kilometres and collapsed the rifle division facing it.

Rather than continuing the attack, Raus prudently turned to clear his left flank of the reinforced remnant of 4th Cavalry Corps and at the same time overrun the masses of Soviet vehicles and batteries attempting to flee the battlefield. The booty was immense in captured guns and horses as well as field kitchens from which the Germans grabbed a quick meal.

As the battle had begun that morning, a battalion of 6th Panzer's 4th Panzer grenadier Regiment had engaged the Soviet defenders of the fortified village of Verkhne-Yablochniy where the 4th Cavalry Corps was concentrated. Survivors from destruction of the infantry corps streamed into the village spreading panic which the attack of the German battalion only increased. The

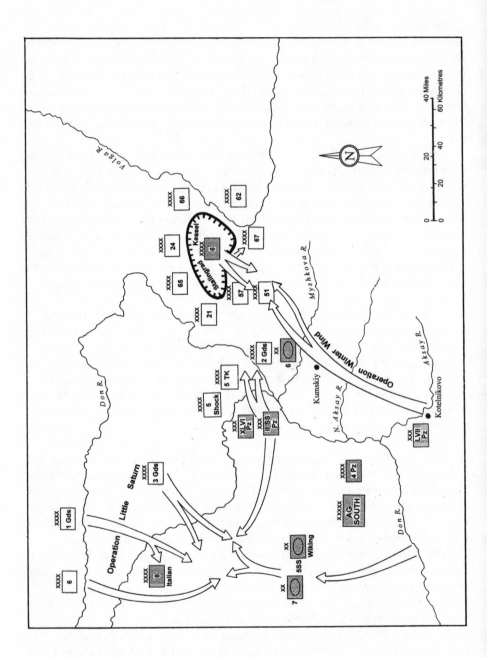

The Stalingrad breakout

response of the Soviet command was just as Raus hoped. They continued to reinforce the village and concentrate against the German infantry which was doing an excellent job of feigning determination to assault the village. All this time 11th Panzer was approaching from behind a small hill range. An hour before nightfall, the panzers charged over the last hill and down into the village. The Soviets with their weapons and tanks pointed the other way never had a chance. After its rampage pulverised the defenders, 11th Panzer returned the way it came leaving the infantry the now easy job of mopping up the village and rounding up the surviving Turkestan cavalry as prisoners.

Der Drehschlacht

13 December 1942
After a short rest 6th Panzer resumed its drive north and seized a bridgehead over the northern arm of the Aksay river where an all-arms battle group, Kampfgruppe Hünnersdorf, built around 11th Panzer Regiment formed and moved north again hidden by the morning fog. Their objective was the village of Verkniy-Kumiskiy nestled in a valley about fourteen kilometres away. Intelligence had informed LVII Panzer Corps that it would be going up against a force of 500 tanks, more than double its number. In addition to Trufanov's 13th Mechanised Corps, 51st Army had been reinforced with the front reserve, 4th Mechanised Corps. Raus knew there was more to the equation than numbers. German training, tactics, and communications were far superior and would be his hidden combat multipliers.

As the column barrelled north in the dissipating fog, reconnaissance reported the village empty, but another reconnaissance elements on the hills flanking the approaching column reported, 'There is a heavy concentration of hostile tanks in a broad depression south of here. More tanks are following.' The Soviets had responded quickly to the German advance, preparing to strike the German column from the flank while another brigade approached from the opposite direction. But the Germans were faster. As the Soviet brigade began to move out of the depression to attack the column, sixty panzers were waiting for them. A dozen Soviet tanks burst into flames from close range hits. The Soviets withdrew back into the depression to form a hedgehog defence which was quickly ringed in by the concentric fire of the Germans. The Germans turned it into a tank graveyard, in which seventy of the metal beasts perished in an hour.

While the fighting in the depression was underway, the rest of the German column entered the village. Unbeknownst to Raus, he had struck into the centre of the assembly area of the two Soviet mechanised corps. The attempt to flank his column was only the first of the violent Soviet reactions to this penetration. What followed was to become known as the *Drehschlacht* or 'revolving battle', one of the masterpiece feats of German arms.

Having poked himself into the Soviet hornet's nest, von Hünnerdorf now prepared to use the nest as pivot. While part of 11th Panzer was fighting in the depression, the rest of the regiment drove into the village just in time to drive off a Soviet tank attack. The panzer grenadiers arrived shortly to take over the defence of the village while von Hünnersdorf manoeuvred against three more Soviet tank brigades attempting to drive past the village to encircle the Germans. The German commander fought off every Soviet attempt to close a ring around the village. At some point, though, numbers would count. From the south, however, the Soviets saw the sixty German tanks fresh from their victory in the depression attacking north in their wedge formations. The Germans struck the Soviets and went for the flanks, eventually pressing them back until they snapped. The Soviets fled down a ravine sacrificing their flank and rearguards and leaving forty smoking tanks behind.

The Soviets were throwing everything into the battle but in an unco-ordinated manner. Had all their forces struck at once, even Kampfgruppe Hünnersdorf's skill would not have availed. But they did not, and the German colonel dominated the field. Informed by air reconnaissance that a strong force was coming from the west due to arrive in an hour, he decided to use that hour to best advantage and turned on the mechanised brigade then attacking from the north-east. Again employing stealth, he slipped his panzers behind the approaching tank element of the brigade and shot it to pieces from the rear. The motorised infantry following the tanks fled in the opposite direction.

Von Hünnersdorf had left a detachment of tanks to block the path of another Soviet mechanised brigade coming from the north-east. The panzers stopped the Soviet tanks cold but began to take losses from the skilfully led enemy motorised infantry and anti-tank units which slipped around the Germans and were inflicting losses. Von Hünnersdorf radioed to hold on. Help was coming. He pivoted his relief force through the village which was itself under heavy tank attack. The lead panzers smashed the attacking Soviets as the rest of the column followed to strike straight north into the flank of the mechanised brigade struggling against the panzer blocking force. They retreated leaving thirty tanks on the field.

While the panzers were driving the mechanised brigade survivors off the field, other Soviet forces had resumed attacks on the village from the west. T34s and combat patrols had already entered the village but were wiped out by the panzer grenadiers. Air reconnaissance also reported strong Soviet tank forces coming from the west to cut off the village and the *Kampfgruppe* from the south.

Von Hünnersdorf threw his panzers, minus a reserve, directly into the path of the Soviets, and both sides reached the dominant terrain feature of Point 140 at the same time. But the Germans knocked the Soviets back and put a hundred tank guns on line to play havoc with the enemy's tanks. The Soviets fed more and more tanks into the fight, but each attack melted back in the face of well-aimed German fire. Finally, the Soviets massed their entire force for one enormous thrust. Now von Hünnersdorf played his trump. He man-oeuvred his panzer reserve into the flank of the attacking Soviet mass and almost immediately threw it off balance. As the Soviets hesitated, the main German tank line attacked. The Soviets fled, leaving the field full of wrecked tanks.

While this fight was going on, the defenders of the village were being pressed hard by Soviet attacks from every side. Guns and anti-tank weapons were lost as tank after tank entered the village. German panzer grenadiers and engineers with magnetic anti-tank mines killed every one. But for every one destroyed another rolled into the village along with dismounted motorised infantry. The panzer commander had heard their calls for help as his own battle was underway, and as soon as the Soviet tanks were driven back, he turned his regiment northward and broke the Soviet encirclement of the village.

The ground battle had been equalled in ferocity by the battle in the air as the German and Soviet air forces in large numbers fought it out in the skies. The swirling ground battle made it difficult for the air forces to directly support the armies struggling below. But they had each other to savage, and the countless burning hulks around the village were matched by planes flaming through the sky to plummet earthward. But the German Luftwaffe was as successful in the air as the army was on the ground. The planes reeling through air were as much a revolving battle, or *Drehschlacht*, as the panzer struggle had been amid the snow and steppe grass.

Now Raus revealed his greatness as a commander. He ordered the *Kampfgruppe* to abandon the village and return to the bridgehead. The rest of the division was still heavily engaged south of the river against remnants of the rifle corps, and there was insufficient ammunition and fuel to continue operations that far from the main body. Besides, he reasoned, terrain was not important. The *Kampfgruppe* had achieved its purpose by savaging the enemy armoured forces concentrated to the north, destroying over 250 tanks to the fewer than thirty lost by 11th Panzer.

'Der Manstein Kommt!'

13 December 1942
The rumble of the guns of the two relieving attacks could be heard by the men of 6th Army. The cry went from man to man, *'Der Manstein kommt!'* (Manstein comes!). They had been keyed to high pitch by the organisation for the breakout, and now the rumble of the guns made that expectation a reality. Almost a week of near-normal rations had put energy back into them, enough energy to light the fires of desperate effort. All through the day they could hear the rumble from the south-west and west in between the Soviet attacks as they put the finishing touches on their breakout preparations.

At the moment 11th Panzer disappeared in the morning fog leading to its *Drehschlacht*, the guns of 6th Army opened a concentrated fire on the two divisions of the Soviet 57th Army hemming in the *Kessel* from the south-west.

XIV Panzer Corps' tanks were already moving forward as the first rounds struck the Soviet positions. The Russians were not used to such a heavy fire. The German gunners had been on such a short allowance for so long that the Soviets no longer felt they had to worry about the normal punch of German artillery. But the order now was to use it up in one crushing drumbeat. The Soviet positions had had to be hacked out of the frozen steppe and were none too deep or well protected. Even Russians needed tools to deal with their winters, and too few had been provided. The Soviet attacks on the *Kessel* in the first week of the month had been costly for 57th Army. The after-action report had stated, 'artillery and infantry did not interact very well when storming the enemy defence line... Soldiers were not well enough instructed on the need to dig trenches.' And this failure had led to 'irreparable losses from German tanks and aeroplanes'.[21] Those losses had not been made up when the 6th Army's artillery started working the shallow Soviet positions that morning.

VIII Flieger Corps' Stuka dive-bombers had taken off at first light to be able to add their weight to 6th Army's guns as the panzers broke out of the city ruins aiming for the positions of the 169th Rifle Division. By mid-morning 16th Panzer Division panzers had broken through and were fighting a running battle with 57th Army's reserve, 90th Tank Brigade. The Austrian 44th (Hoch und Deutschmeister) Infantry Division[22] widened the breach and held it against local counter-attacks as the *Kampfgruppe* of 60th Motorised Division followed the panzers.

Like a dam with a breach, the force of the flood pouring through widened that breach more and more as von Seydlitz forced the pace of the infantry *Kampfgruppen* sent through the broken Soviet front. The breach widened again early that afternoon as the 422nd Rifle Division gave way in the face of attacks by the 24th Panzer Division and the *Kampfgruppe* of the 297th Infantry Division. The Stalingrad Front commander then threw in his last reserves, 235th Tank Brigade and 87th Rifle Division. The fighting was bitter and to the death as the Red Army tankers threw themselves into the path of the Germans. The rifle division came in waves. The artillery of both sides was firing until the barrels glowed. The Germans pressed on despite losses, but they were echeloned in depth, each formation eagerly waiting its turn. The Russian *Hiwis* among them fought with superhuman determination. For them it was truly victory or death. 57th Army, however, had shot its bolt. Already weakened in the last week's fighting, it came apart, its divisions overrun and its tank brigades burned out.

The Soviet front had been broken. Von Seydlitz placed himself along the main route of advance personally hurrying the formations along as they trudged out of the city that only a short time before had seemed to be the army's tomb. Now more than two hundred thousand Germans, Russian *Hiwis*, and Rumanians were on the move south-west. 6th Army's artillery turned to defend the fighting withdrawal of the strong outposts that had kept the Soviets at bay. They could hold out no longer as the rest of the Soviet Stalingrad Front had leapt on the *Kessel* as soon as the breakout became apparent.

XIV Panzer Corps' divisions were now moving through open country shooting up the rear areas of 57th Army and Stalingrad Front. By nightfall they had made fifteen kilometres, stopping only long enough to tank on the last of 6th Army's carefully hoarded fuel. Advance elements just kept moving forward. Behind them in the frigid night endless columns trudged with the city at their backs. The city burned in the night providing an eerie backdrop as they disappeared into the dark.

Moscow, 14 December 1942
Stalin was in a fury. He screamed at Zhukov over the phone. His prize of prizes had just broken out of the trap while the entire front from the Chir to the Aksay seemed to have come apart. The bad news just kept coming in – 57th Army essentially destroyed, 51st Army suffered heavy losses, 5th Tank and 5th Shock Armies were locked in a bitter struggle with the two German corps attacking from the Chir bridgehead and were being driven back. The only reserve, 2nd Guards Army was caught hanging between the Chir fighting and the breakout of 6th Army. *Shto dyelat?* What to do? Lenin's famous question now hung in the air.

Zhukov did not lose his nerve. 'Comrade Stalin, we must commit 2nd Guards Army to hold fast the Fascists attacking from the west.'

Stalin could barely contain his anger. '5th Tank and 5th Shock will just have to hang on. The enemy's 6th Army is getting away. The only way to stop it is throw in 2nd Guards Army. Now that they are in the open, most of them on foot, we have a splendid opportunity to run them down.'

Zhukov picked up the threat in his argument. 'It does not matter that they have broken out. They have nowhere to go. They are still in the bag, but it is just a much larger bag. We must begin Operation LITTLE SATURN immediately. We are not as ready as we would like, but now is the time that the enemy has committed his forces to battle. We shall crush the Italian 8th Army on the upper Don and sweep down upon their rear and trap the entire Army Group. The only enemy forces that could interfere with this move are locked in fighting along the Chir. By committing 2nd Guards we make it impossible for them to redeploy in time.'

Then he threw in a sop to Stalin's prize. 'Remember, Comrade Stalin, 51st Army still lies in the path of the enemy. Trufanov will delay them long enough for our larger trap to catch them all. He still has two mechanised and one rifle corps.' Zhukov did not add that these forces had already been through the Raus meat grinder.

Army Group Don Headquarters

15–17 December 1942
That morning von Manstein fulfilled his two most important roles as a senior commander. The easier of the two was the commitment of Wiking and 7th

Panzer Divisions to the Chir fighting. The Soviets seemed to have committed their reserve in that direction, and he wanted to make sure they kept it there. It would also give him a mass of manoeuvre should the enemy try to enlarge the battlefield.

The second and infinitely more difficult role was that of taking responsibility. Despite the best effort of 6th Army and Army Group Don Headquarters to block outgoing communications of the breakout had reached the Führer Headquarters. Hitler himself had demanded an explanation and was flying out for a personal meeting. Presented with a fait accompli of the breakout, even he could not order 6th Army back into the city. Von Manstein would throw himself upon the defence of nothing succeeds like success.

To say that the meeting was tense was an understatement of the ages. But the edge of Hitler's anger had been taken off by the linking up of 6th Army with LVII Corps. Raus' success in the *Drehschlacht* and von Seydlitz's in the breakout forced Trufanov to fight front and back and be, therefore, too weak in both directions. Raus had broken through to the Myshkova river barely ten kilometres from 6th Army's lead elements on the 15th. A good part of 51st Army found itself trapped in the Myshkova *Kessel* as the rest of it disintegrated the next day. It was just in time, too, for 6th Army had run bone dry on fuel. The Germans were able to film the meeting of the two forces which made for splendid propaganda on the home front. The convoys of resupply vehicles passed through XLVII Panzer Corps' lines to replenish the exhausted but delirious survivors of 6th Army. The men of 6th Panzer Division were quick to tell their comrades in 6th Army who had commanded the relief with the phrase, '*Raus zieht heraus!*' Raus pulls you through! Von Manstein was careful to tell Hitler of the critical contribution in this victory made by the Tiger battalion he had personally ordered to the front. Hitler was further assuaged by the 30,000 Soviet prisoners from the encirclement of 51st Army.

Whatever anger Hitler felt was entirely diverted the next day by the Soviet LITTLE SATURN Offensive. The Italians gave way to no one's surprise, but enough units hung together to slow the Soviets. Instead of then driving through the empty rear area of Army Group Don, the three attacking Soviet armies were intercepted by Wiking and 7th Panzer Divisions quickly diverted from their march to join the fighting on the Chir. They struck 3rd Guards Army in the flank and pushed it back. II SS Panzer Corps followed, and LITTLE SATURN ground to halt in the manoeuvre battles in which the Germans still excelled. By the end of the month the front had stabilised again. A crushing disappointment fell upon Russia as its great triumph at Stalingrad evaporated on the frozen steppes. An opposite wave of euphoria swept Germany.

Hitler, of course, made sure he got all the credit for 6th Army's rescue in which von Manstein and von Seydlitz were tactful enough to oblige him. He did, however, hold a grudge. Von Seydlitz was transferred to command the German garrison of Crete. Von Manstein found a command in France of benefit to his health. Stalin's grudges had a harder edge. Zhukov was arrested and shot. Trufanov, however, was outside of the *Vozd's* revenge. He had taken

Zhukov's advice and died on the Myshkova river.[23]

The more than 200,000 Germans and Russian *Hiwis* of 6th Army spent a very merry Christmas either on leave or recuperating behind the front. The rebuilt army was to play the decisive role under the command of General der Panzertruppen Raus in the victory at Kursk the following June. Soviet losses were to be so heavy that Stalin had sued for peace which was signed in the Treaty of Stockholm that August.[24]

The Reality

The reality of the Stalingrad campaign was that Hitler's grandiose ambitions were supported on a shoestring, and it was in that city on the Volga that that frayed shoestring finally snapped. He committed his most powerful offensive formation in the 1942 summer offensive, 6th Army, to the battle for Stalingrad when the city should have been outflanked by a crossing of the Volga. As long as the Germans made the Soviets play a game of manoeuvre, they kept both the initiative and the advantage which masked serious German manpower shortages. Once 6th Army was locked into city fighting to slake Hitler's desire to humble Stalin by taking his eponymous city by storm, those advantages were cast away. Soviet mass now dropped a huge weight in the scales. The time wasted in the summer and autumn fighting for the city allowed the Soviets to rapidly build up their forces for their great counterstroke of 19 November, Operation URANUS, which trapped 6th Army and a good part of 4th Panzer Army in the Stalingrad *Kessel*.

Von Manstein would later state that had Paulus taken the bit between his teeth to breakout immediately, that operation would have been within 6th Army's combat power at that time, but the consummate staff officer *asked* for permission, and the opportunity evaporated as Hitler emphatically slammed that door shut.

After that the lack of reserves and Hitler's reluctance to commit them early and in the mass necessary to be effective doomed the relief efforts that von Manstein cobbled together. Raus' 6th Panzer Division did indeed perform miracles on the battlefield as this story accurately portrays and eventually drove to within thirty kilometres of the *Kessel* on 24 December. The launching of Operation LITTLE SATURN on 19 December drove deep into Army Group Don's rear forcing the abandonment both of 4th Panzer Army's relief efforts and the dispatch of 6th Panzer Division to shore up the collapsing front to the east.

In this alternate reality, Paulus does the 6th Army his greatest service by having a breakdown early enough for his aggressive senior corps commander, von Seydlitz, to organise the army for a breakout which he had been incessantly urging since the encirclement. Hitler did have a high regard for him and had, as in this story, did plan in September to put him in command after bringing Paulus up to OKW. Von Seydlitz's assumption of command at this point would have been 6th Army's last chance to organise itself for a breakout in conjunction with LVII Panzer Corps' advance. The Soviet Stalingrad Front commander was especially worried about this since his 57th Army, the logical breakout point, had been severely weakened. With a supreme effort, 6th Army probably had the power to break through 57th Army and advance the last 30 kilometres to meet 6th Panzer Division's spearhead.

However, even with this scenario, two critical obstacles remained – the commitment of the Soviet reserve, Stalin's prized 2nd Guards Army, and the launching of LITTLE SATURN. In reality Stalin's commitment of 2nd Guards Army to stop LVII Panzer Corps long enough for LITTLE SATURN to make WINTER STORM completely untenable, was decisive, just as Zhukov had advised.

In this alternate scenario, the Germans are able to unhinge these calculations by drawing enough reserves into the theatre to draw 2nd Guards away from XLVII Panzer Corps and to prevent LITTLE SATURN from collapsing the eastern end of Army Group Don's front. That is the rub. In reality the reserves were few and Hitler stingy with them. Only the timely concentration of reserves could have checked the strategic threat of LITTLE SATURN. In fact, the reserves used in this scenario are the very ones Hitler decided to use on 1 January 1943, far too late.

The personalities of the senior German officers were also critical to the failure of 6th Army to escape. Von Seydlitz who had the moral courage and ability to breakout, remained in a subordinate position. After 6th Army's surrender, his rage against Hitler caused him to join the League of German Officers which called for the overthrow of Hitler and the Nazi state. It was a Soviet propaganda ploy that did the gullible von Seydlitz no good in the end. In 1950 he was purged and thrown into the GULAG, only to be released in 1955 with the other surviving German PoWs. He returned to Germany despised by his former army colleagues and denied the restoration of retired rank and pension by the new *Bundeswehr*.[25]

Paulus' nature as a corporate man ensured that he would never act on his own, and he was convinced of Hitler's infallibility. Von Manstein hinted strongly that Paulus should act on his own, but he would not give such an order himself, despite his loathing for Hitler's incompetence. Thus Stalingrad became not only the grave of the 6th Army but that of the most noble traditions of the German officer corps – the acceptance of responsibility and the initiative embodied in the true story that stated, 'His Majesty made you an officer to know when to *disobey* your orders.'

Notes
1   Beevor, 1999, p. 254.
2   Ibid, pp. 65–6. It was actually Field Marshal von Bock, Army Group South Commander, who convinced the Army chief of staff, Halder, to urge Hitler to mount this audacious counter-attack. However, this did not stop Hitler from claiming the idea as his own.

3   Tsouras, 2000, p. 250.

4   Beevor, ibid., p. 281n. By 6 December the number reported had fallen to 20,300, due probably to heavy casualties and covert incorporation directly into German units.

5   Field-Marshal Lord Carver, 'Manstein,' Barnett, 1989, pp. 233–5.

*6   George S. Patton, *Carthage Must be Destroyed: The US Army in the African Campaign*, Boston: Beacon Hill Books, 1949, p. 231. Had the Allied invasion of North Africa not been postponed until the end of November, it is likely that these divisions would have been used to occupy Vichy France rather than be available for transfer to the Eastern Front.

7   Panzer grenadier Division Grossdeutschland was the German Army's premier division and received priority in the replacement of men and equipment even ahead of the SS. It was formed in April 1939 from Wach Regiment Berlin, the German Army's guard regiment for the capital. In June Hitler ordered it redesignated as *Grossdeutschland* (Greater Germany).

8   Clausewitz, 1976.

9   Raus, 1996, pp. 73, 77.

10   *Vozd*, the Russian word meaning, 'Great War Leader' or as more emotionally translated in the movie *Enemy at the Gates* as 'The Boss'.

11   Raus, 2002, p. 107.

*12   Hermann Hoth, *Stalingrad Victory*, New York: Portland Publishers, Inc., 1949, p. 279. Hoth is our only authority for this conversation with von Manstein who omits it, other than the merest operational details, in his own memoirs.

13   Raus, 2002, pp. 121–2. Both Soviet division commanders had been killed, and the corps commander chased across the Aksay barely escaping capture. The German counted 2,000 captured horses, fifty-six knocked-out tanks, and thousands of prisoners.

14   SS Panzer grenadier Division Wiking (Viking) had been recruited from admirers and anti-communists of Norway and Denmark.

15   Carrell, 1993, p. 338.

*16   Walter von Seydlitz-Kurzbach, *Mein Tat für Deutschland*, Berlin: Potsdamer Verlag, 1953, pp. 201–11.

17   Clark, 1985, pp. 266–7.

18   Ziemke, 1968, p. 71.

19   Ibid., p. 73.

20   Raus, 2002, p. 128.

21   Beevor, ibid., pp. 278–9.

22   Ibid., p. 65. The 44th Infantry Division had been raised around the ancient Austrian Hoch und Deutschmeister Regiment.

*23   In the Treaty of Stockholm, the Soviet Union lost the Baltic States, Ukraine, Belarus and Russia all the way to the lower Volga. It proved fatal to Stalin's prestige. He was overthrown six months later by the Red Army. A subsequent short civil war between the Red Army and NKVD ended the existence of the latter.

*24   Erhard Raus, *Kurskschalcht und Deutscher Sieg*, Vienna: Hoch und Deutschmeister Verlag, 1950, pp. 309–12. Raus' book (published by Infantry Press, Washington, DC, in 1952 as *Kursk: War Winning Victory*) is considered the best written account of this decisive battle. In this book Raus does not discuss his subsequent role as Chief of Staff, OKH, in the overthrow of the Himmler regime in 1948, the year after Hitler's death from Parkinson's disease.

25   Beevor, ibid., pp. 430–31.

Bibliography

Barnett, Correlli (ed.), *Hitler's Generals*, New York: Grove Weidenfeld, 1989.

Beevor, Antony, *Stalingrad, Fateful Siege: 1942–1943*, New York: Viking Press, 1998, Penguin Books, 1999.

Carrell, Paul. *Stalingrad: Defeat of the German 6th Army*, Atglen, PA: Schiffer Military/Aviation History, 1993.

Clark, Alan, *Barbarossa: The Russian-German Conflict 1941–1945*, (New York: Macmillan, 1985.

Clausewitz, Carl von *On War*, trs. Michael Howard and Peter Paret, Princeton, NH: Princeton University Press, 1976.

Raus, Erhard et al. (Peter Tsouras, ed.), *The Anvil of War: German Generalship in the Defense on the Eastern Front*, London: Greenhill Books, 1994.

Raus, Erhard, *Fighting in Hell: The German Ordeal on the Eastern Front*, London: Greenhill Books, 1996

Raus, Erhard, *Panzers on the Eastern Front: Erhard Raus and His Panzer Divisions in Russia 1941–1945*, London: Greenhill Books, 2002.

Tsouras, Peter G., *The Great Patriotic War*, London: Greenhill Books, 1992.

Tsouras, Peter G. *The Greenhill Dictionary of Military Quotations*, London: Greenhill Books, 2000.

Ziemke, Earl F, *Stalingrad to Berlin: The German Defeat in the East*, Washington, DC: Office of the Chief of Military History, 1968.

10 For Want of an Island
The Fall of Malta and German Victory
John D. Burtt

June 1942

A sombre group met at the Governor's Palace in Malta's fortress capital of Valetta. The reason for their graveness: two supply convoys had attempted to break the siege of Malta that month; HARPOON from Gibraltar and VIGOROUS from Alexandria. Of seventeen merchant ships in the attempt, only one slipped through the gauntlet of Axis aircraft and ships – and at last report had hit a mine just off the coast.

Lord Gort,[1] the new governor of Malta on the island only a month, now faced his worst decision. The entry of the final member of the council, the Royal Navy's Vice Admiral Sir Ralph Leatham, interrupted his thoughts.

'Well?' Gort demanded brusquely.

Leatham shook his head, 'Complete loss, sir. The *Orari*[2] is on fire and sinking. We've lost the Polish destroyer and there's damage to three others in that minefield. Salvage possibilities are nil.'

'And the ships from Alexandria?'

'Turned back,' Leatham replied.

'What does London have to say?'

Leatham sighed heavily, 'They regret that another convoy is impossible until mid-August at the earliest. These two operations showed far more support and escort strength is needed. They have too many commitments elsewhere to provide that strength right now.'

Gort turned to his lieutenant governor, 'Sir Edward, can we hold out that long?'

Sir Edward Jackson looked at the notebook in his hands. 'Doubtful, sir. Fodder and white oils will last into July. We are virtually out of all coal now.' He looked up. 'Food – wheat, flour and everything else – will be gone by the end of this month if we continue on the current ration.'

'If we cut it?'

'Cutting the daily bread rations to fourteen ounces will stretch food to mid-July, sir, but...'

'Yes,' Gort interrupted. 'I understand what that means.' He looked at the other members of the council. 'Gentlemen?'

Air Vice Marshal Hugh Lloyd shrugged, 'RAF is in relatively good shape; the Spitfires are more than holding their own. Jerry appears to be focused on Rommel's doings in the desert around Tobruk. We have enough fuel to keep flying for a while.'

Gort nodded and turned away, deep in thought. After a few moments, he turned back. 'My inclination is to fight, gentlemen. Fight to the end. I was told at Gibraltar that I might be coming to oversee another capitulation. But I didn't come to the Island to give her away, not after France...'[3]

Major General Beak cut in, 'Army's ready when you need us, Lord Gort. If Jerry comes, we'll give him a fight.'

'I appreciate the sentiment, General. And I might just borrow a few of your lads and sail off to Sicily to raise what havoc I can.' He sighed. 'But without food...' Gort shook his head. He knew General Beak meant it and that the four brigades on the island would fight; but he also knew the soldiers practised 'sleep parades' to conserve their energy from their meagre rations. A quarter of a million civilians on the island got even less food. 'Send priority to London: Deeply regret failure of VIGOROUS and HARPOON. If no relief received in thirty days, all stores will be exhausted and result inevitable.' He paused. 'Gentlemen, I want you each to prepare potential action lists for your services should surrender become necessary. Have it at this office tomorrow.

'Sir Edward, who is our most prominent clergyman?'

Jackson frowned for a moment, then said, 'Probably Monsignor Salomone, the parish priest in Mgiarr. Known as Dun Edgar to most. Highly respected and revered. Why?'

Gort nodded. 'If we must open surrender discussions, the Church will be our voice. It will help soothe the hurt among the people. Please set up an appointment at his church for tomorrow evening. We must be ready.'[4]

Situation

Early in 1942, the Allies found themselves in dire straits. In the Pacific, Japan took Singapore in February, controlled the Dutch East Indies and its oil by March and finished the Philippines in April. In Europe, Germany successfully survived the Soviet's winter offensive in Russia and struck back hard. In the Mediterranean, the island of Malta came under renewed assault by the Luftwaffe after air and naval units based on the island played a part in strangling Rommel's supply lines to Africa in late 1941. The island's condition worsened under the deluge of bombs; her offensive and defensive power waned and the population starved. A resurgent Desert Fox took back most of the territory he had lost to the British and both sides faced each other at Gazala.

As early as January 1941, prior to the US being an 'active' participant of the war, the two country's leaders, President Franklin D. Roosevelt and Prime

Minister Winston Churchill had agreed that Germany should be dealt with first, then Japan. Despite American public opinion and outcry following the Pearl Harbor disaster, Roosevelt held to that overall goal. To coordinate plans, the two countries created the Combined Chiefs of Staff, headed up by General George Marshall, chairman of the US's newly created Joint Chiefs of Staff, and General Sir Alan Brooke, Chief of the Imperial General Staff.[5] But despite the common goal, severe differences in strategy led to acrimonious debate.

Marshall advocated a direct approach: build up a huge force in Britain, land in France and drive straight into Germany. It was basic Clausewitzian warfare: concentrate at the decisive point directed at the enemy centre of gravity. All other peripheral operations were extraneous to that drive and should be minimised if not eliminated altogether.

Great Britain, on the other hand, remembered all too vividly the effects such a strategy had during World War I – trench warfare and almost a million dead. Churchill and Brooke did not want to bludgeon straight into France and recreate the Great War's western-front abattoir. They wanted to secure the Mediterranean first, taking North Africa to expand the potential for military operations the length of the Axis European holdings. Doing so would secure the Middle East (and its oil) as well as access to India.

Stalin's Soviet Union complicated the debate. Russian winter counter-attacks hurt the German Army, but German ripostes returned the favour. Both Britain and the United States worried about the ability of the Russians to withstand the German offensive they all knew was coming. Keeping the Russians in the fight was paramount. Convoys through the North Atlantic helped, despite the horrendous losses suffered from U-boat attacks. Keeping German forces occupied with other fronts remained a requirement.

In April 1942, Marshall arrived in London bearing the US plan for Western Europe, known afterwards as the 'Marshall Memorandum'. The plan (written by General Dwight D. Eisenhower, chief of Marshall's new Operations division) called for a massive build-up of American forces in Britain (Operation BOLERO) with the goal of a cross-Channel attack by eighteen British and thirty American divisions in spring 1943 (ROUNDUP). The plan also included a smaller assault that could be launched in 1942 (SLEDGEHAMMER) in case German morale collapsed or the Soviet Union appeared to be in grave peril. To Marshall's mind the plan had much going for it: a build-up of force in Britain would get Hitler's attention, drawing him away from Russia, Great Britain's airfield's were plentiful and capable of supporting (and defending) the attackers, and it was the shortest distance between where the allies were and where they needed to go to finish the war.

The Marshall Memorandum put the British in an awkward position. Brooke felt just as strongly as Marshall did about the concentration of force, and both he and Churchill realised that to finally win the war, they would have to put 'boots on the ground' in Europe. But both also saw the plan as premature, leading to disaster. Astute enough to realise that they could not simply reject the plan outright (such a rebuff might make the US turn fully towards the Pacific) they

245

chose an indirect approach: press for action in North Africa (Operation GYMNAST), pay lip service to ROUNDUP/SLEDGEHAMMER, and work to undercut the plan. Churchill knew that Roosevelt wanted American troops in action against the Germans as soon as possible to prevent added pressure for more action in the Pacific. Marshall felt strongly that operations in North Africa would undercut preparations for ROUNDUP. Brooke countered that not invading North Africa allowed the Japanese and Germans to conceivably cut off the entire Middle East.[6]

Debate raged for months. Inserted into the mix was the May visit by Soviet Foreign Minister Vyacheslav M. Molotov who demanded a second front from the Western allies that would drain forty German divisions from the Eastern Front – and recognition of Stalin's Baltic and Polish land-grab prior to the German BARBAROSSA invasion. He got soothing words and no real promises, but the visit added political pressure onto the military planners.

One effective British argument came from Lord Louis Mountbatten, then Director of Combined Operations, who on a trip to Washington, stressed the lack of enough landing craft currently to support a cross-Channel attack. He stated authoritatively that with current craft, it would take twenty-one days to fully land six divisions in France – enough time to allow the Germans to massively respond. This estimate came directly from the planning for an operation he was doing to land a large raiding force to briefly capture the French port of Dieppe in early July. If he wanted American troops in action soon, Mountbatten told the president, attack in North Africa.

Events began to overtake the discussions by the time Churchill himself came to Washington in mid-June. In the Pacific, Japan's advance stalled with the carrier battle in the Coral Sea and stopped forever by the carrier ambush at Midway that saw four front-line carriers and most of their aircraft and crews destroyed. However, in Africa Rommel struck the Gazala line in late May, decisively beating the British 8th Army.

On 21 June, while at lunch with Roosevelt, authorities informed Churchill that Tobruk, the African port famed for withstanding Rommel for seven months in 1941, collapsed in a single day. Over 33,000 troops surrendered. Appended to the news, all but ignored, was the information that the June convoys to Malta failed to get any supplies to the island. As Rommel pursued the British into Egypt, a North African operation appeared to be inevitable to stave off complete disaster.

Japan's Midway defeat led to renewed demands from Australian Prime Minister Curtain, General Douglas MacArthur and Chief of Naval Operations Admiral Ernest King, for Pacific reinforcements to take advantage of the change in initiative in that theatre. Marshall began leaning that way as well as planning for GYMNAST appeared more and more to threaten any cross-Channel operation in 1943. He foresaw that that it would be difficult to disengage from Mediterranean operations once the US had troops committed there. However, Roosevelt, aware of Churchill's tentative political situation, spawned by the Tobruk disaster, stood firmly for GYMNAST as the way to get Americans into combat against the European Axis and to support Churchill.

Marshall was about to admit defeat and sanction an operation he didn't believe in, when events changed the strategic picture once again.

Malta

Churchill travelled home in early July to face a parliamentary vote of confidence, a political move by his opponents to take advantage of the Tobruk disaster. Almost as soon as he landed, he was given Gort's assessment of Malta's situation – more supply by 15 July or surrender is inevitable. The ultimatum was something Churchill did not need. Maltese resilience and fortitude under siege remained an increasingly bright spot through Britain's dark year. In April, as a gesture, King George awarded the entire island the George Cross, Britain's highest non-military honour, to 'bear witness to a heroism and devotion that will long be famous in history'. Churchill immediately sent a strongly worded cable to the Royal Navy, stating another convoy must be attempted; 'Gort,' he signalled, 'must be able to tell the population the Navy will never abandon Malta.'

Churchill survived his vote of confidence 475 to 25 in Parliament, but Malta did not survive the cabinet meeting soon after. Judging that the Royal Navy's commitment of getting convoys through to Russia, to keep Stalin's forces fighting, to be more important than Malta's survival, they prioritised the Navy's assets accordingly. They simply hoped that Gort would be able to tighten Maltese belts sufficiently to survive until August.

He couldn't. On 15 July, 1942 he sent his chosen emissary to Rome to open surrender negotiations. A week later, Malta surrendered: surviving ships and aircraft flew out, ammunition stores destroyed, a single battalion of troops ferried out in fast minelayers and submarines. The Maltese were torn between the anger and frustration of watching Italian warships sail into Grand Harbour, and relief at the food-filled freighters that accompanied them.

Britain had lost her last bastion in the middle of the Mediterranean.

The surrender of Malta had a strong impact on the war, but not in the way the participants immediately anticipated.

Axis leaders felt an initial euphoria in that, first, they did not have Malta-based forces preying on their supply lines, second, they did not have to keep large air forces tied down to keep the island under pressure, and finally, they did not have to invade the island. Both German and Italian commanders assumed that the surrender solved many of the supply problems they had encountered in Africa.

They were wrong.

After taking Tobruk, Rommel advanced another 300 miles, before halting near El Alamein inside Egypt, a mere eighty miles from Cairo. His supply line for his exhausted troops remained under considerable pressure from the

Egypt-based British Desert Air Force, as well as the newly arriving US 13th Air Force. Key to his problem: the lack of transportation of supply from Axis ports, and the vulnerability of those ports to attack.[7] At best his nearest port, Tobruk, could handle only 1,000–2,000 tons of cargo a day; and an air attack on 6 August reduced that to 600 tons for far too long. Malta's capitulation made the sea-lanes to Benghasi and Tripoli safer for Axis shipping, but getting those supplies to Rommel's eight Italian and three German divisions was difficult, especially for units low on internal transport. Although he had entered Egypt confident of driving straight through to the Nile, he began to realise the magnitude of his supply problem.

For the Allies, Malta became another piece of bad news, bringing added pressure on Churchill. However, his opponents, having failed spectacularly in their bid to oust him in the early July vote of confidence, decided not to try again so soon. The British Prime Minister gained a brief reprieve to reverse his political fortunes. He pressed the Americans to work actively on a North Africa invasion. In Washington, Malta's fall added to the pressure Roosevelt felt to get US troops into action soon to help support Churchill and keep resurgent Pacific-ophiles, like Admiral King, at bay. He applied that pressure to Marshall, who reluctantly posted Eisenhower to England to plan the North African invasion. Marshall, still convinced that a North African invasion would mire US troops in the Mediterranean far beyond any 1943 French invasion, began planning on surreptitiously slowing the rate of troops into Britain through his BOLERO plan. However, with Malta lost, he sensed an opportunity to cut the involvement in the Mediterranean. Pointing out that without Malta in Allied hands, additional operations against Axis holdings in the theatre – Sicily, Greece, Italy itself – became more difficult, he advised Roosevelt (and ordered Eisenhower) that ROUNDUP planning should be continued.

Roosevelt, happy with Marshall finally 'on board' with a North African operation, concurred. He also remembered Mountbatten's discussion of a planned invasion raid into France and pressed Churchill for information on its status.

Dieppe

Mountbatten's large-scale raid on France had been in the planning stages for some time. Its purpose remained two-fold. First, keep pressure on the Germans as a way of distracting them from total concentration on the Russians. Second, gain experience against German defences in France. He chose the small port of Dieppe as the target because it was small enough to be taken by a division-sized force and close enough to British air bases to allow the RAF to engage the Luftwaffe in a large air battle.

As originally planned, two brigades of Canadian troops, supported by a battalion of tanks would be landed on either side of the port and proceed to capture it and the airfield. A massive bombing attack just for the landing, followed by bombardment by two battleships, would ensure the troops got ashore against dazed defenders. Paratroops would be dropped on either flank to take out two large batteries of guns protecting the coastline. Twelve hours later, the troops would re-embark for the journey home.

All three British services disliked the plans, especially because of the political pressure to launch it. For the Army, a commander named Bernard Montgomery felt that a flank landing might not be able to take the port and the public would see this as abject failure, regardless of the raid's outcome. He advocated a direct frontal assault on the port.

Royal Navy officers declined to use their battleships in the confined waters of the Channel, having lost too many capital ships during the war already. They provided only gunboats and destroyers for escort and support.

Royal Air Force leaders also declined to provide a heavy bomber force for the raid. Their cited reason: vulnerability of the bombers to Luftwaffe interception near dawn twilight. Their self-imposed rule limited bomber flight to thirty minutes before twilight, giving bombers only five minutes before the landing to hit the target. The real reason for their decline was their continuing battle to regain momentum of their strategic bombing campaign.[8] Their campaign floundered badly due to poor accuracy and high casualties. They had recently been promoting the 'Millennium' campaign – 1,000 plane raids on German cities, capable, they insisted, of bring Germany to her knees.

In addition to refusing the request for a heavy bombing attack, the RAF also cancelled the paratroop drop. The paratroops needed heavy Wellington bombers for their transport and the RAF felt they were better-used dropping bombs. They reasoned that 400 tons of bombs from the two squadrons would help the Allied cause better than dropping paratroops.

This left the raid's planners with a frontal assault and little support. They exchanged commandos for paratroops and continued rehearsals. The operation, called RUTTER, became targeted for early July, but after loading the troops, bad weather closed in for several days. German bombers also found and attacked the raid transports. Mountbatten finally cancelled RUTTER.

Roosevelt's query to Churchill about the raid, however, rejuvenated the plans. The Prime Minister, after a briefing, exploded at the plans for a frontal assault and had the original plans for landing on the flanks reinstated before giving his approval for the raid, now called Operation JUBILEE.

On the night of 18 August 1942, a flotilla of some 250 vessels set out from five British ports heading for Dieppe. Coastal radar spotted a small German convoy near the French coast on a collision course with the invasion fleet, but timely interception by HMS *Brocksley* and Polish destroyer *Slazak* sank two of the trawlers and sent the rest retreating up the coast.

Ashore, the German 302nd Infantry Division, a second-rate unit, manned by press-ganged non-Germans from the East, defended the invasion site. Armed with a wide assortment of foreign and pre-war weapons, concrete defences, built along the shore became this unit's main advantage.

Three Commando landed near the villages of Berneval on the invasion's left flank with the task of eliminating the Goebbel's shore battery of seven big guns. Some of the commandos ran into strong beach defences while another group penetrated to the battery, still recovering from a bombing attack. Destroying the guns, the commandos then hit the beach defenders from the rear clearing the villages. Most of the commandos withdrew following the battle, leaving two companies as road interdiction.

Four Commando landed on the right flank near Vasterival against no opposition and easily overran its target, the Hess shore battery of six 150 mm guns.

At 05:00 hours, the main landings occurred, with the three battalions of the Canadian 6th Brigade landing near Puys and the 4th Brigade landing at Pourville-sur-Mer. The invaders had five basic goals: destroy enemy defences and capture prisoners, destroy the airfield at St Aubyn (two kilometres south of Dieppe), destroy the radar station on the coast, capture or destroy the German invasion barges in Dieppe, and capture the German divisional headquarters, thought to be at Arques la Bataille, four kilometres south of Dieppe.

6th Brigade, made up of battalions from the Les Fusiliers Mont-Royal, Queen's Own Cameron Highlanders and South Saskatchewan Regiments, pushed through Puys fairly easily, aided by Churchill tanks of the 14th Tank Regiment, the Calgary Tanks. By 07:00 hours, the battalions captured Puys and the tanks overran three mobile batteries trying to set up against the invasion. The brigade then moved west against Dieppe itself.

On the other side of the port, 4th Brigade – battalions from the Royal Regiment of Canada, Royal Hamilton Light Infantry, and Essex Scottish Regiments – found itself in a horrendous fight just to get off the beaches. The only exit through the beach cliffs was defended by a machine-gun company and an anti-aircraft battery. It took three hours and many casualties to break out into Pourville. The three sections of tanks accompanying the troops were shot up as they emerged from the village; a local counter-attack cut off the beachhead momentarily before finally being eliminated. However, the Royal Hamilton's suffered almost seventy-five per cent casualties during the breakout.

The Germans immediately counter-attacked with four battalions of troops converging on the embattled port. Four Commando ambushed one battalion, generating a brief fight at Varengeville, before the Germans moved on toward the larger goal. The RAF found another battalion in road march south of the port and shot it up badly. The Germans found that the lack of transport for their static division hurt their response time. A call went out to the 10th Panzer Division, forty miles away at Amiens.

The Cameron Highlanders led the way into Dieppe, struggling against fortress-like defences; but aided by tanks and engineers, the battalion cleared the eastern approach and entered the port.

On the other side of town, the embattled 4th Brigade overran the radar site, turning it over to radar specialists who had landed with them. The Royal Regiment pushed out of Pourville and overran three batteries of mobile guns that had been savaging the landing, and captured the small village of Appeville. But heavy casualties stopped any further advance south. The Essex Scots stumbled across the Quatre Vents Farm, where the German had a non-commissioned-officer school. It took the Brigade's remaining strength to bull into the fortress.

Despite the casualties, Dieppe was in Canadian hands by ten o'clock that morning, but the Germans were closing in. Appeville was retaken and the survivors of 4th Brigade joined the 6th in Dieppe, unable to push toward the airfield. German infantry made two assaults trying to break back into Dieppe, but with their artillery overrun and little support, the attacks did little but savage the attackers. They pulled back to wait reinforcements from the 10th Panzer.

The Canadians, having done as much as they could do, began their withdrawal, which went smoothly from the captured port.

In all, Mountbatten proclaimed the raid a success. The Canadians suffered some thirty per cent casualties, with all their tanks lost or abandoned, but they captured a French port, caused severe casualties on the German defenders, and destroyed all the German coastal defence guns. The Royal Navy lost several landing craft and a destroyer while the Royal Air Force lost over a hundred aircraft during the 2,600 sorties flown, and claimed 130 German planes destroyed. The Germans claimed victory as well having driven the invaders off, despite over 1,200 casualties and the actual loss of forty-eight aircraft.

North Africa

In August, things looked a bit better for the Allies, adding to the successful raid on Dieppe. In the Pacific, American Marines landed at Guadalcanal, taking a partially constructed Japanese airfield in the first offensive step in the theatre. In Russia, German troops began fighting their way into the morass of Stalingrad and their offensive into the Caucasus was slowed significantly.

In North Africa, Rommel faced off against the British 8th Army at Alamein, having failed to break through to the Nile in July. The British had a new commander, Lieutenant General Bernard Montgomery, and were receiving new equipment and troops daily. Rommel was building his forces slowly but knew if he was going to break through, he had to do it quickly. He began planning an offensive for the end of August, telling his superiors they had to improve supply deliveries in order to make the offensive possible.

Enough supply was available in Africa. Rommel simply couldn't get it to the front quickly. The port of Tobruk stayed under attack from the air, limiting deliveries there. Supplies could be delivered to Tripoli and Benghasi, but the Axis needed over half the precious fuel delivered just to get it to the front. The Commander in chief South, Albert Kesselring promised Rommel sufficient fuel and drew up plans with the *Regia Marina* (Italian Navy) staff. But ULTRA intercepts disclosed the transport plans and the Allies sank most of the ships en route. Without enough fuel, Rommel made the hard decision not to attack. With that decision came the knowledge that getting to the Nile would be impossible, something his superiors – especially Mussolini and Hitler – did not want to hear. While he flew to Rome to argue his decision, his forces continued to build defences at Alamein and stockpile supplies. Montgomery continued his own build-up and instituted a massive training program.

Planning for a US–British invasion of North Africa, now called Operation TORCH, began in earnest after Marshall's decision in July. The plan involved three separate landings, at Casablanca, Oran and Algiers. Royal Navy Admiral Cunningham, formerly commander in the Mediterranean, argued unsuccessfully for landings further east near Tunisia, but with Malta under Axis control, planners felt such a landing too risky. Major General George Patton would land with 35,000 American troops at Casablanca, primarily to insure that Spain didn't try to close the Straits of Gibraltar. Major General L. R. Fredendall's 39,000 troops of II Corps would take Oran. Finally a mixed force of 33,000 British and American troops would take Algiers. Allied planners hoped that the Vichy French would not defend vigorously, if at all. The landings were scheduled for early November. Once ashore and settled, the troops would move east.

At Alamein, both sides prepared for the inevitable Allied offensive. The newly renamed German-Italian Panzer Army (*Deutsch-Italienisch Panzer Armee*) was currently be commanded by General der Kavallerie Georg Stumme, an East Front veteran and Rommel's deputy. Hitler publicly promoted Rommel to Field Marshal during his trip back to Rome and Berlin, but despite the accolades, he had been effectively relieved of his command for his decision not to attack at the end of August and forced to take medical leave.

However, Stumme, a solid commander, knew how to defend his position. Although he did not have enough fuel to carry out offensive operations, he had enough (eighteen days' supply) to put his four armoured divisions (the German 15th and 21st Panzer, the Italian Littorio and Ariete Divisions) in a central location to provide a reaction force. His infantry, bolstered by the arrival of the German 164th Division, the Ramcke Parachute Brigade and the Italian Folgore Parachute Division, dug in behind half a million mines. Both Stumme and Rommel believed that when the British attacked, they would try to break through in the south and roll the Axis line toward the coast.

Montgomery, by the last week in October, was ready. His fully supplied Eight Army enjoyed a two-to-one superiority in men, tanks and guns. The RAF and US air forces generally held air superiority over the region. His plan, called LIGHTFOOT, was an unsubtle assault on the Axis forces in front of him. The attack focused on the north where XXX Corps' three infantry divisions would penetrate the Axis front line and minefields, behind a massive artillery barrage, and cut lanes for X Corp's two armoured divisions, the 1st and 10th, to break into the Axis rear areas. The attack would be aided by large dummy supply dumps and diversionary attacks in the south.

On 23 October 1942, 2,000 British guns opened fire, heralding the start of LIGHTFOOT. The hurricane barrage devastated Axis front lines, artillery positions, and communications. Infantry assaults were generally slow but successful. However, the armoured divisions became bogged down, allowing the Axis to recover from the initial shock and react. In the middle of the first day,

Stumme disappeared, victim of a heart attack while travelling between positions; Generalleutnant Wilhelm Ritter von Thoma, commander of the *Deutsches Afrikakorps* (DAK) took over. In Berlin, following initial reports, Hitler contacted Rommel and asked him to return to Africa and reassume command.

Five days into the assault no breakthrough had occurred, despite the gains. Thoma and then Rommel, upon his arrival on 26 October, skilfully used their centralised mobile reserves to blunt attacks. But the attrition-style battle had its effect as did air superiority, where Allied sorties numbered ten times their opponents. The Axis lost more tanks and vehicles to air attack than to armoured combat. Montgomery shifted directions on the 28th, trying to break through to the coast (SUPERCHARGE), but Rommel stymied him again. He chose to back off, regroup and attack again where LIGHTFOOT had nearly broken through. Both sides took a breather, having suffered severe casualties.

Rommel could see the battle taking a bad turn and ordered a portion of the DAK to fall back to Fuka and start preparing defensive positions. He sent a personal representative back to Berlin to discuss the situation and ask for complete freedom of action.

Hitler's response reached him the same time Montgomery launched his new series of attacks, spearheaded by the 51st Highland Division. Predictably, Hitler's order was 'Not one step back.' Rommel, disgruntled and depressed, obeyed. Fortunately, a strong counter-attack by 21st Panzer, stopped the new Allied attack cold, but suffered heavy losses from air and artillery doing so, reducing Rommel's effective tanks to about fifty. Kesselring, after visiting the front, agreed with Rommel that the Alamein front was now indefensible and 'suggested' Rommel treated Hitler's order as advice, not a direct order. For the moment again, Montgomery stopped. However, informed that TORCH would kick off within days, he husbanded his forces, having lost some 600 tanks and 14,000 troops during the two-week battle. Rommel tried to do as well, but he had lost a third of his infantry, ninety per cent of his tanks and most of his guns. He continued sending troops westward toward Fuka and Tobruk.

On 8 November 1942, Operation TORCH caught the Axis by surprise. While the French resisted in places, the landings were generally successful, and sparked significant reaction in Rome and Berlin. Hitler accepted Rommel's withdrawal (with ill grace) and made plans to send troops into Tunisia to stop the allies. Without any interference from Malta, the airlift went without a hitch, Allied airfields being too far away to be effective. As November ended, the Germans had Allied advances stopped in the mud of the Tunisian autumn. To the east, Rommel fell back, reaching El Aghiela, with 8th Army in pursuit. Montgomery followed cautiously, having been dealt a bloody nose at Fuka.

Casablanca

As weather slowed operations in Tunisia, Roosevelt and Churchill decided to meet again to sort out the next steps in their world war. The Anfa Hotel, five miles outside Casablanca, served as the conference site. Considerable optimism surrounded the conference, a far cry from six months previously. Now the Allies stood firmly ashore in Africa with Axis forces barely holding on to Tripoli and its hinterland. The Soviets had the German 6th Army surrounded at Stalingrad on the verge of annihilation. In the Pacific, Japan's thrust at Port Moresby failed and her attempts to retake Guadalcanal led to a bloody battle of attrition that the Japanese lost.

For all that optimism, animosity and division separated the Allies over their next step. Churchill was still worried of any signs of an American shift away from their Germany first focus and toward the Pacific. Most telling was a late 1942 assessment by the US that accommodations for only 500,000 US troops would be needed in England through 1943 rather than the million that BOLERO had called for.

Brooke, speaking for the British, put their European plans on the table – threaten Germany's southern marches, knock Italy out of the war, and convince Turkey to join the Allies. After clearing Tunisia, multiple targets presented themselves: Sicily, Sardinia, Corsica, Greece or the Dodecanese islands in the Adriatic. Air Chief Marshal Portal pointed out that operations throughout the Mediterranean made Germany spread its forces out as well.

General Marshall countered with the US position on the European front: finish the Tunisian operation, then go defensive in the Mediterranean, build-up, and then cross the Channel into France. Anything else simply diverted resources from and postponed the only war-winning strategy – the cross-Channel attack.

Well prepared, the British raised their objections to a 1943 invasion of France: the U-boat threat, scarcity of landing craft, not enough Allied divisions in England, too many German divisions in France, and a French rail system for easy transport of troops. Disingenuously, Brook and his other chiefs minimised Allied reinforcement potential and maximised the effectiveness of the forty plus German divisions in France, most of which were low quality rebuilding units. Underlying these arguments was the main British concern: that American troops were simply not blooded enough to go straight into a showdown fight in France.

Admiral King then shifted the focus of the discussions by asking Brooke exactly what he thought the next step should be.

'Sardinia or Sicily,' Brook responded quickly. 'From Sicily, invade Italy. From Sardinia, Italy or southern France is possible.'

'What about Malta?' King asked. 'Sardinia is useless as a base. And you cannot attack Sicily without dealing with Malta.'

Marshall then put it plainly. To invade Sicily and Italy, the Allies had to have Malta. Adding an invasion of that island would postpone any operation in France beyond the foreseeable future. 'It's one island too many,' he stated flatly, then continued, 'Postponing a second front wouldn't help the Soviets, or the allied cause. Without dealing with Malta, the Allies had no use for more US troops in Mediterranean; without plans for a cross-Channel attack in 1943, they needed no more US troops in Europe. They would be sent to the Pacific.'

Brooke had no immediate answer for the Americans; the issue of Malta was political as well as military. Italians kept their word in bringing food to the island, but they also used Malta's three main airfields for the Regia Aeronautica bases with a garrison of two divisions. Ultimately, the decision remained with Churchill.

Malta presented Churchill with a major dilemma. Throughout the discussion of strategy, the question of a second front had been prominent, abetted by pressure from the Soviets. Churchill wanted a large-scale operation somewhere; his staff had essentially convinced him that an operation in France simply was not feasible in 1943, so the focus needed to stay on the Mediterranean. But his staff had stayed very quiet about Malta.

The Maltese endured more than their share of misery on behalf of the Allies, much of it at Churchill and the Royal Navy's behest. Virtually all other sections of the British government had written the island off at the start of the war. But she had endured and played a significant role in British fortunes in the Mediterranean and Africa. And politically, he had to consider the George Cross.

But to fulfil the need for large-scale operations in the Mediterranean, Malta had to be a target. Ultimately, Churchill felt he could not politically survive planning any action against the island, and that left a second front landing in France.

Thus Casablanca provided the following Allied priorities: finish the African campaign, launch deception operations to keep Italy engaged, concentrate on beating the U-boats and bombing German industry, and prepare for cross-Channel operations. Stalin, who had been demanding the Allies open a significant second front to take some of the pressure off his nation, exploded when informed that no other major operations would take place until later in 1943. He told the Allied leaders that their delay made his people feel alone against the Fascists. He pointed to the horrendous casualties suffered by the Red Army and called Allied casualties thus far 'insignificant'. He needed an attack that diverted a significant number of the German divisions facing him. Despite reassurances from both Roosevelt and Churchill, Stalin remained angry, accusing the West of deliberately delaying action and trying to destroy his country.

The Allies could do little, except push their planning staffs to finalise second front plans. ROUNDUP was solidly on the agenda.

Build-up

Decisions made, the Allies began detailed planning for their cross-Channel assault. In the meantime African operations went on.

In February, the Axis struck hard at the inexperienced US troops of II Corps, attacking at the Kasserine Pass, and inflicting a severe repulse to them. The offensive aimed primarily at delaying the inevitable in Tunisia because Hitler began regretting his impulsive decision to defend his Axis's North African holdings. His 6th Army had surrendered near Stalingrad and the Eastern Front – the troops in Tunisia would be needed.

However, Hitler could not just abandon Tunisia as that would unsettle his ally, Mussolini. The Italian leader, who six months earlier had been ready to enter Cairo in triumph, had now lost everything Italy had in Africa. The political cost of that defeat began emerging as several political enemies (and one or two political 'friends') began shuffling for position against him. German intelligence picked up bits and pieces of a wide variety of conspiracies against Mussolini, all highly vocal but totally disorganised. The logical next step for the converging allies in North Africa: Italy itself through Malta and Sicily, the threat of which made things even dicier. Hitler needed Italy stable while he shored up his Eastern Front. The cost became operations in Tunisia, but he sent word to his commander in chief in the south, Kesselring, to pull out good troops slowly if they could.

The Kasserine defeat and the poor performance of the US II Corps troops made the British all the more convinced that a 1943 cross-Channel attack would be a disaster. They started floating objections and alternative plans, hoping to catch the US reeling from the losses and more susceptible to change; but the US held firm to their demands for ROUNDUP, even while replacing an ineffective Fredendall with aggressive George Patton in Tunisia. Over the next several months the Allies pushed inexorably toward Tunis.

In March, Allied intelligence began picking up mentions of a major offensive planned by the Germans around the Kursk salient on the Eastern Front. ULTRA and on-the-scenes spy rings brought word of a massive build-up in the area. Marshall keyed on that as just the thing to promote a successful crossing – rather than the second front 'saving' the Soviets from disaster, he saw the landing now as taking advantage of a Soviet victory.

By May 1943, Axis resistance neared collapse in Tunisia; Allied air power and encroaching sea power all but isolating the African country, especially for incoming supply. Kesselring began pulling his best troops out while he could – the Hermann Goering Panzer, 15th and 21st Panzer veterans were among those that got out sans equipment.

Axis aircraft operating out of Malta supported the pullout as they had the supply attempts and caused concern among Allied commanders, who pushed the limit of operations against the island. Low-level bombing runs combined with fighter sweeps tried to interdict the island. But over 200,000 Axis troops became trapped in Tunisia when Tunis fell. The operation had cost Italy some 400 ships and the Axis nearly 2,000 aircraft.

While the battle in Tunisia concluded, planning and preparations for future operations continued. The process keyed on an effort to make sure the Axis believed that the Mediterranean would continue to see most of the Allied attention. Two deception programs were particularly effective:

Operation MINCEMEAT: launched at the end of April, MINCEMEAT consisted of floating a corpse ashore off Spain complete with 'secret plans' showing the Allies were planning to invade Greece, then Sicily.

Operation BARCLAY: a bogus army group established in Egypt preparing operations in the Balkans.

While the Germans struggled to escape Tunisia and absorbed disinformation about the next Allied objective, Marshall diligently revised his BOLERO plans to augment US troops in Britain. Eight divisions had been already earmarked for England (101st Airborne, 2nd, 8th, 28th, 45th, plus 3rd and 4th Armored). He stripped four others from previous assignments in the Pacific (6th, 7th, 33rd, 1st Cavalry). In addition, he pencilled-in four divisions from Tunisia for relocation back to Britain (1st, 9th, 82nd Airborne, and 2nd Armored). Britain's two fast passenger liners, the *Queen Mary* and *Queen Elizabeth*, aided transport immeasurably.

A full headquarters (Supreme Headquarters, Allied Expeditionary Force, SHAEF) was established in England for the coming assault, headed up by a newly promoted Lord Mountbatten on the basis of his success at Dieppe and the fact that most of the troops involved would be British and Commonwealth. The 21st Army Group, commanded by Eisenhower, composed Mountbatten's ground forces, made up of the US 1st Army under Patton and British 2nd Army under Montgomery. As part of the overall deception plan, both Patton and Montgomery, who had earned kudos from their German opponents for their battlefield performances, stayed in the Mediterranean until the last minute to continue the appearance of major Allied operations there.

Air and naval operations continued in the Mediterranean as part of the plans to keep the Axis attention focused there. In early June, for example, air and naval bombardment – 5,300 tons of bombs in five days – forced the surrender of the Italian island of Pantelleria and its 11,000-man garrison. Brooke used the easy victory to suggest going after Sicily for real, landing an American-British force on the western end of the island and moving east. The US argued that most of the Axis airfields were in the east and threatened any beachhead in western Sicily. They countered with a plan to land at Syracuse – following a Pantelleria-style neutralisation of Malta. Brooke's plan died out.

However the argument did bring about an alteration in the US posture of no-more-Mediterranean operations. US planners saw the benefit of a smaller operation to continue pinning the Axis down. The discussions bore Operation BRIMSTONE, the invasion of Sardinia. Marshall agreed to the plan only when Eisenhower showed him that it would not interfere heavily with the ROUNDUP plans, using US troops allocated for garrison duty in Africa.

On 5 July 1943, Hitler finally launched his oft-delayed offensive at the Kursk salient on the East Front. By delaying to allow new weapons to make it to the battlefield, he also allowed the Soviets to turn the salient into as massive death-trap. Over two million men, 6,000 tanks and 4,000 aircraft participated in the massive battle.[9] After a week of fighting, the German pincers, 9th and 4th Panzer Armies had made minimal progress toward each other.

And on 10 July 1943, the Allies launched Operation BRIMSTONE, landing infantry divisions with armoured support at four separate locations on Sardinia: Oristano Bay, Cape Altano, Cape Pecora and Palmas Bay. The attack caught the Axis by surprise; Operation MINCEMEAT convinced them that Sicily would be the next target and they had reinforced their presence on that island. The invasion overmatched the two Italian divisions on Sardinia, but the 155th Panzer grenadier Regiment put in a spirited assault against the US 34th Infantry Division at Oristano before being repulsed by naval gunfire.

A day later, Hitler called off the Kursk assault; ambivalent about the offensive just prior to the attack, the Sardinian surprise made him pause and pull back. The various deception operations spun by the Allies had forced a number of redeployments in and around the Mediterranean theatre. In addition, Mussolini began recalling his legions from their occupation duties in Greece and Yugoslavia in preparation for defending Italy itself. With Sardinia falling to the Allies (Hitler had no doubt it would) the next step could be northern Italy itself or southern France.

With operations in the west becoming active again, Hitler could no longer simply focus on the east as his armed forces stretched thin. In mid-July, some 210 divisions remained on the East front, forty-four in France, twenty in Scandinavia, seventeen in the Balkans and five in Italy. He needed to keep troops in Scandinavia, especially Finland, to safeguard precious nickel and iron deliveries. The Balkan partisans absorbed additional troops by threatening transportation lines to the East front. He needed troops in Italy to back up Mussolini and help forestall any quick Allied thrust there. His troops in France kept the Allies at bay from a major second front, while serving as a rebuilding and recovery area for decimated and exhausted Eastern Front formations. He found replacement soldiers harder to come by. The use of Russian volunteers, called *Hiwis* (*Hilfsfreiwilligen*, or volunteer helpers) to replace Germans in service elements became prevalent, as did the use of recruited Russian prisoners. Orders went to his generals to begin developing some sort of an East Wall against the Soviets, while he rearranged and reinforced his forces. He issued orders to Rommel to form a command in Northern Italy to react to anything the Allies did next. Because he did not trust the Italians he also created Operation ALARIC – a plan to hold the western Alpine passes open and disarm his allies if necessary.

In August, the Soviets launched a massive attack on the Orel salient, seeking to take advantage of the German losses suffered at Kursk. Although they had also suffered heavily during the German offensive, the massive reserves they had collected gave them the means to continue their counter-attack and pursuit.[10] The Germans fought a skilled fighting withdrawal to the Dnieper river throughout the month, inflicting horrendous casualties on the attacking Soviets. The loss of 430,000 troops and another 2,500 tanks led Stalin to increase his demands for a substantial second front.

Operation ROUNDUP

While the Germans retreated toward the Dnieper, Mountbatten and his staff finalised their plans for the cross-Channel assault, now scheduled for early September. Mountbatten's plan called for two widely separated landings, Patton's 1st Army near Dieppe and Montgomery's near Dunkirk. The two armies would expand their beachhead; drive on Paris, then on toward Germany, cutting off any German forces further south. Several of the planning staff protested the landing sites, arguing that the coastal ports were too small to adequately handle the logistic and troop build-up, that autumn storms could disrupt the transfer, and most importantly, that the two armies were too far apart to support one another. With Eisenhower's (and Marshall's) support, however, the plan was approved. The landings would take place under an air umbrella from Britain and the troops would be closest to their ultimate goal, Germany. His Dieppe raid had shown Mountbatten that Hitler's Atlantic Wall was nearly all fiction.

Montgomery's 2nd Army would open channel ports from Boulogne to Ostende. His plans called for the British 3rd and 15th Divisions to directly assault Dunkirk (GOLD beach) while the 43rd landed beside them on SWORD beach. The Guards Armoured Division and 49th Division would follow up the landings. In the wings the Canadian 1st Army waited. The Commonwealth's primary post-landing target: the Dutch port of Antwerp. Patton's 1st Army would revisit Dieppe with the 1st Division and 4th Divisions landing on OMAHA and UTAH beaches, respectively. The US 2nd Armored and 2nd Infantry would follow up the assaults. Patton's initial targets: Dieppe itself and La Havre, and expanding between the Somme and Seine Rivers to take Rouen and Amiens. De Gaulle's Free French 2nd Armoured Division along with nine other US infantry and four US armoured divisions remained in reserve for subsequent operations in the direction of Paris.

Facing them were something over forty divisions, operating under the Commander in Chief-West, Field Marshall Gerd von Rundstadt. Their immediate opponent was the German 15th Army which had responsibility for the French coast around Pas de Calais. The army had recently switched commanders, with Colonel-General Hans von Salmuth arriving from the Eastern Front to take command in early August. He inherited defences that were still being built. Allied Intelligence pinpointed most of the Salmuth's divisions and assessed them as weak, undermanned, and underequipped. The rebuilding Panzer divisions, including the 24th at Le Mans and 21st near Caen, generated most of the concern but Mountbatten felt strongly that air power would delay them long enough to allow the beachheads to develop and get Allied armour ashore. Intelligence, unfortunately, missed several key units. In particular, the 25th Panzer at Beauvais and the 10th SS Panzer Division at St. Quentin had not been located, nor the extent of Rommel's buildup in Northern Italy, which included two rebuilding Panzer divisions from Tunisia and the 17th SS Panzer Division.

After a week's delay due to bad weather, ROUNDUP's D-Day began the night of 15 September 1943, with the dropping of the British 1st Airborne and the US 101st Airborne into France behind the landing beaches. The drops went

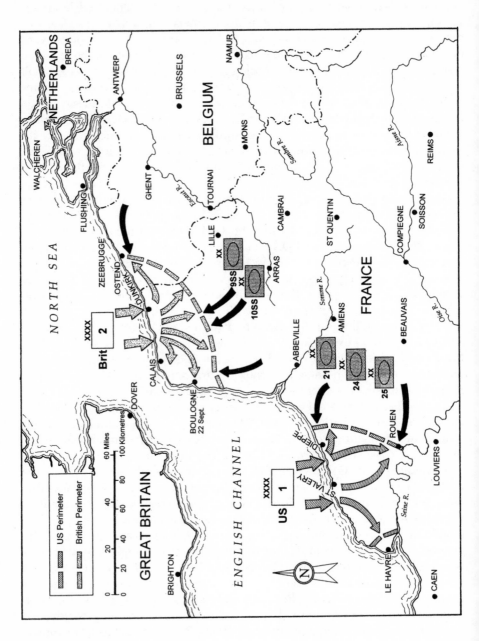

Operation ROUNDUP

poorly, as transport crews had no real experience with large-scale paradrops. Both divisions were scattered badly, losing much of their cohesion and fighting power. However, both units were able to achieve significant gains. The British, landing miles behind their intended drop zones, took the town of Lille, while the 101st fought their way into Dieppe against the 348th Division. The initial fighting began to show that the Germans had learned lessons from the raid on Dieppe – the fortifications were heavier and better-sited for all-around defence.

Royal Navy and US Navy ships opened fire as dawn broke on their targeted beaches in an intense barrage to prepare the way for the troops. In the skies above both air forces kept the Luftwaffe at bay. In all the landings went fairly well.

The US 1st Division landed successfully at OMAHA beach without heavy casualties, aided by the battle the Germans were fighting with the 101st. Trouble arrived as the 2nd Armored Division began to follow up – they found the beaches restrictive and armour had a problem getting off. On UTAH beach the 4th Division had a much harder time smashing through the defences of the 245th Division, but managed to push them back enough to get start landing the 2nd Infantry Division and 1st Army Headquarters.

At the SWORD beaches, two British divisions had a savage fight to take Dunkirk from the 18th Luftwaffe Field division, but with the aid of the specialised armour, took the town and began the process of landing the Guards Armoured Division. To west, fighting on GOLD beach bled the 43rd Division white due to heavy counter-attacks coming out of Calais, but the beachhead held long enough to get the 49th Division ashore and into line.

German reaction showed that Dieppe's lesson of slow response had been learned as well. Mobile units, especially artillery, arrived to take the beach-heads under fire. Lille was retaken after four days of fighting, delaying the 10th SS Panzer Division's movement toward Dunkirk. Other mobile divisions began their move as well – pre-D-Day bombing had been insufficient to seriously disrupt France's well developed transportation net.

Both the US and British beachheads began to expand outward, but ran into serious opposition. The Germans repulsed 2nd Infantry Division's assault on Le Havre with heavy casualties; 2nd Armored and 4th Infantry pushed their way into Rouen, while the 1st Division secured Dieppe against scattered counter-attacks. Mountbatten delayed additional US armoured units to allow more infantry to land. The first British attack on Calais failed, although the Guards Armoured overran one German training division en route to the port. To the east, the Belgian port of Ostende fell to the 15th Division. The Canadian 2nd and 3rd Divisions landed to replace the battered assault divisions. Bad weather and Luftwaffe attacks delayed reinforcement on the beaches. The air battle claimed more and more aircraft, with the Allied effort hurt by their limited time over the battlefield flying in from Britain.

Rommel arrived from Northern Italy four days after the landings to assume command of the German reaction. Under his energetic leadership, German armour began a series of concerted attacks on the beachheads. The 9th and 10th SS Panzers made an assault on the Guards Armoured that ended in stalemate with heavy losses to both sides. Armoured forces backed up German infantry to retake Ostende, threatening the western flank of the British beaches. The 12th SS Panzer struck at Dieppe, almost carrying the town, but was destroyed as was the defending 1st Division. Only timely reinforcement by the 8th Infantry Division held the town. Rouen changed hands as the 25th Panzer caught the 2nd Armored overextended and scattered their supporting 4th Division infantry. Patton was killed as he moved forward to rally his troops.

The Canadians moved forward to support the growing battle with the two SS panzer divisions, while the 7th Armored and 50th Divisions landed to capture Calais that had been cut off. The British held their own against the counter-attacks but could not advance. Luftwaffe bombers created havoc on the Allied supply situation.

On 1 October, 1943, disaster struck as two panzer divisions, the 21st and 24th, launched a heavy assault on Dieppe and the 8th Infantry line collapsed. Only the newly landed Free French 2nd Division and naval bombardment held the panzers away from the US beaches, as more German troops arrived. In the plains behind Dunkirk and Calais British and German forces continued their savage stalemate, each suffering heavy casualties, with the 10th SS and the Guards Armoured Divisions virtually annihilated.

The crisis at the US beaches forced a decision on Mountbatten and his staff. They found that the chosen beaches were too restricted to allow a continuous flow of troops and supplies, especially in the US sector, due to bad weather and Luftwaffe attacks. They were also unable to completely disrupt the flow of German mobile units to the battlefields and those units were far more effective than previously estimated. ULTRA intercepts let them know that substantial reinforcements were in the way from Italy – the Allied forces remaining in the Mediterranean were unable to take advantage of the redeployment. Newly arrived 1st Army commander Hodges, who took over when Patton was killed, estimated he could only hold for another week against Rommel unless more troops and armour arrived. At Dunkirk, Royal Engineers worked frantically to get captured ports into operation to ease supply problems that Montgomery faced. He held his own but was suffering heavy casualties. Eisenhower knew, however, that collapse of the US beachhead would release more German divisions to hit the British.

Mountbatten made the hard decision to withdraw from France. German pressure stayed heavy as the troops came off. The free French division declined to be withdrawn and died protecting the beachhead as a rearguard. By 20 October the last troops had been taken off, completing the disaster. In all, three armoured divisions, and ten infantry divisions had been virtually destroyed, over 100,000 casualties and masses of equipment. In return they had smashed eight smaller static divisions on the French coast and burned out six German panzer divisions.

The Allied withdrawal from France had a horrific effect on the Allies. The British criticised the US troops and leadership that had forced them into a premature invasion. The US became equally adamant that the fault lay with British that had landed them in wholly inadequate beaches. Both Mountbatten and Eisenhower were sacked; Montgomery infuriated the US even further declaring he knew the Dieppe landings were going to be a disaster all along.

The truth, of course, lay in between. The Germans had learned their lesson's from the 1942 Dieppe raid better than the Allies and had prepared better counter-attack plans. Especially damaging was the inability of the Allied air forces to keep the Luftwaffe from hammering the supply ports – all the more so, since the British had learned that lesson in their 1940 Norwegian debacle.[11]

In the midst of the discussions, a major change occurred within the British Government; aided by the cross-Channel disaster, Churchill's opponents, able to gather their strength and armed with 'one disaster too many' ousted the Prime Minister. Lord Halifax[12], recalled from his post as ambassador to the United States, formed an interim government.

Stalin reacted with even more anger than Churchill's opponents. The Soviets had suffered massive casualties in the Orel offensives and several attempts to penetrate the German defences on the Panther-Wotan line.[13]With the withdrawal of the Western Allies from their bloody beaches in France, Stalin knew that Hitler could now substantially reinforce his forces in the East since the threat of another Allied invasion was virtually nil for at least six months to a year. Stalin did the only thing he could and directed Molotov to begin making peace-feelers through Sweden.

The news of an impending Russo-German truce struck the Allies like a bombshell. With the Soviet Union out of the war, there was little hope of Anglo-American forces alone defeating Germany on the Continent. Admiral King took advantage of the iron logic of the situation and of a depressed Marshall to gain approval for a major US shift toward the Pacific.

The Third Reich would survive a few more years.

The Reality

In reality, two ships from Operation HARPOON made it to Malta in June 1942, landing some 15,000 tons of supplies. That made it possible for the Maltese to endure until Operation PEDESTAL fought through to the island in August. They suffered terrible losses despite a powerful Royal Navy escort.

It might be counterintuitive that Malta's surrender would not have helped Rommel very much, but when the island capitulates in our story, Rommel had advanced already into Egypt and his supply line became then a matter of arithmetic. He needed something like 110,000 tons of supply a month. Tobruk could handle, at most, 20,000 tons – the rest had to come from Tripoli and the Axis simply did not have that many trucks. Factor in Allied bombing and you get a DAK with a lousy logistics picture.

The strategic arguments between the British and American Chiefs of staff are very real. The British came to the conferences well prepared, and, with Roosevelt wanting to get troops into action, Marshall had to capitulate. He did however slow troops crossing to England as a result, making it virtually impossible to mount ROUNDUP in 1943. The delay in a Second Front angered Stalin, but new information appears to indicate he expected it and used the anger as a political bargaining chip. Most historians (for example, Dunn 1980) who believe the Allied shouldn't have dabbled in the Mediterranean, believe that the Soviets were able to occupy most of East Europe as a result.

Hitler, of course, did very little reassessing of his decisions, leaving far more Axis troops in Tunisia to be trapped than allowed here. Rommel did have doubts about attacking at the end of August 1942 at Alam Halfa, but did anyway, giving in to his boss's demands for the Nile and his own desire to reestablish ascendancy over the 8th Army. Hitler's decision to form an Eastern Wall also came far too late to do more that delay the Soviets.

The plans for ROUNDUP came from the original preliminary plans drawn up during the aforementioned Allied debate. All of the objections put forth on the plan were real, but the plan never got past the 'here's what we want to do' phase, as the Mediterranean focus stayed in place. The BRIMSTONE plan against Sardinia had been drawn up as an option following the invasion of Sicily.

Finally, the raid at Dieppe failed badly with almost sixty-six per cent of the Canadians involved killed or captured. The small convoy intercepted above in actuality had been detected but that information was not passed on to the raiders. Third Commando's convoy ran into them, delaying their assault and alerting the Germans. The minimal support described above is real, as was the final plan for a frontal assault on the port. The original plan called for a pincer assault and *might* have had a better chance for success. Churchill's comment that changed the plan above was actually made in the 1950s as he was writing his memoirs. There is still a lively debate on exactly why Dieppe was attempted with such a ridiculous plan.

Notes

1   General John Standish Surtees Prendergast Vereker, Viscount Gort. He earned a Victoria Cross for valour in World War I.

2   British merchant ship *Orari* carried 10,350 tons of supply as part of the six ship HARPOON convoy that entered the Mediterranean the night of 11 June, 1942.

3   Gort was the commander of the British Expeditionary Force in 1940. He has been made one of the chief scapegoats of the defeat, especially by the French, who felt his withdrawal from the Arras line ended all hopes of breaking the German trap. In fact, Gort received *no* orders from his Allied superiors for some nine days during the crisis and made the best choices he could given his situation and the information he had.

*4   From *Besieged and Betrayed: The World War II Ordeal of Malta, 1940-1944* by Charles Jellison, University Press of New England, 1981.

5   The Combined Chiefs of Staff consisted of the heads of each country's armed services. For the British, this was Brooke for the Army, Admiral Sir Dudley Pound for

the Royal Navy and Air Chief Marshal Sir Charles Portal for the RAF. The US portion included Marshall, Lieutenant General Henry 'Hap' Arnold for the Army Air Forces, and Admiral Ernest King, Chief of Naval Operations and Commander-in-chief of the US Fleet. The Combined Chiefs met in continuous session in Washington, where Field Marshal Sir John Dill, acted as chairman of the British.

6   Both the Germans and the Japanese had plans to reach for each other. In Germany, Admiral Raeder and General Jodl pushed for Operation ORIENT, a drive through the Middle East. Japan had their Western Plan to set up bases on Madagascar. Both plans, feasible in 1941, fell victim to the questionable priorities of their leaders – Hitler's demand for BARBAROSSA, Japan's for their continuing war in China.

7   For an excellent discussion of Rommel's supply situation and his dependence on African port capacity and land transport, see van Creveld, 1977.

8   The Royal Air Force had based its existence on strategic bombing in the 1930s and had fought tooth and nail for funding to support that goal against her sister services. Her entire pre-war strategy was based on destroying an enemy from the air. Thus the RAF leadership was mortified when France refused to allow strategic bombing during the battle of France, 1940, because of fears of massive German retaliation. With the army pushing for better close ground support, like the Luftwaffe, the RAF leaders were still fighting for prominence and for vindication of their pre-war plans.

9   The Germans massed 900,000 men, 2700 tanks and armoured fighting vehicles, and 1,700 aircraft for their offensive. The Soviets countered with 1,330,000 men, 3,300 tanks, 13,000 artillery guns, 6,00 anti-tank guns, and 1,000 Katyusha rocket-launchers, all supported by 2,500 aircraft. More importantly, the Soviets sowed some 1,700 anti-personnel and 1,500 anti-tank mines *per kilometre* of their defensive front. See Glantz and House, 1999.

10   The Soviets had lost 180,000 men and 1,600 tanks at Kursk; the Germans had lost the same number of tanks and only 50,000 men, but could ill afford those losses. Ibid., note 9.

11   In April, 1940, the British landed troops at the Norwegian ports of Namsos and Åndalsnes in a attempt to capture Trondheim with an indirect approach. Luftwaffe bombers virtually destroyed Namsos the next day cutting the 146th Brigade off from its supply.

12   Edward Frederick Lindley Wood, 1st Earl of Halifax, had been Foreign Secretary from 1938–40 and supported former Prime Minister Neville Chamberlain's policy of appeasement toward Nazi Germany.

13   The Panther-Wotan line was a defensive line that was intended to act as an eastern wall against the surging Soviet juggernaut. The line ran from Narva on the Gulf of Finland to Melitopol on the Sea of Azov and tried to follow defensive river lines as much as possible.

Bibliography

Bradford, Ernle, *Siege Malta: 1940–1943*, New York: Wm Morrow & Company, 1986.

Bruce George, *Second Front Now! The Road to D-Day*, London: MacDonald & Janes, 1979.

Dunn, Walter Scott, Jr, *Second Front Now 1943*, Tuscaloosa, AL: The University of Alabama Press, 1980.

Eisenhower, John S. D., *Allies: Pearl Harbor to D-Day*, New York: Doubleday & Company, Inc, 1982.

Glantz, David and Jonathan M. House, *The Battle of Kursk*, Lawrence, KS: The University Press of Kansas, 1999.

Harrison, Gordon A., *Cross Channel Attack*, Washington, DC: Center for Military History, 1951.

Levine, Alan J., *The War against Rommel's Supply Lines, 1942–1943*, Westport, CT: Praeger, 1999.

Perowne, Stewart, *The Siege within the Walls: Malta 1940–1943*. London: Hodder and Stoughton, 1970.

Pogue, Forrest C., *George C. Marshall: Organizer of Victory, 1943–1945*. New York, Viking Press, 1973.

Van Creveld, Martin, *Supplying War: Logistics from Wallenstein to Patton*, Cambridge, UK: Cambridge University Press, 1977.

Villa, Brian Loring, *Unauthorized Action: Mountbatten and the Dieppe Raid*, New York: Oxford University Press, 1989.

11 Ike's COCKADE
The Allied Invasion of France 1943
Stephen Badsey

Casablanca

18 January 1943

'I am afraid that Eisenhower as a general is hopeless! He submerges himself in politics and neglects his military duties, purely, I am afraid, because he knows little if anything about military matters.'[1] It was two o'clock in the afternoon of Monday, 18 January 1943, and in his villa not far from Casablanca, General Sir Alan Brooke, Chief of the Imperial General Staff and principal military adviser to Prime Minister Winston S. Churchill, reflected on his diary entry of almost a month before. Churchill was at Casablanca to meet President Franklin D. Roosevelt and his advisers for the Anglo-American planning conference, code-named SYMBOL, which would decide their agreed strategy for the next year. Their military chiefs had made considerable progress in promoting Anglo-American unity, including an agreement on a Combined Bombing Offensive to be mounted from the United Kingdom. But on the main Allied land campaign for 1943 there was no agreement at all, and time was running out.

Since the Axis invasion of the Soviet Union in June 1941, Marshal Josef Stalin had taunted the British with being afraid to face the Germans, demanding a 'Second Front' to relieve pressure in the east. In fact the British were already fighting on five land, sea and air fronts all around the world. It had been the Germans who had prudently refused to face the British directly, turning away from an invasion in favour of a protracted naval battle in the Atlantic. Italy's attempts to threaten the British Empire's communications through the Suez Canal had turned into the main British land war in the Western Desert, a war which by December 1942 the British had decisively won. Now their manpower and industrial mobilisation were reaching their peak. From Churchill downwards the British understood that their fortunes had been transformed by Hitler's strategic blunder in declaring war on the United States on 11 December 1941, a week after Pearl Harbor. It was a British axiom that 'we *must* get on with the Americans', on whose troops and equipment they would increasingly depend.[2]

In December 1941 at the ARCADIA Conference in Washington the British and Americans had agreed on the defeat of 'Germany First', before Japan. This was good strategy given the relative strengths of their enemies (and, for the few who knew the secret, because the Germans might develop an atomic bomb), but for the American public it was not easy to understand: Germany had not attacked the United States, whereas the Japanese were still on the advance in the Pacific and the Far East. For the British and their Empire 1942 was a year of survival, and they were content for the United States to fight anywhere it wanted, including in the Pacific to help remove the Japanese threat to India and Australia. At Casablanca, despite their own considerable problems, they responded to the American shortage of fleet aircraft carriers by loaning their latest carrier, HMS *Victorious* (temporarily renamed USS *Robin*) to join the USS *Saratoga* in the South Pacific. But juggling forces between the Pacific and Europe like this meant taking decisions many months in advance. The British, who had come well prepared to the Casablanca Conference, found to their dismay that their American opposite numbers seemed unable to grasp what was involved. Only two days before, General Brooke and his colleagues had listened to the US Chief of Naval Operations, Admiral Ernest King, followed by the US Army Chief of Staff General George C. Marshall, complain that only fifteen per cent of the American war effort was going to the Pacific and that this needed to be doubled, leaving the remaining seventy per cent for the rest of the war; hardly a scientific way of approaching strategy! Brooke at least expected senior officers to have mastered these issues and to deal frankly with their allies. But Admiral King had simply made up his statistics: the whole US Marine Corps overseas, half the US Army overseas and one-third of all US combat air groups were in the Pacific, where the vast distances meant that three times as much shipping was needed to transport and supply them as for Europe.

The strategy agreed at ARCADIA had been for a build-up of American forces in the United Kingdom code-named Operation BOLERO, to be followed by an Anglo-American invasion of northern France code-named Operation ROUNDUP. The British were at first bemused to find General Marshall championing a plan for this invasion to take place in 1942. Roosevelt's policy was that as a democracy the United States should win the war with as few losses to its own citizens as possible, and this had been translated into military terms as adopting the shortest, fastest and most direct route to victory. The British policy also was to win with the fewest possible losses, but they planned to do this by training their troops and commanders, husbanding their assets, minimising their risks, and striking only when they were certain. Perhaps the differing strategies were the legacies of the United States entering World War I in 1917 as opposed to 1914. The British were also aware of the complexity and risks of any cross-Channel operation. On 19 August 1942, Combined Operations Headquarters under Vice Admiral Lord Louis 'Dickie' Mountbatten had mounted Operation JUBILEE, an attempt to capture the port of Dieppe for a few hours before withdrawing. Of about 6,000 troops involved some 3,500 were killed, wounded or captured, mostly from Canadian 2nd Infantry Division which was virtually wiped out. The experience left the Canadians with strong suspicions about the British, and the British with an equally strong dislike of rushed planning. They produced unanswerable arguments to show that an invasion of northern France simply could not be mounted in Marshall's time-frame.

Just before the British failure at Dieppe, in July 1942 President Roosevelt agreed (in defiance of his own military advisers) on the next main Allied effort being a landing in North Africa, the territories of Morocco, Algeria and Tunisia controlled by Vichy France, in the expectation that the French forces would mostly change sides and join the Allies. Code-named Operation TORCH, the North Africa landings were a compromise between the military need to create and build up US transport and supply around the world, and the political need not to remain inactive against Germany for the entire year. The plan for ROUNDUP remained in existence, including Operation SLEDGEHAMMER, a possible much smaller invasion of France to attract German forces away from the Eastern Front, especially if the Soviet Union came close to collapse. After failing to get TORCH cancelled, Marshall insisted on appointing as Supreme Allied Commander for the North African theatre his own protégé and fellow advocate of a 1942 cross-Channel attack, Lieutenant General Dwight D. 'Ike' Eisenhower, a man who had never heard a shot fired in anger, whose largest previous command had been (briefly) that of a battalion, and of whom Brooke had rapidly formed such a low opinion. Realising that Marshall would not dispense with Eisenhower, the British solution was to encourage the Americans to promote him, in the hope that he would be pushed into the stratosphere of policy and organisation, and as far away from strategy and operations as possible.

While the Allied leaders met at Casablanca, Lieutenant General Sir Frederick Morgan, commanding British I Corps as Eisenhower's strategic reserve, received the American plan for his deployment, 'which I read and re-read and studied until it dawned upon me that I did not understand one single word of it.'[3] British and American military staff terminology and practices were very different. As for a common language, that was also a matter for sour jokes and occasional bewilderment: did 'gas' mean petrol or poison?[4] TORCH had been a military and political minefield that had come close to failure and to farce, but most of the Vichy French had agreed to change sides, and fortunately the Allied troops were safely ashore. Now, British 1st Army under Lieutenant General Kenneth Anderson, including US II Armored Corps under Major General Lloyd R. Fredendall, faced the Germans and Italians defending Tunis. Meanwhile, British 8th Army under Brooke's own protégé Lieutenant General Bernard 'Monty' Montgomery was pursuing Field Marshal Erwin Rommel's Panzer Army Africa westwards, squeezing the Axis forces between them. It would be an important and crushing Allied victory, but it would take time.

Crisis

November 1942 to January 1943

The British had come to Casablanca with the argument that the war in Europe could be won, perhaps even in 1943, if the Americans actually honoured the 'Germany First' strategy, but that the next main Allied effort should be made in the Mediterranean. If the Axis powers had evacuated Tunisia immediately after the TORCH landings then another major Allied offensive might have begun early in 1943. As it was, no one knew when the fighting in North Africa would end; Eisenhower's estimate was not before mid-May, possibly June. With the forces available, it would be an unacceptable risk for the Allies to attack anywhere else before they had secured Tunisia. Redeploying their forces back to Great Britain would take too long, especially as the Battle of the Atlantic was still raging, and losses from U-boats made it impossible to estimate the progress of the build-up under BOLERO. The British also hoped to weaken the Axis by internal revolts in occupied Europe; and they had for some time been negotiating with senior Italian figures plotting a coup to overthrow Benito Mussolini, and for Italy to join the Allies as the Vichy forces in North Africa had done. Finally, the British needed to secure their sea communications through the Suez Canal and the Mediterranean into the Atlantic, saving the equivalent of a million tons of shipping. All this, they had decided, meant that once North Africa was cleared the main Allied effort should be the occupation of Sicily, a plan code-named Operation HUSKY.

For reasons of Allied solidarity, the British would not use their strongest argument: the US Navy and Royal Navy were between them the best and strongest in the world, and the RAF had already defeated the Germans in the Battle of Britain; but the British Army, created almost from scratch since 1939, had only recently got the equipment (some of it American-made) and the experience it needed to beat the Germans; the US Army Air Force (USAAF) was only just getting into its stride; and the barely trained US Army was simply not ready to face the best the Germans had. The Anglo-American alliance was also far from secure. Perhaps in reaction to their sense of weakness, American generals in North Africa openly vied with each other in insulting and belittling their British allies. 'Goebbels could hardly have felt more intensely about the Jews,' Brooke was told, than one American general 'felt about the Limeys,' and the same man had openly called Lieutenant General Sir Harold 'Alex' Alexander, the British Commander-in-Chief (C-in-C) Middle East, 'a coward'.[5] At Fredendall's II Armored Corps headquarters and down the chain of command, American officers and soldiers mocked British accents (failing utterly to distinguish Australians and other nationalities from British), and reminded each other that back in 1917–18 AEF (American Expeditionary Force) had really stood for 'After England Failed'.[6]

The British were astonishingly relaxed about this; they knew all about the pressures of alliance warfare: indeed, given the politics of the Dominions and India, the British Empire itself was almost an alliance at war. Soldierly pride, the belief that you and your unit were the best in the world, had to come from somewhere, and it was an American practice to encourage denigration of the next platoon, or battalion, or division. Contempt for your allies was just the culmination of the process. Given time, the British hoped that American insults would become a grudging respect. But it was hard to get on with fellows who showed no inclination to get on with you.

The strongest argument that the British could use, and one reason that Eisenhower had argued against landing in North Africa, was that TORCH had set back BOLERO by almost a year. Mounting the North Africa landings needed 116 troopships and supply ships, with 195 warships to support them, most of which were still in the North African theatre. The British Army had twenty-two divisions in Great Britain itself, plus four Canadian divisions, but these were all in various states of training and readiness, and represented the entire British strategic reserve for the war. After the transfer of troops to North Africa only one American combat division remained in the United Kingdom, the 29th 'Blue and Gray' Infantry Division, a National Guard formation.[7] The USAAF also was still assembling in Great Britain, and its 8th Air Force, the main American contribution to the Combined Bombing Offensive, had yet to carry out a single raid over Germany. The Allies simply did not have the experience, nor the troops and transport in the right place, to launch an invasion of northern France in 1943. Delivered over and over again in a slow patient British monotone across the conference table, backed by tables of figures and staff studies, it was a rock-crusher argument; but it simply would not crush. Instead, Brooke and his team were horrified to hear Marshall raise yet again the issue of whether the war against Japan should take priority. To still have no agreed common strategy after a year of war was a recipe for defeat. The Casablanca talks were in stalemate.

Close to despair on 18 January, after lunch Brooke met with the British permanent military staff representative in Washington, Field Marshal Sir John Dill, and the RAF Chief of Air Staff, Air Marshal Sir Charles 'Peter' Portal, in an effort to find a solution. 'You know that you must come to some agreement with the Americans,' Dill advised Brooke, 'and that you cannot bring unsolved problems to the Prime Minister and the President. You know as well as I do what a mess they would make of it!'[8] Between them they worked out an offer, most of which depended on careful phrasing: the Americans would recognise the primacy of Europe in return for the British conceding the importance of the Pacific; the British would confirm their commitment to ROUNDUP in return for the Americans agreeing to the next blow falling in the Mediterranean. In addition, as a symbol of their commitment to ROUNDUP, the British recommended the immediate creation of a joint planning headquarters in London, to be headed by an American officer, and to investigate the possibility of a large-scale raid or small landing in northern France later in 1943.

At the afternoon meeting of the Combined Chiefs of Staff the Americans agreed to this wording, with General Marshall putting forward Eisenhower's name to command the new headquarters, to be known as COSSAC (Chief of

Staff to the Supreme Allied Commander). The British in turn put forward Lieutenant General Morgan to be Eisenhower's deputy. On 21 January the Combined Chiefs discussed the idea in detail, with the Americans in particular favouring a small invasion over a mere raid. The British put forward an already existing plan for a small landing, code-named HADRIAN and drawn up two months earlier, giving it a planning date of 1 August 1943. Churchill expressed himself completely in favour, 'so as to be able to profit by favourable August weather for some form of SLEDGEHAMMER'.[9] General Marshal promised that by July there would be five or six American divisions in Great Britain ready to take part in an attack, although two days later the Americans altered this slightly to four divisions by 1 August, and seven by 15 September. In return, and after some debate as to whether Sardinia was a better objective than Sicily, the Americans agreed to HUSKY on the understanding that the British wanted only to secure their communications through the Mediterranean, and were not interested in an invasion of Italy.

It is a matter of historical dispute whether the British offer was a genuine move towards a Second Front, or an attempt to call what they saw as an American bluff. The issue was complicated by the fact that no Supreme Allied Commander for the European theatre was discussed, leaving COSSAC without a commander. The British believed that they had a gentleman's agreement at Casablanca that the post would go to one of their officers, and Churchill had advised Brooke that he might expect the appointment. But within weeks it became apparent that the Americans were thinking in terms of General Marshall to command ROUNDUP. If Eisenhower made a success of a cross-Channel landing in 1943 he might reasonably expect to keep his post of Chief of Staff under Marshall.

At the final press conference for SYMBOL, Roosevelt had planned to tell the press the Civil War story of Ulysses S. Grant and his call for 'Unconditional Surrender,' making the same demand from Germany, Italy and Japan. But given the success in securing the defection of Vichy forces during TORCH, and the delicacy of the continuing negotiations with the Italians, Churchill prevailed on Roosevelt to drop the phrase, which he had only meant as a good press headline rather than a considered policy. So events ended in apparent Allied harmony, but the underlying problems had only been masked. 'The Casablanca Conference did not produce a definitive long-range strategy,' an official American study concluded, 'Rather, a firm decision between the Mediterranean and north-west Europe was deferred, as the Allies tried to accommodate both'.[10]

COSSAC

January to August 1943
Set up in London almost as soon as SYMBOL ended, COSSAC drew heavily on the experience of Mountbatten's Combined Operations Headquarters. Dickie

Mountbatten himself was in his element in a wonderfully ill-defined role as go-between for COSSAC and the Chiefs of Staff. As a British official historian later stressed, if the Allies intended to make a small lodgement, and 'the purpose was to remain on the Continent, the only possible objective was the Cotentin peninsula'.[11] This limestone promontory juts out northward for twenty-five miles from the Bay of Biscay into the western approaches of the English Channel, with the port of Cherbourg in the centre of its northern face, and it was narrow enough to be held by a handful of divisions. The British knew Cherbourg well, having used it as a supply port and to evacuate some of their own troops in 1940; the biggest port on the coast of northern France, it had a capacity to discharge 8,500 tons a day, more than enough to land reinforcements and to keep Allied forces ashore supplied. But a frontal assault on Cherbourg from the sea was out of the question. It was the base for 5th and 9th E-Boat Flotillas with five torpedo boats each, and six *Elbing* class destroyers. A chain of four forts along its outer harbour wall, each with four 75 mm guns, protected the entrance, and it was dominated by three medium batteries and by Fort Roule with four 105 mm guns on a promontory overlooking the town. The approaches to Cherbourg were defended to the east by two heavy and two medium coastal batteries, and to the west by four further batteries including the 'York' Battery with four 170 mm guns. There were Luftwaffe airfields at Malpertus-sur-Mer to the east of Cherbourg and Querqueville to the west with about thirty Me 109 or FW 190 fighters, although the countryside was otherwise largely unsuitable for airfields.

Other than the Cherbourg naval garrison, the Cotentin was only weakly defended by 709th Infantry Division, a low-quality *Bodenständige* or 'static' division with no motorised transport or armour. But less than thirty miles to the west were the Channel Islands, occupied by the Germans in 1940 and the only British territory under German control. With the same mentality that had governed his behaviour towards Stalingrad, Hitler was convinced that the British would try to retake these islands, and on his personal orders they were defended by the largest division in the German Army, the 319th Infantry Division with 40,000 troops plus torpedo boats, submarines, anti-aircraft guns and long-range coastal artillery. Too well-defended to be captured or bombed except from very high altitude, these coastal guns threatened any landing on the western Cotentin.

By 1 August the Allies could assemble enough specialist transport shipping for two infantry divisions and an armoured brigade, and enough landing craft for a first assault wave of two (American) regiments or (British) brigades. The key to success, as Lieutenant General Morgan noted, was 'that we should command the resources to reduce Cherbourg within forty-eight hours'.[12] Unfortunately, the peninsula on either side of Cherbourg and for some distance south along both sides was almost entirely rocky cliffs and shoals, with nowhere to land sufficient troops from the sea. The only way to capture Cherbourg was to drop sizeable airborne forces behind it and take it from the landward side; the HADRIAN plan estimated the equivalent of two airborne divisions with 1,116 transport aircraft and 518 gliders, while amphibious forces landed further south to form a defensive line across the peninsula.[13] The northern Cotentin was excellent defensive country, with plenty of woods, hills and broken ground; the problem was not getting Allied footsoldiers ashore, but landing artillery and tanks with enough ammunition to stop a German counter-attack from breaking through.

Even so, a landing operation this small would be no help to Stalin. In west and north-west Europe including Germany were forty-one Axis divisions plus about 1,600 combat aircraft, of which about thirty divisions were in France together with 750 aircraft. COSSAC's staff studies showed that the Germans could concentrate fifteen divisions against such a landing within fourteen days, without moving troops from Russia or Italy. To avoid being overwhelmed in the Cotentin the Allies needed to land at least five brigades on the first day, and no fewer than eight follow-up divisions with all their equipment and supplies on the second day. This was a larger landing than that planned for HUSKY. Not only were the troops and ships not available, even if Cherbourg were captured intact and fully functional within forty-eight hours the port could never discharge that quantity of troops and cargo so quickly: it would be like forcing a bucket of water through a drinking straw.

To add to Eisenhower's problems, by mid-February it was clear that the American promise at Casablanca of four divisions in Great Britain by 1 August had been optimistic, based on the assumption that there would be no continuing major losses to U-Boats in the Atlantic, and no campaign in Sicily. In reality, 2nd 'Indianhead' Infantry Division might arrive to join 29th Infantry Division in September, followed by 4th 'Cloverleaf' Infantry Division a month later. Eisenhower obtained Marshall's agreement that 1st 'Big Red One' Infantry Division and 82nd 'All American' Airborne Division must be redeployed to Great Britain from North Africa; and that by delaying other movements, including troops and supplies for North Africa, 2nd Infantry Division could arrive in August.

While Eisenhower developed his plan, in North Africa the Germans attacked through the Kasserine Pass on 14 February, and inexperienced American troops, badly led and badly deployed, broke and ran. Amazingly, Major General Fredendall commanding II Armored Corps remained throughout the battle in a deep cave that constituted his headquarters, specially dug into a ravine wall, fifty miles from the fighting. General Alexander's assessment was that the Americans were 'soft, green and quite untrained'; more critical reports suggested that 'the United States Army might benefit from a good stiffening of British officers'.[14] The combination of Eisenhower's departure for COSSAC, the shock of Kasserine, and the American decision to scale back HUSKY now had considerable consequences. The British and French announced that Eisenhower's deputy, Lieutenant General Mark Clark, was not acceptable as his successor, and General Alexander was appointed. The Americans had also hoped to create an Army command in North Africa, but with fewer troops they settled for a reinforced II Armored Corps (1st and 2nd

Armored and 3rd and 5th Infantry Divisions), now under Lieutenant General George S. Patton Jr. Given the American lack of confidence in 1st Army after Kasserine, as 8th Army arrived in Tunisia from the Western Desert Alexander took the unusual decision to place II Armored Corps under Montgomery. Patton hated the British as much as his fellow generals, and reportedly the two commanders loathed each other at first sight. But within a month the coupling of Montgomery's mastery of planning and firepower with Patton's gift for armoured manoeuvre had torn the southern German defences in Tunisia apart. 'Monty holds them by the nose' went the saying in II Armored Corps, 'while Patton kicks them in the ass!'[15] It was a combination repeated several times in the course of the year, with Montgomery describing Patton and his troops as 'quite first class, and I have a very great admiration for the way they fight'. Their friendship remained strong even at the war's end, when Patton rose 'to propose a toast to the health of General Montgomery and express our satisfaction in serving under him'.[16] Despite the reduction in American forces, Tunis fell to the Allies on 12 May.

Just as Allied victory in Tunisia was announced, the British and Americans met again for the TRIDENT Conference in Washington DC. The British expected praise for the North Africa success, and that the conference would be chiefly concerned with the future war against Japan. Instead, they found the entire Allied war strategy once more under question. 'The Americans are taking up the attitude that we led them down the garden path taking them to North Africa!' wrote General Brooke in his diary, 'That at Casablanca we again misled them by inducing them to attack Sicily!!' and 'before long they will be urging that we should defeat Japan first!'[17] Roosevelt's Chief of Staff, Admiral William Leahy, who chaired the Combined Chiefs meetings, was dismissive even of the threat of a German atomic bomb. 'The bomb will never go off,' Leahy told the meeting, 'and I speak as an expert in explosives!'[18]

It was in this strained atmosphere that Eisenhower, with the support of Mountbatten and Morgan, presented the COSSAC plan for a landing in the Cotentin, under the code-name of COCKADE. Eisenhower argued that during summer 1943 the British already intended to mount a series of deception plans to draw German attention away from the Eastern Front and from Sicily. These included HARLEQUIN, a major land exercise in early September, linked to STARKEY, a simulated assault on the French coast. Since these exercises were happening anyway, the British troops involved together with their naval and air support could join the American troops already promised to make the COCKADE landing in the Cotentin.

Eisenhower accepted that the Allied landing forces available for COCKADE fell far short of those needed to establish a permanent beachhead, but he compensated for this by three arguments. First, intelligence showed that the Germans had a highly exaggerated idea of the Allied forces in the United Kingdom: at least nine to fourteen armoured divisions and twenty-five to forty infantry divisions, of which fifteen could be used as amphibious assault formations.[19] Together with the deceptions already planned, this should be enough to keep substantial German reinforcements away from COCKADE for some time after the landings. Secondly, since the British were so keen on national uprisings to support their war effort, they could help provoke one in northern France by using the networks built up by their Special Operations Executive (SOE), estimated at potentially 10–20,000 armed Resistance fighters. Next, while the Allies had persistently failed to bring the Luftwaffe to battle by mounting fighter sweeps over northern France, the Dieppe raid had included a major air battle with a hundred German aircraft or more shot down. If the resources of the RAF and USAAF in Great Britain were used to support COCKADE, then as Morgan argued 'The Luftwaffe, thanks to the increasing necessity being forced upon it by our bomber offensive to defend the Father-land, would be at an even greater disadvantage operating over Normandy than would we'.[20] Mountbatten joined in to say that addition to this air support, a special task force of battleships and aircraft carriers would deploy off the northern Cotentin coast, and this amount of firepower would be quite enough to hold off any German counter-attack. Eisenhower concluded that if after three or four days Cherbourg still held out and COCKADE had not achieved its objectives, then the Allies could simply withdraw their troops; if Cherbourg fell to them early then they could stay for as long as seemed appropriate.

There has always been a strong suspicion that Eisenhower, and Marshall above him, believed that COCKADE would achieve much more than this outline plan suggested: and that they expected the Germans in France to collapse before the weight of American firepower. The British Chiefs of Staff were horrified. It seemed to them that the whole Allied global strategy was being distorted to mount a small operation that had little chance of success. 'Battleships by daylight off the French coast?' First Sea Lord Admiral Sir Dudley Pound exploded at Mountbatten, 'You must be mad, Dickie!'[21] Disagreement was not entirely on national lines: COCKADE continued to have Churchill's utter support, as well as Mountbatten's; while one American general, recalling the original SLEDGEHAMMER code-name, dismissed Eisenhower's plan as 'TACKHAMMER would have been more descriptive'.[22] But it rapidly became apparent to the British Chiefs that COCKADE was not negotiable; that if they attempted to block it the Americans might well turn against HUSKY and argue again for a greater commitment against Japan, a change that Brooke was convinced would lose the war. Reluctantly, they agreed to COCKADE for early September.

The scaled-back version of HUSKY began on 9 July, with Montgomery's 8th Army including Patton's II Armored Corps landing on the southern coast of Sicily, supported by British 1st Airborne Division. The airborne landings were not a great success, one lesson learned being that 'operations in the European theatre would probably have to be carried out at night'.[23] There was also a severe problem with shortage of transport aircraft and experienced crews; the USAAF C-47 Dakotas used for HUSKY lacked the range to fly to southern England, and would not be available for COCKADE. The British also dealt fairly with the Italian conspirators against Mussolini, not wishing to be seen to encourage a revolt and then leave it unsupported for fear of the reaction elsewhere in Europe; the planned coup, which had depended on an Allied landing in Italy, was called off. Instead the British mounted two deception operations, BAYTOWN, a supposed crossing into Italy once Sicily was secure, and BRIMSTONE, a supposed invasion of Sardinia. Together with the fighting in Sicily and hints received of the Italian plot, this was enough for the Germans to transfer two Panzer divisions, three Panzer grenadier divisions and three Parachute divisions from France to Italy between June and August.

With the last of the Battle of the Atlantic still raging in June and July, the realities of Allied global commitments cut back on Eisenhower's plan for battleship and carrier support for COCKADE. With no coup against Mussolini, the Italian fleet remained active in the Mediterranean and Aegean, meaning that Force H at Gibraltar, the main British naval presence in the Mediterranean, could not be reduced, as well as forcing the British to cancel some plans for Greece and the Balkans. The Home Fleet at Scapa Flow had five battleships, one aircraft carrier, two cruiser squadrons and three destroyer flotillas, augmented by two US Navy battleships, the USS *South Dakota* and USS *Alabama*, and the fleet carrier USS *Ranger*, guarding against the constant threat from Norway of the battleship *Tirpitz*, the battlecruiser *Scharnhorst* and the heavy cruiser *Lützow* all breaking out simultaneously into the Atlantic to attack Allied convoys. Eisenhower demanded the return of the carrier *Victorious* to British home waters from the South Pacific together with the *Saratoga*, and that the *South Dakota* and *Alabama*, which had been meant for the Pacific by August, should stay with the Home Fleet. Admiral King had no intention of releasing the *Saratoga*, then his only carrier in South Pacific waters, and several US Navy officers now joined the British in wondering how a junior lieutenant general in London had come to dictate Pacific strategy. After further debate COCKADE was allocated two British battleships from the Home Fleet, HMS *Duke of York* and HMS *Anson*, and two carriers, HMS *Illustrious* and USS *Ranger*.

In their typical fashion, once they were committed to COCKADE the British threw their full weight behind it. To accompany HUSKY, on 8 July they mounted deception plan TINDALL, sailing the Home Fleet towards Norway as if it were escorting an amphibious landing force in the hope of tempting the big German warships out into the open. There was little German response, although the Allies were impressed that the carrier HMS *Furious* could provide fighter protection for the fleet even close in to the enemy shoreline. At the end of July the Home Fleet repeated the deception manoeuvre, with the same degree of success and lack of German response. Meanwhile, arms and equipment drops to the two largest SOE networks in France, code-named respectively PROSPER stretching across the north, and SCIENTIST down through the south-west, increased ten-fold in April and May, and then twenty-fold in June and July.[24] The corresponding massive increase in Resistance activity attracted great German attention, leading to disaster in July as the Germans penetrated the PROSPER and SCIENTIST networks and rolled them up. There would be no uprising to accompany COCKADE, although it would take SOE in

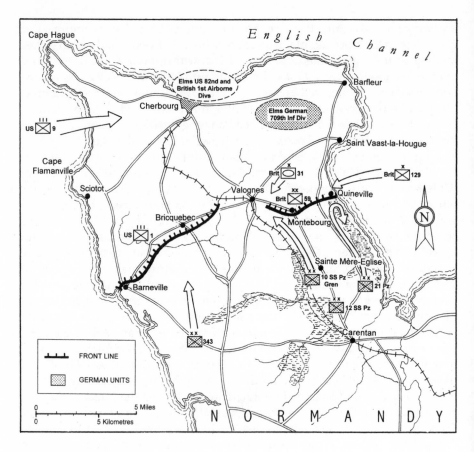

Operation COCKADE

London some months to realise how much their commitment to the plan had cost them. With American political backing, on 3 June the French Committee of National Liberation was established in London, and in August General Charles de Gaulle became its sole head, fuelling British suspicions about a possible hidden agenda behind COCKADE. These suspicions became anger when persistent leaks to the press from both London and Washington culminated on 19 August with a *New York Times* banner headline 'Armies ready to go, says Eisenhower'.[25]

All this finally became too much for General Brooke, who in a stormy interview with Churchill demanded a senior field command. Brooke was sent out to head the new South-East Asia Command (SEAC) and was replaced by General Alexander, with Mountbatten being moved to become C-in-C Middle East. As far as the Americans were concerned, their worst enemy had been sent to direct the British war against Japan, while their best friend (and the British top man in amphibious warfare) had been sent to the Mediterranean!

Looking for a showdown with the British, they demanded a further Allied planning conference, code-named QUADRANT, to take place in August. The British response was that with COCKADE so imminent QUADRANT should be held in London. Roosevelt, who never visited Great Britain throughout the war, rejected this, and QUADRANT was put on hold. On 5 August, Admiral Pound suffered a severe stroke and was replaced as First Sea Lord by Admiral Sir Andrew 'ABC' Cunningham. Like Alexander, Cunningham accepted that it was far too late to change the COCKADE plan.

COCKADE

September 1943
The first Allied troops to land in France at the start of Operation COCKADE were 505th Parachute Infantry of 82nd Airborne Division, jumping just after dusk at 9:00 p.m. on 8 September from their aircraft over the rugged plateau just five miles inland from Cherbourg and west of its main road. Winds and cloud were reasonable, a three-quarter moon provided enough visibility, enemy anti-aircraft fire was light, and most of the regiment made it down safely. Next, the leading brigade of British 6th Airborne Division dropped to the east of Cherbourg, with the objectives of seizing Maupertus airfield and knocking out the coastal batteries in the area. Barely 300 transport aircraft were available, and this had led to two hair-raising Allied decisions: first that the airborne assault should take place simultaneously with night bombing of targets all across the Cotentin, and second that there should be three airborne landings that night, with the same aircraft returning at 1:00 a.m., bringing with them the remainder of 82nd Airborne Division including gliders with heavy weapons, and again at 6:00 a.m., just before dawn, bringing the remainder of 6th Airborne Division with their gliders. Air Marshal Sir Trafford Leigh-Mallory, COSSAC's senior airman, warned Eisenhower that as surprise was impossible these waves 'would suffer some seventy per cent losses in glider strength and at least fifty per cent in paratroop strength' if not fully pro-tected.[26] 82nd Airborne's mission was to take Cherbourg including Fort Roule and the batteries to the west; 6th Airborne's mission, once its first objectives were taken, was to push southwards to Valognes to link-up with the seaborne landings. British and French Commandos also landed on a few small beaches along the north coast to attack the coastal batteries and Querqueville airfield.

At first, and despite their anxieties, the Allies achieved considerable surprise. Shortly after midnight, a listening post in southern England reported that 'a German coastal artillery subaltern on the far shore had been heard calling his captain on the radio to ask if anybody knew what all this fuss was about,' just before all transmission from that battery ceased.[27] But as the first reports of Allied paratroopers came in, the Luftwaffe directed its night-fighters into the Cotentin, and as the second wave arrived many of the Me 109s and Me 110s broke through the RAF escorts. Most of the unarmed transports scattered in self-defence, almost one in five was shot down, and those paratroopers who managed to jump, some from burning aircraft, landed spread far across Normandy. To their eternal honour, the surviving transport crews returned at dawn for a third attempt. Total losses among the paratroopers were over sixty per cent, and of 200 gliders fewer than fifty made it down intact. Leigh-Mallory protested to Eisenhower at 'what he termed the "futile slaughter" of two fine divisions'.[28] An epic air battle that would rage by day and night for the next seventy-two hours had been joined.

As this was happening, two Allied landing flotillas had embarked their troops and were sailing for either side of the Cotentin coast. British 59th (Staffordshire) Infantry Division recorded that 'when units began to move, they found themselves passing with unusual smoothness right through the system of staging camps' down to the coast to embark.[29] By 2:00 a.m. the amphibious landings had started, with the British division coming ashore on the wide beaches of the eastern Cotentin just south of Saint Vaast-la-Hougue, and US 1st Infantry Division on the beaches of the western coast at Sciotot, south of Cape Flamanville. The objective over the next forty-eight hours was for the British to capture Montebourg and then Valognes, and for the Americans to secure the high ground north of Barneville and then Bricquebec, both linking up with British 1st Airborne Division just west of the main Cherbourg road. At first this Allied assault from the sea also went better than expected. The leading troops got ashore without difficulty, the German beach defences were weak with a few earth-and-wood bunkers, and the widely stretched units of 709th Infantry Division were no match for the British and Americans at night. By dawn the South Staffordshires of 177th Infantry Brigade had secured the little harbour of Quinéville and were half-way to Montebourg, while 16th Infantry Regiment leading the Big Red One had advanced about the same distance, reaching the main west coast road. As the light improved the first bombers of the 8th Air Force appeared overhead to the south of the Allied landings, striking at the heart of each little town to create choke-points for any German counter-attack.

The British and Americans now sought to turn round their landing craft and bring in the remainder of each division, together with the tanks of British 31st Armoured Brigade on special floats, under increasing harassment from the Luftwaffe. Already too many landing craft had been lost or damaged, and the likelihood of getting either division completely ashore before the next nightfall was rapidly fading. The first of the surviving American paratroopers had already begun to fight their way into Cherbourg, but they were held up by Fort Roule, and without heavy weapons they had no way to take it. During mid-morning, in response to repeated radio calls, HMS *Duke of York* closed in to Cherbourg from the north and opened fire on the fort, partly reducing it to rubble together with the chain of harbour forts.

For the first day all was confusion on the German side. There were no plans for a response to an Allied invasion, and no movement orders were issued to other divisions along the coast in case further landings took place elsewhere. The soldiers of 709th Infantry Division continued to offer little resistance, and by nightfall 59th (Staffordshire) Infantry Division had captured Montebourg, while 1st Infantry Division's leading troops were half-way to Bricquebec. There was still a gap about fifteen miles wide that the two Allied landing forces needed to close, with no help expected from the survivors of the airborne divisions, whose stragglers were largely making their way towards Cherbourg from all over the Cotentin.

In the air a first day's battle had taken place that exceeded even Dieppe. While over 200 Allied fighter-bombers and bombers carried out their attacks. 540 RAF Spitfires and 160 longer-range USAAF P47 Thunderbolts and P51 Mustangs clashed with 225 front-line fighters of the Luftwaffe's 3rd Air Fleet. At the day's end the Allies had lost 106 fighters but shot down forty-eight Messerschmitts and Focke Wulfs, and damaged fifty-five more more, a far greater attrition rate than the Germans could sustain. On the second night RAF Bomber Command's 8 (Pathfinder) Group returned with its Mosquitoes and Lancasters; and, astonishingly, a final parachute and glider landing was also mounted by the remaining handful of transport aircraft, bringing in much needed men and ammunition.

With Cherbourg still being contested and interference from the Luftwaffe, it took until after dawn on the second day for the two Allied assault divisions to complete their landings. Rather than wait off the beaches for another day under German air attack, both landing flotillas opted to withdraw in daylight, the western flotilla coming up through the narrow gap between Cape Hague and the Channel Islands. The Germans had been waiting for this, and at once the destroyers and E-Boats from Cherbourg and the Channel Islands put to sea to intercept the convoy. The 8th Air Force bombers blitzed the Channel Islands' coastal artillery, Royal Navy destroyers engaged the Germans at sea, and the Allies revealed their hand by bringing their two aircraft carriers in from the north to launch an air strike. Every German ship and craft was sunk, at the cost of two British destroyers.

On the ground 1st Infantry Division took up its planned positions along the ridgeline with its western flank on the sea at Barneville and its eastern flank just beyond Briquebec, while 59th (Staffordshire) Infantry Division held the ridge from Quinéville through Montebourg, with 31st Armoured Brigade in reserve to the north. But only a thin patrol line extended through the valley between the two divisions, a distance of about five miles, while at Valognes, which had been reduced to rubble, troops of 709th Infantry Division still held out. In the course of the day the Americans identified a probe up the western coastal road towards their positions by elements of 343rd Infantry Division, another 'static' German formation that was unlikely to trouble the Big Red One. More serious were indicators that assembling south of the British were elements of 21st Panzer Division and 10th SS Panzer grenadier Division 'Karl der Grosse'.[30] Given the lie of the ground, the obvious line of attack for these two divisions was from south-east to north-west along the main Cherbourg road next morning. At Cherbourg the battle still continued; the American and British paratroopers had mostly by-passed Fort Roule and were fighting hand-to-hand with the garrison through the burning streets and down to the harbour, but still the port showed no sign of falling.

The original plan had been for two further amphibious landings during the third night. 43rd (Wessex) Infantry Division would come ashore at Quinéville to reinforce 59th (Staffordshire) Infantry Division against the expected German attack. If Cherbourg was open, then US 2nd Infantry Division would land there; if not it would land on the open beaches north of Cape Flamanville and march directly to Cherbourg. But barely half the landing craft had survived to return to their harbours in southern England, and both complete divisions could no longer be loaded and transported that night. Eisenhower now had an impossibly difficult decision to make, and barely an hour in which to make it. Reassurance came from Admiral Cunningham. 'Now look here, General,' he told Eisenhower, 'during this present war I have already evacuated two British armies and I don't intend to evacuate a third'.[31] Cunningham offered to commit his battleships and carriers to a direct frontal assault on Cherbourg next morning in conjunction with a heavy bomber attack; he would lose some ships and the port would be badly damaged, but at least it would be opened. With this reassurance, Eisenhower chose to split his landing craft to carry one regiment or brigade each of 2nd Infantry Division and 43rd (Wessex) Infantry Division to their respective beaches. Loading started late in the afternoon amid scenes that verged on chaos as men and equipment had to be moved at short notice, but the flotillas sailed just before midnight.

The crucial day of the battle would be 10 September. The landings by 2nd Infantry Division and 43rd (Wessex) Infantry Division began just before dawn, while 8 (Pathfinder) Group carried out more raids in an attempt to slow down the German reinforcements. With little warning to the troops fighting in Cherbourg, at dawn American medium bombers carried out a saturation raid, followed by a shore bombardment by the *Duke of York* and *Anson*, with fighters and light bombers from the carrier group joining in. Then two British destroyers, replacements for the losses of the previous day, steamed alongside the forts along the harbour wall and blasted each of them individually before landing Commando assault teams. One of the destroyers was literally blown apart by shells from the 'York' Battery, and the Commandos lost more than half their men, but by mid-afternoon they had made contact with the paratroopers. Cherbourg was mostly in ruins and still partly under German control, but at least the smaller Allied warships could fight their way into the harbour. The German reaction was to send over seventy medium bombers with fighter escorts to attack the port and the Allied heavy warships. The *Duke of York* was badly damaged, and a lucky bomb sent USS *Ranger* to the bottom of the Atlantic.[32]

Along the ridge at Montebourg the British awaited the main German armoured attack. This came in mid-morning in a classic pincer movement, with 21st Panzer Division driving to the east of the Cherbourg road, and the brigade-sized 10th SS Panzer grenadiers to the west. The British had local command of the air by now, and 59th (Staffordshire) Infantry Division had enough artillery to stop 21st Panzer's attack short. As the leading tanks of 10th SS Panzer grenadiers cut round the open western flank, crossing the main road between Valognes and Montebourg, they were counter-attacked by 31st Armoured Brigade, and in a duel of Panzer IVs with Shermans they were also halted. Taking a considerable risk, 1st Infantry Division thinned out and extended its line almost to Valognes to provide flanking fire onto the stalled German attack. But with a lodgment between the two Allied forces, the Waffen-SS were not about to give up so easily. Fighting to the east and west through the hedgerows, they slowly bent the two halves of the Allied line back away from each other.

By early afternoon, 129th Infantry Brigade from 43rd (Wessex) Infantry Division was ashore and had joined the British defensive line against 21st Panzer Division. But the Allies had no defence against what happened next. After landing north of Cape Flamanville, US 9th Infantry Regiment was marching overland to within sight of Cherbourg when it was crashed into by the training cadre of 12th SS Panzer Division 'Hitler Jugend' – the new Hitler Youth division that was forming in Normandy. Barely more than a weak brigade in strength, the tanks and motorised infantry of the Hitler Youth had been behind 10th SS Panzer grenadiers as they made their attack, and had by-passed Valognes to the west and sped up the Cherbourg road looking for the enemy. Mostly strung out in march formation on the narrow roads, 9th Infantry Regiment was badly cut up before it could even respond. The Americans had never encountered troops like these before; averaging barely seventeen years old, the Hitler Youth expected only to kill or die.[33]

A gaping hole had been ripped in the Allied defensive line, and the only possible value of Cherbourg now was to evacuate as many soldiers as could be saved, together with those who could be got out over the British beaches. But on the far side of the English Channel Eisenhower would not give the order. The decision was effectively taken from him by Winston Churchill, whose every instinct rebelled against both retreating and abandoning his allies in trouble. Instead, in a fraught meeting with Churchill present, Alexander proposed to Eisenhower that the British forces ashore should fall back north-eastwards with the objective of securing the small ports of St-Vaast-la-Hougue and Barfleur as a base for supply, while during the night the remainder of 43rd (Wessex) Infantry Division could be embarked on British warships and used to reinforce Cherbourg directly through the harbour. 1st Infantry Division and any survivors from 9th Infantry Regiment would conduct a fighting withdrawal to the beaches north of Cape Flamanville. Rather than leave the Allied troops in the Cotentin to their fate, the Royal Navy and RAF would bear the cost, whatever it might be. 'It takes the Navy three years to build a ship,' Cunningham remarked sombrely, 'It would take three hundred to build a new reputation'.[34]

Cherbourg

September to November 1943

The agony of Cherbourg was not quick in ending. By the morning of 11 September, Americans and British from the remains of four divisions, plus the surviving Commandos, had carved out a perimeter that included Fort Roule, taken after repeated assaults. Against this barricade the Hitler Youth threw themselves for the next two days and nights, until finally ordered to withdraw. For the next week there was no lull in the fighting, but a marked pause in major attacks as more German reinforcements arrived. Losses in the air had been massive on both sides, but with barely thirty front-line fighters left 3rd Air Fleet was temporarily grounded, and under the Allied air umbrella both the British retreat towards Barfleur and the American retreat towards the Flamanville beaches were not heavily contested. Each night British warships ran the gauntlet of German submarine and air attack to take troops and supplies into Cherbourg, and by day and night 8th Air Force and Bomber Command sought to destroy or delay the encircling German forces.

As Adolf Hitler was quick to realise, at Cherbourg the British and Americans had made their own Stalingrad, but on the far side of the English Channel rather than the Volga. 1st Infantry Division was pulled off the western beaches on 16 September, leaving almost all of its equipment behind, but still intact as a division. Clearing the last survivors of 709th Infantry Division out of St Vaast and Barfleur, the British established their base and perimeter in the north-east. At Cherbourg there was no way to land vehicles or heavy weapons. Instead, the remaining infantry of 43rd (Wessex) Infantry Division and 2nd Infantry Division, and then 29th Infantry Division, were fed into the meat grinder over the next two weeks, pitting rifles and bazookas against tanks and artillery. Each day the Americans demanded to know what the British were doing to relieve Cherbourg. The British replied that the RAF and Royal Navy were taking heavy losses, that three precious British divisions were being destroyed, and that most of the US Navy was on the far side of the world.

With Marshall's backing, Eisenhower now argued that the Allies should hold Cherbourg through the winter, by which time enough American ground, naval and air reinforcements would have arrived to break out of the bridgehead; but after the experience of COCKADE the British were no longer inclined to believe American promises. The deciding factors were the onset of bad weather in the English Channel, and the increasing impossibility for the British of maintaining such a rate of attrition. On 30 September, Churchill advised Roosevelt by transatlantic telephone link that no more British ships or divisions could be provided for Operation COCKADE.

The Allied withdrawal, code-named Operation WADHAM, was surprisingly straightforward, leading to another American gibe that this was what the British did best. Having already thinned out their eastern lodgement the Allies took the last troops off from Barfleur on the night of 8 October, together with 27,000 uninjured men that were all who remained of the Cherbourg garrison.

Eisenhower issued a brief statement, 'Our landings in the Cherbourg area have failed to gain a satisfactory foothold and I have withdrawn the troops. My decision to attack at this time and place was based upon the best information available. The troops, the air and the navy did all that bravery and devotion to duty could do. If any blame or fault attaches to the attempt it is mine alone.'[35] Even so, there are today many American veterans who say that the British let them down, and historians who have agreed with them.

Consequences

December 1943
As the Allies prepared to meet for the rescheduled QUADRANT Conference in Quebec in December 1943 a position paper was circulated to President Roosevelt and his senior staff and advisers which argued that if Stalin could be induced to declare war on the Japanese the war would be considerably shortened and many American lives saved, that 'the most important factor that the United States has to consider in relation to Russia is the prosecution of the war in the Pacific'.[36] No one was ready to say the words yet, but the humiliating failure of COCKADE made it almost certain that ROUNDUP could not be mounted until late 1944, and the damage done to Anglo-American trust might take even longer than that to rebuild. With Italy still in the war, a revival of the Mediterranean strategy was equally pointless. With no threat any longer from the west, Hitler could afford to strengthen his forces on the Eastern Front, and there was a good chance of stabilising the German line close to the River Dnieper. It would be a bitter thing for Stalin to swallow, but if he waited too long the Germans might reach a deal with the United States first. Now the Americans were in a position to offer Stalin Manchuria and other territory in the east in return for a declaration of war against Japan, perhaps after a cease-fire agreement with Hitler. It was a diplomatic revolution of some magnitude, but the American people had always seen the war against Japan as the real conflict, and after the British had let them down so badly they would understand. Even as the proceedings opened at Quebec, American officials were making their first secret approaches to Hitler and Stalin to end the war in Europe. The British would find out soon enough, but that would be their problem.

The Reality

This scenario has been written with the jaundiced tone of an imaginary British historian (who just happens to share my name) looking back at how his country was defeated in a counterfactual World War II. It is based on three historical events: the Anglo-American differences over strategy at SYMBOL and TRIDENT; the discussion of the HADRIAN plan at Casablanca; and the historical COCKADE, which was the code-name given to the entire deception operation including TINDALL, STARKEY, HARLEQUIN and the real WADHAM (a fictitious American landing in Brittany in October 1943). Events are entirely factual up to 18 January 1943, and largely factual after that. Footnotes marked with an asterisk (*) are fictional, and I have had a little fun with authors, titles and page numbers. Otherwise, all footnoted quotations and citations are genuine, although in a few cases I have taken considerable liberties with the context. Eisenhower's press release for COCKADE is adapted slightly from his draft statement in case of failure on D-Day in 1944. The loss of the SOE networks in France during the attempts to sell the COCKADE deception plan to the Germans is real, as is the *New York Times* headline. The German forces available to repel COCKADE are historically accurate; the much heavier 'Atlantic Wall' defences were largely created after November 1943. The Allied forces are those used for HARLEQUIN (except for II Canadian Corps, which took part in the real exercise) and for STARKEY, including the USAAF contribution, plus a British airborne division, a British battleship and aircraft carrier, and all the American ground and naval forces described. The local weather and the phase of the moon are also correct.

In reality Anglo-American relations became rather better than they have been portrayed here. A compromise was worked out and accepted at Casablanca, leading to Roosevelt announcing the unconditional surrender policy. COSSAC was created under Lieutenant General Morgan as a result of the conference, but did not start functioning until April 1943. The Axis forces in Tunisia did surrender on 12 May 1943; Eisenhower remained as Supreme Allied Commander for the invasions of Sicily and Italy; Operation HUSKY was launched on 8 July, the planned coup overthrew Mussolini on 25 July, Italy surrendered on 3 September, and the Allies invasion of the Italian mainland began with the real Operation BAYTOWN on 8 September, the same date as STARKEY. With the Italian surrender, Sardinia was occupied by the Allies, and Corsica was liberated on 4 October, the date that this scenario ends. The real TRIDENT Conference in May confirmed Operation ROUNDUP for 1944 and renamed it OVERLORD; the real QUADRANT Conference took place in Quebec in August; Brooke remained in his post, and it was Mountbatten who went to SEAC in August; Pound did suffer a stroke on 5 August and was succeeded by Cunningham, but not until October. SHAEF (Supreme Headquarters Allied Expeditionary Forces) under Eisenhower replaced COSSAC in December, and completed the planning for Overlord, which took place in June 1944.

If there is a moral to this story, it is how very careful the Anglo-American leaders had to be when planning global strategy; and the very great level of mutual cooperation and trust that they had achieved by 1944.

Notes

1   Danchev and Todman, 2001, p. 351 entry for 28 December 1942.
*2   Badsey, *The Great Betrayal*, p. 9.

3   Morgan, 1950, p. 30.
*4   Smithee, *How To Speak Yank*, p. 45.
5   Bidwell, *The Chindit War*, pp. 32–3.
6   Atkinson, 2003, pp. 273–4.
7   The 29th ('Blue and Gray') Infantry Division was composed of National Guard units from both Maryland and Virginia, states which had fought on opposite sides in the US Civil War (although men from Maryland fought in both armies). The division's 116th Infantry Regiment was the lineal descendent of Lieutenant General Thomas Jackson's famed 1st Virginia 'Stonewall' Brigade.
8   Danchev and Todman, 2001, p. 362 entry for 19 January 1943.
9   Howard, 1972, p. 272.
10   Gropman, 1997, p. 360.
11   Howard, 1972, p. 273.
12   Morgan, 1950, p. 132; Harrison, 1951, p. 442.
13   CAB 88/9 Memorandum 167 'Continental Operations in 1943' Memoranda of the Combined Chiefs of Staff Meetings 1943, UK National Archives.
14   Morgan, 1950, p. 132.
*15   Patton, *Me and Monty: The Story of a Great Military Partnership*, p. 88.
16   d'Este, 1996, pp. 524 and 599.
17   Danchev and Todman, 2001, p. 405 entry for 14 May 1943.
18   Quoted in the frontispiece to Thomas and Morgan-Witts, 1977.
19   Howard, 1992, p. 76.
20   Morgan, 1950, p. 148.
21   Quoted in Stacey, 1955, p. 33.
22   Bradley, 1951, p. 188.
23   Otway, 1990, p. 143.
24   Marshall, 1988, p. 132.
25   Marshall, 1988, p. 212.
26   Eisenhower, 1948, p. 246.
27   Morgan, 1950, p. 108.
28   Eisenhower, 1948, p. 246.
29   Knight, 1954, p. 35.
*30   Cota, *A Beach Too Far*, pp. 109–90; the 10th SS Panzer grenadier Division was renamed the 10th SS Panzer Division 'Frundsberg' later in 1943.
31   Morgan, 1950, p. 28.
*32   Saunders, *Cherbourg! Triumph and Tragedy*, pp. 300–3.
*33   Meyer, *A Good Day To Die: My Life in the Service of Hitler*, pp. 105–55.
34   Warner, 1967, p. 152.
*35   Tsouras, *Eisenhower: From Failure to Redemption 1942–1951*, p. 208; the original document is in the Eisenhower Library, Abeline, Kansas.
36   Quoted in Grigg, 1985, p. 128.

Bibliography

Atkin, Ronald, *Dieppe 1942: The Jubilee Disaster*, London: Macmillan, 1980.
Atkinson, Rick, *An Army at Dawn: The War in North Africa 1942–1943*, New York: Henry Holt, 2002; Little, Brown, 2003.
Bidwell, Shelford, *The Chindit War*, London: Hodder & Stoughton and Book Club

Associates, 1979.

Bradley, Omar N., *A Soldier's Story*, New York: Henry Holt, 1951.

Danchev, Alex and Daniel Todman (eds), *War Diaries 1939–1945 Field Marshal Lord Alanbrooke*, London: Wiedenfeld & Nicolson, 2001.

d'Este, Carlo, *A Genius for War: A Life of General George S. Patton*, London: HarperCollins, 1996.

Eisenhower, Dwight D., *Crusade in Europe*, Baltimore: Johns Hopkins University Press, 1948.

Franks, Norman, *The Greatest Air Battle: Dieppe, 19th August 1942*, London: Grubb Street, 1997.

Grigg, John, *1943: The Victory That Never Was*, London: Methuen, 1985.

Gropman, Alan (ed.), *The Big L: American Logistics in World War II* Washington DC: National Defense University Press, 1997.

Harrison, Gordon A., *Cross-Channel Attack*, Washington DC: Center of Military History US Army, 1951.

Howard, Michael, *Grand Strategy, Volume IV, August 1942–September 1943*, London: HMSO, 1972.

Howard, Michael, *Strategic Deception in the Second World War*, London: Pimlico, 1992.

Huston, James A., *Out of the Blue: U.S. Army Airborne Operations in World War II*, West Lafayette IN, Purdue University Press, 1998.

Knight, Peter, *The 59th Division: Its War Story*, London: Frederick Mueller, 1954.

Marshall, Robert, *All the King's Men*, London: William Collins, 1988.

Mitcham, Samuel W., *Hitler's Legions: German Order of Battle in World War II*, London: Leo Cooper, 1985.

Morgan, Lieutenant General Sir Frederick, *Overture to Overlord*, London: Hodder and Stoughton, 1950.

Otway, Lieutenant Colonel T. B. H., *Airborne Forces*, London: Imperial War Museum, 1990.

Roskill, S. W., *The War at Sea 1939–1945: volume III: The Offensive: part I*, London: HMSO, 1960.

Saunders, Anthony, *Hitler's Atlantic Wall*, Thrupp: Sutton, 2001.

Stacey, C.P., *Six Years of War* Ottawa: The Queen's Printer, 1955.

Thomas, Gordon and Max Morgan-Witts, *Ruin From the Air*, London: Hamish Hamilton, 1977.

Warner, Oliver, *Cunningham of Hyndhope: Admiral of the Fleet* London: John Murray, 1967.

The Flower Painter's
Essential Handbook

JILL BAYS

D&C
David and Charles

A DAVID & CHARLES BOOK
Copyright © David & Charles Limited 2006

David & Charles is an F+W Publications Inc. company
4700 East Galbraith Road
Cincinnati, OH 45236

First published in the UK in 2006

Text and illustrations copyright © Jill Bays 2006

Jill Bays has asserted her right to be identified as author of this work in
accordance with the Copyright, Designs and Patents Act, 1988.

A catalogue record for this book is available from the British Library.

ISBN-13: 978-0-7153-2246-8 hardback
ISBN-10: 0-7153-2246-X hardback

ISBN-13: 978-0-7153-2248-2 paperback
ISBN-10: 0-7153-2248-6 paperback

Printed in Singapore by KHL Printing Co Pte Ltd.
for David & Charles
Brunel House   Newton Abbot   Devon

Commissioning Editor Freya Dangerfield
Project Editor Ian Kearey
Assistant Editor Louise Clark
Art Editor Lisa Wyman
Senior Designer Sarah Underhill
Production Controller Kelly Smith

Visit our website at www.davidandcharles.co.uk

David & Charles books are available from all good bookshops; alternatively you
can contact our Orderline on 0870 9908222 or write to us at FREEPOST EX2
110, D&C Direct, Newton Abbot, TQ12 4ZZ (no stamp required UK only); US
customers call 800-289-0963 and Canadian customers call 800-840-5220.

*'Has anyone ever seen anything like Winsor & Newton's cups of Chrome
and Carnations and Crimsons loud and fierce as a war-cry, and Pinks tender
and loving as a young girl?'*
Charles Dickens

Contents

Introduction

Painting flowers is not just about creating a still life of some blooms in a vase or jar: it opens a whole new world of painting. Think of the variety of shapes, sizes and patterns, and the range of colours and settings you can explore. There are also many ways of painting, from being free and loose with the brush, to being a super-realist and painting every detail. However you feel, there is a way to achieve the result you want.

your subjects

Even in a small window box or tiny garden, there is an amazing variety of shapes and colours. As an artist, how do you go about selecting your subject? You are probably familiar with your own garden of plants, but even in this situation a lot can depend on outside factors such as light, heat, shade and the weather; and in public gardens, other people walking around can be distracting. Start by finding something that appeals to you immediately, and get the ball rolling by making small sketches of your subject.

There are various approaches to painting flowers and plants. You can choose to paint a close-up of a single subject, in isolation or with the hint of a further dimension, or you can go for the long view, a landscape interpretation that includes flowers or foliage. Keep your options open, and always make sketches to help get your thoughts in order and organize your priorities.

inspiration and challenge

When faced with a new subject to paint, you really should want to paint it, but sometimes inspiration doesn't come immediately, you should be open to becoming more interested as you paint. Don't be put off when this happens, as we can all get stuck in the same ways, and it can be difficult to break out.

Look for the challenge that can come from investigating new shapes and forms, perhaps in a way you haven't explored before. Using different paper and deviating from your usual colours can often inspire you to innovative approaches.

Sometimes painting in a completely free way – going straight in with the brush without any preliminary drawing, for example – can start you off. At other times, carefully thinking out your strategy beforehand can be useful: a considered still life and selection of colour combinations, with preparation in the form of colour roughs and drawings, can be a great help.

WATERCOLOUR VERSATILITY
This painting shows a variety of colours and applications; some paint is thick and dark, other washes are light and pale; some colours are painted straight on to the paper, while others are painted over one another.

working outdoors

If you are like me, then a great deal of your outdoor sketching is likely to take place in your own garden, or a garden or situation that you know well, so you become very familiar with its particular viewpoints and thus have plenty of time to think about the subjects you want to paint. Away from such familiar places, however you have to choose more rapidly.

Outdoor sketching is great fun: you have to gamble on the weather and be prepared for anything. Travel light and cut down on equipment, but always take something to sit on, a hat and sun cream. Go with the right attitude, be prepared to make lots of thumbnail sketches, and don't worry if you don't complete anything in situ.

a word about sketchbooks

A sketchbook is an essential part of your equipment – use it for ideas, sketches, even painting. It is your primary source book, so carry it everywhere and make sure it is readily to hand. Some artists use their sketchbooks as a kind of diary, and draw in them every day.

There are many different sizes of sketchbook. I find one with A4 cartridge paper very useful for most purposes, and also have some containing heavier weights of watercolour paper, which are perfect for taking on holidays as they don't need to be stretched. Smaller books are excellent too as they can be slipped into a pocket or bag and used in crowded places. There is also a choice of bindings, the two most popular being spiral bound or pads with soft or hard covers. You could also make your own sketchbooks using your favourite papers, which will then become very personal records.

how to use this book

Starting with a brief look at the equipment available to you – paper, paints, brushes and accessories – I suggest a useful selection. The next section covers the basic techniques: the brushstrokes you can make, and how to create a variety of washes. The two fundamentals of watercolour painting are then illustrated – working wet into wet and wet on dry. A study of flower shapes and patterns and the details of stems, leaves and grasses follows, with advice on colours and how to create them for flower painting. Tips and advice on light and shade and tone, two invaluable allies of the painter, conclude this section.

The main part of the handbook takes an in-depth look at 50 flowers, ranging from humble daisies to exotic orchids and luscious peonies. Each spread features drawings and sketch studies with pointers on what to look for; a watercolour study, again annotated; a palette of recommended colours and step-by-step instructions on how to paint the flower. To inspire your own work, a finished painting, in a style ranging from loose and free to more detailed, features the subject in a variety of approaches.

WHITE DAISIES

Against a dark background, these flowers are always dramatic; the study above was painted in my sketchbook while on holiday.

PLANT STUDY

The sketch below right of Iris foetidissima, *with its decorative seed pods, was made in pencil and watercolour.*

SKETCHBOOK STUDIES

Coloured pencils are useful – but don't forget to take some water when using watersoluble crayons or pencils.

Materials

paper

Paper, in all its variations, is a fascinating subject. There are so many types, from tissue paper, so thin and yet so tough, through to thick and speckled recycled paper. Paper can be glossy or matt, thick or thin.

stretching paper

1 Wet the paper: either soak it in the bath for a few minutes, then shake off surplus water and position it on a board, or place dry paper on the board and wet it all over with a sponge or damp cloth.

2 Stick the damp paper down with a gummed paper strip (not masking tape or sticky tape). Cut the strip into four lengths 12mm (¹/₂in) longer than each side of the paper. Wet each length with a sponge or damp cloth and stick it down, overlapping the ends and starting with the two longer sides.

what type of paper?

You need a paper that is thick enough to take one or more washes; for sketchbook work, cartridge paper can be drawn on and can take the odd wash of paint, although it is not designed to take too much water. You can buy sketchbooks of watercolour paper, which are more suitable but more expensive.

Both watercolour and cartridge paper can be bought as pads or single sheets; the latter are cheaper and can be cut to size. You can also buy paper in blocks, stuck together on all four sides and with a substantial base; these are ideal for painting away from home as you don't need to stretch the paper beforehand. To remove a sheet from the block, slip a knife around all the edges and lift the sheet away.

It is well worth taking time to get to know different papers and their attributes; art shops usually stock sample sheets and 'pochettes' (manufacturers' packs of a range of papers) you can try. Whatever you choose, be generous when buying paper – people starting out often cramp their style by buying small pads because they are unsure of themselves and unwilling to work freely and boldly.

watercolour paper

There are three basic surfaces of watercolour paper:

- Hot-pressed (HP) is smooth and suitable for more detailed work.

- Cold-pressed (CP) or NOT (not hot-pressed) has a slight 'tooth', the tiny peaks and hollows in the surface, and is ideal for general-purpose painting.

- Rough paper has a more pronounced tooth and is suitable for broad work, such as landscapes.

Watercolour paper is available in different weights. I find the heavier the better, but lightweight papers can always be stretched. To avoid cockling (where the paper shrinks and buckles when washes are applied), it's best to use a paper of 300gsm (140lb) or heavier.

3 Finish with the two shorter sides, then leave the paper to dry naturally. You can place it near a radiator to speed up the drying, but don't use a hairdryer as the gummed strip will tear away from paper.

paints

Paint can be the most confusing part about watercolours; one look at a catalogue or the selection available in a shop is at the same time tempting and alarming. Where to start? The simple answer is to begin with just a few colours, and gradually to build up your own palette of colours as you need them.

types of paint

Watercolour paint is made from pigment, water, gum and glycerine. Some artists make their own paints, but the vast majority buy and use ready-mixed paints, which are available in either tube or pan form. Tube paint is semi-liquid and can be used neat (although it is most often diluted), while pans are dry and require the addition of water before you can paint.

You can buy ready-made selections of pan colours, but a good way to start is to get an empty pan case and fill it with your own selection of colours; this way you won't waste space with colours you may never use or which are unsuitable. Run a brush loaded with clean water over pans before starting, as this helps to soften the paints and make them run more smoothly.

You do not have to stick exclusively to either tubes or pans. If you find that a mixture of these works best for you, go ahead and use it.

The price of each colour varies, depending on the cost of the pigment, and paints are sold in artists' or students' grades. Although artists' paints are more expensive, they are better, as the paint flows more smoothly and the colours are purer.

A basic palette is discussed on pages 14–15, but you need the three basic primary colours to start with – cadmium red, cadmium yellow and ultramarine – plus yellow ochre and burnt sienna as extras.

qualities of paint

No two colours are the same when it comes to how they behave on the paper: some are transparent, some more opaque; some are pretty well permanent – they do not fade when exposed to sunlight over time – and others are fugitive – they need to be protected from light if they are to keep their intensity of colour; some can be washed off the paper without leaving much of a mark, while others stain the paper and are thus impossible to remove. Manufacturers have different methods of grading each of these qualities, but most people find these out for themselves as they go along.

WATERCOLOUR TUBE PAINTS

brushes

Getting used to working with a brush is essential. Whatever the subject you want to paint, it is your most important tool. Remember, if you can draw with a pencil, you can draw with a brush.

Look in any art shop or catalogue, and you'll see an overwhelming number of brushes to choose from. I mainly use no more than three round brushes: from smallest to largest a No. 4 or No. 6, a No. 8 and a No. 12. The No. 12 will do almost anything as it is firm and flexible, holds plenty of water and has a good point; start with this size, even if it seems to be large when you begin.

The best material for watercolour brushes is sable, but this is expensive; there are many good synthetic substitutes and sable/synthetic blends. When buying brushes, check the point, as you should be able to use this as well as the body of the bristles. I use the smaller sizes for very fine details, but be warned, using very small sizes can hinder your progress if you want to achieve fresh, clean and clear watercolours. So take courage and work with the large brush almost exclusively at first, and reserve the smaller sizes for later.

Practise making as many sorts of strokes as you can, from long, flowing marks to short, dabbing ones – time spent doing this is invaluable. Draw with your brushes, and try to become as used to working with a brush as with a pencil.

VERSATILE BRUSHES: NOS 12, 8 AND 4
The brushstrokes at top show the different kinds of strokes you can achieve with just one brush, the No. 12 round, in addition to laying all kinds of washes.

other equipment

There are a few other pieces of equipment, some of which are essential, that are useful either to save time or to achieve certain effects.

drawing board
It is important to have the right drawing board for the task. My main board is a lightweight 'rigid' wooden board measuring a generous 380 x 510mm (15 x 20in). Hardware stores usually cut board to size.

palettes
Some form of a clean, white palette is essential. A white plate works well for tubes. Squeeze each colour around the outside, and use the centre for mixing.

useful accessories
• Two water pots: jam jars will do, but plastic ones won't break.
• Grades B and 2B pencils are best for sketching and preliminary drawing. Keep them sharp.
• A knife, scalpel or pencil sharpener.
• A soft eraser.
• A ruler for measuring and judging angles.
• Masking fluid.
• A natural sponge for dampening paper: the flow is better than that from artificial sponges.
• Kitchen paper or clean cloths or rags for blotting off paint or mopping up spills.
• A hairdryer dries washes quickly, but is not vital.

Techniques
brushstrokes

It's now time to get down to work and practise using the brush to draw flowers and leaves. Ideally you should work from a flower and some leaves in front of you; alternatively, follow the examples on this page.

Either way, try to work life-size, and don't worry if you make a mistake or a blot, just concentrate on getting the shape in one go. Use a No. 12 round brush except where specified. For inspiration, look at the leaves on trees and imagine how you could represent each of the types, from pine needles and the narrow leaves of a willow, to apple or oak leaves; each requires a different kind of mark.

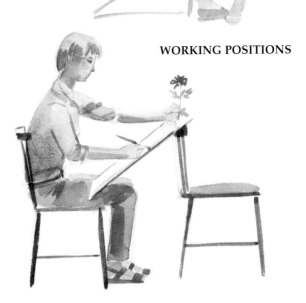

WORKING POSITIONS

Alternate between brushes as you practise painting leaves. I used a No. 4 round to create very thin leaves, using the same method of a single brushstroke for each leaf.

When switching to a larger brush for bigger shapes, don't forget that you can leave a white line between the colours so they don't run; but again try to be bold with your brushstrokes, getting them right each time.

To give the appearance of a mass of grassy leaves, you may need to blend together different, single, short strokes. Try not to hesitate, and resist the temptation to touch up the results. If it doesn't work, start again.

Putting a second wash over a dry one. Note the hold of the brush, which is loose and quite unlike the standard pencil grip, and which helps when making short, dabbing strokes like this.

Here I use a No. 4 brush to make fine, grass-like lines. There should be no stopping and starting, but continuous sweeps of the brush.

washes

A wash is basically any layer of colour on the paper, large or small, applied with a brush or sometimes a sponge. All watercolour paintings are made up of a number of washes, either laid side by side or applied in overlapping layers. The two washes most used are flat washes, where the paint is laid down in as even a colour as possible, and graduated washes, where deliberate variations on the flat colour are created. All watercolours dry about 50 per cent lighter than when applied.

flat wash

Painting even a simple wash of colour needs thought and preparation, and there are several basic things you should do before you put brush to paper. First, always mix plenty of colour – more than you think you will need – and have a large container for water. Test the colour on scrap paper. Set the drawing board at a slight angle as gravity will help the wash to flow, but not so much that you lose control of the wash when it is applied, and make sure the No. 12 round brush is fully loaded.

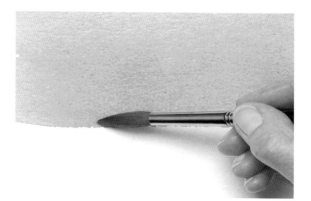

Starting from the top, apply an even stroke across the paper, then repeat this a little lower so that the top of the new stroke joins on to the bottom of the top one. Continue down the paper, and don't go back and touch up the wash in any way. Allow to dry.

graduated wash

Painting a graduated wash, one that gets lighter as you progress down the paper, is a matter of adding clean water to the layers of the original wash colour, using a similar technique as for a flat wash. You can also use different colours in a graduated wash, which is particularly useful for painting flowers and leaves where a smooth transition of colours is needed. The main thing to bear in mind is that you must use plenty of loose, fluid colours if you want to achieve a good result.

Mix up plenty of colour and start as for a flat wash. As you work down the paper with even strokes, add a little clean water to the brush; work quickly, so that the paint has no chance of drying on the paper between the strokes.

For a colour-graduated wash, instead of adding clean water, apply a different colour; practice and experience will enable you to make a smooth blend and transition.

wet-into-wet and wet-on-dry washes

Once you have learned how to apply single layers of washes, you have the choice of working wet into wet or wet on dry. The former technique is what makes watercolours unique as the results are unpredictable: this unpredictability of wet into wet is all part of the process. Mistakes, runs and blotches can sometimes be incorporated into a painting, and keeping one eye open for such happy accidents keeps you on your toes.

It is fun to experiment with applying wet colours onto other wet ones: some colours react against each other, pushing the paint away, and others mix gently to give soft effects. Certain colours, such as ultramarine and burnt sienna, separate when they are mixed and create a granular texture on the paper.

Working wet on dry is more straightforward, as long as you remember to work in layers from the lightest colours to the darkest ones. Always let each wash dry completely before you paint over it, or you will find that the new wash picks up the underneath colour and runs and bleeds, making the edges indistinct and fuzzy.

Here the colour blends smoothly because the wash underneath is still wet when the new colour is applied. Use a paper towel to blot off paint for lighter areas.

Wet-into-wet blending is useful for creating shadow colours on a flower. Allow the colours to mix on the paper to produce a vibrant effect.

These light green leaves were overpainted with a darker green and a touch of red-brown while still wet. You have to work quite quickly to achieve this effect successfully.

In this variation on wet into wet, the petal shape was initially painted with clean water; the pink was just touched in on the petal tips and ran into the water. When this had dried completely, the green centre was painted in the same way.

The red flower and green stem were painted on a completely dry yellow wash – wet on dry – giving sharp edges to the colours. The first wash must dry thoroughly: this could take an hour or so, depending on the room temperature, unless you use a hairdryer to dry the first wash.

flower structures

Knowing the basic structure of a flower or plant, although not absolutely necessary for most purposes, will help you get to know its character – whether it has five or six leaves, whether the leaves are alternate or opposing, and their shape.

The painting of a tulip here shows the principal parts of a flower: the petals, stamens and pistil, and anther, stem and leaves.

As an artist it is vital for you to know the basic shape of the flower you intend to paint – even if you do not know its name, being able to identify its simplified shape and characteristics will help you enormously when you come to draw or paint it.

patterns

Nature creates patterns in the arrangements of how petals and leaves grow – they may be two-coloured or variegated, and they may overlap; geranium and cyclamen have distinctive patterns on each individual leaf, for instance.

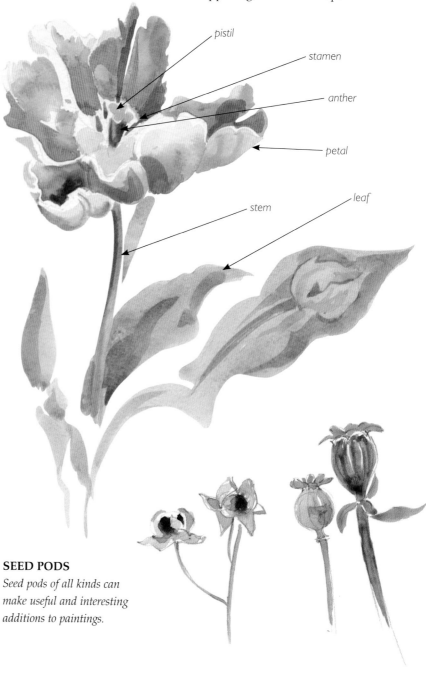

pistil

stamen

anther

petal

stem

leaf

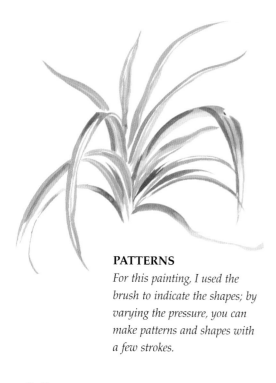

PATTERNS

For this painting, I used the brush to indicate the shapes; by varying the pressure, you can make patterns and shapes with a few strokes.

SEED PODS

Seed pods of all kinds can make useful and interesting additions to paintings.

leaves and stems

When drawing or painting leaves, look for their character: are they glossy and dark or soft and pale? Are they single or in groups, variegated or plain? The edges can be serrated or smooth, while some leaves, like the iris, are sword-shaped.

Leaves of grass can be described with swift, sure strokes of the brush, but leaves that twist and curl are like ribbons – practise and let the brush do the work for you! Try to keep to light, medium and dark shades, and introduce blues and reds to amend the colours if necessary.

SHINY LEAVES

To paint the shine that appears on certain leaves, such as those of camellias or holly, paint an initial light blue-grey wash and allow it to dry before you apply the green.

CROPS AND GRASSES

Practise drawing the fine lines of crops and grasses with brushes that have a good point.

BACKS AND FRONTS

Leaves which present both sides to the observer, like the variegated leaf above, need to be drawn and painted carefully. Look closely, and draw what you see.

STEMS

Some stems are strong and thick, others slender, and some are hairy. You don't need to put in every detail, but note the dark and light sides, and try to use a single, firm brushstroke.

LEAVES WITH VEINS

This ivy leaf shown is half painted – the first wash of light green represents the veins. The negative shapes of the darker green, applied after the first wash has dried, define the pattern of the veins.

LEAVES AND STEMS

Leaves and stems must join together accurately.

colour

The basics of understanding colour and colour mixing are dealt with thoroughly in many books, so I shall concentrate here on the immediate uses of colour in flower painting.

mood and atmosphere

Some colours are described as 'warm', for instance red, and some as 'cool', such as blue, reflecting the emotions they arouse in the viewer. But there can be differences in colours, with yellows, greys and greens, among others, having a wide spectrum from warm to cool. Experiment to see how you can make warm or cool greys from the different reds and blues in your palette.

You can use the temperature of colours to set the mood and atmosphere of a painting. The most obvious way is to associate each colour with the time of day, from early morning to late evening or night; but you can also use the seasons in the same manner – for instance, spring with fresh, bright, coolish colours and summer with warmer versions of the same greens and yellows, while autumnal reds and browns tend to warm, and winter has cool blues and greys.

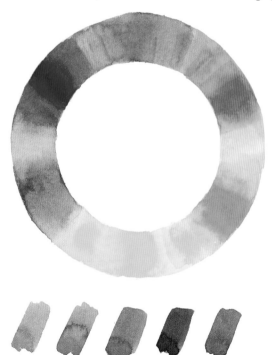

PRIMARY COLOURS

I used only primary colours in this little painting of a poppy – cadmium red, cadmium yellow and ultramarine – to make a harmonious composition.

SECONDARY COLOURS

Here, love-in-a-mist (Nigella) is paired with an orange wallflower. Cobalt blue is one of the cooler blues, a primary which combines well with the warm cadmium orange, a secondary colour.

basic palette

It is vital to develop a basic palette of colours for your subject; you can always add to this when necessary. One of the main reasons for having just a few colours is that doing so means that with practice you will become adept at mixing and thus understanding how colours combine and work together, in nature and on paper.

My basic palette consists of ultramarine, cadmium red, magenta, yellow ochre, burnt sienna, cadmium yellow and a green mixed from cadmium yellow and ultramarine. Make a colour chart for yourself, using the basic palette to become familiar with the colours and the many hues that can be achieved through different combinations and concentrations. Generally in painting, it is the tonal values of a colour that are important – the relationships of each colour to its neighbour – and the local colour, the actual colour of an object, less so.

SATURATED COLOUR

The darkest version of ultramarine, on the left of the bar, is the saturated colour, with no water used to dilute it. You can see how gradually diluting the pure colour changes the tint and makes it lighter.

natural greens

Most leaves and stems are green, so it is an important colour to understand when painting flowers – you will need to have a range from light to dark, and need to know how to make greens. I prefer to mix my own, and try to stick to a light, medium and dark green, with the addition of blues or reds as required: the light green is not a watered-down version of the others – light does not mean watery.

Among readily available greens are sap green, a useful, bright and cheerful green, but liable to fade; olive green, a flat but pleasant green; viridian, a light and clear emerald green that is useful for mixing with earth colours; and Hooker's green, also useful when mixed with earth colours. There are all sorts of mixes you can make up, so experiment by varying the colours you use.

earth colours

The earth colours – siennas, ochres and umbers – are basic to painting natural subjects. While they should be essential in your palette, be careful how you use them, as they can muddy flower tints when overemployed.

Of the basic earth colours, raw sienna is a beautiful transparent yellow; yellow ochre is similar, but more opaque; raw umber is a clear brown with a touch of green; burnt sienna, a reddish brown, is very useful for combining with blues to make greys, or with green-blues to make dark greens; and burnt umber is a darker red-brown that has similar uses to burnt sienna.

WARM AND COOL

A purple cornflower (made by mixing Winsor violet and ultramarine) is paired here with wild flowers, the ox-eye daisy and charlock. The warmth of the purple and the background contrasts well with the cool Winsor yellow used for the charlock.

RED AND GREEN

The primary red and its complementary colour green always work well together. The geranium here is painted with magenta, while the green is a mixture of sap green and burnt sienna.

GREENS

The two top greens here, olive green and sap green, are ready-made shades; all the others are mixes. Second row: ultramarine and cadmium yellow, ultramarine and yellow ochre, and Prussian blue and Winsor yellow. Bottom row: Prussian blue and burnt sienna, Winsor yellow and olive green, and cerulean blue and Winsor yellow.

EARTHS

Top row: yellow ochre; raw umber; burnt sienna Bottom row: burnt umber; raw sienna

light and shade

Light helps us to see our subject in the first place, and light combined with shade helps to define the form or shape. Light and shade also produce other effects, such as drama and variations in colour.

Colour can change under different lighting conditions, and you can affect this when painting indoors by using artificial light to your advantage. For example, you can direct light onto a particular area you wish to highlight, and make silhouettes or reverse flowers out of a background. Light and shade also create patterns, and can be used to promote abstract shapes. I find it helpful to work in three tones – light, medium and dark – and to constantly remind myself to try to see light to dark and dark to light.

This bromeliad has been worked in an abstract way; the light and shade make interesting patterns and shapes without the use of direct light.

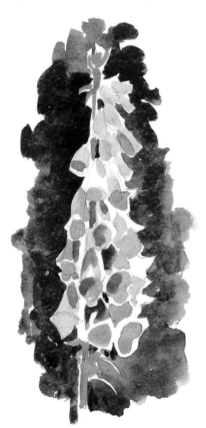

The sunlight behind this pelargonium throws it into shadow. The dark tones suggest form and depth, achieved with minimal detail.

Although there is a fair amount of shade on this white foxglove dramatically lit by sunshine, the flower is obviously white. The clear silhouette helps to throw it into relief from the background.

The dark areas on these leaves help to define their shape and create form.

tone

Whatever you are painting, it is easy to be seduced by the idea of the flower shape and to forget all the colours and tones that make it so attractive. When the sun is shining onto a flower it is possible to see the lights and darks, but where there is no strong light you have to rely on the actual colour that you see – for example, a light-coloured flower can be contrasted with a darker background of leaves. If you are painting a white flower, using a darker background makes it possible to define the edges.

I often look for the darkest tone in a painting, paint it in early on and use it as the basis for the rest of the work. This is pretty well the opposite of the classic watercolour technique of working from light to dark, but it need only be employed over a small area.

DIRECTED LIGHT

With this campanula the light was coming from the right, making the back of the flower darker; on the front-facing flower, the inside of the bell is correspondingly dark.

USING BACKGROUND

This hibiscus was painted in a greenhouse with no direct light on the flower – the painting relied on the tonal values of the dark colours behind the subject. Lighter greens provide a sense of distance.

MONOCHROME AND COLOUR

Rough, monochrome, thumbnail sketches such as these give some idea of tonal values; they don't take too long, and save time when you start to work in colour. I used Payne's grey for the tonal studies. These small sketches are also useful as compositional aids, as they help to clear the mind of extraneous detail.

The Flowers

Agapanthus

Also known as the African blue lily, agapanthus is a striking plant, not only for its colour and size, but also for its character. It has strap-like foliage and handsome flowers of various shades of blue, white, pink and purple. It is large (over 1m/3ft high) and a delight to paint.

Colour palette

French ultramarine   sap green   permanent rose   yellow ochre

➤ *This pot of white agapanthus provided a marvellous subject to paint while sitting in the sun!*

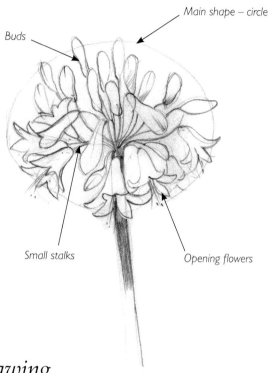

Main shape – circle

Buds

Small stalks

Opening flowers

Wet into wet

Soft-focus flowers

Hard-edged flowers

Drawing

First, make an overall shape – a dome or a circle – and work into that with individual flowers and buds. The flowers are bell-shaped and held on short stalks from the stem. Make the stem strong, as this can be a tall plant.

> **Tip:** *Keep your water clean, and don't go on painting with dirty water; use two pots of water if necessary.*

Painting an agapanthus

1 Draw the main shape as a dome or circle, then the individual flowers or buds.

2 Use a sponge to paint over the flower area with clean water.

3 Drop in a light mix of French ultramarine and permanent rose.

4 When this wash is either dry or still damp, paint the flowers or buds with a darker mix of ultramarine and rose.

5 Make a mix of sap green and yellow ochre, and use this to paint the stem and small stalks.

6 If required, add some more detail and darker tones.

Amaryllis

Amaryllis take your breath away: you can watch them coming out day by day until the whole flower appears and you are mesmerized by their beauty. They cheer you up on cold winter mornings and are marvellous to paint – flamboyant and striking in red, pink or white.

Colour palette

 cadmium red

 cadmium yellow

 brown madder

 sap green

 yellow ochre

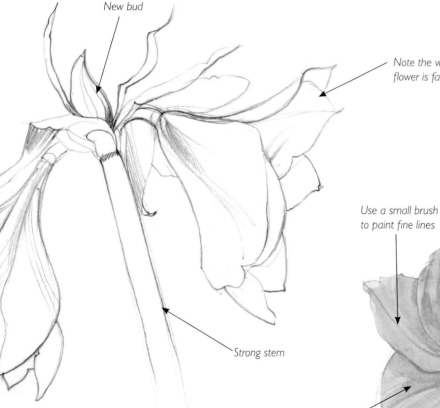

New bud

Note the way the flower is facing

Strong stem

Use a small brush to paint fine lines

Second wash

Deeper colour

First wash

Trumpet shape

Painting an amaryllis

1 Be aware of the direction of light, which gives the flower shape and form.

2 Draw carefully before noting the spaces between petals.

3 Using a large (No. 12) brush, paint the flower using light, medium and dark tones of colour.

4 Put in any detail at the end.

5 Check the tonal values and increase them if necessary.

6 Paint the stamens and pistil; alternatively, draw them lightly with a pencil.

Drawing

The amaryllis is trumpet-shaped and large. Draw it as it emerges, and draw it life size from every angle; see how the flower joins the stem, and practise getting the front view right.

➤ *As here, I paint amaryllis life-size; but, like Georgia O'Keeffe, you could paint them much larger. You can always change the picture size and format: flowers often call for long, narrow picture shapes, so try it.*

Anemones

The rich, jewel-like colours of anenomes have always attracted me; the lovely, striking reds, purples and magentas, combined with a simple shape, make them ideal flowers to paint. The leaves are cut and divided, giving the appearance of halos around the flower.

Colour palette

Winsor violet   magenta   alizarin crimson   carmine

sap green   yellow ochre   Prussian blue   burnt sienna

Cup shape

Folded and crinkled petals

Leaves coming from base of flower

Thick stem

Five to nine petals

Direction of light

Transparent petals

Shallow bowl shape

Frill of divided leaves

Stamens in centre are almost black, depicted by very strong wash

Note two carmine washes for petals, one medium strength, the other darker

Divided leaves come from base of thick stem and are of varying shades of green

Drawing

Using a 2B pencil, draw lightly as you get to know the flower shape — depending on the flower, the shape can vary between a shallow bowl, a cup and a disc. Note the number of petals, and draw the detail last. Finally, add in the centre and the leaves and stems. Always check for errors and make any corrections if required.

Painting anemones

1 Draw the flowers using a light pencil line, referring to your studies and drawings; draw guidelines that can be erased later.

2 Using a No. 12 round brush, paint the first wash of the flowers using a medium wash of carmine or Winsor violet and lots of water. Allow to dry.

3 Paint shadows using a darker mix of the same colour, softening the edges with water on a clean brush.

4 Paint the shadows in the centre using a mix of Prussian blue and burnt sienna.

5 For the stems and leaves use varying mixes of sap green and yellow ochre; add some magenta for any pink stems.

6 Mix Prussian blue and alizarin crimson to paint the stamens with a No. 4 round brush and the centre of the flowers with a No. 8 round brush.

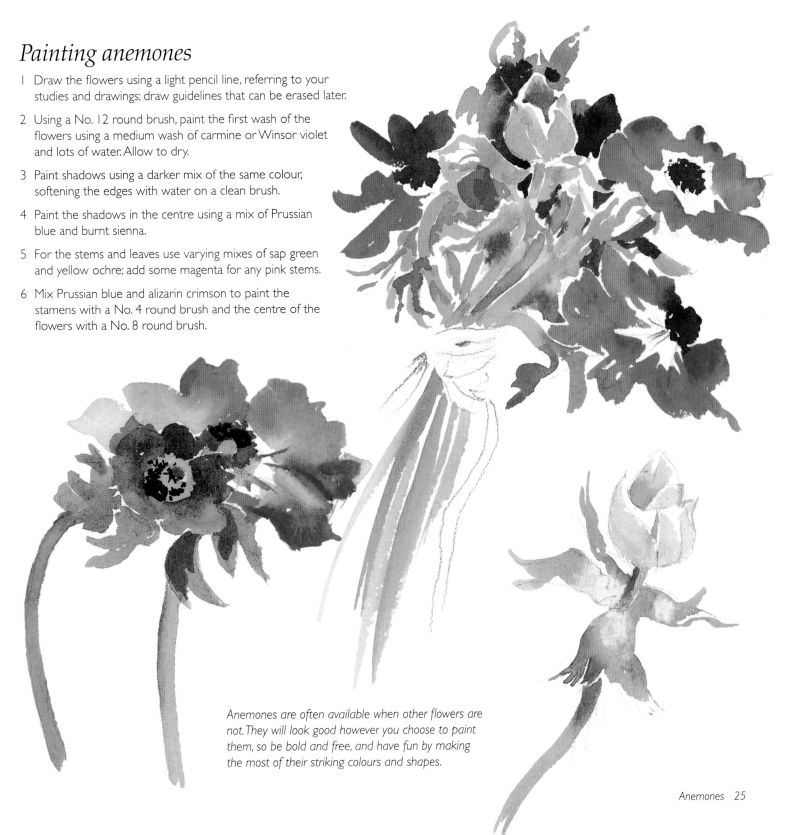

Anemones are often available when other flowers are not. They will look good however you choose to paint them, so be bold and free, and have fun by making the most of their striking colours and shapes.

Begonias

Although begonias originate in tropical forests, the ones we grow are mostly for summer bedding or are pot plants. They have numerous flowers, which can be single or double, some with beautifully marked lopsided leaves. Begonias are bright and colourful, good for hanging baskets.

Colour palette

scarlet lake

cadmium lemon

sap green

olive green

French ultramarine

Drawing

This particular begonia has very decorative leaves but very small pink flowers, so I chose to draw the leaf using a sharp pencil on hot-pressed (HP) paper.

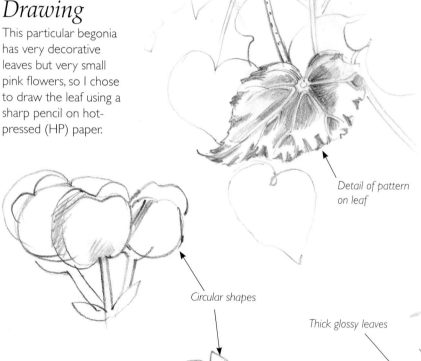

Detail of pattern on leaf

Circular shapes

Thick glossy leaves

Pale stems

Pencil details added

Painting begonias

1 Draw the single or double flowers carefully.

2 Paint over the flower area with a wash of scarlet lake.

3 Blend in sap green and cadmium lemon on the leaves.

4 Strengthen the wash on the flowers to help delineate the petals.

5 Paint the stems with a pale wash of olive green and sap green.

6 Strengthen the green by adding more pigment and a touch of French ultramarine.

This semi-tuberous begonia is a pot plant
and has small spiralling petals on the flowers.
It can be red, pink, orange or white, and
appears in spring to cheer you up.

Delicate colour

Dark and light greens

Blending in

Blossoms

The first spring blossom comes out in February, and what a welcome sight it is! Once it is followed by other blossoms, you know that spring is on its way. The flowers usually appear first, and when they fade the leaves take over. Direct painting with a brush is often the best way to approach blossoms.

Colour palette

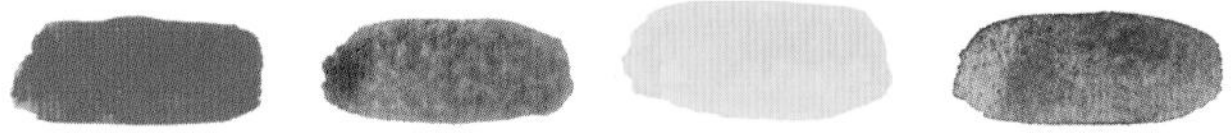

permanent rose   raw umber   Winsor yellow   French ultramarine

Painting blossoms

1 Draw an indication of positioning with a pencil.

2 Load the brush fairly full with a pale wash of permanent rose, and paint the petal and flower shapes confidently and without hesitation.

3 Link the blooms together by painting the twigs and branches with raw umber; you may need to stand and sweep with your whole arm to do this.

4 Put in any shadow on the petals with a grey made by a mix of permanent rose, Winsor yellow and French ultramarine.

5 Add details such as stamens by either painting or drawing them.

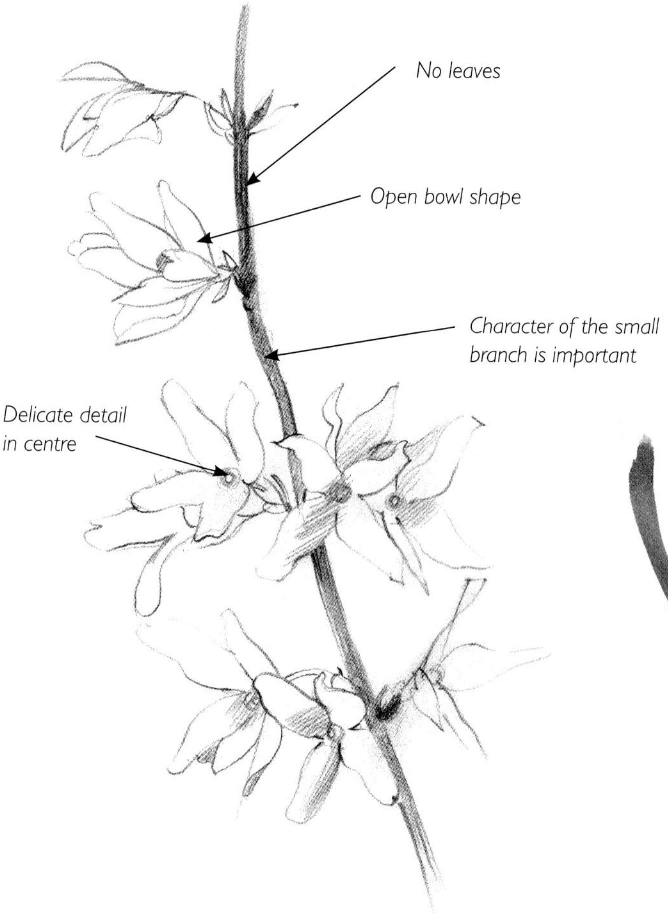

No leaves

Open bowl shape

Character of the small branch is important

Delicate detail in centre

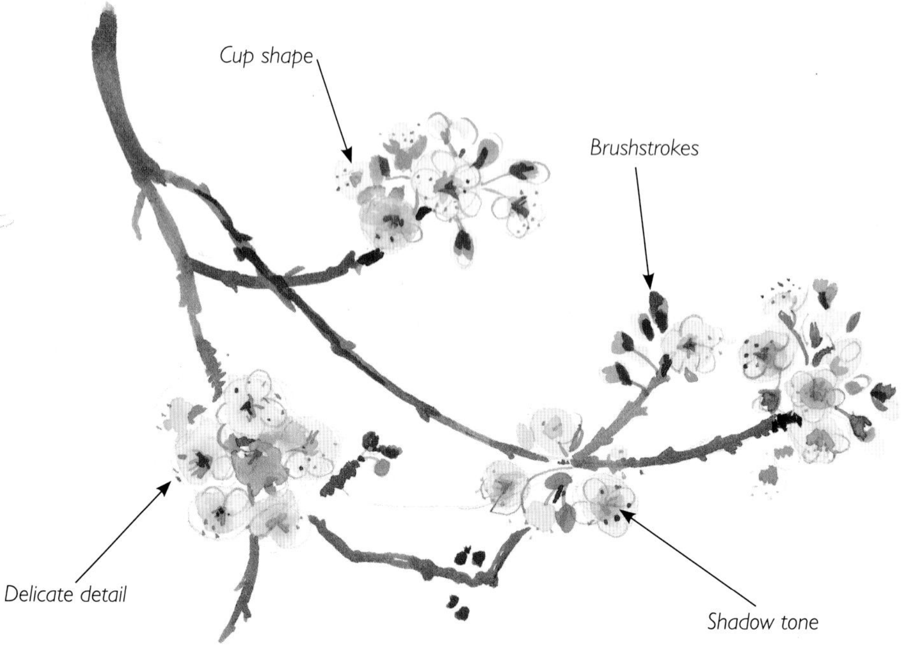

Cup shape

Brushstrokes

Delicate detail

Shadow tone

Drawing

Draw carefully to fix the shape of the flower, which is often a simple cup or bowl shape; the leaves usually follow the blossom. The drawing here is of forsythia, which is a brilliant yellow.

Flowering quince (Chaenomeles) is a striking shrub when in flower. The branches have strong thorns so you must be careful when handling it, but the lovely flowers can be red, orange, pink or white.

Bluebells

The blueness in a bluebell wood is truly amazing – each individual flower contributes to the overall colour, which, when combined with the soft spring green of trees, makes the sight unforgettable. When painting single bluebells, the perfect bell shapes of the flowers are fascinating.

Colour palette

French ultramarine   alizarin crimson   sap green

Painting bluebells

1 Draw one or two bluebells and leaves.

2 Dampen the paper with clean water and drop in a mix of French ultramarine and alizarin crimson to tint the paper gently.

3 Paint the individual flowers with a stronger mix of the ultramarine and crimson.

4 For the stem, mix sap green with a little French ultramarine.

5 Put in the shadows with a darker mix of ultramarine and crimson.

6 Paint the leaves with light and dark mixes of sap green and ultramarine.

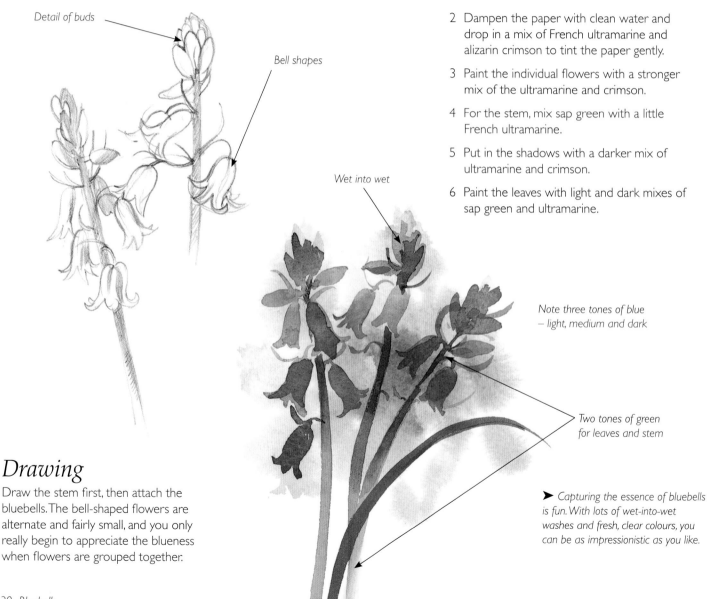

Detail of buds

Bell shapes

Wet into wet

Note three tones of blue – light, medium and dark

Two tones of green for leaves and stem

➤ *Capturing the essence of bluebells is fun. With lots of wet-into-wet washes and fresh, clear colours, you can be as impressionistic as you like.*

Drawing

Draw the stem first, then attach the bluebells. The bell-shaped flowers are alternate and fairly small, and you only really begin to appreciate the blueness when flowers are grouped together.

Carnations

Elegant and glamorous, carnations are used as symbols of love and thanks. They come in lovely colours, have a delightful scent (the genus includes cottage pinks and sweet williams) and a distinctive shape; the petals, which may be frilled, are held above blue-green sepals.

Colour palette

permanent rose   Winsor violet   French ultramarine   sap green

Painting a carnation

1 Draw the shape, stem and leaves.

2 Using a No. 12 or No. 8 round brush, wet the carnation shape with clean water and drop in a pale mix of permanent rose to spread and fill the area.

3 When this is nearly dry, blot out some of the paler petal shapes with a folded piece of tissue.

4 Define the other petal shapes with a darker wash of permanent rose.

5 Paint the leaves and stems with a blue-green mix of French ultramarine and sap green, darkening the mix for the shadows.

6 Define the petals further with a mix of Winsor violet and permanent rose, using a No. 4 round brush.

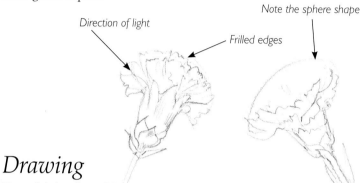

Direction of light

Frilled edges

Note the sphere shape

Drawing

Draw lightly using a 2B pencil, looking for the overall sphere shape and noting the direction of light. Because there are so many small and toothed petals it is difficult to be precise, but be aware of small shadows and darks and lights. The large calyx is important, but the evergreen leaves are fairly insignificant.

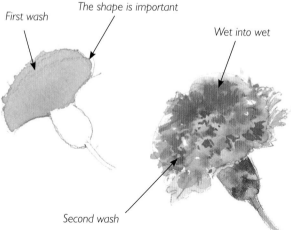

First wash

The shape is important

Wet into wet

Second wash

Keep paint fresh by changing the water frequently

▶ *These carnations were part of a larger bunch of mixed flowers. The long, slender stems of carnations are often best covered by foliage, or they can look isolated and spindly.*

Third wash

Use brushstrokes to make shapes

Chinese lanterns

This intriguing plant produces very decorative orange lanterns in the autumn – each attractive, papery lantern is a calyx that carries seeds. Often used as winter decorations, Chinese lanterns can keep their colour right through to the following spring.

Colour palette

cadmium red   cadmium orange   yellow ochre

raw umber   brown madder

Drawing

The lanterns are teardrop-shaped and can be quite large, up to 4cm (1½in). Concentrate on finding the shape, and use the thin ribs to find the form.

Fine stem

Ribs

Different shapes

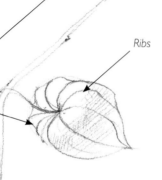

Fine stem

➤ When other flowers are in short supply, Chinese lanterns are useful subjects; you can use all the reds in your palette and even discover new ones! I chose to paint a spray of lanterns against a white wall – the autumn sun made lovely shadows on the wall, and I painted these in a blue-grey.

Light tone

Painting a Chinese lantern

1 Draw the shape and stem lightly and accurately.

2 Using a No. 8 round brush, paint the lantern with a pale tone of cadmium red or cadmium orange.

3 Note the direction of the light, and paint the dark side of the lantern with a darker mix of red or orange.

4 Paint the ribs with cadmium red, using a No. 4 round brush.

5 Paint the stem next, using yellow ochre and raw umber.

Darker tone

Tip: You can make an orange by mixing cadmium red with cadmium yellow; use brown madder to make a darker red.

Chrysanthemums

The chrysanthemum is an extraordinarily versatile flower. The variety of flower shapes is amazing – from single, daisy-like blooms to multi-petalled varieties – and there are many colours; some flowers are scented. Chrysanthemums are always available to paint and draw, unlike the majority of flowers, so you can choose them at any time of year.

Colour palette

permanent rose   magenta   sap green

burnt sienna   cadmium orange

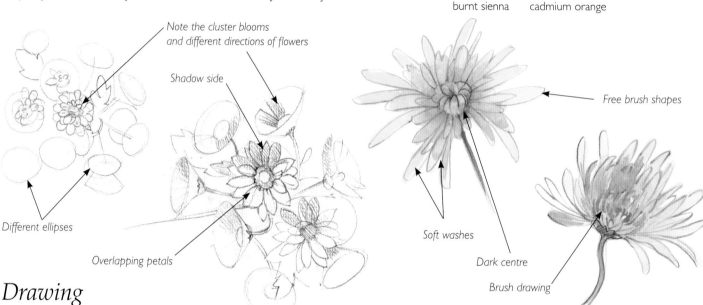

Note the cluster blooms and different directions of flowers

Shadow side

Different ellipses

Overlapping petals

Free brush shapes

Soft washes

Dark centre

Brush drawing

Drawing

Good observation is essential: look at the basic shape and draw it with a sharp B pencil. Single blooms, which are mostly a shallow bowl or disc shape, are easiest to draw; others, such as pom-pom or ball shapes, are more complicated, and some have very spiky petals. Make sure the stems are placed correctly.

Painting chrysanthemums

1 Draw lightly, then dampen the flower areas with clean water.

2 Using a No. 12 brush, paint the general flower shapes with a very pale wash of permanent rose.

3 While this wash is still wet, drop in the centre using a touch of permanent rose and magenta.

4 If the colour spreads too much, blot it out with a paper tissue to make petal shapes.

5 Using a No. 4 round brush, draw in the petal shapes in a darker pink and indicate the dark petal centres with cadmium orange.

6 Make up a mid-green mix from sap green and burnt sienna, and use this to paint the leaves and stems, with the brush making the shapes.

These chrysanthemums were part of a larger bunch of flowers and were the softest shade of pink. I tried to capture the frothiness of the petals with loose wet-into-wet washes, using rose madder genuine, a transparent colour; the centres were pure cadmium orange.

Clivias

Clivias grow well in greenhouses and conservatories, and the striking flowers make a welcome addition in spring. The bright orange-red flowers are like small trumpets on top of a strong stem, and the leaves are strong, strap-like and glossy.

Colour palette

 cadmium yellow

 cadmium red

 sap green

 yellow ochre

 burnt sienna

 scarlet lake

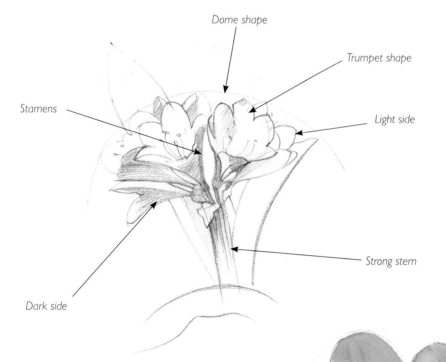

Dome shape

Trumpet shape

Stamens

Light side

Strong stem

Dark side

Painting clivias

1 Draw the shapes carefully.

2 Paint the centre of the flower with a pale wash of cadmium yellow.

3 Follow this with a pale cadmium red, blending in this wash where necessary.

4 Complete the flowers using a darker shade of cadmium red on the shadow side.

5 Paint the stamens and centres using a pale mix of sap green and cadmium yellow.

6 The leaves and stem can be painted using different shades of green, from dark to light, basing the colour on sap green, yellow ochre and burnt sienna.

Working wet into wet

Working wet on dry

Drawing

Draw the trumpet shapes with a round dome – there can be as many as ten blooms on one head. The trumpets are attached to a single strong stem; unusually for a trumpet shape, the throat is light in colour.

Wet base

Tip: *You can substitute scarlet lake for cadmium red if you wish; scarlet lake is a transparent colour, whereas cadmium red is opaque.*

It was pleasant to paint this clivia sitting in the warmth of a large greenhouse; the leaves of the plant behind it made an effective contrast to the clivia petals.

Cyclamens

Cyclamens can be in flower for most of the year and are always delightful. Larger cyclamen in pots can be any shade of pink, red, purple and white, and the smaller, wild varieties are just as entrancing. The heart-shaped leaves are often beautifully patterned.

Colour palette

alizarin crimson Winsor violet brown madder

Prussian blue   yellow ochre

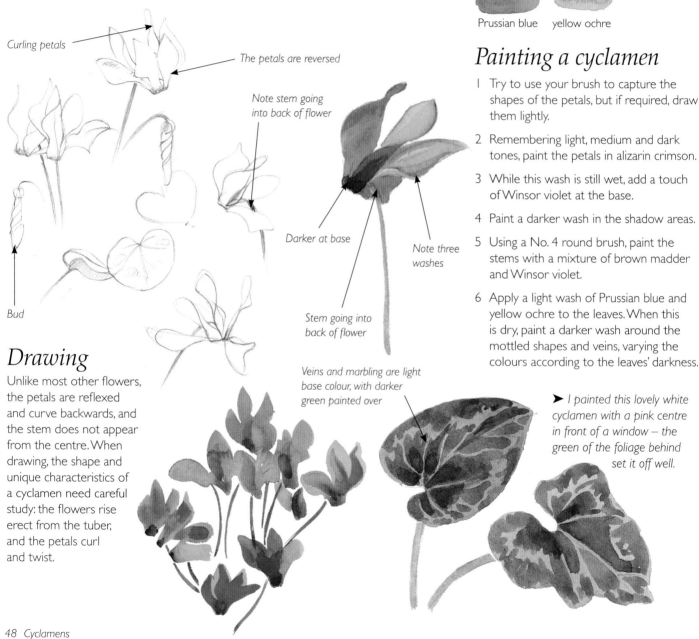

Curling petals

The petals are reversed

Note stem going into back of flower

Darker at base

Note three washes

Bud

Stem going into back of flower

Veins and marbling are light base colour, with darker green painted over

Painting a cyclamen

1 Try to use your brush to capture the shapes of the petals, but if required, draw them lightly.

2 Remembering light, medium and dark tones, paint the petals in alizarin crimson.

3 While this wash is still wet, add a touch of Winsor violet at the base.

4 Paint a darker wash in the shadow areas.

5 Using a No. 4 round brush, paint the stems with a mixture of brown madder and Winsor violet.

6 Apply a light wash of Prussian blue and yellow ochre to the leaves. When this is dry, paint a darker wash around the mottled shapes and veins, varying the colours according to the leaves' darkness.

➤ *I painted this lovely white cyclamen with a pink centre in front of a window – the green of the foliage behind set it off well.*

Drawing

Unlike most other flowers, the petals are reflexed and curve backwards, and the stem does not appear from the centre. When drawing, the shape and unique characteristics of a cyclamen need careful study: the flowers rise erect from the tuber, and the petals curl and twist.

Daffodils

Daffodils are eagerly awaited in spring. We all love to paint them, but it is easy to get into difficulties with the colours and shadows. There are many different yellows, and you should take time to get to know their individual properties: their shades and colours, their transparency or opacity, and their paleness and brightness.

Colour palette

Winsor yellow   cadmium yellow   permanent rose   cobalt blue

French ultramarine   sap green   yellow ochre

Painting a daffodil

1 Either draw the shapes with a pencil or paint them directly with a brush, using Winsor yellow.

2 Add any darker areas using a little cadmium yellow.

3 To make a pale shadow colour, mix permanent rose, cobalt blue and Winsor yellow.

4 Note the direction of the light and paint in the shadow areas.

5 When this wash is dry, add pleats and folds to the shadows, drawing carefully with a B pencil.

6 Paint the stem with a mix of sap green and a little yellow ochre. Next, darken the shadow side with French ultramarine.

▶ *This free and vigorous treatment of a spring bouquet was painted on Rough paper. I used a red watercolour pencil to define the edges of the three nearest flowers.*

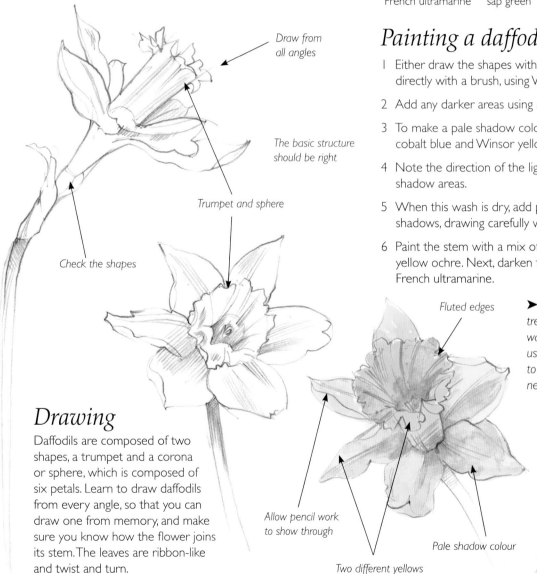

Draw from all angles

The basic structure should be right

Trumpet and sphere

Check the shapes

Fluted edges

Drawing

Daffodils are composed of two shapes, a trumpet and a corona or sphere, which is composed of six petals. Learn to draw daffodils from every angle, so that you can draw one from memory, and make sure you know how the flower joins its stem. The leaves are ribbon-like and twist and turn.

Allow pencil work to show through

Two different yellows

Pale shadow colour

Tip: *It is important to know which yellows are opaque (such as cadmium yellow) and which are transparent (such as aureolin).*

Fuchsias

Also known as Californian fuchsias, these graceful hanging flowers are single or double in reds and purples, and are popular in many gardens. The flowers consist of a tube that opens into sepals and then petals; the stamens are long. There are many varieties of fuchsia, and the plants are easy to grow.

Colour palette

alizarin crimson   Winsor yellow   sap green   burnt sienna

Drawing

Fuchsias usually hang down; observe and draw carefully the three parts – the tube, sepals and petals. The more you observe and draw, the better you will understand the flower and be able to paint it effectively.

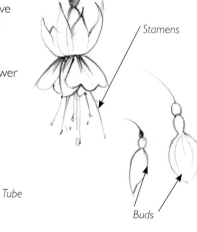

Stamens

Buds

Outer sepals

Tube

Inner petals

Painting fuchsias

1 Draw with the brush or, if you don't feel confident enough yet, indicate the positions with a pencil.

2 You may need to stand up to get a good sweep with the brush.

3 Use a mix of alizarin crimson and a touch of Winsor yellow for the petals.

4 Vary the colour of the petals between light, medium and dark.

5 Use a brush with a fine point to paint the stamens.

6 For the stem and leaves, use a mix of sap green and burnt sienna.

Different tones of red

Fuchsias hang down

Distinctive stamens

Tip: *Why not try painting directly with a brush? Your painting will look fresh and vigorous, and you won't be painting up to edges.*

This was painted entirely with a No. 8 round brush, using the brush to make the shapes. If you decide to go for a free painting of this sort, remember to change your water every time you change colour.

Geraniums

Geraniums are equally popular plants in gardens and in pots on windowsills and balconies; their brilliant colours, ranging from white to pink to the deepest red, are very attractive, and sometimes the leaves are scented. The flowers vary in size, and the leaves are either ivy-leaf-shaped or heart-shaped with attractive markings.

Colour palette

permanent rose   sap green   burnt sienna   alizarin crimson

Drawing

When drawing geraniums, note carefully how the flowers come from a single stem; they often form a dome shape, but not always.

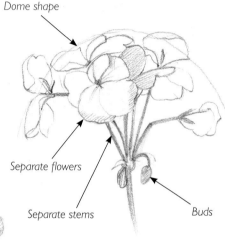

Dome shape

Separate flowers

Separate stems

Buds

Scalloped-edge leaves

Painting geraniums

1 Draw directly with a brush or, if you don't feel confident enough yet, indicate the positions with a pencil.

2 Paint over the whole flower area with a pale wash of permanent rose.

3 With a medium tone of permanent rose, paint the separate flowers, reserving the light pink of the first wash for the lightest tone.

4 Mix sap green and burnt sienna for the stems and buds.

5 Add details such as the centres of the flowers.

6 For further shadows use alizarin crimson to make a deeper shade of pink.

Overall shape

Separate flowers and buds

Brushstroke shapes

➤ White geraniums will need a background to hold the flower shapes. In this painting, simple one-tone shadows help to create the form.

Gladioli

'White' gladioli are not really white, but have subtle tints of the palest greens and pinks. They are an artist's delight, arching and curving in an intriguing way; and because they are tall, large and showy, they can be painted roughly life size, as opposite. Painting very pale and white flowers is all about negative painting – creating the spaces between and around flowers.

Colour palette

French ultramarine   brown madder   permanent rose

sap green   Winsor yellow   yellow ochre

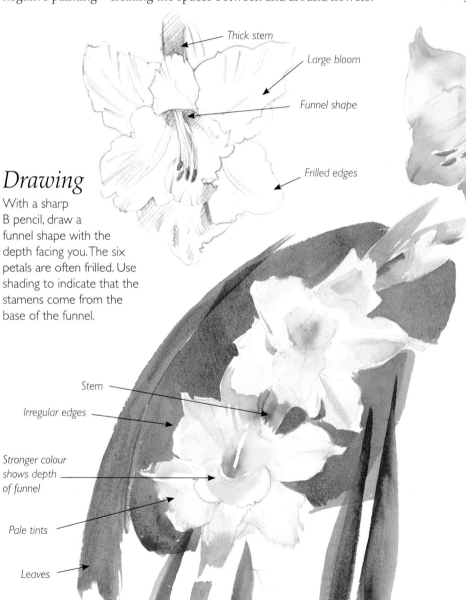

Thick stem

Large bloom

Funnel shape

Frilled edges

Drawing

With a sharp B pencil, draw a funnel shape with the depth facing you. The six petals are often frilled. Use shading to indicate that the stamens come from the base of the funnel.

► *With a white background, emphasize the subtle colours of the flower; contrast white flowers with a colourful background.*

Stem

Irregular edges

Stronger colour shows depth of funnel

Pale tints

Leaves

Painting gladioli

1 Draw the flowers, including the stems and leaves, using a light pencil line.

2 If the flower is white or pale-coloured, paint around the shape using a suitable background colour; I used varying washes of blue and grey (brown madder and ultramarine), applying them with a No. 12 round brush.

3 Delicately tint the petals with a suggestion of permanent rose, and use a very weak grey wash for the shadows and creases.

4 Darken the centres of the flowers with a pale mix of Winsor yellow and sap green.

5 Paint the stems and leaves with varying mixes and strengths of sap green, Winsor yellow and ultramarine, adding yellow ochre to warm up the colours.

6 Paint the stamens to finish, using diluted blue.

Hellebores

These delicate flowers are a welcome sight in January; they are cup- or saucer-shaped, and vary from the small green flowers of *Hellebore foetidus* to the lovely white, pink and purple flowers of the 'Lenten rose'. The stems are often a reddish green, and the leaves are divided and distinctive.

Colour palette

Naples yellow

permanent rose

Winsor violet

French ultramarine

sap green

Drawing

Draw a hellebore from every angle as the simple-looking shape of the flower can be deceptive. Get the shape right, then put in the centre, leaving the petals and details until last. Note where the light strikes, and remember that shallow cup shapes and saucer shapes can have more depth than appears at first glance.

Flowers mostly hang down, creating shadows underneath

Cup shape

Detail of veins and spots

Painting a hellebore

1. Draw the flower, then use a No. 8 round brush to paint the centre and stamens with Naples yellow.

2. When this is completely dry, mask out the centre and stamens with masking fluid.

3. Wait until the masking fluid is completely dry before painting the petals with a very pale mix of permanent rose and Winsor violet.

4. Make a darker mix of the rose and violet to paint the darker tones on the petals.

5. To capture the form and shape of the petals, paint an even darker mix on the underside.

6. When everything is completely dry, gently rub off the masking fluid, then paint the details around the stamens with a mid-green wash mix of sap green and French ultramarine.

Masking fluid

Light hitting top of flower

Tip: *Don't leave masking fluid on paper for too long or it will disturb the surface; if possible, rub it off the same day you apply it.*

Note shadow underneath

Add deeper tones

Use a small brush for the spots

*I painted these hellebores larger than life size
to show the lovely shapes and the stamens.*

Hibiscuses

The hibiscus is an exotic flower found all over the world and is lovely to paint. The large flower, which may only last for a day, comes in a variety of colours, red, white, pink, purple and even yellow, and the trumpet-shaped flower has striking stamens on a central column. Some hibiscuses are hardy shrubs, but many are grown as pot plants in conservatories and greenhouses.

Colour palette

Winsor yellow   cadmium red   alizarin crimson

sap green   burnt sienna   yellow ochre

Drawing

The hibiscus is basically a trumpet shape; the five petals can have frilled edges, but the most striking part of the flower is the column from which the stamens and pistil spring. There are veins and pleats, and some flowers can feature stripes on the petals.

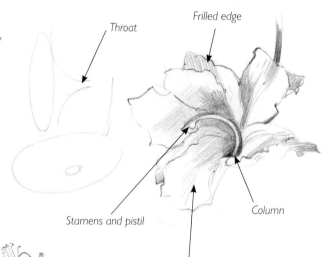

Throat

Frilled edge

Stamens and pistil

Column

Veins and pleats

Painting a hibiscus

1 Draw the shape, including some buds, leaves and stems.

2 Paint the whole flower with a light wash of Winsor yellow.

3 While this is wet, drop in a darker mix of Winsor yellow and cadmium red to make soft shadows.

4 When this is dry, use the same wash to paint the pleats and folds wet on dry.

5 Use alizarin crimson to softly indicate the dark centre of the flower.

6 Paint the leaf and stem using a mix of sap green, burnt sienna and yellow ochre.

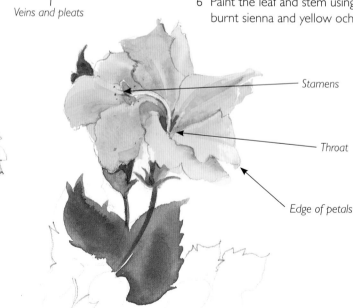

Stamens

Throat

Edge of petals

I fell in love instantly with this stunning red hibiscus and its striking central column. The leaves were glossy and deep green and caught the light, and I could have spent hours just looking at it!

Honeysuckles

The sweetly scented honeysuckle has delicate, tubular flowers that bloom over a long period. The stamens are often very noticeable and add to the charm of the plant. The flowers are attractive to bees and moths, and can be white, cream, yellow or tinged with red.

Colour palette

Naples yellow   alizarin crimson   oxide of chromium

Drawing

This honeysuckle (*Lonicera fragrantissima*) blooms in winter and is, as its name suggests, highly scented. The flowers are small and tubular, and flare out; study it carefully and use a sharp pencil when drawing it.

Delicate flowers

Leaves hardly emerging

Stamens

Two tones on flowers

Painting a honeysuckle

1 Draw the shape.

2 Using Naples yellow, paint the petals, blending in a little alizarin crimson towards the throat of each flower.

3 Draw in the stamens with a sharp pencil.

4 Paint the leaves using a light and a medium tone of oxide of chromium.

5 Use oxide of chromium to paint the stem.

6 Add a shadow side to the stem using a touch of alizarin crimson.

Tip: *When painting small flowers such as this, contrast is all-important: you need to think about light flowers on dark, and dark flowers on light.*

Stamens drawn with pencil

Flowers have five lobes

Irises

There are many different types of iris, all of which are delightful to draw and paint. A particular favourite is the bearded iris, which comes in a variety of beautiful colours, including mid-blue, purple, white and yellow, and has large flowers and lovely buds. The flowers are intriguing and need to be studied closely: they have three inner petals and three outer petals that hang down.

Colour palette

Winsor violet   gamboge   sap green   burnt sienna

Drawing

Study the shapes and draw them life size. Use the leaves as a foil to the flowers: the leaves are stiff and sword-shaped, while the petals can be irregular and be blown by wind, making them hard to draw.

Varied line

Inner petals

Veining

Note different arrangement of petals

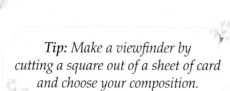

Light tone

Dark tone

Water iris has upright petals

Painting an iris

1 Draw the shape in pencil, noting the arrangement of petals.

2 Paint the petals with a pale wash of Winsor violet.

3 While this first wash is drying, paint the yellow parts of the petals with gamboge.

4 Mix a darker shade of violet and use this to show the shaded parts and bring out the form of the petals.

5 Paint the stem and leaf with a mix of sap green and burnt sienna.

6 Add a little burnt sienna to gamboge for the darker parts of the yellow petals.

➤ *This bearded iris has the most beautiful petals, which wave about in the wind. The background in this painting uses pale washes of the same colours as the iris petals.*

Tip: Make a viewfinder by cutting a square out of a sheet of card and choose your composition.

Lilacs

Lilac (*Syringa vulgaris*) appears in late spring and has a lovely scent. The flowers, which are small and can be either single or double, grow in clusters around central stems – when painting them, you have to treat them as a mass. The tubular flowers can be white, purple, lilac or dark red.

Colour palette

ultramarine violet   alizarin crimson   olive green

sap green   raw umber   burnt umber

Drawing

Start by drawing a general shape, a dome or plume, and then fit the flowers, buds and tiny stems into this shape; the small, tubular flowers grow around the stems, and you don't have to draw all of them to give a convincing impression.

Flowers open at different times

Note light and dark areas

Flowers have four small petals on a tubular stem

Light and dark areas

Three tone washes

Indication of buds and flowers

Painting a lilac

1   Draw the shape in pencil, or paint straight away using a light wash of ultramarine violet.

2   Note the light areas and either darken the adjacent parts with the violet or alizarin crimson, or blot out some colour from the wet wash with a tissue.

3   Indicate the individual flower buds by using a darker wash.

4   To give structure to the flower heads, paint small and large stems with a mix of olive green and sap green.

5   Paint the leaves with a medium wash of the two green colours.

6   Mix raw umber and burnt umber to paint the other stems.

Tip: When painting a lot of small florets as in this lilac, don't attempt each flower, but paint the whole shape and indicate several flowers.

➤ *These purple and white lilacs were growing side by side on top of a tall bush; their heady fragrance was quite overwhelming.*

Lilies

Whether fragrant or unscented, lilies are beautiful. The flowers are mainly trumpet-shaped and the buds are often decorative, and lilies are reasonably simple to draw. Try painting the lovely shapes any way you can; in a landscape or in pots on a patio, for example.

Colour palette

| permanent rose | cobalt blue | Winsor yellow |
| sap green | burnt sienna | cadmium orange |

Drawing

Lilies are trumpet-shaped when seen in profile, but from the front they are more difficult to draw; try to achieve the depth of the trumpet using shading. It's easier to draw life size, drawing a box shape and then defining the petals.

Six petals

Draw a box shape with petals radiating from the centre

Stamens

Turned-over petals

➤ *When regale lilies flower I am overwhelmed by the scent and the pure shapes – no wonder lilies are popular as symbols of purity and grace. The petals can curve in different ways, with the flowers pointing up or down.*

Tip: When painting white flowers, you can define the edges with a pencil line.

Tones

Curly petals

Detail in centre

Painting lilies

1 Indicate the shapes with fine pencil lines.

2 Mix a shadow colour from permanent rose, cobalt blue and Winsor yellow, and paint this, keeping to a single tone.

3 Add details: paint the stamens using cadmium orange, and the stalks are a pale green made up of sap green and Winsor yellow.

4 For the pinky-mauve petals, use a light wash of permanent rose and cobalt blue.

5 Paint the stem and leaves using a mix of sap green and burnt sienna.

6 Add more tone to the existing shadows with a darker version of the shadow mix.

7 Dampen the background area to make the washes run more easily, and then drop in darkish shadow mixes, working quickly so the washes blend.

Lupins

Lupins are impressive, imposing flowers that can grow as tall as 1m (3ft); the garden varieties have a stunning array of colours – some are bi-coloured – and make a vivid display. The many individual flowers, which are often scented and which grow around a central stem, are sweet-pea-shaped, and are best painted as a mass.

Colour palette

Winsor yellow   cadmium red   French ultramarine   sap green

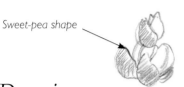

Sweet-pea shape

Buds at the top

Flowers arranged in tiers around stem

Drawing

You can draw a lupin as a botanical specimen or treat it quite loosely – whichever method you choose, capturing the character of the flower is important. The top of the spike is tightly packed, and the pea-like flowers open as they go down the stem. The leaves are distinctive and decorative.

Painting lupins

1   Draw the shapes loosely in pencil.

2   Paint the flowers as a mass with a pale wash of Winsor yellow and cadmium red.

3   When this wash is dry, paint in some individual flowers with a deeper wash.

4   Add a little French ultramarine to the wash for the shadows.

5   Paint the stems and leaves using a mix of sap green and ultramarine.

6   To show the contours of the lupins, paint in a background wash of ultramarine and drop a little sap green into it here and there.

Overall spike shape

Bi-coloured flowers
around a central stem

Pea-like flowers
in two parts

➤ When painting lupins, getting the
overall distinctive shape is important
to show the character. In this rather
free painting, detail is not essential
to the mood.

Magnolias

Around Easter, magnolia flowers appear, shaped like small wine glasses in white, pink and purple, and lasting a long time before they fade; if attacked by frost, the waxy petals turn brown. The buds have lovely shapes, and sometimes you can see full-blown flowers, half-open ones and buds in varying stages on the same branch. When painting magnolias against a spring sky, the question is whether to paint the background before or after the flowers: try it both ways.

Colour palette

permanent rose   French ultramarine   cobalt blue   raw umber

sap green   magenta   raw sienna

Drawing

Magnolias start as a goblet shape and open right out in the sun, so try to draw them at all stages of this process if possible. Note particularly the stamens and small leaves.

Bud

Sepals

Goblet shape

Light

Tone and shadow

Wet into wet

Painting magnolias

1 Draw or indicate the shapes loosely in pencil.

2 The flower is basically white; paint on pale pink or purple washes using permanent rose or magenta.

3 Deepen the colours towards the centre, possibly adding a little French ultramarine to the wash.

4 Tones and shadows indicate the form, but the background makes the shape. Working wet on dry, mix up a large cobalt blue wash and speedily paint around the flowers.

5 To work wet into wet, dampen the paper around the flowers with clean water, then drop the paint onto the wet areas.

6 Paint the stems and sepals using sap green and raw umber, and use raw sienna for the stamens.

This beautiful pink magnolia has large, waxy flowers that open out in sunny weather, and turn the tree into a mass of colour – a fantastic sight!

Nasturtiums

Nasturtiums are easy to grow, and their bright colours – yellow, orange and red, and often a mixture – and rounded leaves make them a favourite in any garden. The flowers have appealing and distinctive spurs at the base that give them the appearance of monks' hoods.

Colour palette

cadmium red   cadmium yellow   sap green   alizarin crimson

Drawing

The flower is basically trumpet-shaped and has five petals. Note the spur at the base and the fact that the petals have cut-out bases where they go into the sepal. In comparison, the leaves are flat and circular and are thus easier to draw, but look carefully at the quite intricate veining.

Spur at base

Shape based on trumpet

Circular leaf

Sepals

Veining and cut-outs

Painting nasturtiums

1 Draw or indicate the shapes loosely in pencil if you like; otherwise, go straight in with a brush.

2 Cadmium red and cadmium yellow are strong, opaque colours, so use them boldly as you paint the petals; alizarin crimson is less opaque, but you can use it in the same way.

3 Use a No. 4 round brush to paint the stems in a pale sap green.

4 Mix up a clear, bright green from sap green and cadmium yellow, and paint over the leaves.

5 When the leaf is dry, mix a darker green and go over the leaves again, this time leaving the veins as the pale first wash.

6 Finish by adding any details and shadow areas, using darker versions of the mixes.

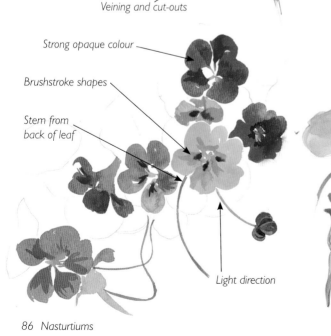

Strong opaque colour

Brushstroke shapes

Stem from back of leaf

Light direction

➤ Nasturtiums always seem to grow in a tangle of stems, leaves and flowers. In this painting I included buds, seed pods and the spurs at the base of the flowers.

Orchids

Orchids are very beautiful, striking flowers, and some varieties, such as the lovely moth orchid shown here, can be grown indoors on a shady window sill; others can be found outdoors or in greenhouses. The flowers grow on a long stem, away from the glossy leaves, and often have intriguing details on their inner petals.

Colour palette

permanent rose   Winsor yellow   cobalt blue   olive green

sap green   burnt sienna   magenta   Winsor violet

Drawing

Close observation is needed with orchids: there are five petals, of which the central lower one is marked and is quite different to the others. In general the flower is a flat disc shape that faces forwards; practise drawing it from all angles.

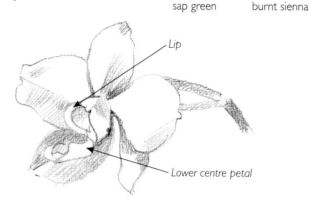

Lip

Lower centre petal

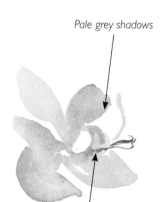

Pale grey shadows

Centre with tongue shape

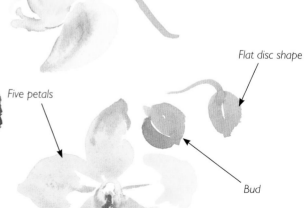

Five petals

Flat disc shape

Bud

▲ These beautiful flowers grew on a long stem away from the leaves, so I accentuated this characteristic by painting the stem with no background. The lip and tongue petal was delicate and intricately marked.

Although I used very few colours on the orchids themselves, the colourful background suggests that the palette was larger.

Painting an orchid

1 Draw or indicate the shapes carefully in pencil.

2 Paint the shadows on the white petals using a mix of permanent rose, Winsor yellow and cobalt blue.

3 For the touch of green near the centres, use either olive green or sap green.

4 Mix sap green and burnt sienna for the stems.

5 Working carefully, use a mix of magenta and Winsor violet for the darker details on the petals.

6 Dampen the background area around the orchids with clean water, and then drop in permanent rose, Winsor yellow and cobalt blue; work rapidly to let the colours blend on the paper without forming hard edges.

Pansies

Who could not like pansies? Their faces seem to look like small cats, and their velvety texture comes in many colours – blue, purple, white, yellow, red and orange. A pansy's flat face is held more or less parallel to the stem and actually faces you, unlike many other flowers, which look up or down.

Colour palette

Winsor violet   sap green   burnt sienna   cadmium yellow

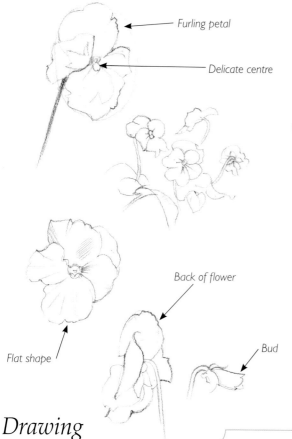

Furling petal

Delicate centre

Flat shape

Back of flower

Bud

Drawing

Draw with a soft pencil and turn the pansy this way and that, studying it from every angle. The basic shape is a disc, but the pansy looks different every way it turns. Try to capture the soft, furling petals, and note where the stem springs from. The leaves are often heart-shaped.

Tip: Become familiar with complementary colours as you can use them to your advantage when painting flowers and backgrounds.

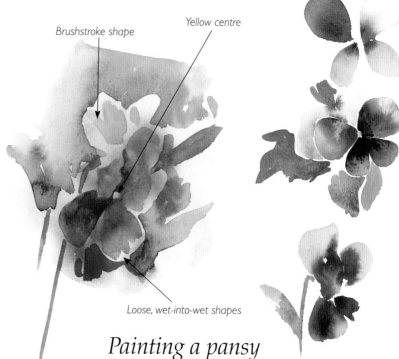

Brushstroke shape

Yellow centre

Loose, wet-into-wet shapes

Painting a pansy

1 Try to avoid drawing, but use a No. 8 round brush to make all the shapes.

2 Using a mid-toned mix of Winsor violet, wash in the petals shapes, leaving a small white space in the centre.

3 While the wash is wet, drop in a darker wash of violet nearer the centre.

4 Paint the leaves and stem with a mid-toned mix of sap green and burnt sienna.

5 Use a darker version of the green mix for the shadows and any details.

6 To finish, add a small dot of strong cadmium yellow in the centre of the pansy.

This simple little painting was mostly painted without drawing, using the brush to make the shapes. It shows various views of pansies and includes a bud.

Peonies

Whether perennials or shrubs, peonies are always eye-catching. There are single, semi-double and double varieties in reds, pinks, white and yellow, and they have golden stamens and lovely leaves. If you are, like me, loath to pick them and prefer to paint them in situ, be aware of your eye level as you will be looking down on the flowers.

Colour palette

alizarin crimson French ultramarine Prussian blue

Winsor yellow yellow ochre burnt sienna

Drawing

Like most peonies, the tree peony is loosely a cup or bowl shape. Draw the flower life size and carefully check the light direction as the centre, which is full of stamens, is quite dark. There are two rows of strong, waxy petals.

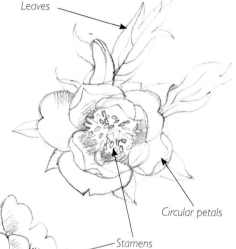

Leaves

Circular petals

Cup shape

Stamens

Tip: Practise making really dark tones, using Prussian blue, burnt sienna, French ultramarine and alizarin crimson.

Painting a peony

1 Draw the flower, sepals and leaves in pencil.

2 Paint the petals with a light wash of crimson lake or alizarin crimson.

3 While the wash is wet, paint the dark tones and shadows in a stronger wash.

4 When this is dry, paint the stronger darks and shadows with a dark mix of alizarin crimson and French ultramarine.

5 Mix light and darker washes of Winsor yellow and Prussian blue for the leaves, and add a touch of yellow ochre to paint the sepals.

6 Paint the stamens with yellow ochre, and use a mix of Prussian blue and alizarin crimson on the dark side.

Light tone

Dark tone

Stamens

Leaves

▶ *This tree peony, with its lovely feathery petals, was painted wet-into-wet on stretched paper; the beautiful rich, golden-yellow stamens really stood out.*

Poinsettias

The actual flowers of a poinsettia are small and insignificant – it is the bracts that are colourful, and these can be brilliant red, pink or white. Poinsettias make very striking house plants; the stems are upright, and the leaves are quite large and form a frame for the colourful bracts.

Colour palette

carmine   French ultramarine   sap green   oxide of chromium

Star shape

Irregular spaces between the leaves

Small flowers in the centre

Overlapping leaves

Painting a poinsettia

1 Draw the bracts in pencil, remembering that they make a sort of star shape; there are six main leaf bracts, with others in between.

2 Using a No. 8 round brush, paint the bracts with a medium wash of carmine.

3 When the wash is dry, paint a darker carmine wash where you see shadows; you can paint this second wash while the first is wet if you leave a tiny gap between the two washes.

4 Mix sap green with a touch of French ultramarine and paint the tiny flowers in the centre.

5 Paint the green leaves using oxide of chromium; this is an opaque green, so paint very carefully using varying tones.

6 As an alternative to using oxide of chromium, you can mix up your own choice of greens to paint the leaves.

Drawing

The leaf-shaped bracts form a star shape around the tiny flowers; note the veins and how the bracts appear on the stem. Using a 2B pencil, practise drawing them as if they are leaves.

Second and third washes

White space

Use a No. 12 or No. 8 round brush to paint the first wash

Dark green

The bright red bracts are stunning, but you must be careful to keep your eyes open to see the shapes and spaces between them or you may lose your way.

Poppies

Poppies are amazing and are always on the list of flowers to paint. In summer, the beautiful, large, bright petals of the oriental poppy invite the brightest of reds, maybe with an underwash of yellow. Annual poppies are just as inviting, and have a tremendous colour range, from red and orange, through pink and purple to white; the seeds, leaves and stems are all decorative.

Drawing

Poppies are bowl-shaped and fairly simple to draw. The soft, furling petals are often veined or pleated; the centres are interesting and have many stamens; and the seed heads and buds can be included. In the case of opium poppies, the blue-grey leaves often wrap around the stem.

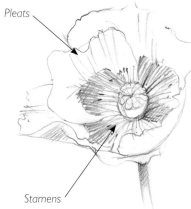

Pleats

Stamens

Colour palette

French ultramarine   alizarin crimson   cerulean blue   Winsor yellow

Painting poppies

1 Draw lightly with a pencil, and include the leaves, buds and seed heads.

2 Mix a purple from French ultramarine and alizarin crimson, and paint over the petals with one pale wash.

3 Using a deeper purple mixed from the same colours, paint the shadows on the petals.

4 Place the 'smudge' at the base of the petals with an even darker tone of purple.

5 Paint the stems, leaves and buds with a blue-green wash mixed from cerulean blue and Winsor yellow.

6 Mix a darker green wash and darken the stems beneath the poppies, then use varying mixes of blue and yellow for shadows on the leaves.

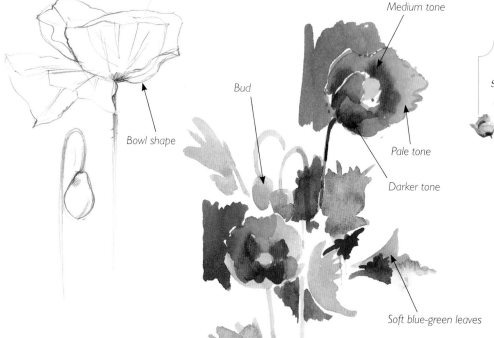

Bowl shape

Bud

Medium tone

Pale tone

Darker tone

Soft blue-green leaves

> **Tip:** *For detail, try using a water-soluble coloured pencil – you can draw a line and wet it afterwards for a soft, paint-like effect.*

➤ *These large white poppies were growing with others just as impressive and made a striking statement against a darkish background. This was painted quite freely.*

Primrose

The primrose is an early spring flower; the delicate stems hold the flowers mostly upright, and the leaves are crinkled and veined. Wild primroses have very pale yellow flowers with orange markings at the base of each petal; they grow on roadside verges, in ditches and in woodlands. It can be difficult to paint them in situ, but you can find them in the wild flower departments of garden centres.

Colour palette

lemon yellow   Payne's grey   brown madder

oxide of chromium   cadmium orange

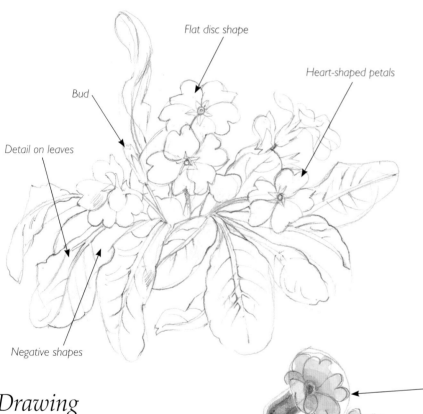

Flat disc shape

Heart-shaped petals

Bud

Detail on leaves

Negative shapes

Painting primroses

1   Draw carefully with a sharp B pencil.

2   Paint the petals with a pale wash of lemon yellow.

3   For the shadows on the petals use a pale wash of Payne's grey.

4   Use a medium wash of brown madder for the stalks, and a pale wash of oxide of chromium for the leaves.

5   While the green is wet on the leaves, paint on a medium wash of the same colour to show the veins and crinkles. Leave some of the first wash showing for the central veins.

6   Mix a darker green wash and continue to paint the leaves, including the smaller veins.

7   Paint the flower centres with cadmium orange, and add a tiny bit of green for the very middle.

Drawing

Draw life size using a sharp 2B pencil. The flowers have pretty heart-shaped petals and are flat disc shapes with a longish calyx. Make a study of the whole plant, including the leaves.

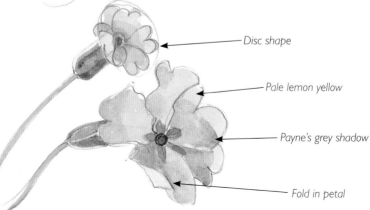

Disc shape

Pale lemon yellow

Payne's grey shadow

Fold in petal

➤ *This was difficult to paint in a free way, but I wanted to capture a feeling of spring and so included a blue sky. In your paintings you can include items of interest such as leaves, twigs, small branches and grass.*

Tip: To paint such a delicate subject, use stretched lightweight hot-pressed (HP) paper, which has a very smooth surface.

Red hot pokers

These spectacular flowers really live up to their name, with lovely shades of red, orange and yellow. Some are tubular in shape, others more rounded, but they are all fascinating to paint. The heads are composed of many small florets, so practise making an overall wash and then adding to this either while it is wet or when it has dried – both ways can reward you with striking results.

Colour palette

cadmium orange

cadmium yellow

cadmium red

raw umber

sap green

Treat flower as a shape

The silhouette is important

First wash

Second wash

Separate flowers within the shape

Detail

Wet into wet

Strong stem

Painting a red hot poker

1 Using a No. 12 round brush, make the shape of the flower with a pale wash of cadmium orange.

2 While this is wet, drop in further washes of cadmium yellow and cadmium red.

3 Use a mix of raw umber and sap green to paint the shadow side and underneath of the flower; no detail is needed at this stage.

4 Depending on the background, decide on the silhouette and cut in with a dark background or define the edges on a light background.

5 Now add detail with a small brush, painting some of the individual florets with darker tones of orange or red.

6 Paint the stem with a mix of sap green and raw umber, remembering that it should look strong enough to bear the weight of a heavy flower.

➤ Painting these Kniphofia raised the question of backgrounds; the flowers hardly need one, but the leaves of this plant were in a clump at the base and looked untidy. I painted the sky, the flowers and grasses, and finally the background.

Drawing

Draw life size using a sharp 2B pencil, looking for the overall shape; the contour depends on the variety of flower. Don't be put off by the many intricate florets, which are tubular and flower from the base first. The stems are strong and the strappy leaves come from the base.

Tip: When painting a positive shape for a background, as here, be careful with the edges of the silhouette that is your subject.

Rhododendrons

Rhododendrons appear in clusters, and the individual flowers are bell-shaped and strikingly beautiful. The colours are delicate; sometimes the flowers are spotted or the flowers graduate from one colour to another. The stamens and pistil are very decorative. Azaleas are grouped with rhododendrons – they usually have smaller flowers and make very decorative indoor plants.

Colour palette

alizarin crimson   permanent rose   French ultramarine

sap green   yellow ochre   burnt sienna

Drawing

Note the direction of light and draw the individual, bell-shaped flowers in clusters with a 2B pencil, noting the shape of the petals. The leaves are important and act as a foil to the flowers. Choose a size of paper to suit the subject – don't draw too small – and avoid using an eraser as this can roughen the paper surface.

Bowl shapes

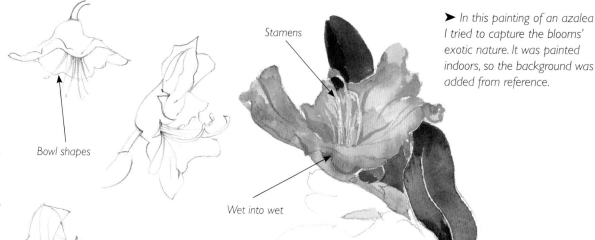

Stamens

Wet into wet

➤ In this painting of an azalea I tried to capture the blooms' exotic nature. It was painted indoors, so the background was added from reference.

Darker tone

Painting rhododendrons

1. Draw the shapes lightly in pencil.

2. Dampen the flower clusters with clean water, then use a No. 12 round brush to drop in a pale pink wash of alizarin crimson that fills the area.

3. While this is wet, paint the shadows and centres with a mix of permanent rose and French ultramarine, paying attention to the direction of light.

4. Mix a light green from sap green and yellow ochre, and paint the leaves.

5. When this wash is dry, mix a darker green from sap green and burnt sienna and paint over the leaves, leaving the first wash to indicate the veins.

6. Strengthen the flowers using varied washes of pink and pale grey, mixed from ultramarine and permanent rose.

7. Use a smaller brush, such as a No. 4 round, to paint the stamens in yellow ochre, the buds in a darker pink, and the stems in burnt sienna.

Romneyas

These stunning white flowers, also known as Californian tree poppies, are an artist's dream. They may take a while to become established in a garden, but once there, they provide many subjects. The beautiful, large flowers have delightful, crinkled petals, which shimmer in even a light breeze, and the stamens are a brilliant yellow – in fact, the flower vaguely resembles a poached egg.

Colour palette

cerulean blue   Winsor yellow   Prussian blue

brown madder   cadmium yellow   yellow ochre

Drawing

These flowers are based on a circular shape; be aware of the petals, and practise drawing ellipses. The leaves are decorative and divided; the details of the petals and the centre can be added later.

Crimped and pleated petals

Disc shape

Large, central stamens

Ragged edges

Painting romneyas

1 Draw lightly, preferably life size.

2 Paint the centres using cadmium yellow.

3 White flowers need some sort of colour behind them to stand out: I used the leaves as a background. Contrast is very important here.

4 Paint the leaves where required using a mix of cerulean blue and Winsor yellow; mix a darker version of this by adding Prussian blue and use for the shadows.

5 Use a grey, made of cerulean blue and brown madder, for the wrinkles and pleats on the petals.

6 Make a light green mix from cerulean blue and cadmium yellow for the stems, and use yellow ochre for the detail on the centres and stamens.

Allow pencil drawing to show through

Colour around flower to highlight white

Large, central stamens: cadmium yellow with a little yellow ochre

Ragged edges

Veins and pleats in mid-tone grey: cerulean blue and brown madder

➤ *For the grey-green leaves I mixed cerulean blue and Winsor yellow, strengthening the colour with Prussian blue. The actual background consisted of a very dark and dense laurel hedge. Painting the flowers at different times of day meant that I used a range of colours and mixes.*

Roses

Roses have such perfect colours and are so beautiful from bud to full-blown flower. Roses with many petals have to be drawn carefully – the petals spiral and overlap and turn gracefully at the edges – while single-petalled roses are much easier to draw. Small, single roses that bloom en masse can be useful as background flowers.

Colour palette

 permanent rose   French ultramarine   Winsor yellow

yellow ochre sap green brown madder

Drawing

Draw the main shapes first, recognizing the essential cup or bowl shape, and work around petals that overlap and spiral; practise capturing this. The petals also fold over at the edges.

Most roses open right out

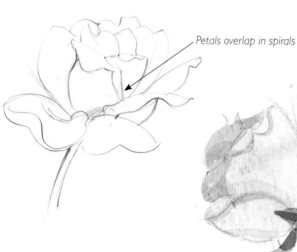

Petals overlap in spirals

Painting a rose

1 Draw the shapes lightly in pencil.

2 Paint over the entire flower shape with a pale wash of permanent rose.

3 Using a darker tone, such as a pinky-grey mixed from permanent rose, French ultramarine and Winsor yellow, paint in the shadows to give an idea of form.

4 Make up a mix of sap green, yellow ochre and ultramarine for the sepals, buds and leaves.

5 Paint the stems with a pale wash of brown madder, using single brushstrokes.

6 Using a No. 4 round brush and darker mixes of the colours, put in any fine details.

Pinks and greys indicate shadows and depth

Loosely based on a cup shape

There are several approaches to painting roses: the botanical, free but controlled, and one that uses a free brushstroke. This lovely yellow rose with overlapping petals was painted quite wet before touches of a darker yellow were dropped in. The shadows were grey, and some detail was added with a pencil.

Snapdragons

The snapdragon is a lovely summer flower, delighting children and adults alike with its playful shape. The flower is in two parts and is known as a lipped flower. The flowers grow around a single stalk, rather like a foxglove, and come in an array of mouth-watering colours.

Colour palette

magenta

cadmium red

alizarin crimson

sap green

burnt sienna

French ultramarine

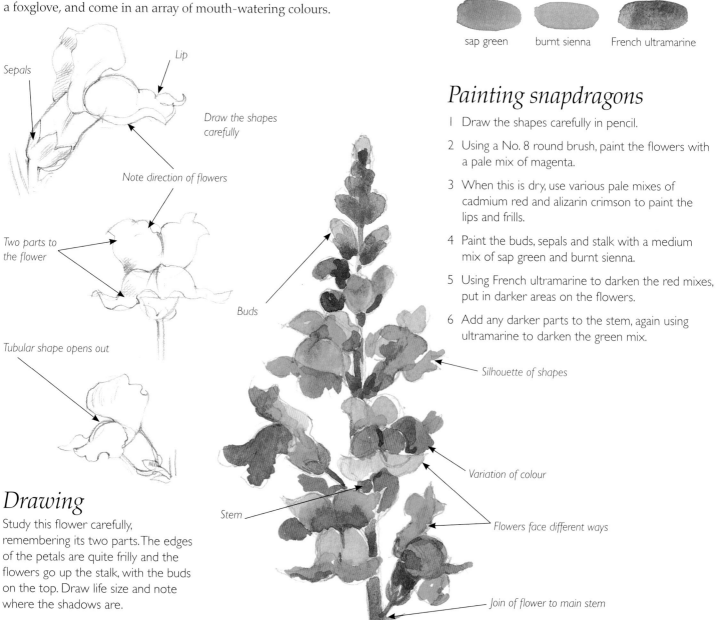

Sepals

Lip

Draw the shapes carefully

Note direction of flowers

Two parts to the flower

Tubular shape opens out

Buds

Silhouette of shapes

Variation of colour

Flowers face different ways

Stem

Join of flower to main stem

Painting snapdragons

1 Draw the shapes carefully in pencil.

2 Using a No. 8 round brush, paint the flowers with a pale mix of magenta.

3 When this is dry, use various pale mixes of cadmium red and alizarin crimson to paint the lips and frills.

4 Paint the buds, sepals and stalk with a medium mix of sap green and burnt sienna.

5 Using French ultramarine to darken the red mixes, put in darker areas on the flowers.

6 Add any darker parts to the stem, again using ultramarine to darken the green mix.

Drawing

Study this flower carefully, remembering its two parts. The edges of the petals are quite frilly and the flowers go up the stalk, with the buds on the top. Draw life size and note where the shadows are.

Snapdragons look good as a mass
display in a garden. You can be quite
impressionistic in your approach and use
wet-into-wet techniques to your advantage.

Snowdrops

Snowdrops appear around the New Year and are the classic winter flowering plant, loved by everyone. The small white flowers have petals of incredible purity, and the inner petals have green markings. Snowdrops grow in clumps of grass and, being small, are quite difficult to paint.

Colour palette

burnt sienna   sap green   brown madder   French ultramarine

Painting snowdrops

1 Draw the shapes in pencil on hot-pressed (HP) paper.

2 Leave the white of the paper for the petals, or use masking fluid to make the shapes.

3 Use a No. 4 round brush to paint the stem and calyx with a mix of burnt sienna and sap green.

4 Paint the leaves with a similar mix, only slightly more blue.

5 Mix French ultramarine and brown madder to make a light grey for the shadow areas.

6 After removing the masking fluid, the white flowers may need a background – a light grass green or a soft grey are good choices.

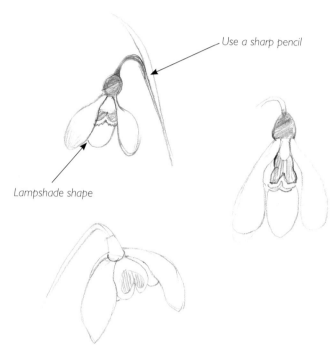

Use a sharp pencil

Lampshade shape

Drawing

Use a sharp 2B pencil to draw snowdrops both in bud and open. The buds are teardrop-shaped, but the open flowers resemble a hanging lampshade. Some snowdrops have double petals.

Tip: *It is quite difficult to get the scale of snowdrops right – they are small, and you really need to have them at eye level to appreciate their size. To achieve the detail, it's important to have good points on your brushes.*

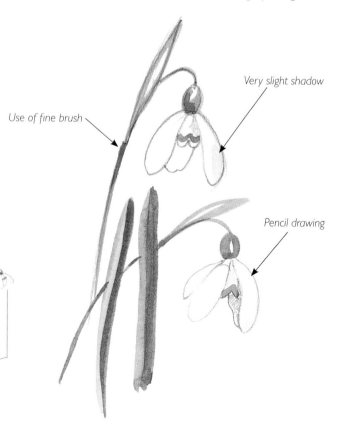

Use of fine brush

Very slight shadow

Pencil drawing

These snowdrops were growing amid grass, so I dug them up, along with the grass and some ivy, and placed them at a low eye level to make an indoor still life. The scale of the ivy is important as the flowers really are quite small.

Sunflowers

No matter how many times they have been painted, sunflowers are still a perenially popular subject. They can be painted as they are, in vases, as still lifes, in fields, or simply as decorative seed heads. The colours of sunflowers range from yellow to dark red, and the centres can be dark sepia, umber and green. Cadmium yellow, used here, is a bright opaque colour – use it pale or dark – and cadmium orange has a rich brilliance.

Colour palette

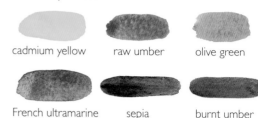

cadmium yellow   raw umber   olive green

French ultramarine   sepia   burnt umber

➤ *The brilliance of these sunflowers is enhanced by the dark background; they were painted at eye level. There is a great range of colours available, with at least seven different yellows you could use; match the flowers' yellow against a colour chart. I love strong colour, but if you prefer to work in a paler key, make sure you keep all the tonal values in keeping.*

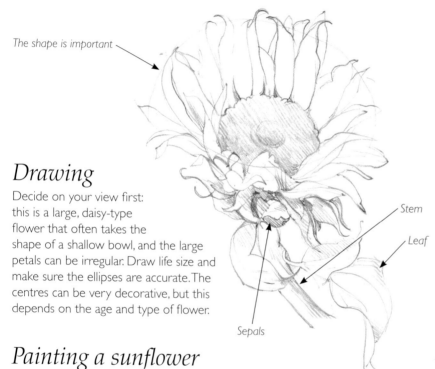

The shape is important

Stem

Leaf

Sepals

Drawing

Decide on your view first: this is a large, daisy-type flower that often takes the shape of a shallow bowl, and the large petals can be irregular. Draw life size and make sure the ellipses are accurate. The centres can be very decorative, but this depends on the age and type of flower.

Painting a sunflower

1 Draw from life with a pencil, taking care with the shapes.

2 Paint the petals with a pale wash of cadmium yellow.

3 Use a darker shade of cadmium yellow to indicate the shadow side of the petals; you can do this wet on dry or wet into wet.

4 Paint the detail on the petals with raw umber.

5 The stem and sepals should be olive green, with a touch of French ultramarine added to strengthen any dark areas.

6 Mix sepia and burnt umber to paint the centre of the flower; you may want to use olive green for the middle part.

> **Tip:** *To mix a really dark colour without using black, try using Prussian blue, burnt sienna and alizarin crimson.*

Very dark centre

Brilliant colour

Water lilies

Water lilies always look easy to paint as they are laid out on the water; the leaves are simple shapes, and mostly you look down on them. Decide on a viewpoint and don't deviate from it as there is a certain amount of perspective in the leaves. You can paint a landscape view or a close-up. Buds add variety, and you can include other water plants and even fish.

Colour palette

cadmium red

Winsor yellow

French ultramarine

brown madder

yellow ochre

sap green

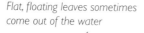
burnt sienna

Drawing

Depending on the variety, water lilies are often cup- or bowl-shaped; when looking down on the flower, it can appear star-shaped. The stamens are often prominent. Draw the shape first, and then add the petals. The leaves are rounded and flat.

Flat, floating leaves sometimes come out of the water

Cup shape

Stamens

Painting a water lily

1 Draw the shape and petals with a pencil.

2 Use a pale apricot mix of cadmium red and Winsor yellow to paint the whole flower except the stamens.

3 When this wash is dry, use a medium tone of the mix to paint the shadow side.

4 Mix French ultramarine and brown madder to make a grey, and use this to paint details on the flower.

5 Paint the stamen area with Winsor yellow.

6 When this is dry, use yellow ochre for the details.

7 Make varying mixes of sap green and ultramarine for the water and the petals, adding burnt sienna for the brown areas.

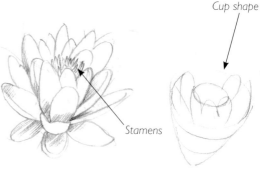

Petals

Cup or bowl shape

Shadows on petals

Silhouette is important

➤ *In this painting of water lilies on a pond, I lightened the leaves as they were mottled and varied in colour.*

Closing thoughts

It has been a privilege to take part in the production of this book. I have been able to draw and paint both common and unusual flowers and plants, and it has been good to have a goal and direction. I've learned that one's style can change quite dramatically, but one thing remains constant: watercolour is a challenging medium, but its colour, light and transparency are ideal for flowers. I hope that you will also learn from these examples and get as much pleasure from painting them as I have.

I would like to thank the staff at David & Charles for their help and support, and also my family and friends, who encourage me so much.

Index